THE COMPLETE WORKS OF OSCAR WILDE

VOLUME I

THE COMPLETE WORKS OF
OSCAR WILDE

General Editors: Russell Jackson and Ian Small

VOLUME I
POEMS AND POEMS IN PROSE

EDITED BY
BOBBY FONG
AND
KARL BECKSON

OXFORD
UNIVERSITY PRESS

OXFORD
UNIVERSITY PRESS

Great Clarendon Street, Oxford OX2 6DP

Oxford University Press is a department of the University of Oxford.
It furthers the University's objective of excellence in research, scholarship,
and education by publishing worldwide in

Oxford New York

Athens Auckland Bangkok Bogotá Buenos Aires Calcutta
Cape Town Chennai Dar es Salaam Delhi Florence Hong Kong Istanbul
Karachi Kuala Lumpur Madrid Melbourne Mexico City Mumbai
Nairobi Paris São Paulo Shanghai Singapore Taipei Tokyo Toronto Warsaw

and associated companies in Berlin Ibadan

Oxford is a registered trade mark of Oxford University Press
in the UK and certain other countries

Published in the United States
by Oxford University Press Inc., New York

Introduction © Ian Small 2000
Editorial Introduction and textual editing © Bobby Fong 2000
Commentary © Karl Beckson 2000

The moral rights of the author have been asserted
Database right Oxford University Press (maker)

First published 2000

British Library Cataloguing in Publication Data

Data available

Library of Congress Cataloging in Publication Data

Wilde, Oscar, 1854–1900.
[Works. 2000]
The complete works of Oscar Wilde / general editors Russell Jackson and Ian Small.
p. cm.
Includes indexes.
Contents: v. 1. Poems and poems in prose / edited by Karl Beckson and Bobby Fong
I. Jackson, Russell, 1949– II. Small, Ian.
PR5810. G00 828'.809—dc21 00-025689

ISBN 0-19-811960-7

1 3 5 7 9 10 8 6 4 2

Typeset in Ehrhardt
by Jayvee, Trivandrum, India
Printed in Great Britain
on acid-free paper by
Biddles Ltd.,
Guildford and King's Lynn

ACKNOWLEDGEMENTS

We are most grateful to Mr Merlin Holland, representative of the Estate of Oscar Wilde, for permission to quote from the unpublished manuscripts. We also wish to thank the Viscountess Mary Hyde Eccles, Mr Jeremy Mason, and Mr Mark Samuels Lasner for their kindness and co-operation in permitting us access to manuscripts in their possession.

Our gratitude extends to the Bibliotheca Bodmeriana, Cologny; the British Library; the Brigham Young University Library; the William Andrews Clark Memorial Library of the University of California, Los Angeles; the Dartmouth College Library; the Houghton Library at Harvard University; the Harry S. Dickey Collection of the Milton S. Eisenhower Library at the Johns Hopkins University; the Huntington Library, San Marino, California; the Frederick R. Koch Foundation, New York City; the Henry W. and Albert A. Berg Collection of the New York Public Library, Astor, Lenox and Tilden Foundations; the Firestone Library at Princeton University; the Philip H. & A. S. W. Rosenbach Foundation, Philadelphia; the Poetry Collection of the Lockwood Memorial Library, State University of New York at Buffalo; the Harry Ransom Humanities Research Center of the University of Texas; and the Beinecke Library at Yale University for permission to quote from material in their possession.

ACKNOWLEDGEMENTS

CONTENTS

INTRODUCTION

IAN SMALL

This edition collects for the first time all the known extant poems of Oscar Wilde together with their textual histories; included are 21 poems which were, for various reasons, unpublished during his lifetime. This undertaking is more significant than it initially appears, for most accounts of Wilde's writing have tended to be dismissive of his early work, particularly the poetry, which has often been regarded as second-rate and derivative. This judgement has a long history and can be traced back to the frequently quoted comments made by Oliver Elton when Wilde presented a copy of his *Poems* (1881) to the Oxford Union. Elton complained about Wilde's plagiarisms, that the poems were 'by a number of better-known and more deservedly reputed authors'.[1] Other contemporary critics pointed to his dilettantism, his 'unmanliness', and his vulgarity.[2] Osbert Burdett, looking back in 1925 to what he called 'the Beardsley period', baldly asserted that Wilde's 'lines were full of coloured phrasing, the phrasing of an imagination that can produce its finest effects only in prose, and all that was factitious was enchanting to the people whose ears lacked the sensitiveness to discern the counterfeit. For Wilde's verse will not bear a moment's critical attention.' By 1970 this judgement had hardly changed; in his *Penguin Book of Irish Verse*, Brendan Kennelly concluded that in 'his short pieces', Wilde 'tends to simper stylishly like many another *fin-de-siècle* poet'. A little later, in their review of research on Wilde, Ian Fletcher and John Stokes noted that 'Wilde's poetry has never been highly regarded'; and as recently as 1989 Isobel Murray merely repeated what had then become a commonplace, that 'on the whole, Wilde reads better . . . without the early poems'.[3] In these arguments, Wilde's 'real' gifts are those of wit, dramatist, and raconteur, talents held to be unsuited to the art of poetry.

---

[1] Elton's comments were recorded by Henry Newbolt; see *My World as in My Time* (London, 1932), 96–7.

[2] See Karl Beckson (ed.), *Oscar Wilde: The Critical Heritage* (London: Routledge, 1970; 1977), 33–53.

[3] Osbert Burdett, *The Beardsley Period* (London: The Bodley Head, 1925), 57; Brendan Kennelly (ed.), *The Penguin Book of Irish Verse* (Harmondsworth: Penguin, 1970), 38–9; Ian Fletcher and John Stokes, 'Oscar Wilde', in *Anglo-Irish Literature: A Review of Research*, ed. Richard J. Finneran (New York: MLA, 1976), 121; Isobel Murray (ed.), *The Oxford Authors: Oscar Wilde* (Oxford: OUP, 1989), p. xix. For details of the reception of *Poems* (1881), see Beckson (ed.), *Critical Heritage*.

In recent years Wilde's achievements have been treated with more interest and seriousness, and as a consequence his reputation has changed significantly. As Richard Ellmann noted, Wilde is now bracketed with Nietzsche as one of the most significant figures in the European *fin de siècle*. At the same time, however, the poetry has continued to be neglected. So few modern Wilde scholars have based their reassessments of his career on a rereading of the poetry. On the contrary, recent revaluations typically take as their point of departure Wilde's work and life between 1888 and 1897. It is the drama, the fiction, the sexual politics, and Wilde's apparent anticipation (in his critical writing) of some of the ways of thinking associated with postmodernism which have formed the basis of his new reputation. The only poem held to be an exception to this pattern of judgement is *The Ballad of Reading Gaol*, a work which is the least representative of Wilde's poetic *œuvre* (in both subject and style), and which appeared only at the end of his writing career.

To judge Wilde's poetic achievement against that of contemporaries such as Thomas Hardy and W. B. Yeats, who made poetry their central creative activity, inevitably tends to reflect poorly on him. It is much more appropriate to evaluate Wilde's poetry in relation to his *own* development as a writer—to see it in the context of the successful author he became in his criticism, fiction, and drama. In this respect, the aim of this edition is not to attempt to revalue Wilde as the equal of, say, Swinburne or Hopkins. Rather this volume, when seen in relation to the complete Oxford English Texts edition of Wilde's work, will demonstrate through its textual apparatus that some writing practices evident in the early poems are the first examples of a strategy which Wilde later developed in more sophisticated ways. Wilde's early poetry exhibits qualities which turn out to be fundamental to the famous and successful writer he later became, and whom modern critics value so highly. In other words, those features of Wilde's poetry which Elton judged pejoratively can be seen in a more positive light, as an attempt to renegotiate the relationship between concepts such as originality and creativity, journalism and art. To put matters at their simplest, this edition will help to explain the conundrum of why, in the face of widespread critical hostility, Wilde *himself* took his role as a poet seriously.

It is possible to argue that by the late 1870s, when Wilde was trying to establish a career, poetry as a cultural practice was becoming marginal: when seen in the context of the growing popularity of genres such as the short story, the readership of poetry (relative to the whole of the reading public) was in decline. Nevertheless, for the aspiring author both in Dublin and Oxford in the mid-1870s, poetry was still the ultimate test of the serious literary artist. Initially, then, for one as clearly ambitious and able as Wilde, a commitment to poetry was logical, understandable, and almost certainly inevitable. Less consistent with that commitment is Wilde's early perception that a literary reputation (no less than his blossoming social celebrity) had to be actively manufactured or cultivated. In this sense Wilde was quite unlike Hardy and the poets of a generation earlier (such as Hopkins), for he seemed to equate status and achievement directly with publication and publicity. Wilde wanted the best of two increasingly incompatible ambitions: to achieve the status which poetry, as the highest form of literary art, had traditionally bestowed, but without forgoing the social and commercial opportunities made possible by new forms of mass culture.

As early as his undergraduate days at Trinity College, Dublin, Wilde appears to have been actively seeking a public. Moreover, the habitual modern dismissal of his early poetry disguises the fact that for one so young he enjoyed significant success in placing his poems. Between 1877 and the appearance of *Poems* in 1881, he published some forty poems in Irish, American, and English periodicals. In fact, his first published poem was as early as 1875 when he had just turned 21. In the following year, eight poems appeared in print, seven in Irish publications (in the *Dublin University Magazine* and in *Kottabos*) and one in the English *Month and Catholic Review*. His most successful year prior to the publication of *Poems* (1881) seems to have been 1877 when he published nine poems in Ireland and at least two (and perhaps three) in the United States.[4] The next year (1878) saw two more poems published in Ireland as well as his Newdigate Prize poem at Oxford, *Ravenna*. In 1879 Wilde published two further poems in Ireland and five in England. In 1880 and 1881, this success continued with eight more poems appearing in England. By any standards, this was an impressive body of work for a man only in his mid-twenties.

It is therefore understandable that Wilde should have taken from this experience the sense that he was building a literary reputation, one which a volume of collected poems would help to consolidate. The pattern of his early publications suggests a growing confidence in which he moves from a local, university, Dublin, and Oxford audience towards the more cosmopolitan markets of London and Boston (in publications such as *Biograph and Review* and the Boston *Pilot*). When Wilde was considering publishing a volume of poems in England in the early 1880s the occasion must have seemed propitious. As a young poet, already widely published, and flushed with success from Oxford, it must have been tempting for him to believe that he was the latest upholder of the tradition of earlier Newdigate winners such as John Ruskin, Matthew Arnold, and John Addington Symonds.

However, it is worth noting that in the late nineteenth century to publish a collection of poems was a significantly different undertaking from placing

---

[4] The uncertainty over Wilde's American publications derives from the fact that Stuart Mason (Christopher Millard) suggests in a manuscript note to his own copy of the *Bibliography of Oscar Wilde* (London: T. Werner Laurie Ltd., 1914) that 'Italia' was published in the Boston *Pilot* in 1877, a detail which (because of the extreme rarity of that publication) the present editors have been unable to confirm. The full publishing history of each poem is given in the appropriate explanatory notes.

single works in a variety of periodicals. In the first place the readership and market for a volume of poetry were very different from the readership for a periodical. The market for such books was much smaller, more critical, and not bound by loyalty to a title which periodicals aimed to exploit. Moreover the economics of publishing a book of poetry was wholly different from that of periodical publishing. With the exception of the Bodley Head in the 1890s, publishers found poetry, particularly the work of new poets, unprofitable. Katharine Tynan, a contemporary of Wilde (and like him a Bodley Head author), commented that the late nineteenth century was 'an age as stony to poetry as the ages of Chatterton and Richard Savage'.[5] Finally, individual poems, when collected, possessed a very different identity and status from that conferred by their occasional publication. In this period, the reading and buying public, as well as the publishing industry, enforced a very strong distinction between 'literary art' and journalism, one which was based on taste, money, and the contrast between popular and élite readerships.

Perhaps the most important of these three was money, because price effectively defined readerships and therefore canons of taste. Significantly the periodicals in which Wilde had published his poems were in the middle-price range: most cost between 6d. and 1s. They were more expensive than mass circulation titles, but cheaper than 'quality' or élite journals. It is also worth noting that the periodicals in which Wilde's work had appeared were of a general, rather than an exclusively literary, appeal. By contrast, *Poems* (1881), with a price of 10s. 6d. and an initial print-run of just 750 copies (of which only a third was sold as the first edition), seems to have been aimed at a more discriminating and wealthier market. Indeed, it is significant that Wilde's first successful publications, the short fiction, were markedly cheaper: *The Happy Prince and Other Tales* (1888) was priced at 5s. with a print-run of 1,000; *Lord Arthur Savile's Crime and Other Stories* (1891) was only 2s. and had a larger print-run (2,000 copies, of which 500 were intended for the American market). Moreover these prices correspond closely to those of the periodicals, such as *World* and the *Court and Society Review* (both of which sold at 6d.), in which the stories in the latter volume first appeared. Even *Intentions* (1891) was priced at 7s. 6d. with a print-run of 1,500.[6] The slightly higher price seems to

---

[5] Tynan's comments appeared in the *Irish Daily Independent*; they are quoted in James G. Nelson, *The Early Nineties: A View from the Bodley Head* (Cambridge, Mass.: Harvard University Press, 1971), 84.

[6] See Mason, 331–62. It is worth noting, however, that the advertised print-runs, which Mason cites, are not always the same as actual print-runs (see n. 15). Nine hundred copies of *Intentions* were intended for the British market and 600 for the North American. For clarity, it should be noted that there were 240 old (i.e. pre-decimal) pence to the pound, and 12 old pence to the shilling; 2.4 old pence (d.) correspond to one new penny, and 5 new pence correspond to one shilling. It is difficult to make simple comparisons between the value of money in the 1890s

match the wealthier market of the periodical—the *Nineteenth Century* (priced at 2*s.* 6*d.*)—in which some of the essays first appeared. In other words, in the later works there seems to be a more precise correspondence between the first periodical readership and the marketing strategies behind the books. By contrast, the pricing of *Poems* (1881) suggests a different audience from those readers who might have encountered the poems in periodicals.

To Wilde the decision in the early 1880s to put together a volume of poetry may have represented a strategy to identify and establish himself as an *artist* (in his later words, as a 'lord of language') addressing an exclusive market, rather than a mere journalist who could put together an occasional poem to satisfy the demands of a periodical editor.[7] It is certainly of a piece with other aspects of the self-fashioning which took place throughout his life—from the suppression of his Dublin accent at Oxford, his cultivation of various styles of dress, haircuts, and 'looks', to his attempts to ingratiate himself with members of the English aristocracy, and his assiduous self-promotion within London literary society. However, this strategy brought problems, not the least of which was whether poems initially conceived for occasional publication would bear the scrutiny which would automatically follow from their presentation as a *collection*. Interestingly, the attempt to effect their transformation into literary art can be seen in the physical characteristics of the book itself. Although the publisher, David Bogue, was a strictly commercial house, considerable care was taken over the appearance of the volume: contemporary reviewers noted the typeface, the hand-made paper, and the parchment covers.

There is some evidence that in the early 1880s Wilde had overestimated the nature of the exposure and reputation he had achieved as a poet in the English periodical press, and had misunderstood the cultural differences between English, Irish, and American readerships. In 1878 he had tried to use his undergraduate friendship with George Macmillan to persuade the house of Macmillan to republish *Ravenna*, a tactic which he would repeat with *The Picture of Dorian Gray*. That he was unsuccessful despite the personal connection should perhaps have alerted Wilde to the fact that his poetry would be subjected to rather different criticism when removed from the occasion of its initial publication (whether as the winner of an

and the present day. A rough indication, however, is to be found in the fact that a labourer could earn as little as (and on occasions less than) 6*d.* per hour, and that the lowest middle-class occupation had a salary of around £70–£80 p.a.—in the title of John Davidson's poem, 'thirty bob a week'.

[7] Later, in his essay 'The Soul of Man Under Socialism', Wilde contrasted run-of-the-mill journalists with 'men of education and cultivation' who were forced to pander to the 'gross popular appetite'. Oscar Wilde, 'The Soul of Man Under Socialism', in *Intentions and the Soul of Man* (*Collected Edition*, Vol. 8), ed. Robert Ross (London: Methuen, 1908), 314.

undergraduate prize or as a 'literary' item for a periodical of general appeal). He should also have realized that English (and particularly London) readers might have different tastes from their Irish and American counterparts. Although by 1881 Wilde had published ten poems in the English press, most of the periodicals involved were minor. *Waifs and Strays* (priced at 2*s*.) was provincial (its subtitle was *A Terminal Magazine of Oxford Poetry*, and it was published by Thomas Shrimpton and Son in Oxford, the publisher of *Ravenna*); it was also short-lived (1879–82). *Biograph and Review* (1*s*.), which reprinted two poems originally published in Ireland, was also marginal; it too only survived from 1879 to 1882. *Pan* (6*d*.) was an even more ephemeral phenomenon, only lasting from September 1880 until June 1881. *Time* (1*s*.) and *World* (6*d*.) were more secure publications; both, however, were just as much a part of the entrepreneurial and commercial culture characteristic of late nineteenth-century periodical publishing. Both titles were under the control of Edmund Yates, with whom Wilde made contact via his brother Willie.[8] Although there is good evidence that Wilde was approached by Yates and was therefore (to some degree, at least) a 'name', it is difficult to avoid the conclusion that he had not really established himself among major English publishers on his own merits, but (as with his attempt to place *Ravenna*) still depended on personal contacts. In other words, the cultural capital which accrued from the periodicals in which Wilde's poems appeared was perhaps not as great as he imagined. Indeed, the most mainstream title to publish his work at this time was *Routledge's Christmas Annual* (1*s*.); of course it carried the prestigious name of a well-established and distinguished publishing house, but it reproduced Wilde's least characteristic work so far, what purported to be a translation from the Polish of a poem by Helena Modjeska.

When Wilde put together his collection of poems in 1881, he had to underwrite all of the printing costs that the publisher, David Bogue, would incur. Such a practice was not particularly unusual in the nineteenth century, and we should resist the temptation to interpret it as evidence of a simple lack of faith on the part of Bogue. There is some evidence that Bogue did not ask Wilde to put as much money 'up front' as was usually the case.[9]

---

[8] See Mason, 225–6.

[9] The details of the actual contract which Wilde signed with Bogue are given below and they are evidence of what is perhaps a compromise between the two men. A standard and printed contract was altered in ways which must have helped Wilde, and what he was required to pay Bogue was certainly less than Bogue routinely asked. Manuscript emendations (shown below as underlining) and deletions (shown by angle brackets) to the printed contract which Wilde signed indicate how much the standard charges were changed. The relevant clauses are as follows:

Memorandum of Agreement, made this seventeenth day of May 18 81 BETWEEN Oscar Wilde, Esq

of Keats House, Tite St, Chelsea, London on the One Part, and DAVID BOGUE, of 3, St Martin's Place, Publisher, on the Other Part.

It might be that Bogue's contract indicates his sense of Wilde's promise as a poet. If so, a balance needs to struck between those omens which were favourable for *Poems* (1881)—that Wilde was already widely published, and enjoyed some kind of reputation (even if it was an ambivalent one)—and those which were unfavourable: that no major English publisher had shown confidence in him, and that his name, such as it was, had been linked much more firmly to the world of the emergent mass media than to the world of literary art. Moreover almost half of the works in *Poems* (1881) appeared there for the first time. It is only this balance of factors which can explain the relatively poor sales of the volume and the critical hostility to it, as well as Wilde's disappointment at its fate.[10]

Poems went through three editions in 1881. This is not evidence of the volume's popularity: rather the opposite. The second and third editions were made up of unsold copies of the first edition. It was not an uncommon practice for nineteenth-century publishers to 're-package' unsold material in a new edition to stimulate sales. As Allan C. Dooley has argued, the meanings of terms such as 'edition' and 'impression', when used by nineteenth-century publishers, often do not correspond to their modern usage.[11] For example, publishers would routinely advertise as new editions what in practice were simple impressions (that is, reprintings made from

It is agreed:-
I.—That the said DAVID BOGUE shall be the sole Publisher of a Work entitled
    Poems by Oscar Wilde
of which the said Oscar Wilde is Proprietor.
II.—That all charges in relation to the Work be paid by the said Proprietor.
III.—That <half> one third of the estimated cost be paid when the MS is sent to the Printer, and <the balance> one third when the work is ready for issue and the balance two months after the date of publication.
IV.—That the said David Bogue shall account for all the copies he may dispose of at <half the published price> the trade sale price and thirteen as twelve deducting a commission of ten per cent.
V.—That the said David Bogue shall take upon himself the risk of bad debts.
The remaining two clauses specify dates when accounts were to be rendered, and nominate procedures for the arbitration of disputes between author and publisher. It is tempting to interpret what seem to be generous terms as a willingness on Bogue's part to take account of Wilde's lack of resources in 1881. (Manuscript held in the William Andrews Clark Memorial Library, UCLA (Wilde W6721Z M533 1881 May 17). Stuart Mason (p. 283) printed the first clauses of the contract and noted that there were manuscript changes made to it. He failed to note, however, the original terms of the standard contract.)

[10] Evidence that Wilde was anxious about the reception of the volume can be seen in his log-rolling letters to Matthew Arnold, Oscar Browning, Robert Browning, W. E. Gladstone, and William Ward. See *The Letters of Oscar Wilde*, ed. Rupert Hart-Davis (London: Hart-Davis: 1963), 77–9. His disappointment at the volume's fate can be seen in his letter to the librarian of the Oxford Union Society. See *More Letters of Oscar Wilde*, ed. Rupert Hart-Davis (London: John Murray, 1985), 36–7.
[11] See Allan C. Dooley, *Author and Printer in Victorian England* (London: University Press of Virginia, 1992), 86–9.

the same plates) in order to boost sales; they would—as Bogue did—also divide first print-runs into separate editions if a book did not sell.[12]

In 1882 Bogue printed a further 500 copies which did incorporate textual revisions to some poems (the details of which can be found in the appropriate textual note in the present volume). These copies made up Bogue's fourth and fifth (1882) editions.[13] The unsold sheets of the 1882 editions

---

[12] Bogue's first three (1881) editions of *Poems* are identical except for the addition of 'SECOND EDITION' and 'THIRD EDITION' to the appropriate title-pages. All the 1881 editions are divided into sections as follows:

ELEUTHERIA	p. 1
GARDEN OF EROS	p. 17
ROSA MYSTICA	p. 35
BURDEN OF ITYS	p. 61

(Pp. 83 and 84 are blank, indicating a section break, but with no subtitle. The poems in this 'group' are: 'Impression du Matin'; Magdalen Walks'; 'Athanasia'; 'Serenade'; 'Endymion'; 'La Bella Donna della mia Mente'; 'Chanson'.)

CHARMIDES	p. 101

(Pp. 143 and 144 are blank, again indicating a section break, and again with no subtitle. The poems in this 'group' are: 'Impressions: I. Les Silhouettes'; II. La Fuite de la Lune'; 'The Grave of Keats'; 'Theocritus'; 'In the Gold Room'; 'Ballade de Marguerite'; 'The Dole of the King's Daughter'; 'Amor Intellectualis'; 'Santa Decca'; 'A Vision'; 'Impression du Voyage'; The Grave of Shelley'; 'By The Arno'.)

IMPRESSIONS DU THÉATRE [*sic*]	p. 165
PANTHEA	p. 173

(Pp. 187 and 188 are blank, indicating a section break, but with no subtitle. The poems in this 'group' are: 'Impression. Le Reveillon'; 'At Verona'; 'Apologia'; 'Quia Multum Amavi'; 'Silentium Amoris'; 'Her Voice'; 'My Voice'; 'Taedium Vitae'.)

HUMANITAD	p. 203

(Pp. 231 and 232 are again blank, indicating a new section for the final poem.)

Each section has as a running head the title of that section; the parts of the volume which are not marked off formally by a titled section (pp. 83–100, pp. 143–163, and pp. 187–202) have the title of the appropriate poem as a running head. This practice was continued through Bogue's two 1882 editions as well as that of the Bodley Head edition in 1892, despite the fact that these last three editions identify new sections in the contents page, and have new half-title pages tipped in to mark off the new sections. The tops of all the 1881 editions are trimmed and gilded, and all are of 236 pages; the endpaper identifies the printer as the Chiswick Press (C. Whittingham and Co. Tooks Court, Chancery Lane).

An American edition by Roberts Brothers of *Poems* was also published in 1881. Its contents page follows that of the first Bogue edition; however, a section which in Bogue's first edition is untitled (pp. 83–100), and which in the fourth and fifth editions is entitled 'Wild Flowers', is in the American edition called 'Impression du Matin', and the blank sheet at p. 143 is removed (as is the blank sheet at p. 187). Otherwise the edition follows the section subtitles and running heads of the 1881 Bogue editions. The volume was bound in green cloth with an embossed gold motif on its front; the endpapers have a green leaf decoration.

[13] The fourth and fifth editions have the same title-page as his first three, except for the lines 'FOURTH EDITION' or 'FIFTH EDITION'; additionally the date of 1882 replaces that of 1881. The contents page is changed, but set in the same typeface as the earlier editions. More sections are introduced in the volume. As a consequence of Wilde's revisions to 'Charmides' the pagination from p. 109 on differs from first three editions. The fourth and fifth editions have 234 pages with two end-pages of advertisements from Bogue's list. Once more the volume was printed at the Chiswick Press.

(probably, although not certainly, from the fifth edition) formed the basis for Elkin Mathews and John Lane's reissue of the volume as *Poems* (1892). Wilde began negotiating with Mathews at the end of 1891 and secured the following contract:

To Oscar Wilde, Esq

Poems

Dear Sir,

I undertake to issue your volume of Poems on the following terms viz:-
To instruct printer to supply Title-page with my imprint for 230 copies.
On receipt of artist's Designs for cover at cost of £5–5–0.
Block to be prepared from same the cost of which as well as that of Title-page, Binding and Advertising to be first charges on the amount received for copies sold. The cost of advertising not to exceed £5–5–0.
For my Commission I agree to take 20% on the net published price, it being agreed that the book shall be brought out as a net one the price to be fixed when bound.
After the above charges have been met the balance to be remitted quarterly the first balance to be struck six months after publication.

> I am yours faithfully,
> Elkin Mathews[14]

The edition had a new half-title, and a new title-page designed by Charles Ricketts; Bogue's advertisements were cut out of the end matter and the volume was bound in violet cloth boards.

The modest reception of *Poems* (1881) did not lead Wilde to abandon poetry altogether, only to be much more circumspect in what he attempted. After *Poems* (1881) he published no more collections (except for the 1892 reissue by the Bodley Head). Instead, he reverted to his habit of publishing poems singly, although his productivity dropped as he concentrated on more profitable and successful genres, such as fiction and drama. After his average of two poems per year throughout the 1880s, Wilde published no

The organization of the sections for the fourth and fifth editions differed from that or the first three and are as follows:

ELEUTHERIA	p. 1	FLOWERS OF GOLD	p. 141
GARDEN OF EROS	p. 17	IMPRESSIONS DU THÉATRE [*sic*]	p. 163
ROSA MYSTICA	p. 35	PANTHEA	p. 171
BURDEN OF ITYS	p. 61	FOURTH MOVEMENT	p. 185
WIND FLOWERS	p. 83	HUMANITAD	p. 201
CHARMIDES	p. 101	FLOWER OF LOVE	p. 229

[14] Manuscript held in the William Andrews Clark Memorial Library, UCLA (Wilde M429L W6721 [1892?] ALS Elkin Mathews to Oscar Wilde). The Clark Library also has an ALS from Leighton Hodge to Elkin Mathews (dated 13 Feb. 1892) which gives a quotation for the gilding of the tops of the 1892 edition, a decoration which Bogue had also employed.

Dear Sir,

Oscar Wylde [sic] Poems

The extra price for gilding the tops of the above will be 4/- per 100 making our estimate for binding 66/- per 100.

poems between 1889 and 1894, apart from the prose poems printed in 1893 and 1894 in the *Spirit Lamp* and the *Fortnightly Review* which are included in this volume. However, it can be argued that they are short prose narratives as much as poems; certainly they are quite unlike the rest of Wilde's poetic *œuvre*.

Wilde's next major poetic work, *The Sphinx*, was published by the Bodley Head in June 1894 (that is, well over a decade after *Poems* (1881)). The price of the first edition of this work was high (£5. 5s. and £2. 2s. for the large-paper and small-paper editions respectively) and it was advertised as a limited edition (of which 50 were for the American market). Copies of the books themselves, each of which was numbered, state that the large paper edition was limited to twenty-five copies, the small paper edition to 200.[15] *The Sphinx* was an elaborately produced volume. Both editions had vellum covers tooled in gold with a design by Charles Ricketts (the larger edition had a decorative margin, also by Ricketts). Both editions were printed on handmade paper with uncut edges, and the print was in three inks: red, green, and black, with elaborate illustrations, again by Ricketts. Some pages had only 2, 4, or 5 lines of text, all of which was in small capitals. Unlike *Poems* (1881), which seems to have been directed towards a serious literary readership, *The Sphinx*, with its elaborate and costly production values, was clearly trying to exploit a rather different fashion which had emerged in the 1890s, one which the Bodley Head had been instrumental in establishing—a collector or connoisseur market for select editions of poetry, where the materiality of the book was as important as the text itself. The earlier success of the Bodley Head's 1892 reissue of *Poems* (the edition of 220 signed and numbered copies sold out within days) may have persuaded Wilde, Mathews, and Lane that Wilde's work was well suited to this developing market.

The Bodley Head took pains over the physical appearance of all their books, and were prepared to commit substantial resources to their production. Nevertheless, the price of most of the works on their list was competitive, the average being around 5s.[16] For a small number of books, however, the price was considerably higher: *The Sphinx* was the Bodley Head's most expensive book, while *Salomé* (the English edition of which

[15] In fact the records of the Bodley Head taken on 30 June 1894 prior to the dissolution of the partnership between Mathews and Lane indicate that 303 quarto copies of *The Sphinx* had been printed, although only 175 had been bound. See Nelson, *The Early Nineties*, 322–3. The strategy of the Bodley Head appears to have been to order a significantly larger print-run than their prospectus advertised; it is safe to assume that if demand had proved sufficient, the remaining unbound sheets of *The Sphinx* would have been used to form a second, and perhaps subsequent, editions.

[16] The specialized economics of publishing poetry in the 1890s, where considerable savings could be made on typesetting, allowed for large profits to be made on small print-runs; this in turn permitted significant investment in high-quality materials, such as paper, bindings, and commissioned art-work, without a publisher having to resort to the kind of high pricing necessary for a comparably sized volume of prose.

they had brought out in an edition of 500 copies in February 1894), at 15s., turned out to be their most profitable. The print-run for each was small compared with those for works by some Bodley Head authors (such as Francis Thompson, Richard Le Gallienne, George Egerton, and John Addington Symonds), who were selling up to ten times as many copies as Wilde. On the other hand, a work such as Katharine Tynan's *Cuckoo Songs* (1894), which had a print-run comparable to that of *Salomé*, was produced more economically (at 1s. 1¾d. per copy rather than *Salomé*'s 3s. 7¼d.) and consequently was sold much more cheaply at 5s. Lane, who was in charge of the commercial strategies of the business, clearly had a sharp sense of the amount of money it was worth investing in particular authors. For Wilde's work, he was prepared to invest significant sums because he was sure of high returns on limited editions.

Certainly the Bodley Head's marketing of Wilde's poetry was quite distinct from that of Bogue; moreover, although Wilde disliked Lane, he was more than happy with the way his work was marketed by the firm. The Bodley Head had also published *Lady Windermere's Fan* in 1893; and when the partnership split up, Lane (who assumed ownership of the Bodley Head name) published *A Woman of No Importance* as well as holding the rights to 'The Portrait of Mr W. H.'. By the early 1890s, then, Wilde had a very different sense of his importance as a writer and therefore a different sense of how his work should be presented to the public. When he returned the contract for *The Sphinx* to Lane, Wilde commented that 'the maker of a poem is a "poet," not an "author" . . . A book of this kind—very rare and curious—must not be thrown into the gutter of English journalism'.[17] This presentation of *The Sphinx* as a collector's item suggests that Wilde (as much as Mathews and Lane) saw financial as well as artistic opportunities in its publication. In comparison with the less than generous terms offered by Bogue, the Bodley Head contract specifies a 10 per cent royalty on the trade price (one usual for Bodley Head authors, although not for other publishing houses).[18] Had *The Sphinx* sold out, the deal could have earned

---

[17] For Wilde's letter, see Hart-Davis (ed.), *Letters*, 318. For further bibliographical details of *The Sphinx*, see Mason, 392–4. Charles Ricketts later commented that the unusual qualities of the book were made partly from choice and partly by necessity: 'This is the first book of the modern revival printed in three colours, red, black, and green: the small bulk of the text and unusual length of the lines necessitated quite a peculiar arrangement of the text.' Charles Ricketts, *Defence of the Revival of Printing* (1909); quoted in Mason, 398.

[18] James G. Nelson prints the contract for *The Sphinx* in full; unusually, it was drawn up by lawyers, indicating Wilde's growing business acumen:

(1) The publishers shall pay the poet a royalty of 10% on the gross sum received on the sales rendering accounts every six months.

(2) The publishers shall determine all details respecting the publication, the price at which copies are to be sold and the number of copies for publication in this country, America and elsewhere.

(3) The artist will before the 1st day of October 1892 submit to the publishers for their

Wilde a substantial royalty, although one dwarfed by his earnings from the theatre.

This evidence of a changing strategy in presenting his poems to the public justifies an examination of the ways in which Wilde tried initially to fashion a poetic identity, and of why he was not entirely successful in that attempt. It is not unreasonable to see the failure of *Poems* (1881), compared with the success of the repackaged Bodley Head edition of 1892, together with the resources invested in the publication of *The Sphinx*, as confirmation of the suspicion of Wilde's contemporaries that in transforming himself into an artist he kept a sharp eye on the commercial values normally associated with the mass media. What constituted literary success had certainly changed over the decade following the publication of *Poems* (1881), and houses such as the Bodley Head were perceived to have been complicit in those changes. They were held to have compromised literary judgement by conflating literary value with a material rarity brought about by an adroit manipulation of the market for books. Mathews and Lane were obliged to defend the literary merits of their list when charged by the popular press that their books were issued 'on the principle that rarity, not excellence, involves a speedy rise in price'.[19] The publication by the Bodley Head of Wilde's work, particularly his poetry, implicated him in this controversy, and laid him open to the accusation that his 'success' was in part the result of astute marketing. At the same time, some of the differences between the failure of *Poems* (1881) and the instant selling out of its 1892 reissue must be attributed to the growing public interest in Wilde as a fiction writer and newly emerged playwright (he had made his London début with *Lady Windermere's Fan* in February 1892 to considerable acclaim). Yet it remains a moot point among critics even today whether Wilde is best understood as

approval ten designs for decorating[,] colouring and fully illustrating the Poem also specimens of paper or other material and binding.

(4) The artist will execute and see to the reproduction of the designs when approved and prepare for and superintend through the press the said work and will make arrangements for the supply of all materials and labour for printing[,] issuing and binding the first and other editions thereof according to his own judgment but at the expense of the publishers with the stipulation that their total expenditure exclusive of advertisements[,] sales and fees paid to the author and artist shall not exceed £150 for an edition of 300 copies or less and £50 per 100 for any larger number which they may decide to produce.

(5) The publishers shall pay to the artist the sum of £45 which shall be paid as follows[:] £10 [£30 marked out by John Lane and £10 inserted] on the 18th of July 1892 and £10 on the eighteenth of each month until the total amount shall have been paid.

(6) The copyright of the work and of the illustrations and designs and of all future editions thereof shall belong absolutely to the publishers [Wilde has written in here: 'personally.' In the margin by (6) Wilde has written: 'the publishers are not to have the right to sell the copyright of the poem, without the poet's sanction.']

Quoted in Nelson, *The Early Nineties*, 96–7.

[19] The accusation appeared in the 'Literary Notes' of the *Pall Mall Gazette*, LVII, no. 8846 (29 July 1893), 4; quoted in Nelson, *The Early Nineties*, 83.

a literary artist or as a representative cultural figure. Some of the strongest arguments for Wilde's importance have been made by critics (such as Richard Dellamora, Jonathan Dollimore, Regenia Gagnier, and Alan Sinfield) who see Wilde as a prototypical product of the media, who is admired for the way he and his publishers market or 'package' his works, as much as for the works themselves.[20]

Two of the most frequent contemporary criticisms of *Poems* (1881) were that the volume was derivative and thin. Many critics were disappointed at Wilde's failure to establish a new voice in the volume, reactions very different from the reception which his drama and critical essays would receive some years later in the 1890s. It is worth noting that the kind of reader for whom these critics claimed to be speaking was quite distinct: he or she was assumed to have expectations unlike those of the periodical reader (or indeed the theatre-goer). In brief, Wilde's critics employed criteria of judgement which they deemed appropriate to the permanence and value implicit in the publication of a book of poems. The tart observation which Elton made at the Oxford Union about Wilde's plagiarisms exemplifies these different criteria. Wilde's poems were being judged for the first time against the work of established and serious poets.

There were several ways in which the volume exhibited a lack of originality. There were the 'uses' of lines by earlier authors, which this edition documents in its explanatory notes; there was also a form of self-plagiarism, where lines from one poem are repeated virtually verbatim in later poems. In 1914 Stuart Mason noted that some lines from 'Humanitad' were taken from *Ravenna*, and others in 'Humanitad' were repeated in *The Duchess of Padua*, then in 'The Critic as Artist', and then again in 'The Young King'.[21] There is also a process of self-revision in which poems are divided and given new titles and identities, or in which passages are distributed between different poems. This economy in the use of his material was a practice which Wilde would repeat throughout his career, a circumstance which suggests that it was more deliberate and strategic than his contemporaries realized.[22]

An early example of such manipulation of existing material is to be found in the genesis of the poem which appears in *Poems* (1881) as 'Sonnet on

---

[20] See Richard Dellamora, *Masculine Desire: The Sexual Politics of Victorian Aestheticism* (Chapel Hill: University of North Carolina Press, 1990); Jonathan Dollimore, *Sexual Dissidence: Augustine to Wilde, Freud to Foucault* (Oxford: Clarendon Press, 1991); Regenia Gagnier, *Idylls of the Marketplace: Oscar Wilde and the Victorian Public* (Aldershot: Scolar Press, 1987); Alan Sinfield, *The Wilde Century* (London: Cassell, 1994).

[21] See Mason, 314.

[22] The composition of the plays in the early 1890s shows Wilde reusing passages of dialogue from the book version of *The Picture of Dorian Gray* in *A Woman of No Importance*, and moving blocks of dialogue between various drafts of *An Ideal Husband* and *The Importance of Being Earnest*.

Approaching Italy'. It was first published as 'Salve Saturnia Tellus' in the *Irish Monthly* in 1877, with the place and date 'Genoa, 1877' appended to it. Wilde revised it for the *Biograph and Review* in 1880 as 'Sonnet Written at Turin'. At first sight the occasion of the poem seems intrinsic to its effect; it suggests that the poem ought to derive some of its power from the specificity of its setting. However, the fact that virtually the same lines are seen by Wilde to be equally applicable to more than one location suggests a pragmatic and opportunist attitude towards writing. A more complex example of this opportunism is to be found in the work (originally of two sections) which appeared as a three-part poem in the *Dublin University Magazine* in 1876 as 'Graffiti d'Italia: I. San Miniato'. In *Poems* (1881) it becomes two 'new' works. The first part is slightly revised and is entitled simply 'San Miniato'; the second and third parts are also slightly revised and retitled 'By the Arno'. Importantly Wilde separated them in *Poems* (1881) by some 120 pages: he seems, then, to be deliberately disguising the fact that they had their origins in a single poem which had already been published.

There are a number of ways of understanding this plagiarism.[23] The most obvious is to attribute it, as Wilde's early critics did, to a simple lack of originality and inventiveness. Those more generously disposed towards Wilde might be tempted to argue that imitation derived from his sense of immaturity and insecurity, feelings which combined with his anxiety to be published: in simple terms, he may have been quite consciously appropriating styles which in his estimate had already 'worked'. There are, however, several problems with this account. First, although explaining his motives, it does not exculpate Wilde from the charge of lack of originality. Second, Wilde's 'debts' are more specific than stylistic imitations. He copied phrases and whole lines. Finally, as I have suggested, it does not explain why Wilde plagiarized in his later more successful drama, fiction, and criticism—a phenomenon which contemporary reviewers continued to remark upon but gradually ceased to object to. One reason for this change of attitude may relate to the increasing blatancy of Wilde's borrowings in his later works; effectively it opened both his intentions and practice of plagiarism to public scrutiny, and in so doing turned it into a game.[24] A deceit acknowledged was no longer a deceit; reviewers could hardly be offended. Another reason for the change relates to the genres in which

---

[23] For recent discussions of Wilde's plagiarism, see Lawrence Danson, *Wilde's Intentions: The Artist in His Criticism* (Oxford: Clarendon Press, 1997), and Josephine M. Guy, 'Self-Plagiarism, Creativity and Craftsmanship in Oscar Wilde', *ELT*, 41, 1 (1998), 6–23. For an alternative account of Wilde's writing practices, see Sos Eltis, *Revising Wilde: Society and Subversion in the Plays of Oscar Wilde* (Oxford: Clarendon Press, 1996).

[24] The best example of this knowing game is to be found in a passage in one of the drafts of *A Woman of No Importance*, where Wilde has Lord Illingworth claim that 'a cigarette, as someone says, is the perfect type of the perfect pleasure'. The 'someone' was Wilde himself in *The Picture of Dorian Gray*. The passage was deleted in later drafts of the play.

Wilde was writing. Critical essays and short fiction were more intrinsically linked to the topicality and insistent self-referentiality of the periodical press. The *raison d'être* of the critical essay was that it formed part of a debate: and consequently it was automatically circumscribed by terms of reference already established. So the unattributed use of sources in 'The Critic as Artist' in *Intentions* was (and is) rarely described as plagiarism. Likewise, Wilde's fiction aligned itself with popular sub-genres which play upon expectations of plot, character, and setting. So the very familiarity of the devices in *The Picture of Dorian Gray* may well have contributed to its success. In both criticism and popular fiction, genres in which the skill of the writer consists in an ability to manipulate the familiar and expected, it can be hard (and is often pointless) to distinguish between lack of originality and topicality.[25]

Wilde's own explanation of his plagiarism is also worth considering. He distinguished between plagiarism as simple thieving by a lazy writer from plagiarism understood as a creative use of sources. In '*Olivia* at the Lyceum', a review published in 1885, Wilde explained that the 'originality . . . which we ask from the artist, is originality of treatment, not of subject. It is only the unimaginative who ever invents. The true artist is known by the use he makes of what he annexes, and he annexes everything.'[26] In other words, Wilde suggested that rather than invention it was the reworking of existing material which constituted real originality, and he kept with this theory ruthlessly throughout his career. The proper distinction to draw, then, is not between plagiarism and originality, but between what Wilde saw as creative and uncreative plagiarism. He may have learned from the relatively poor reception of *Poems* (1881) that poetry as a genre was less accommodating to his concept of creativity than other genres were; in poetry what was generally understood to be originality was much less susceptible to negotiation.

Finally, Wilde's poems contain many examples of revision which bear testimony to a conscientiousness and craftsmanship, qualities which are not easily compatible with plagiarism. Wilde's writing practices in *Poems* (1881) are characterized by a pattern of frequent and scrupulous revisions from manuscript to first periodical publication to book publication (which the textual apparatus of the present edition documents fully). They are the first examples of what was to become a lifelong habit. Generally speaking, there are three kinds of revision, although of course they constantly shade into each other: those made to individual lexical items, those made to the

---

[25] These very qualities have been identified as the principal reasons for the success of the Society Comedies; see Kerry Powell, *Oscar Wilde and the Theatre of the 1890s* (Cambridge: Cambridge University Press, 1990).

[26] '*Olivia* at the Lyceum', *Dramatic Review*, 30 May 1885; reprinted in *Reviews* (*The First Collected Edition of the Works of Oscar Wilde*, Vol. 13), ed. Robert Ross (London: Methuen, 1908), 29.

line, and those made to the stanza or pattern of the poem. Changes to individual words are to be found in most of the poems and they can have a significant effect on a poem's tone and meaning. For example, the relatively early 'By the Arno' (No. 6) sees Wilde revising 'golden mist' in line 18 of both the manuscript and *Dublin University Magazine* versions to 'sea-green mist' in the first edition of *Poems*, to 'sea-green vest' in the 1882 edition. Another early poem, 'Rome Unvisited' (No. 7), shows a slightly different pattern of revision (one found also in the plays) where Wilde's final text is a reversion to his first intentions. The line 'Is garnered into yellow sheaves' (line 50) in one manuscript becomes 'The reapers garner into yellow sheaves' in a second manuscript version, and is retained in the poem's first publication in the *Month and Catholic Review*. In his revisions for the book publication of the poem, Wilde reverted in part to his first thoughts by changing the line to 'Is garnered into dusty sheaves'. Many poems also reveal what was to become a common feature of Wilde's later writing practices—the addition, deletion, or rearrangement of material for different occasions and different publications. The *Time* version of 'Athanasia' (No. 59), for example, has a final stanza which Wilde omitted when the poem was reprinted in the 1881 and 1882 editions of *Poems*. In addition to these three categories, there is what can be called 'radical' revision, where combined textual changes are so thoroughgoing that it can be argued that the last version constitutes a different work. This sort of revision is to be found in the prose-poem 'The Disciple' (No. 113), although it is perhaps best seen in Wilde's novel, *The Picture of Dorian Gray*.

The history of the composition of *The Sphinx*, for which there are eleven surviving groups of manuscripts, is complex. Textual evidence and the watermarks of the paper of early manuscript drafts suggest that the poem (under the title *The Sphynx*) was begun during Wilde's Oxford years (1874–8) and a fair copy of it made. A letter to Robert Sherard confirms that Wilde took the poem up again in Paris in 1883, and made a further fair copy. (This Paris version contains thirteen stanzas omitted from the final published work.) After Wilde came to an agreement with the Bodley Head to publish the poem, he changed its quatrain structure to two-line stanzas, a feature which survives in a fair copy draft (with sketches by Charles Ricketts) now in the British Library (Add. MS. 37942). Wilde sent this copy to John Lane, requesting that a typewritten copy of it be made.[27] Wilde made further changes to the typescript; the text of this document is essentially that of the published poem, except for lines 75–88, which Wilde almost certainly added in proof, when a decision was made to standardize the spelling of the title). We cannot be

---

[27] *Letters*, 319. Details of the composition of *The Sphinx* derive from a paper entitled 'Wilde the Craftsman: Textual History of The Sphinx' given by Bobby Fong to a conference on 'Wilde Writings: Attributions, Editions, and Revisions' at UCLA in January 1999.

sure of the exact date of the poem's completion, except that it was at
some time between June 1893 and its publication in September 1894.

The Sphinx has some similarities with Poems (1881), especially in its
sensual imagery, ornate vocabulary, and an interest for what recent
critics have called 'orientalism', which Wilde developed in A House of
Pomegranates (1891), and in parts of The Picture of Dorian Gray (1890). At
the same time, there are other subjects in Poems (1881) which Wilde did not
pursue in his later poetry. These are to be found in a number of poems on
topical political subjects (such as events in Turkey and Bulgaria) and in a
further group occasioned by Wilde's visits to Italy and Greece in the late
1870s. Reviewers did not recognize Wilde as a new or significant mediator
of Italian or Greek culture as they had Swinburne or Elizabeth Barrett and
Robert Browning. Likewise, the 'political' poems attracted little attention.
These circumstances may have been responsible for Wilde's decision to
limit the thematic range of his later work to mainly classical, pastoral, and
Decadent subjects.

By contrast, the entire range of Wilde's poetry, from Poems (1881) to
The Sphinx (and, indeed, The Ballad of Reading Gaol (1898)), testifies to his
enduring interest in formal matters, and to his impressive mastery of tech-
nique. He was competent in a wide variety of lyric forms, from sonnets and
ballads to the complex sixteen-syllable lines of The Sphinx, each of which
has an internal (and often virtuoso) rhyme. He also demonstrated that he
was equally at ease with the tradition of Victorian discursive poetry (in
'Humanitad') as well as the more experimental work of contemporary
French writers such as Paul Verlaine and Stéphane Mallarmé (in, for
example, 'Impression du Matin').[28]

Wilde's last poem, The Ballad of Reading Gaol, is often seen as a new
departure—as a renewed commitment to poetry at the end of his career. In
terms of sales alone, it was by far the most successful of all his poetic works,
with the first six English editions (of which all but 99 were priced at 2s. 6d.)
selling in total over 5,000 copies in four months (between February and
May 1898).[29] This success may have had something to do with the publicity

[28] Wilde made an extended trip to Paris in early 1883 and made the acquaintance of a number of writers and painters whose work he already knew. As well as Verlaine and Mallarmé, he
met Alphonse Daudet, Edgar Degas, Edmond de Goncourt, Victor Hugo, and Emile Zola.
For accounts of the general importance of French culture in Wilde's work, see Malcolm Brad-
bury and Ian Fletcher (eds.), Decadence and the 1890s (London: Edward Arnold, 1979). For the
specific influence of French poetry, see Patricia Clements, Baudelaire and the English Tradition
(Princeton: Princeton University Press, 1985); and Lothar Hönnighausen, The Symbolist
Tradition in English Literature, condensed and trans. Gisela Hönnighausen (Cambridge:
Cambridge University Press, 1988).

[29] See Mason, 409–22. Commenting on an advertisement for The Ballad of Reading Gaol in
the Athenaeum in 1897 which was headed '3,000 copies sold in three weeks', Wilde wrote to
Leonard Smithers, the publisher of the poem, that 'the Athenaeum advertisement is
admirable; I feel like Lipton's tea' (Hart-Davis (ed.), More Letters, 171).

generated by Wilde's trials and imprisonment (the poem was first published under Wilde's prison number—'C.3.3.'—and not his name). Nevertheless, reviews were generally more favourable than those of his earlier work. This reaction might have been caused by Wilde's decision to abandon his Decadent preoccupations with the exotic and esoteric, and to revert to the Christian moralizing and robust, melodramatic sensationalism which he had explored in his successful short fiction and drama. It might also have related to his decision to base the poem on his own experience: reviewers noted a sincerity absent from his earlier poetry. Further evidence for this change of direction is to be seen in Wilde's use of the ballad form. Although Wilde clearly owes much to the work of English Romantic poets and to Thomas Hood (a detail once more noted by reviewers), he also drew inspiration from the example of contemporaries such as Rudyard Kipling, who had demonstrated the appropriateness of popular vernacular forms for addressing contemporary political and social issues.[30] In a letter to Edward Strangman written when he was finishing the poem, Wilde confessed that he was 'out-Henleying Kipling', suggesting that he was only too aware that he was writing for a new audience.[31]

It is impossible to say whether Wilde's poetry would have continued in the direction indicated by *The Ballad of Reading Gaol*. It is also impossible to conceive of the poem in isolation from the events which gave Wilde its subject-matter—his disgrace, trials, and subsequent imprisonment. In this sense, *The Ballad of Reading Gaol* is perhaps better seen as the culmination of a long-held career strategy, in which Wilde's eclecticism and frequent changes of direction are motivated by an attempt to find a public—to find what was in fashion and therefore what would sell. One can argue that *The Ballad of Reading Gaol* was simply the most astutely marketed of all Wilde's poems: that its popularity at the turn of the century cannot be understood in isolation from the notoriety of its author. At the same time, however, the more sympathetic readings of Wilde's life by modern critics have sustained the poem's appeal: it is now valued for the same pathos and poignancy which modern readers see in Wilde's final years.

[30] For example, Kipling's immensely popular *Barrack-Room Ballads*, published in 1892, drew attention to topical issues such as the calibre of army recruits and their experiences in India.

[31] See Hart-Davis (ed.), *More Letters*, 150.

EDITORIAL INTRODUCTION

The texts of Oscar Wilde's poetry and poems in prose are based on a fresh collation of available manuscripts and printed versions with textual authority, that is, versions of poems published during Wilde's lifetime with warranted assumption that the text had been submitted by him to the publishers. Copy text for much of the poetry is the fifth edition of *Poems*, a collection which included both revisions of poetry previously published in periodicals as well as poems making their first appearance in print. *Poems* was published by David Bogue in June 1881, and the second and third editions—actually two issues identical to the first edition except for title-pages and covers—appeared later that year. Wilde then ordered revisions made to standing type, and a run of five hundred copies was printed in January 1882. Half of these copies became the fourth edition; the remainder became the fifth; and both were issued in 1882. A variant, however, had been introduced into the poem 'Silentium Amoris' due to loosening of type during the run (see 'Textual Footnotes and Commentaries' below). The pages with this variant were the last printed and the first to be bound into volumes. Hence, certain copies of the fourth edition are more corrupt than those of the fifth. David Bogue went bankrupt shortly after, and in 1892 Wilde contracted with Elkin Mathews and John Lane of the Bodley Head to bring out as a new 'author's edition' two hundred and twenty copies of the fifth edition which had not been sold. The original covers and title-pages were cut out and a new design by Charles Ricketts substituted. Otherwise, the fifth edition and the author's edition are identical.

The fifth edition has been overruled as copy text only where the manuscript pages still exist from which type for *Poems* was set, for these pages represent the latest versions of those poems traceable to Wilde's hand (we do not have page proofs, which might have included further revisions by Wilde). Still, given Wilde's reliance on publishers' corrections of his accidentals and his own tendency to revise in proof, all of the substantives (variants in words) and most of the accidentals (variants in punctuation, spelling, and capitalization) have been decided in favour of the printed version. Wilde had initiated the negotiations for publishing *Poems* in 1881, and he paid all costs. The financial stake he had in the venture, the revisions he made to previously published poems, and the hope he had that the volume would establish him among the ranks of young poets all suggest that in general the fifth edition represents the most authoritative version of the poems contained therein.

Emendation of substantives, as well as changes in accidentals in the published poetry, has invariably been taken from other manuscript or earlier published versions of the poem in question. The sole exception is in line 570 of 'Charmides', where all manuscript and printed versions omit the closing quote, an obvious grammatical necessity which has been added by the editors. All emendations of substantives and accidentals are listed in the textual footnotes, along with variants from published versions during Wilde's lifetime with textual authority, and from all manuscript versions, no matter how fragmentary. Not included were those instances where Wilde used a fragment from a longer published poem in personalizing a presentation copy of one of his books.

Copy text for published poetry not included in *Poems* and for the poems in prose has generally been the last printed version with textual authority. The texts of poetry not published during Wilde's lifetime have been taken from manuscript. Wilde's handwriting is both distinctive (important in winnowing out forged manuscript poems signed 'Oscar Wilde' but not in his hand), and generally legible, even in desultory jottings (the few exceptions are indicated as *illegible* in the textual footnotes). Titled manuscripts, and untitled manuscripts of more than a stanza, which do not correspond to published poems are presented as independent poems, albeit sometimes incomplete. Some of these poems have been punctuated by the editors since Wilde sometimes neglected even such basics as periods and capitalization in early drafts. Such editorial emendations are indicated in the textual footnotes.

A word should be said regarding the hitherto standard edition of the poetry and poems in prose: that prepared by Robert Ross for the *Collected Edition* of Wilde's works, published by Methuen in 1908. While his selection of copy text is similar to that of the present edition, Ross haphazardly changed both substantives and accidentals without indicating such emendations. Almost two-thirds of the poems in the *Collected Edition* vary from the copy texts, sometimes without discernible reason. The new poems introduced for the first time in subsequent issues of the Ross edition were based on manuscripts to which we had access. In short, the *Collected Edition* has no textual authority in itself, and its variants have not been included in the textual footnotes.

The present edition, more complete than any of its predecessors, also has twenty-two poems not found in Ross's work. After Wilde's conviction in 1895, the family effects were auctioned off and, among other things, his literary manuscripts were dispersed. Some manuscripts were lost; many disappeared into private collections; a portion has been acquired by institutions and individuals willing to permit scholars to examine them.

The chronological arrangement given the poetry and poems in prose is, to some extent, speculative. Wilde's letters and allusions in the poems have provided some guide, but in many cases we could only narrow the date of composition for a particular work to a span of years. Since Wilde, like most writers, worked on several poems simultaneously, the dating of a specific poem was a balance between when it was begun and when it was published.

Textual Footnotes and Commentaries

The commentary for each poem includes a description of the manuscripts and publishing history of the text, along with the assignment of sigla to the various versions of the poem that have textual authority. Variants in the textual footnotes are keyed to these sigla. An introduction to each poem discusses the personal circumstances under which the work was composed and the historical or literary background necessary for understanding the poem. Annotations follow for specific lines.

In the textual notes, certain symbols, summarized in the list of 'Abbreviations and Symbols', give some sense of the sequence of Wilde's revisions in draft. A word or phrase which has been crossed out is indicated by angle brackets: < >. A word or phrase which has been superseded by another but not crossed out is indicated by curly brackets: { }. A word or phrase which has been added to an existing line by being placed before or above the line is indicated by single quotes: ' '. An incomplete line is indicated by square brackets: [ ]. Note, however, that the square brackets are a standard length: there is no attempt to reflect the particular length of what is omitted. Take, for example, line 22 of No. 78, 'Sen Artysty':

<blockquote>I had no joy in Nature; what to me,</blockquote>

One manuscript has the following:

<blockquote>in nature—
I had no joy for   the</blockquote>

where the *in nature* was written in above the initial line at a later time. In the textual notes, this is rendered:

<blockquote>I had no joy {for} 'in nature—' the [ ]</blockquote>

Except in the case of No. 118, *The Sphinx*, which has an unusually complex provenance (see commentary and textual footnotes to that poem), only variant readings are listed in the textual footnotes, and not readings which agree with the copy text.

Finally, a number of variants can confidently be ascribed to compositorial error or loose type rather than to Wilde. In all editions of *Poems*, the word *flight* in line 273 of 'The Garden of Eros' is printed *flght*. This has been silently emended. As noted above, during the run for the fourth and fifth editions of *Poems*, the period after *sung* in line 4 of 'Silentium Amoris' fell out, so some copies of the fourth edition are corrupt in this one regard since they were bound with the topmost sheets that were printed last. Similarly, the type used in *The Sphinx* was unusually small in order to accommodate the elongated lines. In the run for a deluxe large paper edition, which took place after the regular edition of the poem was printed, three exclamation marks dropped out: those following *Nile* in line 74, *lips* in line 127, and *paramour* in line 142. Since in the regular edition the exclamation marks serve as end-stops to the lines, the loss of these marks renders the sentences grammatically incorrect. These too are instances of variants introduced by loosening of type, not by authorial intention. None of the variants caused by loosening of type has been included in the textual footnotes.

NB Manuscript material relating to the dating of, and revisions to, some of Wilde's early poems—2, 3, 5, 7, 9, 14, 16, 17, 20, 25, 26, 27, 28, 29, 31, 32— was brought to the attention of the editors while the present volume was in final proof. A description of it and its relevance is given in the Addendum on pp. 329 ff.

ABBREVIATIONS AND SYMBOLS

For the sigla used in textual notes, see Commentary.

Berg	Henry W. and Albert A. Berg Collection, New York Public Library
BL	British Library
Bodmeriana	Bibliotheca Bodmeriana (Cologny-Geneva, Switzerland)
Buffalo	State University of New York (Buffalo, NY)
Clark	William Andrews Clark Memorial Library, University of California (Los Angeles, California)
Dartmouth	Dartmouth College Library
Dulau	Dulau & Co., *A Collection of Original Manuscripts, Letters, and Books of Oscar Wilde*, Cat. No. 161 (1928)
Ellmann	Richard Ellmann, *Oscar Wilde* (London, 1987; New York, 1988). Since pagination differs in these editions, we cite page numbers of both in the order listed above.
ELT	*English Literature in Transition, 1880–1920.*
Harvard	Houghton Library, Harvard University
Huntington	Henry E. Huntington Library (San Marino, California)
Hyde	Mary Hyde (Lady Eccles) Collection
Johns Hopkins	Milton S. Eisenhower Library, Johns Hopkins University
Letters	*Letters of Oscar Wilde*, ed. Rupert Hart-Davis (London and New York, 1962)
Mason	Stuart Mason (pseud. of Christopher Millard), *Bibliography of Oscar Wilde* (London, 1914; rpt. 1967)
More Letters	*More Letters of Oscar Wilde*, ed. Rupert Hart-Davis (London and New York, 1985)
MS (pl. MSS)	An autograph manuscript (or holograph)
P1	*Poems* (London, 1881), 1st to 3rd editions
P2	*Poems* (London, 1882), 4th and 5th editions
Poems (1908)	Vol. 9 of the *Collected Edition*, ed. Robert Ross, 14 vols. (London, 1908)
Princeton	Firestone Library, Princeton University
Rosenbach	Rosenbach Library and Museum (Philadelphia)
Texas	Harry Ransom Humanities Research Center, University of Texas (Austin)
TS (pl. TSS)	Typescript
Yale	Beinecke Rare Book and Manuscript Library, Yale University

Symbols used in Textual Notes

~	word preceding punctuation is unchanged
^	punctuation omitted
< >	word or phrase crossed out
{ }	word or phrase superseded by another but not crossed out
' '	word or phrase added to existing line by being placed before or above the line
[ ]	rest of line unfinished
/	line break

Ye Shall be Gods

Before the dividing of days
    Or the singing of summer or spring
God from the dust did raise
    A splendid and goodly thing
Man—from the womb of the land   5
    Man—from the sterile sod
Torn with a terrible hand—
    Formed in the image of God.
But the life of man is a sorrow
    And death a relief from pain   10
For love only lasts till tomorrow
    And life without love is vain.

Στροφὴ ά

And your strength will wither like grass
    Scorched by a pitiless sun
And the might of your hands will pass   15
    And the sands of your life will run.
O gods not of saving but sorrow
    Whose joy is in weeping of men
Who shall lend thee their life, or who borrow
    From others to give thee again?   20
O gods ever wrathful and tearless
    O gods not of night but of day
Though your faces be frowning and fearless
    Thy kingdom shall pass—men say.

’Αντιστροφὴ ά

The spirit of man is arisen   25
    And crowned as a mighty King.
The people have broken from prison
    And the voices once voiceless now sing.
Cry aloud, O dethroned and defeated,
    Cry aloud for the fading of might   30
Too long were ye feared and entreated
    Too long did men worship thy light.

Aye weep for your crimes without number
   The loving and luring of men
For your greatness is sunken in slumber   35
   Your light will n'er lighten again.

Στρόφὴ β΄

But as many a lovely flower
   Is born of a sterile seed
In a fatal and fearful hour
   There grew from this creedless breed   40
Love—fostered in flame and in fire
   That dies but to blossom again
Love—ever distilling desire
   Like wine from the eyelids of men.
We kneel to the great Iapygian   45
   We bow to the Lampsacene's shrine
For hers is the only religion
   And hers to entice and entwine—

’Αντιστροφὴ β΄

There once was another, men tell us,
   The giver and taker of life   50
A lovingless God and a jealous
   Whose joy was in weeping and strife.
He is gone; and his temple tis sunken
   In ashes and fallen in dust
For the souls of the people are drunken   55
   With dreams of the Lady of Lust—
We kneel to the Cyprian Mother
   We take up our lyres and sing
Thou art crowned with the crown of another
   Thou art throned where another was King.   60

35 your] yr. *M*   36 Your] Yr. *M*   44 men.] ~‸ *M*   49 another,] ~‸ *M*
us,] ~‸ *M*   52 strife.] ~‸ *M*

2 *Chorus of Cloud-Maidens*

('Aριστοφάνους. Νεφέλαι 275–290. 298–313.)

Στροφή

Cloud-maidens that float on for ever,
    Dew-sprinkled, fleet bodies, and fair,
Let us rise from our Sire's loud river,
    Great Ocean, and soar through the air
To the peaks of the pine-covered mountains where the
        pines hang as tresses of hair.   5
Let us seek the watchtowers undaunted,
    Where the well-watered cornfields abound,
And through murmurs of rivers nymph-haunted
    The songs of the sea-waves resound;
And the sun in the sky never wearies of spreading his radiance
        around.   10
        Let us cast off the haze
            Of the mists from our band,
        Till with far-seeing gaze
            We may look on the land.

'Αντιστροφή

Cloud-maidens that bring the rain-shower,   15
    To the Pallas-loved land let us wing,
To the land of stout heroes and Power,
    Where Kekrops was hero and king,
Where honour and silence is given
    To the mysteries that none may declare,   20
Where are gifts to the high gods in heaven
    When the house of the gods is laid bare,
Where are lofty roofed temples, and statues well
        carven and fair;

---

2 *Chorus of Cloud-Maidens.* Copy text: *O*, collated with *D*   *Title* Cloud-Maidens]
Cloud‸Maidens *D* (*The text of D is inconsistent in this regard, printing a hyphen in line 1 and omit-
ting it in line 15.*)   *Subscript* 275–290. 298–313] 275–287 and 295–307 *D*   2 Dew-
sprinkled] Dew‸sprinkled *D*   3 river,] ~‸ *D*   4 Great] Of *D*   8 through] the *D*
9 The songs] With the crash *D*   sea-waves] sea‸waves *D*   10 radiance] bright
rays *D*   11–14 *Printed as two anapaestic tetrameter lines in D*   12 mists] clouds *D*
13 far- seeing] far‸seeing *D*   15 Cloud-maidens] Cloud‸maidens *D*   rain-shower]
rain‸shower *D*   23 temples,] ~; *D*   fair;] ~. *D*

Where are feasts to the happy immortals
When the sacred procession draws near,   25
  Where garlands make bright the high portals
At all seasons and months in the year;
  And when spring days are here,
Then we tread to the wine-god a measure,
  In Bacchanal dance and in pleasure,   30
'Mid the contests of sweet singing choirs,
  And the crash of loud lyres.

Oxford, 1874.

3   *From Spring Days to Winter*

(For Music.)

In the glad spring when leaves were green,
  O merrily the throstle sings!
I sought, amid the tangled sheen,
Love whom mine eyes had never seen,
  O the glad dove has golden wings!   5

Between the blossoms red and white,
  O merrily the throstle sings!
My love first came into my sight,
O perfect vision of delight,
  O the glad dove has golden wings!   10

The yellow apples glowed like fire.
  O merrily the throstle sings!
O Love too great for lip or lyre,
Blown rose of love and of desire,
  O the glad dove has golden wings!   15

But now with snow the tree is grey
  Ah, sadly now the throstle sings!
My love is dead: ah! well-a-day,
See at her silent feet I lay
  A dove with broken wings!   20

26 high] *D*; bright *O*   29 wine-god] wine‸god *D*   30 Bacchanal] Carnival *D*
31 choirs] quires *D*   *Postscript* Oxford, 1874] Magdalen College, Oxford *D*
  3 From Spring Days to Winter. Copy text: *D*

Ah, Love! ah, Love! that thou wert slain—
Fond Dove, fond Dove return again.

Magdalen College, Oxford.

4   *Requiescat*

Tread lightly, she is near
    Under the snow,
Speak gently, she can hear
    The daisies grow.

All her bright golden hair   5
    Tarnished with rust,
She that was young and fair
    Fallen to dust.

Lily-like, white as snow,
    She hardly knew   10
She was a woman, so
    Sweetly she grew.

Coffin-board, heavy stone,
    Lie on her breast,
I vex my heart alone,   15
    She is at rest.

Peace, Peace, she cannot hear
    Lyre or sonnet,
All my life's buried here,
    Heap earth upon it.   20

Avignon.

    4 Requiescat. Copy text: *P2*, collated with *P1*, *M*   1 lightly,] ~: *M*   near₍ₐ₎ ~, *M*
2 snow,] ~: *M*   3 gently,] ~: *M*   6 rust,] ~: *M*   14 breast,] ~: *M*   15 alone,]
~₍ₐ₎ *P1*   17 Peace, Peace] Peace, peace *M*   18 sonnet,] ~: *M*   *Postscript* Avignon.]
not in M

5   *San Miniato*

See, I have climbed the mountain side
Up to this holy house of God,
Where once that Angel-Painter trod
Who saw the heavens opened wide,

And throned upon the crescent moon   5
The Virginal white Queen of Grace,—
Mary! could I but see thy face
Death could not come at all too soon.

O crowned by God with thorns and pain!
Mother of Christ! O mystic wife!   10
My heart is weary of this life
And over-sad to sing again.

O crowned by God with love and flame!
O crowned by Christ the Holy One!
O listen ere the searching sun   15
Show to the world my sin and shame.

6   *By the Arno*

The oleander on the wall
Grows crimson in the dawning light,
Though the grey shadows of the night
Lie yet on Florence like a pall.

The dew is bright upon the hill,   5
And bright the blossoms overhead,
But ah! the grasshoppers have fled,
The little Attic song is still.

---

5 San Miniato. Copy text: *P1–2*, collated with *M, D*   1 mountain‸side] mountain-side *D*
3 once that Angel-Painter] the Angelic Monk has *M*; that Angelic Monk once *D*   trod‸] ~, *D*
4 wide,] ~, *M*   5–16 *not in M*   6 Virginal white Queen of Grace,—] Queen of heaven
and of grace‸—*D*   7 Mary!] ~, *D*   face‸] ~, *D*   9 O‸] ~! *D*   pain!] ~, *D*
10 Christ!] ~, *D*   O‸] ~! *D*   wife!] ~, *D*   11 life‸] ~, *D*   13 O‸] ~! *D*   flame!]
~, *D*   14 O‸] ~! *D*   Holy One!] holy one, *D*   15 O‸] ~! *D*   listen‸] ~, *D*
    6 By the Arno. Copy text: *P2*, collated with *M, D, P1*   2 dawning light,] morning
light; *M*   3 Though the grey] The silver *M*   4 yet on] upon *M*   like] as *M, D*
5–8 *not in M*   7 But‸] ~, *D*   grasshoppers have] luccioli are *D*   8 little Attic]
grilli's merry *D*

Only the leaves are gently stirred
By the soft breathing of the gale,   10
And in the almond-scented vale
The lonely nightingale is heard.

The day will make thee silent soon,
O nightingale sing on for love!
While yet upon the shadowy grove   15
Splinter the arrows of the moon.

Before across the silent lawn
In sea-green vest the morning steals,
And to love's frightened eyes reveals
The long white fingers of the dawn   20

Fast climbing up the eastern sky
To grasp and slay the shuddering night,
All careless of my heart's delight,
Or if the nightingale should die.

7   *Rome Unvisited*

I

The corn has turned from grey to red,
Since first my spirit wandered forth
From the drear cities of the north,
And to Italia's mountains fled.

And here I set my face towards home,   5
For all my pilgrimage is done,
Although, methinks, yon blood-red sun
Marshals the way to Holy Rome.

---

9 Only the leaves] The myrtle-leaves *M*   stirred∧] ~, *M*   10 soft] sad *M*   breathing]
blowing *M, D*   13 soon,] ~∧*D*   14 O∧] ~! *D*   love!] ~, *M, D*   16 Splinter
the] Fall the bright *M, D*   17 Before] While yet *M*   18 sea-green vest] golden mist
M, D; sea-green mist *P1*   morning] moonlight *M*   19 to love's frightened] from love-
wearied *M*; to love's wearied *D*   reveals] conceals *M*   20 The long white] How the
long *M*   21 Fast] Come *M*   eastern] Eastern *M*   sky∧] ~, *D*   23 heart's] hearts
M   24.1 *Postscript* Magdalen College/ Oxford. *M*; Magdalen College, Oxford. *D*
    7 Rome Unvisited. Copy text: *P2*, collated with *M1, M2, C, P1*   *Title* Rome
Unvisited] Graffit<t>i d'Italia/ II. Arona. July 10*th* 1875. *M2*   1–44 *not in M1*
1 red,] ~∧ *M2*   2 forth∧] ~, *M2*   3 north] North *M2*   6 For all,] Alas! *M2, C*
done,] ~—*M2*   7 blood-red] bloodred *M2*   8 Marshals] Marshalls *M2*

O Blessed Lady, who dost hold
  Upon the seven hills thy reign!   10
  O Mother without blot or stain,
Crowned with bright crowns of triple gold!

O Roma, Roma, at thy feet
  I lay this barren gift of song!
  For, ah! the way is steep and long   15
That leads unto thy sacred street.

II

And yet what joy it were for me
  To turn my feet unto the south,
  And journeying towards the Tiber mouth
To kneel again at Fiesole!   20

And wandering through the tangled pines
  That break the gold of Arno's stream,
  To see the purple mist and gleam
Of morning on the Apennines.

By many a vineyard-hidden home,   25
  Orchard, and olive-garden grey,
  Till from the drear Campagna's way
The seven hills bear up the dome!

III

A pilgrim from the northern seas—
  What joy for me to seek alone   30
  The wondrous Temple, and the throne
Of Him who holds the awful keys!

---

9 Lady,] ~∧ *M2*   10 reign!] ~, *M2*   11 Scarlet with blood of martyrs slain, *M2*
12 Crowned with bright] And bright with *M2*   gold!] ~. *M2*   14 song!] ~, *M2*
15 For,] ~∧ *M2*   16 thy] the *M2*   street.] ~: *M2*   18 my feet] <my feet> again
M2   19 towards] toward *M2*   Tiber∧mouth∧] Tiber-mouth, *M2*   20 again]
<again> <and> 'in' pray'er' *M2*   Fiesole!] ~. *M2*   21 And] Or *M2, C*   22 break
the gold of Arno's] hang o'er Arno's yellow *M2*   26 Orchard,] ~∧ *M2*   27 from the
drear] rise from the *M2, C*   Campagna's] Campagnas *M2*   28 hills∧bear up the]
hills, the golden *M2, C*   dome!] ~. *M2*   30 seek alone∧] climb the street, *M2*
31 And kneel in homage at the feet *M2*   32 who] Who *C*   keys!] Keys∧ *M2*

When, bright with purple and with gold,
   Come priest and holy Cardinal,
    And borne above the heads of all   35
The gentle Shepherd of the Fold.

O joy to see before I die
   The only God-anointed King,
    And hear the silver trumpets ring
A triumph as He passes by!   40

Or at the brazen-pillared shrine
   Holds high the mystic sacrifice,
    And shows his God to human eyes
Beneath the veil of bread and wine.

IV

For lo, what changes time can bring!   45
   The cycles of revolving years
    May free my heart from all its fears,
And teach my lips a song to sing.

Before yon field of trembling gold
   Is garnered into dusty sheaves,   50
    Or ere the autumn's scarlet leaves
Flutter as birds adown the wold,

---

33 When,] ~∧ *M2*   gold,] ~∧ *M2*   35 borne] <high> borne *M2*   40 triumph]
Triumph *M2*   He] <h> 'H'e *M2*   passes by!] passeth by. *M2*   41 brazen-pillared]
altar of the *M2, C, P1*   43 his] a *M2, C, P1*   eyes,] ~, *M2*   44 Beneath the veil of
bread] From the dead fruit of corn *M2, C*   wine.] vine∧ *M2*   44.1–44.8 *M2 has a fourth
section of two stanzas omitted in later versions*:

> But now what good remains for me—
>   Alas! I leave Italia's land,
>   'To' <And> journey to the northern strand,
> And barren wastes of hungry sea.
>
> What idle hope have I to win,
>   Or pass beyond the sacred gate—?
>   Enough for me to sit and wait
> Till Gods own hand shall lead me in.

45 For lo,] And yet∧ *M1*; For lo! *M2*   bring!] ~!—*M1*; ~—*M2*   47 fears,] ~∧ *M1, C*
48 lips] {tongue} lips *M1*   sing.] ~—*M1, M2*   49 field of trembling] field of troubled
{ruined} *M1*; troubled sea of *M2, C*   50 Is garnered into dusty] Is garnered into yellow
M1; The reapers garner into *M2, C*   sheaves,] ~∧ *M1*   51 ere] e're *M1*; e'en *M2, C*
autumn's] autumns *M1, M2*   52 as] like *M1*   adown] a-down *M1*   wold,] ~∧ *M1*

I may have run the glorious race,
　　And caught the torch while yet aflame,
　　And called upon the holy name   55
Of Him who now doth hide His face.

Arona.

8   *Choir Boy*

Every day in the chapel choir
　　Praises to God I sing,
And they say that my voice mounts higher,
　　Than even a bird can sing—

Though the organ be loudly pealing,   5
　　It reaches the heavens blue,
Up through the vaulted ceiling
　　To where God sits out of view.

And they say that S. Michael, great and fair
　　Painted upon the wall,   10
With his golden glory of backblown hair,
　　White as a lily, and tall—

Is not so lovely to the view
　　His lips are not so red,
His eyes are not such wells of blue,   15
　　His

53 may have run the glorious race,] may have won the bitter race‿ *M1*; may have run the glorious race‿ *M2*; shall have run the glorious race, *C*   54 caught the torch while yet aflame]
set my fingers on the goal *M1*; caught the torch while yet a-flame *M2*   55 And] <Or>
And *M2*   called upon the holy name] <looked upon> looking through the Auriole *M1*
56 Of Him who now doth hide His face.] Behold the Father face to face—*M1*; Of Him who
now doth hide his face. *M2*; Of Him Who now doth hide His face. *C*   56.1–56.4 *M1 has
a concluding stanza that is an early version of M2, 44.5–44.8*:

My limbs are overfaint to win
Or pass beyond the sacred gate,
Sleep, sleep, O troubled soul & wait
Till Gods own hand shall lead thee in

Postscript Arona.] *M1*, *C have no postscript*; <Magd> S. M. Magdalen College/ Oxford. *M2*
　8 *Choir Boy*. Copy text: *M*

9   *La Bella Donna della mia Mente*

My limbs are wasted with a flame,
    My feet are sore with travelling,
For calling on my Lady's name
    My lips have now forgot to sing.

O Linnet in the wild-rose brake   5
    Strain for my Love thy melody,
O Lark sing louder for love's sake,
    My gentle Lady passeth by.

She is too fair for any man
    To see or hold his heart's delight,   10
Fairer than Queen or courtezan
    Or moon-lit water in the night.

Her hair is bound with myrtle leaves,
    (Green leaves upon her golden hair!)
Green grasses through the yellow sheaves   15
    Of autumn corn are not more fair.

Her little lips, more made to kiss
    Than to cry bitterly for pain,
Are tremulous as brook-water is,
    Or roses after evening rain.   20

Her neck is like white melilote
    Flushing for pleasure of the sun,
The throbbing of the linnet's throat
    Is not so sweet to look upon.

9 La Bella Donna della mia Mente. Copy text: *P1–2*, collated with *K*   3 Lady's] lady's *K*
5 brake˄] ~! *K*   6 Love] love *K*   melody,] ~; *K*   7 Lark˄] ~! *K*   8 My
gentle Lady] Now my fair lady *K*   8.1–8.4 *K has:*

O almond-flowers! bend adown
    Until ye reach her drooping head;
O twining branches! weave a crown
    Of apple-blossoms white and red.

10 or] and *K*   delight,] ~; *K*   11 Queen] queen *K*   courtezan˄] ~, *K*   14 hair!)]
~), *K*   21–8 *K reverses the two stanzas*   21 neck is like] breasts are as *K*
22 Flushing] Blushing *K*   sun,] ~; *K*   24 sweet] fair *K*

As a pomegranate, cut in twain,   25
    White-seeded, is her crimson mouth,
Her cheeks are as the fading stain
    Where the peach reddens to the south.

O twining hands! O delicate
    White body made for love and pain!
O House of love! O desolate   30
    Pale flower beaten by the rain!

10   *Chanson*

A ring of gold and a milk-white dove
    Are goodly gifts for thee,
And a hempen rope for your own love
    To hang upon a tree.

For you a House of Ivory   5
    (Roses are white in the rose-bower)!
A narrow bed for me to lie
    (White, O white, is the hemlock flower)!

Myrtle and jessamine for you
    (O the red rose is fair to see)!   10
For me the cypress and the rue
    (Fairest of all is rose-mary)!

25 pomegranate,] ~ₐ *K*   twain,] ~ₐ *K*   26 White-seeded, is her crimson] Her open lips and amorous *K*   28 to] at *K*   30 White] Fair *K*   pain!] ~; *K*   32 Pale flower beaten by the] White lily, overdrenched with *K*   32.1–32.8 *K has*:

God can bring Winter unto May,
    And change the sky to flame and blue,
Or summer corn to gold from grey:
    One thing alone He cannot do.

He cannot change my love to hate,
    Or make thy face less fair to see,
Though now He knocketh at the gate
    With life and death—for you and me.

10 Chanson. Copy text: *P1–2*, collated with *K, M*   1 milk-white] milkwhite *M* 4 hang] hangen *K, M*   5 House of Ivoryₐ] house of ivory, *K*; House of Ivory, *M* 6 rose-bower)!] ~,) *K*; roseₐbower)ₐ *M*   7 lieₐ] ~, *K, M*   8 flower)!] ~.) *K*; ~). *M*   9 you,] ~, *K, M*   10 see)!] ~,) *K*; ~)ₐ *M*   11 rueₐ] ~, *K, M*   12 rosemary)!] rosemary.) *K*; rose-mary)ₐ *M*

For you three lovers of your hand
   (Green grass where a man lies dead)!
For me three paces on the sand   15
   (Plant lilies at my head)!

11   See! the gold sun has risen,
   (Ah God! how very fair)
Too soon he has broken from prison—

    Ah Sweet! it is only my hair

Nay, for I see the snow white day   5
   Come from his rosy bower,
And I know that the night has fled away,

    Ah Sweet! 'tis my breast flower

Nay, but the night has surely fled,
   For crimson grows the south,   10
And the gates of dawn are opening red,

    Ah Sweet, it is only my mouth

Then why do I see the sky so blue,
   Flecked where the linnet flies,
Ah love lie nearer, and tell me true   15
   Is it only the light of thine eyes?
For if thou art the dawn and the holy day,
   And thou the golden sun—

Nay but the sun doth o'er us pass
   Turning my blood to wine,   20
As we lie by a stream and the warm soft grass

    Ah Sweet! 'tis my body and thine.

13 hand∧] ~, K   14 dead)!] ~,) K; ~)∧ M   15 sand∧] ~, K   16 head)!] ~.) K; ~). M
  11 See! the gold sun has risen. Copy text: M

12   'Ah God it is a dreary thing
                    To sit at home with unkissed lips,—'

                                        Mrs. Browning

      Sweet I went out in the night,
        Though the wind sang drearilie,
      And I waited beneath the lamp's light,
        For I knew I was fair to see.

      And there came one with eyes of fire,   5
        And a throat as a singing dove,
      And he looked on me with desire,
        And I knew that his name was Love.

      See what I found in the street
        A man child lusty and fair   10
      With little white limbs, little feet,
        And glory of golden hair.

      Red and white as a mountain rose,
        Little brown eyes as bright as wine
      Little white fingers, and little white toes   15
        O he is lovely, this boy of mine.

      What do you say he's the child of sin,
        That God looks on him with angry eyes,
      And never will let him enter in
        To the lilies and flowers and rivers of Paradise.   20

---

12 Sweet I went out in the night. Copy text: *M*   3 lamp's] lamps *M*   7 And he
looked] And 'lips move' he looked *M*   11 With little white limbs] <From his head to the
soles of> *M*   limbs,] ~∧ *M*   12 golden] {yellow} *M*   12.1–12.4 *M has an incomplete stanza that has been omitted*:

                    Naked, and lithe and brown and merry
                        My
                    Little red lips like a summer cherry
                        Little brown

16 mine.] ~∧ *M*   20 To the lilies and flowers and rivers] <The holy garden>
M   Paradise.] ~∧ *M*

13   She stole behind him where he lay
              All tossed and tired from the dance,
          He turned his curly head away
              With pretty boyish petulance.

          She said, 'I loved you all the while,   5
              Rough Colin is a clumsy clout.'
          He twirled his crook, and would not smile
              His cross lips from their rosy pout.

          She said, 'You are more dear to me
              Than are the fat lambs of my flock,'   10
          He would not speak, but sulkily
              Smoothed down his crumpled linen smock.

          She said, 'I love you best of all,'
              And put her little hand in his.
          Her voice was sweeter than the call   15
              At evening of the pigeon is.

          He shook her clinging fingers off:
              (But little maids have little wiles)
          She said, 'I heard your white ewe cough
              Just as I passed beyond the stiles.'   20

          He rose and seized his polished crook,
              She hid her face in birdlike laughter,
          He raced along the sedgy brook
              And she—alas, she followed after.

          She followed, and he ran before,   25
              Carelessly whistling to the wind,
          But ere he closed the sheepfold door
              The gold-haired child crept in behind.

13 She stole behind him where he lay. Copy text: *M1, M2, M3, M4*   1–8 *not in M3, M4*
4 pretty,] *M2*; ~, *M1*   boyish] {wilful,} *M1*   5 said,] *M2*; ~ˏ *M1*   7 smile]
{wile} *M2*   8 cross] <red> *M1*   rosy] {foolish} {boyish} *M1*   9–20 *not in M1,*
M3, M4   9–16 *In M2, lines 13–16 preceded lines 9–12, but Wilde renumbered these stanzas*
10 fat] <white> *M2*   11 but] <and> *M2*   12 smock.] ~ˏ *M2*   13 best of]
<more than> *M2*   18 But . . . wiles] <I saw the [   ]> *M2*   20 passed beyond]
<crossed the broken> *M2*   the] *not in M2*   stiles.] ~ˏ *M2*   21–6 *not in M1, M2, M4*
21 seized] <took> *M3*   22 birdlike] <boyish> *M3*   23 raced along] <ran beside>
M3   24 alas,] ~ˏ *M3*   27–8 *not in M1, M2*   27 ere] e're *M3, M4*   closed]
M4; shut *M3*   sheepfold] *M3*; wattled *M4*   28 gold-haired child] *M4*; *not in M3*
behind.] *M3*; ~ˏ *M4*

There rose a little undertune
    Of singing in the wattled fold,
And through its latticed cloud the moon   30
    Leaned down with naked arms of gold.

14   *The Dole of the King's Daughter*

(Breton.)

Seven stars in the still water,
    And seven in the sky;
Seven sins on the King's daughter,
    Deep in her soul to lie.

Red roses are at her feet,   5
    (Roses are red in her red-gold hair)
And O where her bosom and girdle meet
    Red roses are hidden there.

Fair is the knight who lieth slain
    Amid the rush and reed,   10
See the lean fishes that are fain
    Upon dead men to feed.

Sweet is the page that lieth there,
    (Cloth of gold is goodly prey,)
See the black ravens in the air,   15
    Black, O black as the night are they.

What do they there so stark and dead?
    (There is blood upon her hand.)
Why are the lilies flecked with red?
    (There is blood on the river sand.)   20

29–32 *not in M2, M3, M4*   29 rose] <came> *M1*   30 in] <from> *M1*
31 through] {from} *M1*

14 The Dole of the King's Daughter. (Breton.). Copy text: *M2*, collated with *M1, D, P1–2*
Subtitle (Breton.)] *P1–2; no subtitle in M1, M2;* (For a Painting.) *D*   1–16 *not in M1*
2 sky;] ~, *D*   3 daughter,] ~, *D*   4 lie.] ~—*D*   5 are] *not in D*   feet,] ~, *D*
6 red-gold hair) ,] yellow hair), *D*   7 And O where] And where *D*   meet,] ~,
D   9 who] that *D*   10 reed,] ~; *D*   13 there,] ~, *D*   14 prey,)] ~):
D   15 air,] *D, P1–2;* ~, *M2*   16 black,] ~, *D*   17 Three milkwhite doves are
lying dead, *M1*   18 (There] ,~ *M1*   hand.)] ~, *M1*; ~:) *D;* ~, *P1–2*   19 Why are
the lilies] Three white lilies are *M1*   red?] ~, *M1*   20 (There] ,~ *M1*   sand.)]
D, P1–2; ~. *M1;* ~,) *M2*

There are two that ride from the south and east,
    And two from the north and west,
For the black raven a goodly feast,
    For the King's daughter rest.

There is one man who loves her true,   25
    (Red, O red, is the stain of gore!)
He hath duggen a grave by the darksome yew,
    (One grave will do for four.)

No moon in the still heaven,
    In the black water none,   30
The sins on her soul are seven,
    The sin upon his is one.

15   *Love Song*

Though the wind shakes lintel and rafter,
    And the priest sits mourning alone,
For the ruin that comes hereafter
    When the world shall be overthrown,
What matter the wind and weather   5
    To those that live for a day?
When my Love and I are together,
    What matter what men may say?

I and my Love where the wild red rose is,
    When hands grow weary and eyes are bright,   10
Kisses are sweet as the evening closes,
    Lips are reddest before the night,
And what matter if Death be an endless slumber
    And thorns the commonest crown for the head,
What matter if sorrow like wild weeds cumber,   15
    When kisses are sweetest, and lips are red?

21 There are] *not in M1*   south and east] North and East *M1*; north and east *D*
22 north and west] South and West *M1*; south and west *D*   23 raven] ravens *M1, D*
24 King's] *D, P1–2*; Kings *M1, M2*   25 There is] *not in M1*   who] that
M1, D   26 Red, O red,] Crimson and red‸ *M1*; Red—oh, red‸ *D*   gore!)] ~.) *M1*
28 (One] ‸~ *M1*   four.)] *P1–2*; ~. *M1*; ~). *D, M2*   31 her] *her M1*   seven,] ~‸ *M1*
32.1 *Postscript* S. M. Magdalen College/ Oxford. *M1*; Magdalen College, Oxford. *D*
    15 Love Song. Copy text: *M1, M2*   1–16 *not in M2*   7 my Love and I] <I and>
my Love 'and I' *M1*

I that am only the idlest singer
　　That ever sang by a desolate sea,
A goodlier gift than song can bring her,
　　Sweeter than sound of minstrelsy,　　　　　　20
For singers grow weary, and lips will tire,
　　And winds will scatter the pipe and reed,
And even the sound of the silver lyre
　　Sickens my heart in the days of need,
But never at all do I fail or falter　　　　　　25
　　For I know that Love is a god, and fair,
And if death and derision follow after,
　　The only god worth a sin and a prayer.

And She and I are as Queen and Master,
　　Why should we care if a people groan　　　　30
'Neath a despot's feet, or some red disaster
　　Shatter the fool on his barren throne?
What matter if prisons and palaces crumble,
　　And the red flag floats in the piled-up street,
When over the sound of the cannon's rumble　　35
　　The voice of my Lady is clear and sweet?
For the worlds are many and we are single,
　　And sweeter to me when my Lady sings,
Than the cry when the East and the West world mingle,
　　For clamour of battle, and fall of Kings.　　40

So out of the reach of tears and sorrow
　　Under the wild-rose let us play,
And if death and severing come tomorrow,
　　I have your kisses, sweet heart, today.

Magdalen College, Oxford.

19 her,] *M1*; ~‿ *M2*　　20 sound of minstrelsy,] *M1*; *not in M2*　　21 For . . . tire,] *M2*;
For Love is better than [　　] *M1*　　22–6 *not in M1*　　26 fair,] ~‿ *M2*　　27 And
. . . after] *M1*; [　　] {certainly alter} *M1*; And that [　　] alter *M2*　　after,] ~‿ *M1*
28 The . . . prayer] *M1, M2*; {Love} [　　] *M1*　　god] *M2*; <god> thing *M1*　　prayer.] ~‿
M1, M2　　29–44 *not in M1*　　29 And] <For> *M2*　　31 despot's] despots *M2*
35 When] <For> *M2*　　cannon's] cannons *M2*　　38 And <'Why'> *M2*
40 Kings.] ~‿ *M2*

16   Ἄιλινον, αἴλινον εἰπέ, τὸ δ᾽ εὖ νικάτω

O well for him who lives at ease
    With garnered gold in wide domain,
    Nor heeds the splashing of the rain,
The crashing down of forest trees.

O well for him who ne'er hath known   5
    The travail of the hungry years,
    A father grey with grief and tears,
A mother weeping all alone.

But well for him whose feet have trod
    The weary road of earthly strife   10
    Yet from the sorrows of his life
Builds ladders to be nearer God.

S. M. Magdalen College, Oxford.

17   *The True Knowledge*

....ἀναγκαίως δ᾽ ἔχει
βίον θερίζειν ὥστε κάρπιμον στάχυν,
καὶ τὸν μὲν εἶναι τὸν δὲ μή.

Thou knowest all:—I seek in vain
    What lands to till or sow with seed;
    The land is black with briar and weed,
Nor cares for falling tears or rain.

Thou knowest all:—I sit and wait   5
    With blinded eyes and hands that fail,
    Till the last lifting of the veil
That hangs before God's holy gate.

16 *Ἄιλινον, αἴλινον εἰπέ, τὸ δ᾽ εὖ νικάτω.* Copy text: *L*, collated with *M*, *D*
2 domain,] *M*, *D*; ~! *L*   5 O] And *M*   7 father] Father *M*   9 trod‸] ~, *D*
10 earthly] toil and *M*, *D*   *Postscript* S. M. Magdalen College, Oxford.] *D*; *not in M, L*
    17 The True Knowledge. Copy text: *L*, collated with *I*   1 all:—] ~‸—*I*   2 seed;]
~—*I*   5 all:—] ~‸—*I*   7 veil‸] ~, *I*   8 That hangs before God's holy] And
the first opening of the *I*

Thou knowest all:—I cannot see;
I trust I shall not live in vain: 10
I *know* that we shall meet again
In some divine eternity.

S. M. Magdalen College, Oxford.

18   *Heart's Yearnings*

('Έρως τῶν ἀδυνάτων.)

Surely to me the world is all too drear,
    To shape my sorrow to a tuneful strain,
It is enough for wearied ears to hear
    The Passion-Music of a fevered brain,
    Or low complainings of a heart's pain.   5

My saddened soul is out of tune with time,
    Nor have I care to set the crooked straight,
Or win green laurels for some pleasant rhyme,
    Only with tired eyes I sit and wait
    The opening of the Future's Mystic Gate.   10

I am so tired of all the busy throng
    That chirp and chatter in the noisy street,
That I would sit alone and sing no song
    But listen for the coming of Love's feet.
    Love is a pleasant messenger to greet.   15

O Love come close before the hateful day,
    And tarry not until the night is dead,
O Love come quickly, for although one pray,
    What has God ever given in thy stead
    But dust and ashes for the head?   20

9 all:—] ~ₐ—*I*   see;] ~. *I*   10 vain:] ~, *I*   11 *know*] know *I*   againₐ] ~, *I*
    18 Heart's Yearnings. Copy text: *M2*, collated with *M1*   1 drear,] ~ₐ *M1*
4–5 *M1 has:*

The passion music <of a fevered>
                        rising in the brain
And low [   ]

6–40 *not in M1*   9 <Only with tired eyes to wait> I sit and wait, *M2 has deletion without
another reading to be substituted*   10 <Until> the opening of the 'Future's' Mystic Gateₐ
M2   14 Love's] Loves *M2*   15 Love] <For> Love *M2*   greet.] ~ₐ *M2*

Strain, strain O longing eyes till Love is near,
   O Heart be ready for his entering thee,
O Breaking Heart be free from doubt and fear,
   For when Love comes he cometh gloriously,
   And entering Love is very fair to see.   25

Peace, Peace O breaking heart, Love comes apace,
   And surely great delight and gladness brings,
Now look at last upon his shining face,
   And listen to the flying of his wings
   And the sweet voice of Love that sings.   30

O pale moon shining fair and clear
   Between the apple-blossoms white,
That cluster round my window here,
   Why does Love tarry in his flight
   And not come near for my heart's delight—   35

I only hear the sighing of the breeze
   That makes complaint in a sweet undertune,
I only see the blossom-laden trees
   Splintering the arrows of the golden moon,
   That turn black night into the burnished noon.   40

Magdalen College, Oxford.

19   *The Little Ship*

    Have you forgotten the ship love
       I made as a childish toy,
    When you were a little girl love,
       And I was a little boy?

    Ah! never in all the fleet love   5
       Such a beautiful ship was seen,
    For the sides were painted blue love
       And the deck was yellow and green.

    I carved a wonderful mast love
       From my Father's Sunday stick,   10
    You cut up your one good dress love
       That the sail should be of silk.

31 pale] Pale *M2*   36 hear] <see> *M2*   37 That] <For> That *M2*
19 The Little Ship. Copy text: *M*   10 Father's] Fathers *M*

And I launched it on the pond love
　　And I called it after you,
And for want of the bottle of wine love   15
　　We christened it with the dew.

And we put your doll on board love
　　With a cargo of chocolate cream,
But the little ship struck on a cork love
　　And the doll went down with a scream!   20

It is forty years since then love
　　And your hair is silver grey,
And we sit in our old armchairs love
　　And we watch our children play.

And I have a wooden leg love   25
　　And the title of K. C. B.
For bringing her Majesty's Fleet love
　　Over the stormy sea.

But I've never forgotten the ship love
　　I made as a childish toy   30
When you were a little girl love
　　And I was a sailor boy.

20   *ΘΡΗΝΩΙΔΙΑ*

(Eur. Hec., 444–483.)

Song sung by captive women of Troy on the sea beach at Aulis,
while the Achaeans were there stormbound through the wrath
of dishonoured Achilles, and waiting for a fair wind to bring
them home.

Στροφή
O fair wind blowing from the sea!
　　Who through the dark and mist dost guide
　　The ships that on the billows ride,
Unto what land, ah, misery!
Shall I be borne, across what stormy wave,   5
Or to whose house a purchased slave?

20 *ΘΡΗΝΩΙΔΙΑ.* Copy text: *K*, collated with *M*   1–51 *not in M*

O sea-wind blowing fair and fast
  Is it unto the Dorian strand,
    Or to those far and fabled shores,
     Where great Apidanus outpours   10
  His streams upon the fertile land,
  Or shall I tread the Phthian sand,
Borne by the swift breath of the blast.

Ἀντιστροφή

O blowing wind! you bring my sorrow near,
  For surely borne with splashing of the oar,   15
And hidden in some galley-prison drear
  I shall be led unto that distant shore
    Where the tall palm-tree first took root, and made,
    With clustering laurel leaves, a pleasant shade
  For Leto when with travail great she bore   20
    A god and goddess in Love's bitter fight,
    Her body's anguish, and her soul's delight.

        It may be in Delos,
          Encircled of seas,
        I shall sing with some maids   25
          From the Kyklades,
        Of Artemis goddess
          And queen and maiden,
        Sing of the gold
          In her hair heavy laden.   30
        Sing of her hunting,
          Her arrows and bow,
        And in singing find solace
          From weeping and woe.

Στροφὴ β΄

Or it may be my bitter doom   35
To stand a handmaid at the loom,
  In distant Athens of supreme renown;
    And weave some wondrous tapestry,
    Or work in bright embroidery
Upon the crocus-flower'd robe and saffron-colour'd gown,   40
    The flying horses wrought in gold,
    The silver chariot onward roll'd
That bears Athena through the Town;

Or the warring giants that strove to climb
From earth to heaven to reign as kings,   45
And Zeus the conquering son of Time
Borne on the hurricane's eagle wings;
And the lightning flame and the bolts that fell
From the risen cloud at the god's behest,
And hurl'd the rebels to darkness of hell,   50
To a sleep without slumber or waking or rest.

Ἀντιστροφὴ β΄

Alas! our children's sorrow, and their pain
In slavery.
Alas! our warrior sires nobly slain
For liberty.   55
Alas! our country's glory, and the name
Of Troy's fair town;
By the lances and the fighting and the flame
Tall Troy is down.

I shall pass with my soul overladen,   60
To a land far away and unseen,
For Asia is slave and handmaiden,
Europe is Mistress and Queen.
Without love, or love's holiest treasure,
I shall pass unto Hades abhorr'd,   65
To the grave as my chamber of pleasure,
To death as my Lover and Lord.

21   *Lotus Land*

The sultry noon is amorous for rain;
The golden bee, the lily's paramour,
Sleeps in the lily-bell, which doth allure

51.1 Ἀντιστροφὴ β΄] Ὅλος χόρος M   52 children's] childrens M   53 slavery.] ~ₐ
M   54 warrior sires] warriorsires M   55 liberty.] ~ₐ M   57 Troy's] Troys M
town;] ~, M   58 lances,] ~, M   fighting,] ~, M   59 down.] ~! M   59.1 M
gives this title to lines 60-7: Ἡγέμων   60 Mine is the bondslave's bitter fate,ₐ
M   61 In some strange land for evermore, M   62 Asia is now made desolate,ₐ M
63 Mistress and Queen] conqueror M   64 or love's] and life's M   65 abhorr'd]
abhorred M   67 death] Death M   Lover] lover M   Lord] lord M   67.1 *Postscript* Magdalen College/ Oxford. M
    21 Lotus Land. Copy text: M

And bind its lovers with a honied chain;
How still it is! no passionate note of pain   5
   Comes from the tawny songstress of the brake,
   And in the polished mirror of the lake
My purple mountains see themselves again.

O sad, and sweet, and silent! surely here
A man might dwell apart from troublous fear,   10
   Watching the bounteous seasons as they go
From lusty spring to winter;—Yet you say
That there is War in Europe on this day?
   Red War and Ravenous? Can this be so!

Illaunroe.

22   *Desespoir*

The seasons mend their ruin as they go,
   For in the spring the narciss shows its head
   Nor withers till the rose has flamed to red,
And in the autumn purple violets blow,
And the slim crocus stirs the winter snow;   5
   Wherefore yon leafless trees will bloom again
   And this grey land grow green with summer rain
And send up cowslips for some boy to mow.
But what of Life whose bitter hungry sea
   Flows at our heels, and gloom of sunless night   10
   Covers the days which never more return?
Ambition, love and all the thoughts that burn
   We lose too soon, and only find delight
   In withered husks of some dead memory.

22 Desespoir. Copy text: *M2*, collated with *M1*   1 mend] mark *M1*   go,] ~: *M1*
2 narciss] snowdrop *M1*   its] *M1*; it's *M2*   head,] ~, *M1*   3 Nor] But *M1*   till]
when *M1*   5 the slim crocus stirs the] now the fields are grey with *M1*   snow;] ~: *M1*
6 Wherefore yon leafless trees] Yet am I sure the rose *M1*   again,] ~, *M1*   7 grey] dull
M1   rain,] ~, *M1*   8 cowslips] lilies *M1*   9 But what of Life whose bitter] Not so
with life: Times silent *M1*   10 heels, and gloom of sunless] heels: the blending gloom of
M1   sunless] <blinded> *M2*   11 Covers the days which] Creeps on the joys that *M1*
return?] ~. *M1*   12 love,] ~, *M1*   13 lose] lo<o>se *M1*   soon,] ~: *M1*
14 withered] barren *M1*   withered] <barr> withered *M2*   dead] fond *M1*

23   *Lotus Leaves*

νεμεσσῶμαί γε μὲν οὐδέν
κλαίειν ὅς κε θάνῃσι βροτῶν καὶ πότμον ἐπίσπῃ,
τοῦτό νυ καὶ γέρας οἶον ὀϊζυροῖσι βροτοῖσι
κείρασθαί τε κόμην βαλέειν τ᾽ ἀπὸ δάκρυ παρειῶν.

I

There is no peace beneath the noon.—
    Ah! in those meadows is there peace
    Where, girdled with a silver fleece,
As a bright shepherd, strays the moon?

Queen of the gardens of the sky,   5
    Where stars like lilies, white and fair,
    Shine through the mists of frosty air,
O tarry, for the dawn is nigh!

O tarry, for the envious day
    Stretches long hands to catch thy feet.   10
    Alas! but thou art overfleet,
Alas! I know thou wilt not stay.

II

Eastward the dawn has broken red,
    The circling mists and shadows flee;
    Aurora rises from the sea,   15
And leaves the crocus-flowered bed.

---

23 *Lotus Leaves*. Copy text: *I*, collated with *M1*, *M2*   1 There is] <I had> There was
M2   noon.—] ~ₐ *M1*; ~, *M2*   2 Ah!] But *M2*   those] these *M2*   is there] there is
M1, *M2*   3 Where,] ~ₐ *M1*, *M2*   fleece,] ~ₐ *M1*, *M2*   4 As a bright] Like a young
M2   shepherd,] ~ₐ *M1*, *M2*   moon?] ~. *M1*, *M2*   5 O holy maiden at Whose feet
M1   6 Where] The *M1*   lilies, white and fair,] lilies ₐ white & fair ₐ *M1*; gilded cressets
fairₐ *M2*   7 air,] ~ₐ *M1*   8 Oₐ] *M1*, *M2*; Oh, *I*   tarry,] ~: *M1*; ~ₐ *M2*   dawn is
nigh!] night is sweet. *M1*   9 Oₐ] *M1*, *M2*; Oh, *I*   tarry,] ~ₐ *M1*, *M2*   for the envious day] with us yet a while *M1*   10 Bright wanderer in the fields above *M1*   feet.] ~,
M2   11 An hour—and you wake to love *M1*   Alas!] ~ₐ *M2*   overfleet] over fleet *M2*
12 Endymion in his lonely isle. *M1*   Alas!] ~ₐ *M2*   stay.] ~! *M2*   13–76 *not in M2*
13 Eastward ... broken] See how {the} <envious East> {is} 'the distant hills are' *M1*   red,]
~ₐ *M1*   14 <With> <How the dark> the Envious East with gladness glows—*M1*
15 rises from the sea,] blushing as the rose ₐ *M1*   16 And leaves] Deserts *M1*   bed.]
~<—> *M1*

Eastward the silver arrows fall,
   Splintering the veil of holy night;
   And a long wave of yellow light
Breaks silently on tower and hall,   20

And spreading wide across the wold,
   Wakes into flight some fluttering bird;
   And all the chestnut tops are stirred,
And all the branches streaked with gold.

III

To outer senses there is peace,   25
   A dream-like peace on either hand;
   Deep silence in the shadowy land,
Deep silence where the shadows cease,

Save for a cry that echoes shrill
   From some lone bird disconsolate;   30
   A curlew calling to its mate;
The answer from the distant hill.

And, herald of my love to Him
   Who, waiting for the dawn, doth lie,
   The orbèd maiden leaves the sky,   35
And the white fires grow more dim.

IV

Up sprang the sun to run his race,
   The breeze blew fair on meadow and lea;
   But in the west I seemed to see
The likeness of a human face.   40

A linnet on the hawthorn spray
   Sang of the glories of the spring,
   And made the flow'ring copses ring
With gladness for the new-born day.

17–20 *not in M1*   21 spreading wide across the] <stealing through the silent> spreading wide across the *M1*   22 bird;] ~, *M1*   23 stirred,] ~: *M1*   24 gold.] ~: *M1*
25–8 *not in M1*   29–30 *M1 has:*

> 'Save for the cry that echoes shrill
>   Of some poor bird disconsolate—'
>   {all is still}
> <Save for some cry disconsolate.>

31 mate;] ~: *M1*   32 hill.] ~: *M1*   33 With sounds of streams that murmuring flow, *M1*   34 And with the winds low lullaby *M1*   35 sky,] ~ˌ *M1*   36 grow more dim] <grow more> dimmer grow *M1*   37–76 *not in M1*

A lark from out the grass I trod   45
    Flew wildly, and was lost to view
    In the great seamless veil of blue
That hangs before the face of God.

The willow whispered overhead
    That death is but a newer life,   50
    And that with idle words of strife
We bring dishonour on the dead.

I took a branch from off the tree,
    And hawthorn-blossoms drenched with dew,
    I bound them with a sprig of yew,   55
And made a garland fair to see.

I laid the flowers where He lies
    (Warm leaves and flowers on the stone);
    What joy I had to sit alone
Till evening broke on tired eyes: 60

Till all the shifting clouds had spun
    A robe of gold for God to wear,
    And into seas of purple air
Sank the bright galley of the sun.

V

Shall I be gladdened for the day,   65
    And let my inner heart be stirred
    By murmuring tree or song of bird,
And sorrow at the wild wind's play?

Not so: such idle dreams belong
    To souls of lesser depth than mine;   70
    I feel that I am half divine;
I know that I am great and strong.

I know that every forest tree
    By labour rises from the root;
    I know that none shall gather fruit   75
By sailing on the barren sea.*

S. M. Magdalen College, Oxford.

Postscript S. M. Magdalen College, Oxford] *M1 has no postscript*; Verona *M2*
* πόντος ἀτρύγετος, 'the unvintageable sea.'

24   O Loved one lying far away
            Beyond the reach of human moan,
            Can coffin board and heavy stone
        Turn godlike man to senseless clay?

        Or hast thou eyes to see the light   5
            And feeling quick with joy and pain?
            Alas! I think a lesser gain
        Is mine, if thou can'st see me right.

        Alas! how mean we must appear
            When looked on by the holy dead!   10
            I trust the glory round thy head
        Has kept thine eyes from seeing clear.

                        II

        For in my heart these fancies rise
            That I the singer of this song
            Am weak where thou didst think me strong   15
        And foolish where you feigned me wise.

        Now that I lack thy helping hand
            I shift with every changing creed,
            No better than a broken reed
        Less stable than the shifting sand.   20

        Less stable than the changing sea,
            At every setting of the sun
            I cry in vain, 'What have I done
        This day for immortality?'

25   *A Fragment from the Agamemnon of Aeschylos*

                (Lines 1140–1173.)

[The scene is the courtyard of the Palace at Argos. Agamemnon has
already entered the House of Doom, and Klytaemnestra has followed
close on his heels:—Kasandra is left alone upon the stage. The

---

24 O Loved one lying far away. Copy text: *M*   24 immortality?'] ~ˏ' *M*
25 A Fragment From the Agamemnon of Aeschylos. Copy text: *K*

conscious terror of death, and the burden of prophecy, lie heavy upon her; terrible signs and visions greet her approach. She sees blood upon the lintel, and the smell of blood scares her, as some bird, from the door. The ghosts of the murdered children come to mourn with her. Her second sight pierces the palace walls; she sees the fatal bath, the trammelling net, and the axe sharpened for her own ruin and her lord's.

But not even in the hour of her last anguish is Apollo merciful; her warnings are unheeded; her prophetic utterances made mock of.

The orchestra is filled with a chorus of old men, weak, foolish, irresolute. They do not believe the weird woman of mystery till the hour for help is past, and the cry of Agamemnon echoes from the house, 'Oh me! I am stricken with a stroke of death.']

ΧΟΡΟΣ

Thy prophecies are but a lying tale,
    For cruel gods have brought thee to this state,
    And of thyself, and thine own wretched fate,
      Sing you this song, and these unhallow'd lays,
Like the brown bird of grief insatiate   5
      Crying for sorrow of its dreary days;
Crying for Itys, Itys, in the vale—
    The nightingale! the nightingale!

ΚΑΣΑΝΔΡΑ

Yet I would that to me they had given
    The fate of that singer so clear,   10
Fleet wings to fly up into heaven,
    Away from all mourning and fear;
      For ruin and slaughter await me—the cleaving
      with sword and with spear.

ΧΟΡΟΣ

Whence come these crowding fancies on thy brain,
    Sent by some god it may be, yet for nought?   15
Why dost thou sing with evil-tongued refrain,—
Moulding thy terrors to this hideous strain
    With shrill sad cries, as if by death distraught?
Why dost thou tread that path of prophecy,
    Where, upon either hand,   20
    Landmarks for ever stand,
With horrid legend for all men to see?

ΚΑΣΑΝΔΡΑ

O bitter bridegroom, who did'st bear
   Ruin to those that loved thee true!
O holy stream Skamander, where   25
   With gentle nurturement I grew
   In the first days, when life and love were new.

And now—and now—it seems that I must lie
   In the dark land that never sees the sun;
Sing my sad songs of fruitless prophecy,   30
   By the black stream Kokutos, that doth run
   Through long low hills of dreary Acheron.

ΧΟΡΟΣ

   Ah, but thy word is clear!
   Even a child among men,
   Even a child, might see   35
   What is lying hidden here.
   Ah! I am smitten deep
   To the heart with a deadly blow!
   At the evil fate of the maid,
   At the cry of her song of woe;   40
   Sorrows for her to bear!
   Wonders for me to hear!

ΚΑΣΑΝΔΡΑ

O my poor land, laid waste with flame and fire!
   O ruin'd city, overthrown by fate!
Ah, what avail'd the offerings of my Sire   45
   To keep the foreign foemen from the gate!
Ah, what avail'd the herds of pasturing kine
To save my country from the wrath divine!

Ah, neither prayer or priest availèd aught,
Nor the strong captains that so stoutly fought,   50
   For the tall town lies desolate and low.
   And I, the singer of this song of woe,
Know by the fire burning in my brain,
That Death, the healer of all earthly pain,
   Is close at hand. I will not shirk the blow.   55

26   *A Vision*

Two crownèd Kings, and One that stood alone
    With no green weight of laurels round his head,
    But with sad eyes as one uncomforted,
And wearied with man's never-ceasing moan
For sins no bleating victim can atone,   5
    And sweet long lips with tears and kisses fed.
    Girt was he in a garment black and red,
And at his feet I marked a broken stone
    Which sent up lilies, dove-like, to his knees.
    Now at their sight, my heart being lit with flame   10
I cried to Beatricé, 'Who are these?'
And she made answer, knowing well each name,
    'Æschylos first, the second Sophokles,
    And last (wide stream of tears!) Euripides.'

27   *Sonnet on Approaching Italy*

I reached the Alps: the soul within me burned,
    Italia, my Italia, at thy name:
    And when from out the mountain's heart I came
And saw the land for which my life had yearned,
I laughed as one who some great prize had earned: 5
    And musing on the marvel of thy fame
    I watched the day, till marked with wounds of flame
The turquoise sky to burnished gold was turned.

26 A Vision. Copy text: *P1–2*, collated with *K*, *M*   *Title* A Vision] A <Night> Vision
M   1 kings,] ~; *K*   One] one *K*   5 no bleating victim can] that neither prayer or
priest *K*; <that neither prayer or priest> no bleating victim can *M*   6 fed.] ~, *M*
7 Girt] Clothed *K*; <Clothed> Girt *M*   red,] ~, *M*   8 marked] mark'd *K*
9 dove-like] love-like *M*   10 Now‸] ~, *K*   sight,] ~‸ *K*   being lit with flame‸] did
burn as flame; *K*   11 I cried to Beatricé,] Then she, who lay beside me: *K*   these?'] ~',?
M   12 she] I *K*; She *M*   answer,] ~‸ *M*   name,] ~‸ *M*   13 Æschylos‸]
Æschylus, *K*   first,] ~; *K*   second‸] ~, *K*   Sophokles,] ~; *K*   14 And] The *K*
27 Sonnet on Approaching Italy. Copy text: *P2*, collated with *I*, *B*, *P1*   1 Alps:] ~; *I*, *B*
burned,] *I*, *B*; ~ <*P1*, *P2*   2 name:] ~, *I*   3 came‸] ~, *I*, *B*   5 earned:] ~. *I*; ~;
B   6 And‸] ~, *B*   marvel] stories *I*, *B*; story *P1*   fame‸] ~, *B*   7 day, till] sky
till, *B*   flame‸] ~, *B*   8 burnished gold was turned.] daffodil returned. *I*; burnished
gold was turned, *P1*

The pine-trees waved as waves a woman's hair,
   And in the orchards every twining spray   10
   Was breaking into flakes of blossoming foam:
But when I knew that far away at Rome
   In evil bonds a second Peter lay,
   I wept to see the land so very fair.

Turin.

28   *Sonnet Written in Holy Week at Genoa*

I wandered through Scoglietto's far retreat,
   The oranges on each o'erhanging spray
   Burned as bright lamps of gold to shame the day;
Some startled bird with fluttering wings and fleet
Made snow of all the blossoms, at my feet   5
   Like silver moons the pale narcissi lay:
   And the curved waves that streaked the great green bay
Laughed i' the sun, and life seemed very sweet.
Outside the young boy-priest passed singing clear,
   'Jesus the Son of Mary has been slain,   10
   O come and fill his sepulchre with flowers.'
Ah, God! Ah, God! those dear Hellenic hours
   Had drowned all memory of Thy bitter pain,
   The Cross, the Crown, the Soldiers, and the Spear.

9 pine-trees] pine trees *B*   12 Rome₍₎] ~, *B*   13 second] Second *I* *Postscript*
Turin.] Genoa, 1877. *I*; *B has no postscript*
   28 Sonnet Written in Holy Week at Genoa. Copy text: *P2*, collated with *U*, *P1*
1 through] in *U*, *P1*   far] green *U*, *P1*   retreat,] ~; *U*   2 oranges₍₎] ~, *U*   spray₍₎] ~,
U   3 day;] ~. *U*   4 bird₍₎] ~, *U*   fleet₍₎] ~, *U*   5 Made snow of all the blossoms,] Showered the milk-white blossoms; *U*   6 moons] crowns *U*   lay:] ~; *U*
7 waves₍₎] ~, *U*   great green] sapphire *U*, *P1*   bay₍₎] ~, *U*   9 Outside₍₎the young boy-
priest passed] Outside, a little child came *U*   10 Jesus₍₎the Son of Mary₍₎] Jesus, the
blessed Master, *U*   slain,] ~—*U*   11 O₍₎] ~, *U*   12 Ah, God! those dear
Hellenic] ah, God! these sweet and honied *U*   13 memory] memories *U*   pain,] ~—*U*
14.1 *Postscript* Genoa, 1877. *U*

29   *Impression de Voyage*

The sea was sapphire coloured, and the sky
  Burned like a heated opal through the air;
  We hoisted sail; the wind was blowing fair
For the blue lands that to the Eastward lie.
From the steep prow I marked with quickening eye   5
  Zakynthos, every olive grove and creek,
  Ithaca's cliff, Lycaon's snowy peak,
And all the flower-strewn hills of Arcady.
The flapping of the sail against the mast,
  The ripple of the water on the side,   10
  The ripple of girls' laughter at the stern,
The only sounds:—when 'gan the West to burn,
  And a red sun upon the seas to ride,
  I stood upon the soil of Greece at last!

Katakolo.

30   *The Theatre at Argos*

Nettles and poppy mar each rock-hewn seat:
  No poet crowned with olive deathlessly
  Chants his glad song, nor clamorous Tragedy
Startles the air; green corn is waving sweet
Where once the Chorus danced to measures fleet;   5
  Far to the East a purple stretch of sea,
  The cliffs of gold that prisoned Danae;
And desecrated Argos at my feet.

29 Impression de Voyage. Copy text: *M*, collated with *T, W, P1, P2*   *Title* Impression
de Voyage] *W, P2*; Hellas! Hellas! *T*; Impression d<e>u Voyage *M*; Impression du Voyage *P1*
1 sapphire˄coloured,] sapphire-colored; *T*; sapphire-coloured, *W*   2 Burned] Glowed *T*
air;] *T, W, P2*; ~, *M, P1*   3 sail;] ~, *T*; ~: *W*   4 Eastward] eastward *P1, P2*
5 quickening] eager *T*   6 olive˄grove] olive-grove *T, W*   7 Lycaon's] Lykaon's *T*
8 And all the flower-strewn] Parnassos and the *T*   Arcady] Arkady *T, W*   10 water]
waters *T*   11 at] in *T*   12 sounds:—when] sounds. When *T*   14 soil] strand
W   *Postscript* Katakolo.] *P2*; *Katacolo*, 1877. *T*; *Katokolo*, 1877. *W*; *M, P1* have no
postscript
  30 The Theatre at Argos. Copy text: *M*, collated with *T*   1 seat:] sea˄ *T*   6 stretch
of] *not in T*; sketch of *M*   sea,] *T*; ~˄ *M*

No season now to mourn the days of old,
  A nation's shipwreck on the rocks of Time,   10
    Or the dread storms of all-devouring Fate,
    For now the peoples clamor at our gate,
  The world is full of plague and sin and crime,
And God Himself is half-dethroned for Gold!

Argos, 1877.

31   *Urbs Sacra Æterna*

Rome! what a scroll of History thine has been;
  In the first days thy sword republican
  Ruled the whole world for many an age's span:
Then of the peoples wert thou royal Queen,
Till in thy streets the bearded Goth was seen;   5
  And now upon thy walls the breezes fan
  (Ah, city crowned by God, discrowned by man!)
The hated flag of red and white and green.
When was thy glory! when in search for power
  Thine eagles flew to greet the double sun,   10
  And the wild nations shuddered at thy rod?
Nay, but thy glory tarried for this hour,
  When pilgrims kneel before the Holy One,
  The prisoned shepherd of the Church of God.

Monte Mario.

---

11 Fate,] ~. *T*
   31 Urbs Sacra Æterna. Copy text: *P2*, collated with *U*, *P1*   1 O Rome, what sights and
changes hast thou seen! *U*   3 the whole] all the *U*   span:] ~; *U*   4 the peoples
wert thou royal] thy peoples thou wert noble *U*; thy peoples thou wert crownèd *P1*
5 bearded Goth was] Goth and Hun were *U*   7 Ah,] ~! *U*   man!)] ~‸) *U*
9 glory!] greatness?—*U*   10 greet] meet *U*   11 the wild nations shuddered] all the
nations trembled *U*, *P1*   rod] nod *U*   12 but thy glory tarried for this] glory rather in
the present *U*   *Postscript* Monte Mario] *Rome*, 1877 *U*

32   *The Grave of Keats*

    Rid of the world's injustice, and his pain,
       He rests at last beneath God's veil of blue:
    Taken from life when life and love were new
    The youngest of the Martyrs here is lain,
    Fair as Sebastian, and as early slain.   5
       No cypress shades his grave, no funeral yew,
       But gentle violets weeping with the dew
    Weave on his bones an ever-blossoming chain.
    O proudest heart that broke for misery!
       O sweetest lips since those of Mitylene!   10
       O poet-painter of our English Land!
    Thy name was writ in water—it shall stand:
    And tears like mine shall keep thy memory green,
    As Isabella did her Basil-tree.

Rome.

33   *Sonnet on the Massacre of the Christians in Bulgaria*

    Christ, dost thou live indeed? or are thy bones
    Still straitened in their rock-hewn sepulchre?
    And was thy Rising only dreamed by Her
    Whose love of thee for all her sin atones?

32 The Grave of Keats. Copy text: *M2*, collated with *I*, *M1*, *R*, *P1–2*, *M3*   1 injustice,]
~ₐ *I*, *M1*   his pain,] its pain, *I*; its painₐ *M1*; his painₐ *M3*   2 rests] sleeps *R*   veil]
v<a>eil *M3*   blue:] ~; *I*, *M1*   3 when] while *I*, *M1*, *M3*   4 Martyrs] martyrs *I*,
R, *P1–2*, *M3*   5 Sebastian,] ~ₐ *I*, *M1*   early] foully *I*, *M1*   slain.] ~: *R*; ~ₐ *M3*
6 grave] tomb *M1*   no] *P1–2*, *M3*; nor *I*, *M1*, *R*; <nor> or *M2*   yew,] ~ₐ *M3*   7 gentle violets weeping with the] red-lipped daisies, violets drenched with *I*, *M1*; <violets, poppies, daisies, dimmed with> '<sunlit> gentle violets weeping with the' *M2*; dim-eyed violets
weeping with the *M3*   dewₐ] ~, *I*   8 Weave on his bones an] And sleepy poppies, *I*, *M1*
ever-blossoming chain] catch the evening rain *I*, *M1*; everblossoming chain *M3*   10 O
saddest poet that the world hath seen! *I*, *M1*; O sweetest <singer that > lips since those of
Mitylene *M2*   11 poet-painter] sweetest singer *I*, *M1*; Painter-poet *R*   our] the *I*
Land] land *I*, *M1*, *R*, *M3*   12 Thy name was writ in water on the sand, *I*, *M1*; Thy name
was writ in water: it shall stand: *R*; <Thy name was writ in> Was thy name writ in water? it
shall standₐ *M3*   13 And tears like mine shall] But our tears shall *I*, *M1*; And tears like
mine will *P1–2*   green,] ~ₐ *M3*   14 And make it flourish like a Basil-tree. *I*, *M1*; As
Isabella did her Basil-Tree. *R*; <And make it flourish as thy Basil-tree.> As Isabella did thy
Basil-Tree. *M2*   *Postscript* Rome.] *Rome*, 1877. *I*; Rome: 1877 *M1*; *M3* has no postscript
    33 Sonnet on the Massacre of the Christians in Bulgaria. Copy text: *P2*, collated with *M*, *P1*
1 Christ,] ~ₐ *M*   2 straitened] straightened *M*   3 was thy Rising only dreamed by]
do we owe thy rising but to *M*

For here the air is horrid with men's groans,   5
The priests who call upon thy name are slain,
Dost thou not hear the bitter wail of pain
From those whose children lie upon the stones?
Come down, O Son of God! incestuous gloom
Curtains the land, and through the starless night   10
Over thy Cross a Crescent moon I see!
If thou in very truth didst burst the tomb
Come down, O Son of Man! and show thy might,
Lest Mahomet be crowned instead of Thee!

34   *Easter Day*

The silver trumpets rang across the Dome:
    The people knelt upon the ground with awe:
    And borne upon the necks of men I saw,
Like some great God, the Holy Lord of Rome.
Priest-like, he wore a robe more white than foam,   5
    And, king-like, swathed himself in royal red,
    Three crowns of gold rose high upon his head:
In splendour and in light the Pope passed home.
My heart stole back across wide wastes of years
    To One who wandered by a lonely sea,   10
    And sought in vain for any place of rest:
'Foxes have holes, and every bird its nest,
    I, only I, must wander wearily,
    And bruise my feet, and drink wine salt with tears.'

5 horrid] heavy *M*   6 who] that *M*   slain,] ~; *M*   9 Our prayers are nought: impen-
etrable gloom *M*   10 Covers God's face: and in the star-less night *M*   11 Cross]
<c>Cross *M*   a] the *M*, *P1*   Crescent] <c>Crescent *M*   see!] ~. *M*   12 tomb‸] ~,
M   13 down,] ~‸ *M*   Man!] ~, *M*   14 Thee!] thee. *M*   14.1 *Postscript*
Magdalen College./ Oxford. *M*

    34 Easter Day. Copy text: *P1–2*, collated with *M1*, *M2*, *W*   1 Dome:] dome; *M1*, *M2*,
W   2 with awe:] in awe, *M1*; in awe; *M2*, *W*   3 saw,] ~‸ *M1*, *M2*, *W*   4 Like]
As *W*   God,] ~‸ *M1*, *W*; god‸ *M2*   5 Priest-like,] ~‸ *M1*, *W*; Priestlike‸ *M2*
6 And, king-like,] And‸King-like‸ *M1*; And‸Kinglike‸ *M2*; And‸king-like‸ *W*   royal red,]
royal red; *M2*; Nero's red; *W*   7 upon] above *M1*, *M2*, *W*   head:] ~, *M1*; ~; *M2*
9 years‸] ~, *M2*   11 rest:] ~. *M1*, *M2*; ~‸ *W*   12 its] it's *M2*, *W*   13 only I,] I
alone‸ *M1*, *M2*   wander wearily,] travel wearily‸ *M1*; travel wearily, *W*   14.1 *Post-*
script Rome. *M2*; Rome, 1877. *W*

35   *Sonnet. On Hearing the Dies Iræ Sung in the
Sistine Chapel*

Nay, Lord, not thus! white lilies in the spring,
    Sad olive-groves, or silver-breasted dove,
    Teach me more clearly of Thy life and love
Than terrors of red flame and thundering.
The hillside vines dear memories of Thee bring: 5
    A bird at evening flying to its nest
    Tells me of One who had no place of rest:
I think it is of Thee the sparrows sing.
Come rather on some autumn afternoon,
    When red and brown are burnished on the leaves,   10
    And the fields echo to the gleaner's song,
Come when the splendid fulness of the moon
    Looks down upon the rows of golden sheaves,
    And reap Thy harvest: we have waited long.

36   *Italia*

Italia! thou art fallen, though with sheen
    Of battle-spears thy clamorous armies stride
    From the north Alps to the Sicilian tide!
Ay! fallen, though the nations hail thee Queen
Because rich gold in every town is seen,   5
    And on thy sapphire lake in tossing pride
    Of wind-filled vans thy myriad galleys ride
Beneath one flag of red and white and green.

35 Sonnet. On Hearing the Dies Iræ Sung in the Sistine Chapel. Copy text: *P2*, collated with *M1, L, M2, P1*   1 Nay, Lord, not thus!] Nay‸come not *thus*: *M1*; Nay, come not thus: *L*; Nay, {come} 'Lord,' not thus: *M2*   white] <white> field *M2*   2 Sad] Dark *M2*   olive-groves] olive-gardens *M1, L*; olive-woods *M2*   silver-breasted dove] a murmuring Dove *M1*; the holy dove *L*   3 Thy] thy *M1*   4 red‸flame] red-flame *M2*   thundering.] ~; *M1, L*   5 The hillside vines] Fruit-laden vines *M1*; Wind-shaken reeds *L*; The empurpled vines *M2, P1*   Thee] thee *M1*   bring:] ~; *M1, L, M2*   6 its] it's *M2*   nest‸] ~, *P1*   7 rest:] ~; *M1, L, M2*   8 Thee] thee *M1*   9 afternoon,] ~‸ *M1, M2*   11 fields] woods *M1*; <fields> trees *M2*   to] <with> to *M2*   gleaner's song,] reaper's song: *M1*; reaper's song. *L*; gleaners song: *M2*   12 fulness] fullness *M1, L, M2*   13 sheaves] ~‸ *M1, M2*   14 Thy harvest:] thy Harvest; *M1*; <t>Thy Harvest: *M2*   14.1 *Postscript* Magdalen College/ Oxford. *M1*; Rome. *M2*
    36 Italia. Copy text: *P1–2*

O Fair and Strong! O Strong and Fair in vain!
  Look southward where Rome's desecrated town   10
  Lies mourning for her God-anointed King!
Look heaven-ward! shall God allow this thing?
  Nay! but some flame-girt Raphael shall come down,
  And smite the Spoiler with the sword of pain.

Venice.

37   *Vita Nuova*

I stood by the unvintageable sea
  Till the wet waves drenched face and hair with spray;
  The long red fires of the dying day
Burned in the west; the wind piped drearily;
And to the land the clamorous gulls did flee: 5
  'Alas!' I cried, 'my life is full of pain,
  And who can garner fruit or golden grain
From these waste fields which travail ceaselessly!'
  My nets gaped wide with many a break and flaw,
  Nathless I threw them as my final cast   10
Into the sea, and waited for the end.
  When lo! a sudden glory! and I saw
  From the black waters of my tortured past
The argent splendour of white limbs ascend!

38   *E Tenebris*

Come down, O Christ, and help me! reach thy hand,
  For I am drowning in a stormier sea
  Than Simon on thy lake of Galilee:
The wine of life is spilt upon the sand,

37 Vita Nuova. Copy text: *P2*, collated with *I, L, P1*   2 spray;] *I, L; ~, P1, P2*
4 Burned] Glowed *L*   west;] ~: *L*   piped] sang *L*   drearily;] ~, *I, L*   5 clamorous]
clamoring *L*   flee:] ~. *I*   6 'Alas!'] ∧Alas!, *L*   'my life is full of] ∧my hands are weak
with *L*   7 And who can garner fruit∧] And who can gather fruit∧] *I*; How shall I gather
fruit, *L*   grain∧] *I, L; ~, P1, P2*   8 which] that *I, L*   ceaselessly!'] ~?' *I; ~?∧ L*
9 flaw,] *I, L; ~∧ P1, P2*   11 sea,] ~: *I, L*   12 glory] brightness *I, L*   13 Christ
walking on the waters! fear was past; *I*; Christ walking on the waters; fear was past; *L*; The
argent splendour of white limbs ascend, *P1*   14 I knew that I had found my Perfect
Friend. *I*; I knew that I had found my perfect friend. *L*; And in that joy forgot my tortured
past. *P1*   14.1 *Postscript June,* 1877. *I*
    38 E Tenebris. Copy text: *P2*, collated with *P1*

My heart is as some famine-murdered land   5
　　Whence all good things have perished utterly,
　　And well I know my soul in Hell must lie
If I this night before God's throne should stand.
'He sleeps perchance, or rideth to the chase,
　　Like Baal, when his prophets howled that name   10
　　From morn to noon on Carmel's smitten height.'
Nay, peace, I shall behold before the night,
　　The feet of brass, the robe more white than flame,
　　The wounded hands, the weary human face.

39   *Quantum Mutata*

There was a time in Europe long ago
　　When no man died for freedom anywhere,
　　But England's lion leaping from its lair
Laid hands on the oppressor! it was so
While England could a great Republic show.   5
　　Witness the men of Piedmont, chiefest care
　　Of Cromwell, when with impotent despair
The Pontiff in his painted portico
Trembled before our stern ambassadors.
　　How comes it then that from such high estate   10
　　We have thus fallen, save that Luxury
With barren merchandise piles up the gate
Where noble thoughts and deeds should enter by:
　　Else might we still be Milton's heritors.

40   *To Milton*

Milton! I think thy spirit hath passed away
　　From these white cliffs, and high-embattled towers;
　　This gorgeous fiery-coloured world of ours
Seems fallen into ashes dull and grey,

5 land‸] ~, *P1*
　　39 Quantum Mutata. Copy text: *P1–2*
　　40 To Milton. Copy text: *P1–2*, collated with *M1*, *M2*　　1 Milton!] ~‸ *M1*
2 white cliffs,] white cliffs‸ *M1*; white-cliffs‸ *M2*　　high-embattled] high embattled *M1*, *M2*
towers;] towers: *M1*　　3 gorgeous fiery-coloured] mighty fiery coloured *M1*; gorgeous
fiery coloured *M2*　　4 Seems] is *M1*; Is *M2*　　grey,] ~—*M1*; ~: *M2*

And the age changed unto a mimic play   5
    Wherein we waste our else too-crowded hours:
For all our pomp and pageantry and powers
We are but fit to delve the common clay,
Seeing this little isle on which we stand,
    This England, this sea-lion of the sea,   10
    By ignorant demagogues is held in fee,
Who love her not: Dear God! is this the land
    Which bare a triple empire in her hand
    When Cromwell spake the word Democracy!

41   *Ave Maria Plena Gratia*

Was this His coming! I had hoped to see
A scene of wondrous glory, as was told
Of some great God who in a rain of gold
Broke open bars and fell on Danae:

5–6 *M1 has*:

        We [   ] play
           wherein we waste our [   ] hours

5 And the age changed unto] Or else transformed to *M2*   6 we waste our else too-crowded] {we for<s> idle show we waste our} we waste our else too crowded *M2*   7 and] of *M1, M2*   8 clay,] ~. *M1*   9 on which we stand,] {at the [   ] stand_∧} on which we stand_∧ *M1*; on which we stand_∧ *M2*   9–11 *M1 also has*:

    I think some ancient spirit has passed away
        Seeing this little isle on which we stand,
    This England this sealion of the sea,
        <With>
        Compassed with anarchy on every hand
    By demagogues is held in fee

10 This] Thy *M2*   sea-lion] sealion *M2*   11 *M2 has*:

    Is given over to rabble band
    Of clamorous demagogues who hold in fee
    The [   ]

12–14 *M2 has*:

        who love her [   ]
           Dear God is this the land
      That held the worlds wide empire in her
                 hand
     where Cromwell spake the word
           democracy.

    41 Ave Maria Plena Gratia. Copy text: *P2*, collated with *I, K, P1*   1 this] *this I, K*   coming!] ~? *I, K*   2 wondrous] blinding *K*   3 God] god *I, K*   4 bars_∧] ~, *K*   Danae:] Danaé; *I, K*

Or a dread vision as when Semele   5
    Sickening for love and unappeased desire
    Prayed to see God's clear body, and the fire
Caught her brown limbs and slew her utterly:
With such glad dreams I sought this holy place,
    And now with wondering eyes and heart I stand   10
    Before this supreme mystery of Love:
Some kneeling girl with passionless pale face,
    An angel with a lily in his hand,
    And over both the white wings of a Dove.

Florence.

42   *Wasted Days*

            (From A Picture Painted By Miss V. T.)

A fair slim boy not made for this world's pain,
    With hair of gold thick clustering round his ears,
    And longing eyes half veil'd by foolish tears
Like bluest water seen through mists of rain;
Pale cheeks whereon no kiss hath left its stain,   5
    Red under-lip drawn in for fear of Love,
    And white throat whiter than the breast of dove—
Alas! alas! if all should be in vain.

Corn-fields behind, and reapers all a-row
    In weariest labour toiling wearily,   10
    To no sweet sound of laughter, or of lute;
And careless of the crimson sunset-glow
    The boy still dreams: nor knows that night is nigh:
    And in the night-time no man gathers fruit.

Oxford, Oct. 30th.

5 vision‚] ~, *I, K*   Semele‚] Semelé, *I*; Semelé‚ *K*   6 Sickening for] Hungering with *K*
desire‚] ~, *I, K*   7 Prayed] Pray'd *K*   8 brown] fair *I, K*; white *P1*   utterly:] ~. *I,
K*   9 sought this holy] came into this *K*   10 now‚] ~—*K*   stand‚] ~, *I*
11 Before this supreme mystery] And look upon this Mystery *I*; And look upon this mystery
K   Love:] ~. *I, K*   12 ‚Some] 'A *I, K*; ‚A *P1*   passionless‚] ~, *I*   14 both the
white wings of a Dove.‚] both, with outstretched wings, the Dove.' *I*; both with outstretch'd
wings, the Dove.' *K*; both with outstretched wings the Dove.‚ *P1*   *Postscript* Florence]
Vatican Gallery, Rome, 1877 *I*; St. Marco, Florence *K*
  42 Wasted Days. Copy text: *K*, collated with *E1, E2*   9 Corn-fields behind] *E2*; Behind,
wide fields *K*   10 weariest] *E2*; heat and *K*   11 laughter,] *E2*; ~‚ *K*   lute;] *E2*; ~. *K*
12 The sun is shooting wide its crimson rays, *K*; The sun is shooting wide its crimson glow, *E1*
13 The boy still] *E2*; Still the boy *K*   nigh:] ~, *K*   *Postscript* Oxford, Oct. 30th.] *not in K, E1*

43 *The Grave of Shelley*

Like burnt-out torches by a sick man's bed
    Gaunt cypress-trees stand round the sun-bleached stone;
    Here doth the little night-owl make her throne,
And the slight lizard show his jewelled head.
And, where the chaliced poppies flame to red,   5
    In the still chamber of yon pyramid
    Surely some Old-World Sphinx lurks darkly hid,
Grim warder of this pleasaunce of the dead.

Ah! sweet indeed to rest within the womb
    Of Earth, great mother of eternal sleep,   10
But sweeter far for thee a restless tomb
    In the blue cavern of an echoing deep,
    Or where the tall ships founder in the gloom
Against the rocks of some wave-shattered steep.

Rome.

44 *Santa Decca*

The Gods are dead: no longer do we bring
    To grey-eyed Pallas crowns of olive-leaves!
    Demeter's child no more hath tithe of sheaves,
And in the noon the careless shepherds sing,
For Pan is dead, and all the wantoning   5
    By secret glade and devious haunt is o'er:
    Young Hylas seeks the water-springs no more;
Great Pan is dead, and Mary's Son is King.

43 The Grave of Shelley. Copy text: *M2*, collated with *M1*, *P1–2*   1 burnt-out] *M1*, *P1–2*; burnt out *M2*   torches] <candles> torches *M1*   2 Are the gaunt cypresses which guard the stone: *M1*   3 Here doth the little night-owl make her] The tender hare-bell here hath made it's *M1*   4 With the shrill skylark's song the air is fed, *M1* 5 And,] ~∧ *M1*   chaliced] sun-scorched *M1*   5 red,] ~∧ *M1*   6 In the still chamber of yon] <Sleeps> Lies Adonais by that *M1*   7 Surely some Old-World Sphinx lurks darkly] *P1–2*; In whose still heart some Old-World Sphynx <lies> is *M1*; Surely some Old-World Sphynx lurks darkly *M2*   8 warder] Warder *M1*   pleasaunce] meadow *M1* 9 Ah!] ~∧ *M1*   10 Earth,] *P1–2*; earth∧ *M1*; Earth∧ *M2*   great] grey *M1*   12 the] *P1–2*; some *M1*, *M2*   an] *P1–2*; the *M1*, *M2*   *Postscript* Rome.] *not in M1*

44 Santa Decca. Copy text: *M*, collated with *P1*, *P2*   2 olive-leaves!] *P1*, *P2*; ~; *M* 4 sing,] *P1*, *P2*; ~∧ *M*   6 glade,] *P1*, *P2*; ~, *M*   8 Great] <For> Great *M*   dead,] *P1*, *P2*; ~∧ *M*

And yet—perchance in this sea-trancèd isle,
Chewing the bitter fruit of memory,   10
Some God lies hidden in the asphodel.
Ah Love! if such there be then it were well
For us to fly his anger: nay, but see
The leaves are stirring: let us watch a-while.

Corfu.

45   *Theoretikos*

This mighty empire hath but feet of clay:
Of all its ancient chivalry and might
Our little island is forsaken quite:
Some enemy hath stolen its crown of bay,
And from its hills that voice hath passed away   5
Which spake of Freedom: O come out of it,
Come out of it, my Soul, thou art not fit
For this vile traffic-house, where day by day
Wisdom and reverence are sold at mart,
And the rude people rage with ignorant cries   10

Postscript Corfu.] *P2*; *not in M, P1*
    45 Theoretikos. Copy text: *P1–2*, collated with *M1, M2*   1 <Their golden idol has but feet of clay‸> it's golden idol hath but feet of clay: *M1*; This mighty Empire hath but feet of clay, *M2*   2–4 *not in M1*   2 Of all its ancient chivalry,‸] Seeing of wisdom, reverence, *M2*   3 quite:] ~‸ *M2*   4 its] it's *M2*   bay,] ~—*M2*   5–6 *M1 has:*

> something has passed away
> From flower and field: I think the age of clay
>> Bear up this
>> This golden
>
> <From flower and field that spot has
>> That W
>> Which spake to Wordsworth. O
>>> was
> and from the hills that spirit hath passed
>> that spake of Freedom: O come out of it>
>
> and from it's hills that voice hath passed
>> which spake of freedom: O come out of it

5 its] it's *M2*   6 Freedom:] ~. *M2*   7 *not in M1*   it, my Soul, thou] it‸my soul, Thou *M2*   8 this vile traffic-house,] such a market House‸ *M1*; this vile {marketplace} 'traffic gain'‸ *M2*   9 Wisdom and reverence] Honour and chivalry *M1, M2*   10 rude] <common> vile *M1*

Against an heritage of centuries.
  It mars my calm: wherefore in dreams of Art
And loftiest culture I would stand apart,
Neither for God, nor for his enemies.

46   *Amor Intellectualis*

Oft have we trod the vales of Castaly
  And heard sweet notes of sylvan music blown
  From antique reeds to common folk unknown:
And often launched our bark upon that sea
Which the nine Muses hold in empery,   5
  And ploughed free furrows through the wave and foam,
  Nor spread reluctant sail for more safe home
Till we had freighted well our argosy.
Of which despoilèd treasures these remain,
  Sordello's passion, and the honied line   10
Of young Endymion, lordly Tamburlaine
  Driving his pampered jades, and, more than these,
The seven-fold vision of the Florentine,
  And grave-browed Milton's solemn harmonies.

---

11 an] their *M1*   centuries.] ~: *M1*; ~—, *M2*   12–13 *M1 has:*

      It likes me not: and I shall stand apart
      Fenced round with culture and the dreams of Art,

12 It mars my] {They} 'It' wound {thy} 'my' *M2*   13 loftiest] lofty *M2*   would]
<shall> would *M2*   apart,] ~ᴧ *M2*   14 God, nor] Godᴧor *M1*, *M2*   enemies] Ene-
mies *M1*

    46 Amor Intellectualis. Copy text: *P1–2*, collated with *M1*, *M2*   1–8 *not in M2*
1 we] I *M1*   3 From] On *M1* folk] men *M1*   4 our] my *M1*   5 Muses] Sisters *M1* empery,] ~ᴧ *M1*   6 *M1 has:*

      < Nor spread reluctant sail for more safe home>
      And [   ]

8 we] I *M1*   our argosy.] mine argosyᴧ *M1*   9 Of which despoilèd treasures] as friends
grow treacherous: but *M2*   these remain,] there remainᴧ *M1*, *M2*   10 passion,] ~ᴧ *M1*
11 Of young Endymion, [   ] *M1*; Gray Endymion, Lordly Tamburlaine *M2*
12–14 *not in M1*   12 and,] ~ᴧ *M2*   these,] ~ᴧ *M2*   13 seven-fold] sevenfold *M2*
Florentine,] ~ᴧ *M2*   14 Milton's solemn harmonies] Miltons mighty Harmonies *M2*

47   *At Verona*

How steep the stairs within Kings' houses are
    For exile-wearied feet as mine to tread,
    And O how salt and bitter is the bread
Which falls from this Hound's table,—better far
That I had died in the red ways of war,   5
    Or that the gate of Florence bare my head,
    Than to live thus, by all things comraded
Which seek the essence of my soul to mar.

'Curse God and die: what better hope than this?
    He hath forgotten thee in all the bliss   10
    Of his gold city, and eternal day'—
Nay peace: behind my prison's blinded bars
    I do possess what none can take away,
    My love, and all the glory of the stars.

48   *Ravenna*

A year ago I breathed the Italian air,—
And yet, methinks this northern Spring is fair,—
These fields made golden with the flower of March,
The throstle singing on the feathered larch,
The cawing rooks, the wood-doves fluttering by,   5
The little clouds that race across the sky;
And fair the violet's gentle drooping head,
The primrose, pale for love uncomforted,
The rose that burgeons on the climbing briar,
The crocus-bed, (that seems a moon of fire   10
Round-girdled with a purple marriage-ring);
And all the flowers of our English Spring,
Fond snow-drops, and the bright-starred daffodil.
Up starts the lark beside the murmuring mill,
And breaks the gossamer-threads of early dew;   15
And down the river, like a flame of blue,
Keen as an arrow flies the water-king,
While the brown linnets in the greenwood sing.

47 At Verona. Copy text: *P1–2*
48 Ravenna. Copy text: *Ravenna*

A year ago!—it seems a little time
Since last I saw that lordly southern clime,   20
Where flower and fruit to purple radiance blow,
And like bright lamps the fabled apples glow.
Full Spring it was—and by rich flowering vines,
Dark olive-groves and noble forest-pines,
I rode at will; the moist glad air was sweet,   25
The white road rang beneath my horse's feet,
And musing on Ravenna's ancient name,
I watched the day till, marked with wounds of flame,
The turquoise sky to burnished gold was turned.

O how my heart with boyish passion burned,   30
When far away across the sedge and mere
I saw that Holy City rising clear,
Crowned with her crown of towers!—On and on
I galloped, racing with the setting sun,
And ere the crimson after-glow was passed,   35
I stood within Ravenna's walls at last!

II

How strangely still! no sound of life or joy
Startles the air; no laughing shepherd-boy
Pipes on his reed, nor ever through the day
Comes the glad sound of children at their play: 40
O sad, and sweet, and silent! surely here
A man might dwell apart from troublous fear,
Watching the tide of seasons as they flow
From amorous Spring to Winter's rain and snow,
And have no thought of sorrow;—here, indeed,   45
Are Lethe's waters, and that fatal weed
Which makes a man forget his fatherland.

Ay! amid lotus-meadows dost thou stand,
Like Proserpine, with poppy-laden head,
Guarding the holy ashes of the dead.   50
For though thy brood of warrior sons hath ceased,
Thy noble dead are with thee!—they at least
Are faithful to thine honour:—guard them well,
O childless city! for a mighty spell,
To wake men's hearts to dreams of things sublime,   55
Are the lone tombs where rest the Great of Time.

III

Yon lonely pillar, rising on the plain,
Marks where the bravest knight of France was slain,—
The Prince of chivalry, the Lord of war,
Gaston de Foix: for some untimely star   60
Led him against thy city, and he fell,
As falls some forest-lion fighting well.
Taken from life while life and love were new,
He lies beneath God's seamless veil of blue;
Tall lance-like reeds wave sadly o'er his head,   65
And oleanders bloom to deeper red,
Where his bright youth flowed crimson on the ground.

Look farther north unto that broken mound,—
There, prisoned now within a lordly tomb
Raised by a daughter's hand, in lonely gloom,   70
Huge-limbed Theodoric, the Gothic king,
Sleeps after all his weary conquering.
Time hath not spared his ruin,—wind and rain
Have broken down his stronghold; and again
We see that Death is mighty lord of all,   75
And king and clown to ashen dust must fall.

Mighty indeed *their* glory! yet to me
Barbaric king, or knight of chivalry,
Or the great queen herself, were poor and vain,
Beside the grave where Dante rests from pain.   80
His gilded shrine lies open to the air;
And cunning sculptor's hands have carven there
The calm white brow, as calm as earliest morn,
The eyes that flashed with passionate love and scorn,
The lips that sang of Heaven and of Hell,   85
The almond-face which Giotto drew so well,
The weary face of Dante;—to this day,
Here in his place of resting, far away
From Arno's yellow waters, rushing down
Through the wide bridges of that fairy town,   90
Where the tall tower of Giotto seems to rise
A marble lily under sapphire skies!
Alas! my Dante! thou hast known the pain
Of meaner lives,—the exile's galling chain,
How steep the stairs within kings' houses are,   95
And all the petty miseries which mar

Man's nobler nature with the sense of wrong.
Yet this dull world is grateful for thy song;
Our nations do thee homage,—even she,
That cruel queen of vine-clad Tuscany,   100
Who bound with crown of thorns thy living brow,
Hath decked thine empty tomb with laurels now,
And begs in vain the ashes of her son.

 O mightiest exile! all thy grief is done:
Thy soul walks now beside thy Beatrice;   105
Ravenna guards thine ashes: sleep in peace.

IV

 How lone this palace is; how grey the walls!
No minstrel now wakes echoes in these halls.
The broken chain lies rusting on the door,
And noisome weeds have split the marble floor: 110
Here lurks the snake, and here the lizards run
By the stone lions blinking in the sun.
Byron dwelt here in love and revelry
For two long years—a second Anthony,
Who of the world another Actium made!—   115
Yet suffered not his royal soul to fade,
Or lyre to break, or lance to grow less keen,
'Neath any wiles of an Egyptian queen.
For from the East there came a mighty cry,
And Greece stood up to fight for Liberty,   120
And called him from Ravenna: never knight
Rode forth more nobly to wild scenes of fight!
None fell more bravely on ensanguined field,
Borne like a Spartan back upon his shield!
O Hellas! Hellas! in thine hour of pride,   125
Thy day of might, remember him who died
To wrest from off thy limbs the trammelling chain:
O Salamis! O lone Platæan plain!
O tossing waves of wild Eubœan sea!
O wind-swept heights of lone Thermopylæ!   130
He loved you well—ay, not alone in word,
Who freely gave to thee his lyre and sword,
Like Æschylos at well-fought Marathon:

 And England, too, shall glory in her son,
Her warrior-poet, first in song and fight.   135
No longer now shall Slander's venomed spite

Crawl like a snake across his perfect name,
Or mar the lordly scutcheon of his fame.

For as the olive-garland of the race,
Which lights with joy each eager runner's face,   140
As the red cross which saveth men in war,
As a flame-bearded beacon seen from far
By mariners upon a storm-tossed sea,—
Such was his love for Greece and Liberty!

Byron, thy crowns are ever fresh and green: 145
Red leaves of rose from Sapphic Mitylene
Shall bind thy brows; the myrtle blooms for thee,
In hidden glades by lonely Castaly;
The laurels wait thy coming: all are thine,
And round thy head one perfect wreath will twine.   150

V

The pine-tops rocked before the evening breeze
With the hoarse murmur of the wintry seas,
And the tall stems were streaked with amber bright;—
I wandered through the wood in wild delight,
Some startled bird, with fluttering wings and fleet,   155
Made snow of all the blossoms: at my feet,
Like silver crowns, the pale narcissi lay,
And small birds sang on every twining spray.
O waving trees, O forest liberty!
Within your haunts at least a man is free,   160
And half forgets the weary world of strife:
The blood flows hotter, and a sense of life
Wakes i' the quickening veins, while once again
The woods are filled with gods we fancied slain.
Long time I watched, and surely hoped to see   165
Some goat-foot Pan make merry minstrelsy
Amid the reeds! some startled Dryad-maid
In girlish flight! or lurking in the glade,
The soft brown limbs, the wanton treacherous face
Of woodland god! Queen Dian in the chase,   170
White-limbed and terrible, with look of pride,
And leash of boar-hounds leaping at her side!
Or Hylas mirrored in the perfect stream.

O idle heart! O fond Hellenic dream!
Ere long, with melancholy rise and swell,   175
The evening chimes, the convent's vesper-bell,
Struck on mine ears amid the amorous flowers.
Alas! alas! these sweet and honied hours
Had 'whelmed my heart like some encroaching sea,
And drowned all thoughts of black Gethsemane.   180

VI

O lone Ravenna! many a tale is told
Of thy great glories in the days of old:
Two thousand years have passed since thou didst see
Cæsar ride forth to royal victory,
Mighty thy name when Rome's lean eagles flew   185
From Britain's isles to far Euphrates blue;
And of the peoples thou wast noble queen,
Till in thy streets the Goth and Hun were seen.
Discrowned by man, deserted by the sea,
Thou sleepest, rocked in lonely misery!   190
No longer now upon thy swelling tide,
Pine-forest like, thy myriad galleys ride!
For where the brass-beaked ships were wont to float,
The weary shepherd pipes his mournful note;
And the white sheep are free to come and go   195
Where Adria's purple waters used to flow.

O fair! O sad! O Queen uncomforted!
In ruined loveliness thou liest dead,
Alone of all thy sisters; for at last
Italia's royal warrior hath passed   200
Rome's lordliest entrance, and hath worn his crown
In the high temples of the Eternal Town!
The Palatine hath welcomed back her king,
And with his name the seven mountains ring!

And Naples hath outlived her dream of pain,   205
And mocks her tyrant! Venice lives again,
New risen from the waters! and the cry
Of Light and Truth, of Love and Liberty,
Is heard in lordly Genoa, and where
The marble spires of Milan wound the air,   210
Rings from the Alps to the Sicilian shore,
And Dante's dream is now a dream no more.

But thou, Ravenna, better loved than all,
Thy ruined palaces are but a pall
That hides thy fallen greatness! and thy name   215
Burns like a grey and flickering candle-flame,
Beneath the noon-day splendour of the sun
Of new Italia! for the night is done,
The night of dark oppression, and the day
Hath dawned in passionate splendour: far away   220
The Austrian hounds are hunted from the land,
Beyond those ice-crowned citadels which stand
Girdling the plain of royal Lombardy,
From the far West unto the Eastern sea.

I know, indeed, that sons of thine have died   225
In Lissa's waters, by the mountain-side
Of Aspromonte, on Novara's plain,—
Nor have thy children died for thee in vain:
And yet, methinks, thou hast not drunk this wine
From grapes new-crushed of Liberty divine,   230
Thou hast not followed that immortal Star
Which leads the people forth to deeds of war.
Weary of life, thou liest in silent sleep,
As one who marks the lengthening shadows creep,
Careless of all the hurrying hours that run,   235
Mourning some day of glory, for the sun
Of Freedom hath not shewn to thee his face,
And thou hast caught no flambeau in the race.

Yet wake not from thy slumbers,—rest thee well,
Amidst thy fields of amber asphodel,   240
Thy lily-sprinkled meadows,—rest thee there,
To mock all human greatness: who would dare
To vent the paltry sorrows of his life
Before thy ruins, or to praise the strife
Of kings' ambition, and the barren pride   245
Of warring nations! wert not thou the Bride
Of the wild Lord of Adria's stormy sea!
The Queen of double Empires! and to thee
Were not the nations given as thy prey!
And now—thy gates lie open night and day,   250
The grass grows green on every tower and hall,
The ghastly fig hath cleft thy bastioned wall;
And where thy mailèd warriors stood at rest
The midnight owl hath made her secret nest.

O fallen! fallen! from thy high estate, 255
O city trammelled in the toils of Fate,
Doth nought remain of all thy glorious days,
But a dull shield, a crown of withered bays!

Yet who beneath this night of wars and fears,
From tranquil tower can watch the coming years; 260
Who can foretell what joys the day shall bring,
Or why before the dawn the linnets sing?
Thou, even thou, mayst wake, as wakes the rose
To crimson splendour from its grave of snows;
As the rich corn-fields rise to red and gold 265
From these brown lands, now stiff with Winter's cold;
As from the storm-rack comes a perfect star!

O much-loved city! I have wandered far
From the wave-circled islands of my home;
Have seen the gloomy mystery of the Dome 270
Rise slowly from the drear Campagna's way,
Clothed in the royal purple of the day:
I from the city of the violet crown
Have watched the sun by Corinth's hill go down,
And marked the 'myriad laughter' of the sea 275
From starlit hills of flower-starred Arkady;
Yet back to thee returns my perfect love,
As to its forest-nest the evening dove.

O poet's city! one who scarce has seen
Some twenty summers cast their doublets green, 280
For Autumn's livery, would seek in vain
To wake his lyre to sing a louder strain,
Or tell thy days of glory;—poor indeed
Is the low murmur of the shepherd's reed,
Where the loud clarion's blast should shake the sky, 285
And flame across the heavens! and to try
Such lofty themes were folly: yet I know
That never felt my heart a nobler glow
Than when I woke the silence of thy street
With clamorous trampling of my horse's feet, 290
And saw the city which now I try to sing,
After long days of weary travelling.

VII

Adieu, Ravenna! but a year ago,
I stood and watched the crimson sunset glow
From the lone chapel on thy marshy plain: 295
The sky was as a shield that caught the stain
Of blood and battle from the dying sun,
And in the west the circling clouds had spun
A royal robe, which some great God might wear,
While into ocean-seas of purple air   300
Sank the gold galley of the Lord of Light.

Yet here the gentle stillness of the night
Brings back the swelling tide of memory,
And wakes again my passionate love for thee:
Now is the Spring of Love, yet soon will come   305
On meadow and tree the Summer's lordly bloom;
And soon the grass with brighter flowers will blow,
And send up lilies for some boy to mow.
Then before long the Summer's conqueror,
Rich Autumn-time, the season's usurer,   310
Will lend his hoarded gold to all the trees,
And see it scattered by the spendthrift breeze;
And after that the Winter cold and drear.
So runs the perfect cycle of the year.
And so from youth to manhood do we go,   315
And fall to weary days and locks of snow.
Love only knows no winter; never dies:
Nor cares for frowning storms or leaden skies.
And mine for thee shall never pass away,
Though my weak lips may falter in my lay.   320

Adieu! Adieu! yon silent evening star,
The night's ambassador, doth gleam afar,
And bid the shepherd bring his flocks to fold.
Perchance before our inland seas of gold
Are garnered by the reapers into sheaves,   325
Perchance before I see the Autumn leaves,
I may behold thy city; and lay down
Low at thy feet the poet's laurel crown.

Adieu! Adieu! yon silver lamp, the moon,
Which turns our midnight into perfect noon,   330
Doth surely light thy towers, guarding well
Where Dante sleeps, where Byron loved to dwell.

49 *Magdalen Walks*

The little white clouds are racing over the sky,
    And the fields are strewn with the gold of the flower of March,
    The daffodil breaks under foot, and the tasselled larch
Sways and swings as the thrush goes hurrying by.

A delicate odour is borne on the wings of the morning breeze,   5
    The odour of deep wet grass, and of brown new-furrowed earth,
    The birds are singing for joy of the Spring's glad birth,
Hopping from branch to branch on the rocking trees.

And all the woods are alive with the murmur and sound of Spring,
    And the rosebud breaks into pink on the climbing briar,   10
    And the crocus-bed is a quivering moon of fire
Girdled round with the belt of an amethyst ring.

And the plane to the pine-tree is whispering some tale of love
    Till it rustles with laughter and tosses its mantle of green,
    And the gloom of the wych-elm's hollow is lit with the iris sheen   15
Of the burnished rainbow throat and the silver breast of a dove.

See! the lark starts up from his bed in the meadow there,
    Breaking the gossamer threads and the nets of dew,
    And flashing a-down the river, a flame of blue!
The kingfisher flies like an arrow, and wounds the air.   20

---

49 Magdalen Walks. Copy text: *P2*, collated with *I*, *P1*   2 March,] ~: *I*   3 tas-
selled] feathery *I*   4 Sways and swings] Bends to the wind *I*   hurrying] fluttering *I*
6 The] An *I*   deep wet] leaves, and of *I*, *P1*   brown new-furrowed] newly-upturned
I; newly upturned *P1*   earth,] ~: *I*   8 on] of *I*   10 rosebud] rose-bud *I*
13 some] a *I*   love₍ₐ₎] ~,* *I* [*the* *refers to a footnote*]   14 rustles] quivers *I*   laughter₍ₐ₎]
~, *I*   tosses] rustles *I*   green,] ~; *I*   15 wych-elm's hollow is] elm is broken, and *I*
iris₍ₐ₎sheen] iris-sheen *I*   16 Of a breast and of silver feathers, the signs of the passionate
dove. *I*   17 See!] ~, *I*   his] its *I*   18 threads₍ₐ₎] ~, *I*   dew,] ~: *I*   19 a-
down] adown *I*   river,] ~₍ₐ₎ *I*   ₍ₐ₎a] (~ *I*   blue!₍ₐ₎] ~!) *I*   20 kingfisher] king-fisher *I*
20.01–20.12 *I has*:

> And the sense of my life is sweet! though I know that the end is nigh:
>   For the ruin and rain of winter will shortly come,
>   The lily will lose its gold, and the chestnut-bloom
> In billows of red and white on the grass will lie.
>
> And even the light of the sun will fade at the last,
>   And the leaves will fall, and the birds will hasten away,
>   And I will be left in the snow of a flowerless day
> To think on the glories of Spring, and the joys of a youth long past.

[*continued overleaf*

50   *Cypriots or Folk Making for Malta*

Like a flame-bearded beacon seen from far
By storm-vexed sailors whom some curious wind
Hath beaten from their course, for seven days
O'er the wide waste they wander, day and night
In weary alternation rise and fall   5
And bring but barren comfort save that day
More clearly shows their ruin, till some God
Pitying their fortunes landward turns their prow
And from the towered crest of some high wave
They do descry that flaming torch which burns   10
On Calpé and the cliffs of Herakles
Which are the portals of the terrene sea,
So bright and welcome is thy face to me,
Constrained to wander on a stormier deep
Than is the wild Atlantic. Yet methinks   15
I am not made in some sick port to lie
Where rat and rot and scurvy may creep in,
And sickened bilge breed pestilence for my crew
And worms to eat my timbers: better far
To pail all upon the die and launch   20
Into the white-plumed battle of the waves
And seek new land, as the great Genoan
Who won a second world for jealous Spain
Or Cortes when he sighted Mexico,
And freighted all his galleys with the gold   25
Of Montezuma.

Yet be silent, my heart! do not count it a profitless thing
To have seen the splendour of sun, and of grass, and of flower!
To have lived and loved! for I hold that to love for an hour
Is better for man and for woman than cycles of blossoming Spring.

20.2 *Postscript Magdalen College, Oxford. I*   20.3 *Footnote* * Cf Aristophanes 'ὅταν
πλατάνος πτελέᾳ ψιθυρίζῃ.' *I*

50 Cypriots or Folk Making for Malta. Copy text: *M. W did not capitalize the first letter of the
words beginning lines 4–10, 14, 17–19, 21–7*   *Title* for] <from> for *M*   1 flame-
bearded] flame‸bearded *M*   3 course,] ~. *M*   4 wander,] ~. *M*   7 ruin,] ~. *M*
12 sea,] ~. *M*   13 me,] ~. *M*   15 Atlantic. Yet] Atlantis: yet *M*   16 ‸to lie‸]
(~ ~) *M*   18 sickened] <rotten> sickened *M*   for] <on> for *M*   22 new]
<some> ne<ver>w *M*   23 a second] <another> a second *M*   24 sighted]
<brake> {touched} sighted *M*   Mexico] Mezico *M*   26 Montezuma.] ~‸ *M*

51   *The Burden of Itys*

This English Thames is holier far than Rome,
   Those harebells like a sudden flush of sea
Breaking across the woodland, with the foam
   Of meadow-sweet and white anemone
To fleck their blue waves,—God is likelier there,   5
Than hidden in that crystal-hearted star the pale
     monks bear!

Those violet-gleaming butterflies that take
   Yon creamy lily for their pavilion
Are monsignores, and where the rushes shake
   A lazy pike lies basking in the sun   10
His eyes half shut,—He is some mitred old
Bishop *in partibus*! look at those gaudy scales all
     green and gold.

The wind the restless prisoner of the trees
   Does well for Palæstrina, one would say
The mighty master's hands were on the keys   15
   Of the Maria organ, which they play
When early on some sapphire Easter morn
In a high litter red as blood or sin the Pope is borne

From his dark House out to the Balcony
   Above the bronze gates and the crowded square,   20
Whose very fountains seem for ecstasy
   To toss their silver lances in the air,
And stretching out weak hands to East and West
In vain sends peace to peaceless lands, to restless nations rest.

Is not yon lingering orange afterglow   25
   That stays to vex the moon more fair than all
Rome's lordliest pageants! strange, a year ago
   I knelt before some crimson Cardinal
Who bare the Host across the Esquiline,
And now—those common poppies in the wheat seem
     twice as fine.   30

51 *The Burden of Itys.* Copy text: *P2*, collated with *M1, M2, M3, P1*   1–24 *not in M1,*
M2, M3   25–42 *not in M2, M3*   25 lingering orange] <violet> lingering 'orange'
M1   26 moon∧] ~, *M1*   27 pageants! strange, a year] pageants? strange: a month
M1   29 Host] host *M1*   Esquiline,] ~∧ *M1*   30 wheat] oats *M1*   fine.] ~∧ *M1*

The blue-green beanfields yonder, tremulous
  With the last shower, sweeter perfume bring
Through this cool evening than the odorous
  Flame-jewelled censers the young deacons swing,
When the grey priest unlocks the curtained shrine,   35
And makes God's body from the common fruit of
    corn and vine.

Poor Fra Giovanni bawling at the mass
  Were out of tune now, for a small brown bird
Sings overhead, and through the long cool grass
  I see that throbbing throat which once I heard   40
On starlit hills of flower-starred Arcady,
Once where the white and crescent sand of Salamis
    meets sea.

Sweet is the swallow twittering on the eaves
  At daybreak, when the mower whets his scythe,
And stock-doves murmur, and the milkmaid leaves   45
  Her little lonely bed, and carols blithe
To see the heavy-lowing cattle wait
Stretching their huge and dripping mouths across the
    farmyard gate.

And sweet the hops upon the Kentish leas,
  And sweet the wind that lifts the new-mown hay,   50
And sweet the fretful swarms of grumbling bees
  That round and round the linden blossoms play;
And sweet the heifer breathing in the stall,
And the green bursting figs that hang upon the
    red-brick wall.

---

31 blue-green beanfields] blue‿green beanfield *M1*   32 bring] brings *M1*
33 evening‿] ~, *M1*   the] that *M1*   34 Flame-jewelled censers] <Flame> 'red-'
hearted censer *M1*   deacons swing,] deacon swings‿ *M1*   35 curtained] golden
M1   36 *M1 has:*

          And <these> [   ] Gods body
                  makes the human
                          animate God from <withered> 'common'
                      fruit of corn and vine

39 overhead,] over head‿ *M1*   cool] deep *M1*   41 starlit] star-lit *M1*   flower-starred
Arcady,] flowerstared Arkady—*M1*   43–216 *not in M1, M2, M3*

And sweet to hear the cuckoo mock the spring 55
   While the last violet loiters by the well,
And sweet to hear the shepherd Daphnis sing
   The song of Linus through a sunny dell
Of warm Arcadia where the corn is gold
And the slight lithe-limbed reapers dance about the
     wattled fold. 60

And sweet with young Lycoris to recline
   In some Illyrian valley far away,
Where canopied on herbs amaracine
   We too might waste the summer-trancèd day
Matching our reeds in sportive rivalry, 65
While far beneath us frets the troubled purple of the sea.

But sweeter far if silver-sandalled foot
   Of some long-hidden God should ever tread
The Nuneham meadows, if with reeded flute
   Pressed to his lips some Faun might raise his head 70
By the green water-flags, ah! sweet indeed
To see the heavenly herdsman call his white-fleeced
     flock to feed.

Then sing to me thou tuneful chorister,
   Though what thou sings't be thine own requiem!
Tell me thy tale thou hapless chronicler 75
   Of thine own tragedies! do not contemn
These unfamiliar haunts, this English field,
For many a lovely coronal our northern isle can yield

Which Grecian meadows know not, many a rose
   Which all day long in vales Æolian 80
A lad might seek in vain for overgrows
   Our hedges like a wanton courtezan
Unthrifty of its beauty, lilies too
Ilissus never mirrored star our streams, and cockles blue

Dot the green wheat which, though they are the signs 85
   For swallows going south, would never spread
Their azure tents between the Attic vines;
   Even that little weed of ragged red,
Which bids the robin pipe, in Arcady
Would be a trespasser, and many an unsung elegy 90

Sleeps in the reeds that fringe our winding Thames
   Which to awake were sweeter ravishment
Than ever Syrinx wept for, diadems
   Of brown bee-studded orchids which were meant
For Cytheræa's brows are hidden here   95
Unknown to Cytheræa, and by yonder pasturing steer

There is a tiny yellow daffodil,
   The butterfly can see it from afar,
Although one summer evening's dew could fill
   Its little cup twice over ere the star   100
Had called the lazy shepherd to his fold
And be no prodigal, each leaf is flecked with spotted gold

As if Jove's gorgeous leman Danae
   Hot from his gilded arms had stooped to kiss
The trembling petals, or young Mercury   105
   Low-flying to the dusky ford of Dis
Had with one feather of his pinions
Just brushed them! the slight stem which bears the burden
     of its suns

Is hardly thicker than the gossamer,
   Or poor Arachne's silver tapestry,—   110
Men say it bloomed upon the sepulchre
   Of One I sometime worshipped, but to me
It seems to bring diviner memories
Of faun-loved Heliconian glades and blue
     nymph-haunted seas,

Of an untrodden vale at Tempe where   115
   On the clear river's marge Narcissus lies,
The tangle of the forest in his hair,
   The silence of the woodland in his eyes,
Wooing that drifting imagery which is
No sooner kissed than broken, memories of Salmacis   120

Who is not boy or girl and yet is both,
   Fed by two fires and unsatisfied
Through their excess, each passion being loth
   For love's own sake to leave the other's side
Yet killing love by staying, memories   125
Of Oreads peeping through the leaves of silent
     moon-lit trees,

Of lonely Ariadne on the wharf
   At Naxos, when she saw the treacherous crew
Far out at sea, and waved her crimson scarf
   And called false Theseus back again nor knew   130
That Dionysos on an amber pard
Was close behind her, memories of what Maeonia's bard

With sightless eyes beheld, the wall of Troy,
   Queen Helen lying in the ivory room,
And at her side an amorous red-lipped boy   135
   Trimming with dainty hand his helmet's plume,
And far away the moil, the shout, the groan,
As Hector shielded off the spear and Ajax hurled the stone;

Of wingèd Perseus with his flawless sword
   Cleaving the snaky tresses of the witch,   140
And all those tales imperishably stored
   In little Grecian urns, freightage more rich
Than any gaudy galleon of Spain
Bare from the Indies ever! these at least bring back again,

For well I know they are not dead at all,   145
   The ancient Gods of Grecian poesy,
They are asleep, and when they hear thee call
   Will wake and think 'tis very Thessaly,
This Thames the Daulian waters, this cool glade
The yellow-irised mead where once young Itys
      laughed and played.   150

If it was thou dear jasmine-cradled bird
   Who from the leafy stillness of thy throne
Sang to the wondrous boy, until he heard
   The horn of Atalanta faintly blown
Across the Cumner hills, and wandering   155
Through Bagley wood at evening found the Attic poets'
      spring,—

Ah! tiny sober-suited advocate
   That pleadest for the moon against the day!
If thou didst make the shepherd seek his mate
   On that sweet questing, when Proserpina   160
Forgot it was not Sicily and leant
Across the mossy Sandford stile in ravished wonderment,—

134 ivory] carven *P1*

Light-winged and bright-eyed miracle of the wood!
    If ever thou didst soothe with melody
One of that little clan, that brotherhood   165
    Which loved the morning-star of Tuscany
More than the perfect sun of Raphael
And is immortal, sing to me! for I too love thee well,

Sing on! sing on! let the dull world grow young,
    Let elemental things take form again,   170
And the old shapes of Beauty walk among
    The simple garths and open crofts, as when
The son of Leto bare the willow rod,
And the soft sheep and shaggy goats followed the
        boyish God.

Sing on! sing on! and Bacchus will be here   175
    Astride upon his gorgeous Indian throne,
And over whimpering tigers shake the spear
    With yellow ivy crowned and gummy cone,
While at his side the wanton Bassarid
Will throw the lion by the mane and catch the mountain kid!   180

Sing on! and I will wear the leopard skin,
    And steal the moonèd wings of Ashtaroth,
Upon whose icy chariot we could win
    Cithæron in an hour e'er the froth
Has overbrimmed the wine-vat or the Faun   185
Ceased from the treading! ay, before the flickering
        lamp of dawn

Has scared the hooting owlet to its nest,
    And warned the bat to close its filmy vans,
Some Mænad girl with vine-leaves on her breast
    Will filch their beechnuts from the sleeping Pans   190
So softly that the little nested thrush
Will never wake, and then with shrilly laugh and leap
        will rush

Down the green valley where the fallen dew
    Lies thick beneath the elm and count her store,
Till the brown Satyrs in a jolly crew   195
    Trample the loosestrife down along the shore,
And where their hornèd master sits in state
Bring strawberries and bloomy plums upon a wicker crate!

Sing on! and soon with passion-wearied face
   Through the cool leaves Apollo's lad will come,   200
The Tyrian prince his bristled boar will chase
   Adown the chestnut-copses all a-bloom,
And ivory-limbed, grey-eyed, with look of pride,
After yon velvet-coated deer the virgin maid will ride.

Sing on! and I the dying boy will see   205
   Stain with his purple blood the waxen bell
That overweighs the jacinth, and to me
   The wretched Cyprian her woe will tell,
And I will kiss her mouth and streaming eyes,
And lead her to the myrtle-hidden grove where Adon lies!   210

Cry out aloud on Itys! memory
   That foster-brother of remorse and pain
Drops poison in mine ear,—O to be free,
   To burn one's old ships! and to launch again
Into the white-plumed battle of the waves   215
And fight old Proteus for the spoil of coral-flowered caves!

O for Medea with her poppied spell!
   O for the secret of the Colchian shrine!
O for one leaf of that pale asphodel
   Which binds the tired brows of Proserpine,   220
And sheds such wondrous dews at eve that she
Dreams of the fields of Enna, by the far Sicilian sea,

Where oft the golden-girdled bee she chased
   From lily to lily on the level mead,
Ere yet her sombre Lord had bid her taste   225
   The deadly fruit of that pomegranate seed,
Ere the black steeds had harried her away
Down to the faint and flowerless land, the sick and
     sunless day.

217–22 *not in M1, M3*   217 spell!] ~, *M2*   218 O'r' for the drugs of Circe's secret
shrine, {that Circean shrine} *M2*   219 for <that bloom of purple> pallid blooming
asphodel *M2*   220 Which binds the tired brows] that hid the slumbering hair *M2*
221 and {weeps} sheds such dews at 'wondrous' evening that she *M2*   222 *M2 has:*

> Enna
> seems to forget me the fields of Enna
>   of Sicily
> forgets the fields of Enna
>   and the sea
>   by the blue Sicilian sea.

223–52 *not in M1, M2, M3*

O for one midnight and as paramour
    The Venus of the little Melian farm!   230
O that some antique statue for one hour
    Might wake to passion, and that I could charm
The Dawn at Florence from its dumb despair
Mix with those mighty limbs and make that giant breast
      my lair!

Sing on! sing on! I would be drunk with life,   235
    Drunk with the trampled vintage of my youth,
I would forget the wearying wasted strife,
    The riven veil, the Gorgon eyes of Truth,
The prayerless vigil and the cry for prayer,
The barren gifts, the lifted arms, the dull insensate air!   240

Sing on! sing on! O feathered Niobe,
    Thou canst make sorrow beautiful, and steal
From joy its sweetest music, not as we
    Who by dead voiceless silence strive to heal
Our too untented wounds, and do but keep   245
Pain barricadoed in our hearts, and murder pillowed sleep.

Sing louder yet, why must I still behold
    The wan white face of that deserted Christ,
Whose bleeding hands my hands did once enfold,
    Whose smitten lips my lips so oft have kissed,   250
And now in mute and marble misery
Sits in his lone dishonoured House and weeps, perchance
      for me.

O Memory cast down thy wreathèd shell!
    Break thy hoarse lute O sad Melpomene!
O Sorrow Sorrow keep thy cloistered cell   255
    Nor dim with tears this limpid Castaly!
Cease, Philomel, thou dost the forest wrong
To vex its sylvan quiet with such wild impassioned song!

253–8 *not in M1, M3*   253 Memory] memory *M2, P1*   shell!] shel [*page tear*] *M2*
254 Melpomene!] Melpomen [*page tear*] *M2*   255 Sorrow͵Sorrow͵] sorrow, sorrow,
M2; sorrow͵sorrow͵ *P1*   256 dim] dull *M2*   Castaly!] ~, *M2*   257 cease cease
fond bird you do the woodlands wrong, *M2*; Cease, cease, sad bird, thou dost the forest wrong͵
P1   258 To vex their {f[   ]} sylvan silence {with thy wild} <and passionate> with
impassioned song *M2*

Cease, cease, or if 'tis anguish to be dumb
    Take from the pastoral thrush her simpler air, 260
Whose jocund carelessness doth more become
    This English woodland than thy keen despair,
Ah! cease and let the northwind bear thy lay
Back to the rocky hills of Thrace, the stormy Daulian bay.

A moment more, the startled leaves had stirred, 265
    Endymion would have passed across the mead
Moonstruck with love, and this still Thames had heard
    Pan plash and paddle groping for some reed
To lure from her blue cave that Naiad maid
Who for such piping listens half in joy and half afraid. 270

A moment more, the waking dove had cooed,
    The silver daughter of the silver sea
With the fond gyves of clinging hands had wooed
    Her wanton from the chase, and Dryope
Had thrust aside the branches of her oak 275
To see the lusty gold-haired lad rein in his snorting yoke.

A moment more, the trees had stooped to kiss
    Pale Daphne just awakening from the swoon
Of tremulous laurels, lonely Salmacis
    Had bared his barren beauty to the moon, 280
And through the vale with sad voluptuous smile
Antinous had wandered, the red lotus of the Nile

Down leaning from his black and clustering hair,
    To shade those slumberous eyelids' caverned bliss,
Or else on yonder grassy slope with bare 285
    High-tuniced limbs unravished Artemis
Had bade her hounds give tongue, and roused the deer
From his green ambuscade with shrill halloo and pricking
    spear.

Lie still, lie still, O passionate heart, lie still!
    O Melancholy, fold thy raven wing! 290
O sobbing Dryad, from thy hollow hill
    Come not with such desponded answering!

259–70 *not in M1, M2, M3*   271–4 *not in M1, M2*   271 A moment more, the waking] a moment more the amorous *M3*   272 The] the *M3*   sea⌃] ~, *M3* 273 With [   ] wooed *M3*   274 Her leman from the hunting, [   ] *M3* 275–92 *not in M1, M2, M3*

No more thou wingèd Marsyas complain,
Apollo loveth not to hear such troubled songs of pain!

It was a dream, the glade is tenantless,   295
    No soft Ionian laughter moves the air,
The Thames creeps on in sluggish leadenness,
    And from the copse left desolate and bare
Fled is young Bacchus with his revelry,
Yet still from Nuneham wood there comes that
        thrilling melody   300

So sad, that one might think a human heart
    Brake in each separate note, a quality
Which music sometime has, being the Art
    Which is most nigh to tears and memory,
Poor mourning Philomel, what dost thou fear?   305
Thy sister doth not haunt these fields, Pandion is not here,

Here is no cruel Lord with murderous blade,
    No woven web of bloody heraldries,
But mossy dells for roving comrades made,
    Warm valleys where the tired student lies   310
With half-shut book, and many a winding walk
Where rustic lovers stray at eve in happy simple talk.

The harmless rabbit gambols with its young
    Across the trampled towing-path, where late
A troop of laughing boys in jostling throng   315
    Cheered with their noisy cries the racing eight;
The gossamer, with ravelled silver threads,
Works at its little loom, and from the dusky red-eaved sheds

Of the lone Farm a flickering light shines out
    Where the swinked shepherd drives his bleating flock   320
Back to their wattled sheep-cotes, a faint shout
    Comes from some Oxford boat at Sandford lock,
And starts the moor-hen from the sedgy rill,
And the dim lengthening shadows flit like swallows up
        the hill.

293–4 *not in M1, M3*   293 thou wingèd Marsyas] no more O treacherous bird *M2*
294 loved not to hear such troubled songs] doth not love to hear this troubled note *M2*
295–348 *not in M1, M2, M3*

The heron passes homeward to the mere,   325
   The blue mist creeps among the shivering trees,
Gold world by world the silent stars appear,
   And like a blossom blown before the breeze
A white moon drifts across the shimmering sky,
Mute arbitress of all thy sad, thy rapturous threnody.   330

She does not heed thee, wherefore should she heed,
   She knows Endymion is not far away,
'Tis I, 'tis I, whose soul is as the reed
   Which has no message of its own to play,
So pipes another's bidding, it is I,   335
Drifting with every wind on the wide sea of misery.

Ah! the brown bird has ceased: one exquisite trill
   About the sombre woodland seems to cling
Dying in music, else the air is still,
   So still that one might hear the bat's small wing   340
Wander and wheel above the pines, or tell
Each tiny dewdrop dripping from the blue-bell's
     brimming cell.

And far away across the lengthening wold,
   Across the willowy flats and thickets brown,
Magdalen's tall tower tipped with tremulous gold   345
   Marks the long High Street of the little town,
And warns me to return; I must not wait,
Hark! 'tis the curfew booming from the bell at
     Christ Church gate.

52   *Theocritus. A Villanelle*

     O Singer of Persephone!
       In the dim meadows desolate
     Dost thou remember Sicily?

     Still through the ivy flits the bee
       Where Amaryllis lies in state;   5
     O Singer of Persephone!

338 cling₍₎] ~, *P1*
   52 Theocritus. Copy text: *P1–2*, collated with *M*   1 Singer] singer *M*   *2 not in M*
3 Hast thou forgotten Sicily. *M*   *4–6 not in M*

Simætha calls on Hecate
  And hears the wild dogs at the gate;
Dost thou remember Sicily?

Still by the light and laughing sea   10
  Poor Polypheme bemoans his fate:
O Singer of Persephone!

And still in boyish rivalry
  Young Daphnis challenges his mate:
Dost thou remember Sicily?   15

Slim Lacon keeps a goat for thee,
  For thee the jocund shepherds wait,
O Singer of Persephone!
Dost thou remember Sicily?

53   *Nocturne*

The moon hath spread a pavilion
  Of silver and of amethyst:
But where is young Endymion,
Where are the lips that should be kissed?

The roof of fleecy cloud is spun,   5
  Of silken light the ropes are twist:
But where is young Endymion,
Where are the lips that should be kissed?

To spite her jealous Lord the Sun
  She wears a veil of seagreen mist: 10
But where is young Endymion,
Where are the lips that should be kissed?

7 Hecate] Hecaté *M*   8 And] and *M*   dogs] hounds *M*   gate;] ~ₐ *M*   9 Hast
thou   forgotten   Sicily. *M*   10   All   night   upon   the   wine   dark   [   ]   *M*
11 Polypheme] Poly. *M*   fate:] ~. *M*   12 *not in M*   14 Daphnis] <Lacon>
Daphnis *M*   mate:] ~. *M*   15 O S. [   ] *M*   16 Slim Lacon] Young Hylas *M*
thee,] ~ₐ *M*   17 For thee the [   ] wait. *M*   18–19 *not in M*

  53 Nocturne. Copy text: *M2*, collated with *M1*, *M3*   1–20 *not in M3*   1 The] the
M1   a] her *M1*   2 amethyst:] ~ₐ *M1*   3 Endymion,] ~ₐ *M1*   4 Where] where
M1   kissed?] ~ₐ *M1*   5 The] *not in M1*   fleecy] {sapphire} silken *M1*   spun,] ~ₐ *M1*,
M2   6 of fleecy cloud the skies are turned *M1*   7–8 *not in M1*   7 Endymion,] ~ₐ
M2   9 In secret fear of the deathly sun *M1*   To spite] <Against> To spite *M2*
10 wears a veil of seagreen] hides her face behind the *M1*; <hides her face behind a> wears a veil of
seagreen *M2*   mist:] ~ₐ *M1*   11 Endymion,] ~ₐ *M1*, *M2*   12 where [   ] kissed *M1*

All through the weary hours that run
   She keeps the lingering lover's tryst:
But where is young Endymion,
Where are the lips that should be kissed?   15

Her gold torch-bearers one by one
   Pass from her side and are not missed,
But where is young Endymion,
Where are the lips that should be kissed?   20

Ah down in moonless Acheron
   Pale Proserpine is glad, I wist:
For there is young Endymion,
There are the lips that should be kissed.

Verona.

54   *Endymion*

(For Music.)

The apple trees are hung with gold,
   And birds are loud in Arcady,
The sheep lie bleating in the fold,
The wild goat runs across the wold,
But yesterday his love he told,   5
   I know he will come back to me.
O rising moon! O Lady moon!
   Be you my lover's sentinel,
   You cannot choose but know him well,
For he is shod with purple shoon,   10
You cannot choose but know my love,
   For he a shepherd's crook doth bear,
And he is soft as any dove,
   And brown and curly is his hair.

13 Through [*illegible*] run *M1*   14 in vain she keeps the lover heart tryst. *M1*; {From star to star} She keeps the lingering lover's tryst‸ *M2*   15 But where [   ] *M1* Endymion,] ~‸ *M2*   16 where [   ] *M1* kissed?] ~‸ *M2*   17 torch-bearers] torchbearers *M1*   18 Pass] pass *M1* missed,] ~. *M1*   19–24 *not in M1* 19 Endymion,] ~‸ *M2*   20 should be kissed?] *not in M2*   22 glad, I wist:] glad‸I wist‸ *M2*; fain to list: *M3*   23 Endymion,] ~‸ *M2*   *Postscript* Verona.] *M3*; *not in M1, M2*
   54 Endymion. Copy text: *P1–2*, collated with *M*   1–28 *not in M*

The turtle now has ceased to call   15
   Upon her crimson-footed groom,
The grey wolf prowls about the stall,
The lily's singing seneschal
Sleeps in the lily-bell, and all
   The violet hills are lost in gloom.   20
O risen moon! O holy moon!
   Stand on the top of Helice,
   And if my own true love you see,
Ah! if you see the purple shoon,
The hazel crook, the lad's brown hair,   25
   The goat-skin wrapped about his arm,
Tell him that I am waiting where
   The rushlight glimmers in the Farm.

The falling dew is cold and chill,
   And no bird sings in Arcady,   30
The little fauns have left the hill,
Even the tired daffodil
Has closed its gilded doors, and still
   My lover comes not back to me.
False moon! False moon! O waning moon!   35
   Where is my own true lover gone,
   Where are the lips vermilion,
The shepherd's crook, the purple shoon?
Why spread that silver pavilion,
   Why wear that veil of drifting mist?   40
Ah! thou hast young Endymion,
   Thou hast the lips that should be kissed!

55   *Charmides*

He was a Grecian lad, who coming home
   With pulpy figs and wine from Sicily
Stood at his galley's prow, and let the foam
   Blow through his crisp brown curls unconsciously,
And holding wave and wind in boy's despite   5
Peered from his dripping seat across the wet and stormy night

---

33 its gilded] it's golden *M*   35 O waning moon! O cruel moon! *M*   38 crook, the]
crook‸and *M*   40 drifting mist?] amethyst, *M*   41 Endymion,] ~‸*M*   42 kissed!] ~. *M*
  55 *Charmides.* Copy text: *M2 (lines 511–606), M3 (lines 607–54), P2 (lines 1–510); collated
with M1, P1, P2 (lines 511–654)   1–510 not in M1, M2, M3*

Till with the dawn he saw a burnished spear
　　Like a thin thread of gold against the sky,
And hoisted sail, and strained the creaking gear,
　　And bade the pilot head her lustily　　　　　　　　　　10
Against the nor'west gale, and all day long
Held on his way, and marked the rowers' time with
　　　　measured song,

And when the faint Corinthian hills were red
　　Dropped anchor in a little sandy bay,
And with fresh boughs of olive crowned his head,　　　　15
　　And brushed from cheek and throat the hoary spray,
And washed his limbs with oil, and from the hold
Brought out his linen tunic and his sandals brazen-soled,

And a rich robe stained with the fishes' juice
　　Which of some swarthy trader he had bought　　　　20
Upon the sunny quay at Syracuse,
　　And was with Tyrian broideries inwrought,
And by the questioning merchants made his way
Up through the soft and silver woods, and when the
　　　　labouring day

Had spun its tangled web of crimson cloud,　　　　　　25
　　Clomb the high hill, and with swift silent feet
Crept to the fane unnoticed by the crowd
　　Of busy priests, and from some dark retreat
Watched the young swains his frolic playmates bring
The firstling of their little flock, and the shy shepherd fling　　30

The crackling salt upon the flame, or hang
　　His studded crook against the temple wall
To Her who keeps away the ravenous fang
　　Of the base wolf from homestead and from stall;
And then the clear-voiced maidens 'gan to sing,　　　　35
And to the altar each man brought some goodly offering,

A beechen cup brimming with milky foam,
　　A fair cloth wrought with cunning imagery
Of hounds in chase, a waxen honey-comb
　　Dripping with oozy gold which scarce the bee　　　　40
Had ceased from building, a black skin of oil
Meet for the wrestlers, a great boar the fierce and
　　　　white-tusked spoil

Stolen from Artemis that jealous maid
  To please Athena, and the dappled hide
Of a tall stag who in some mountain glade   45
  Had met the shaft; and then the herald cried,
And from the pillared precinct one by one
Went the glad Greeks well pleased that they their simple vows
    had done.

And the old priest put out the waning fires
  Save that one lamp whose restless ruby glowed   50
For ever in the cell, and the shrill lyres
  Came fainter on the wind, as down the road
In joyous dance these country folk did pass,
And with stout hands the warder closed the gates of
    polished brass.

Long time he lay and hardly dared to breathe,   55
  And heard the cadenced drip of spilt-out wine,
And the rose-petals falling from the wreath
  As the night breezes wandered through the shrine,
And seemed to be in some entrancèd swoon
Till through the open roof above the full and brimming moon   60

Flooded with sheeny waves the marble floor,
  When from his nook upleapt the venturous lad,
And flinging wide the cedar-carven door
  Beheld an awful image saffron-clad
And armed for battle! the gaunt Griffin glared   65
From the huge helm, and the long lance of wreck and
    ruin flared

Like a red rod of flame, stony and steeled
  The Gorgon's head its leaden eyeballs rolled,
And writhed its snaky horrors through the shield,
  And gaped aghast with bloodless lips and cold   70
In passion impotent, while with blind gaze
The blinking owl between the feet hooted in shrill amaze.

The lonely fisher as he trimmed his lamp
  Far out at sea off Sunium, or cast
The net for tunnies, heard a brazen tramp   75
  Of horses smite the waves, and a wild blast
Divide the folded curtains of the night,
And knelt upon the little poop, and prayed in holy fright.

And guilty lovers in their venery
    Forgat a little while their stolen sweets,   80
Deeming they heard dread Dian's bitter cry;
    And the grim watchmen on their lofty seats
Ran to their shields in haste precipitate,
Or strained black-bearded throats across the dusky parapet.

For round the temple rolled the clang of arms,   85
    And the twelve Gods leapt up in marble fear,
And the air quaked with dissonant alarums
    Till huge Poseidon shook his mighty spear,
And on the frieze the prancing horses neighed,
And the low tread of hurrying feet rang from the cavalcade.   90

Ready for death with parted lips he stood,
    And well content at such a price to see
That calm wide brow, that terrible maidenhood,
    The marvel of that pitiless chastity,
Ah! well content indeed, for never wight   95
Since Troy's young shepherd prince had seen so
      wonderful a sight.

Ready for death he stood, but lo! the air
    Grew silent, and the horses ceased to neigh,
And off his brow he tossed the clustering hair,
    And from his limbs he threw the cloak away,   100
For whom would not such love make desperate,
And nigher came, and touched her throat, and with
      hands violate

Undid the cuirass, and the crocus gown,
    And bared the breasts of polished ivory,
Till from the waist the peplos falling down   105
    Left visible the secret mystery
Which to no lover will Athena show,
The grand cool flanks, the crescent thighs, the
      bossy hills of snow.

108.1–108.6 *P1 has*:

    Those who have never known a lover's sin
      Let them not read my ditty, it will be
    To their dull ears so musicless and thin
      That they will have no joy of it, but ye
    To whose wan cheeks now creeps the lingering smile,
    Ye who have learned who Eros is,—O listen yet a-while.

A little space he let his greedy eyes
    Rest on the burnished image, till mere sight   110
Half swooned for surfeit of such luxuries,
    And then his lips in hungering delight
Fed on her lips, and round the towered neck
He flung his arms, nor cared at all his passion's will to check.

Never I ween did lover hold such tryst,   115
    For all night long he murmured honeyed word,
And saw her sweet unravished limbs, and kissed
    Her pale and argent body undisturbed,
And paddled with the polished throat, and pressed
His hot and beating heart upon her chill and icy breast.   120

It was as if Numidian javelins
    Pierced through and through his wild and whirling brain,
And his nerves thrilled like throbbing violins
    In exquisite pulsation, and the pain
Was such sweet anguish that he never drew   125
His lips from hers till overhead the lark of warning flew.

The moon was girdled with a crystal rim,
    The sign which shipmen say is ominous
Of wrath in heaven, the wan stars were dim,
    And the low lightening east was tremulous   130
With the faint fluttering wings of flying dawn,
Ere from the silent sombre shrine this lover had withdrawn.

Down the steep rock with hurried feet and fast
    Clomb the brave lad, and reached the cave of Pan,
And heard the goat-foot snoring as he passed,   135
    And leapt upon a grassy knoll and ran
Like a young fawn unto an olive wood
Which in a shady valley by the well-built city stood.

And sought a little stream, which well he knew,
    For oftentimes with boyish careless shout   140
The green and crested grebe he would pursue,
    Or snare in woven net the silver trout,

126.1–126.6 *P1 has*:

    They who have never seen the daylight peer
        Into a darkened room, and drawn the curtain,
    And with dull eyes and wearied from some dear
        And worshipped body risen, they for certain
    Will never know of what I try to sing,
    How long the last kiss was, how fond and late his lingering.

And down amid the startled reeds he lay
Panting in breathless sweet affright, and waited for the day.

On the green bank he lay, and let one hand   145
   Dip in the cool dark eddies listlessly,
And soon the breath of morning came and fanned
   His hot flushed cheeks, or lifted wantonly
The tangled curls from off his forehead, while
He on the running water gazed with strange and secret smile.   150

And soon the shepherd in rough woollen cloak
   With his long crook undid the wattled cotes,
And from the stack a thin blue wreath of smoke
   Curled through the air across the ripening oats,
And on the hill the yellow house-dog bayed   155
As through the crisp and rustling fern the heavy cattle strayed.

And when the light-foot mower went afield
   Across the meadows laced with threaded dew,
And the sheep bleated on the misty weald,
   And from its nest the waking corn-crake flew,   160
Some woodmen saw him lying by the stream
And marvelled much that any lad so beautiful could seem,

Nor deemed him born of mortals, and one said,
   'It is young Hylas, that false runaway
Who with a Naiad now would make his bed   165
   Forgetting Herakles,' but others, 'Nay,
It is Narcissus, his own paramour,
Those are the fond and crimson lips no woman can allure.'

And when they nearer came a third one cried,
   'It is young Dionysos who has hid   170
His spear and fawnskin by the river side
   Weary of hunting with the Bassarid,
And wise indeed were we away to fly
They live not long who on the gods immortal come to spy.'

So turned they back, and feared to look behind,   175
   And told the timid swain how they had seen
Amid the reeds some woodland God reclined,
   And no man dared to cross the open green,
And on that day no olive-tree was slain,
Nor rushes cut, but all deserted was the fair domain.   180

Save when the neat-herd's lad, his empty pail
    Well slung upon his back, with leap and bound
Raced on the other side, and stopped to hail
    Hoping that he some comrade new had found,
And gat no answer, and then half afraid   185
Passed on his simple way, or down the still and silent glade

A little girl ran laughing from the farm
    Not thinking of love's secret mysteries,
And when she saw the white and gleaming arm
    And all his manlihood, with longing eyes   190
Whose passion mocked her sweet virginity
Watched him a-while, and then stole back sadly and wearily.

Far off he heard the city's hum and noise,
    And now and then the shriller laughter where
The passionate purity of brown-limbed boys   195
    Wrestled or raced in the clear healthful air,
And now and then a little tinkling bell
As the shorn wether led the sheep down to the mossy well.

Through the grey willows danced the fretful gnat,
    The grasshopper chirped idly from the tree,   200
In sleek and oily coat the water-rat
    Breasting the little ripples manfully
Made for the wild-duck's nest, from bough to bough
Hopped the shy finch, and the huge tortoise crept across
        the slough.

On the faint wind floated the silky seeds   205
    As the bright scythe swept through the waving grass,
The ousel-cock splashed circles in the reeds
    And flecked with silver whorls the forest's glass,
Which scarce had caught again its imagery
Ere from its bed the dusky tench leapt at the dragon-fly.   210

But little care had he for any thing
    Though up and down the beech the squirrel played,
And from the copse the linnet 'gan to sing
    To her brown mate her sweetest serenade,
Ah! little care indeed, for he had seen   215
The breasts of Pallas and the naked wonder of the Queen.

205 seeds₎] *P2*; ~, *P1*

But when the herdsman called his straggling goats
　　With whistling pipe across the rocky road,
And the shard-beetle with its trumpet-notes
　　Boomed through the darkening woods, and seemed to bode　　220
Of coming storm, and the belated crane
Passed homeward like a shadow, and the dull big drops of rain

Fell on the pattering fig-leaves, up he rose,
　　And from the gloomy forest went his way
Past sombre homestead and wet orchard-close,　　　　　　225
　　And came at last unto a little quay,
And called his mates a-board, and took his seat
On the high poop, and pushed from land, and loosed the
　　　dripping sheet,

And steered across the bay, and when nine suns
　　Passed down the long and laddered way of gold,　　　230
And nine pale moons had breathed their orisons
　　To the chaste stars their confessors, or told
Their dearest secret to the downy moth
That will not fly at noonday, through the foam and
　　　surging froth

Came a great owl with yellow sulphurous eyes　　　　235
　　And lit upon the ship, whose timbers creaked
As though the lading of three argosies
　　Were in the hold, and flapped its wings, and shrieked,
And darkness straightway stole across the deep,
Sheathed was Orion's sword, dread Mars himself fled
　　　down the steep,　　　　　　　　　　　　　240

And the moon hid behind a tawny mask
　　Of drifting cloud, and from the ocean's marge
Rose the red plume, the huge and hornèd casque,
　　The seven-cubit spear, the brazen targe!
And clad in bright and burnished panoply　　　　　245
Athena strode across the stretch of sick and shivering sea!

To the dull sailors' sight her loosened locks
　　Seemed like the jagged storm-rack, and her feet
Only the spume that floats on hidden rocks,
　　And, marking how the rising waters beat　　　　　250
Against the rolling ship, the pilot cried
To the young helmsman at the stern to luff to windward side.

250 And,] *P2*; ~ ‸ *P1*

But he, the over-bold adulterer,
    A dear profaner of great mysteries,
An ardent amorous idolater,   255
    When he beheld those grand relentless eyes
Laughed loud for joy, and crying out 'I come'
Leapt from the lofty poop into the chill and churning foam.

Then fell from the high heaven one bright star,
    One dancer left the circling galaxy,   260
And back to Athens on her clattering car
    In all the pride of venged divinity
Pale Pallas swept with shrill and steely clank,
And a few gurgling bubbles rose where her boy lover sank.

And the mast shuddered as the gaunt owl flew   265
    With mocking hoots after the wrathful Queen,
And the old pilot bade the trembling crew
    Hoist the big sail, and told how he had seen
Close to the stern a dim and giant form,
And like a dipping swallow the stout ship dashed
        through the storm.   270

And no man dared to speak of Charmides
    Deeming that he some evil thing had wrought,
And when they reached the strait Symplegades
    They beached their galley on the shore, and sought
The toll-gate of the city hastily,   275
And in the market showed their brown and pictured pottery.

II

But some good Triton-god had ruth, and bare
    The boy's drowned body back to Grecian land,
And mermaids combed his dank and dripping hair
    And smoothed his brow, and loosed his clenching hand, 280
Some brought sweet spices from far Araby,
And others bade the halcyon sing her softest lullaby.

And when he neared his old Athenian home,
    A mighty billow rose up suddenly
Upon whose oily back the clotted foam   285
    Lay diapered in some strange fantasy,
And clasping him unto its glassy breast,
Swept landward, like a white-maned steed upon a
        venturous quest!

Now where Colonos leans unto the sea
   There lies a long and level stretch of lawn,   290
The rabbit knows it, and the mountain bee
   For it deserts Hymettus, and the Faun
Is not afraid, for never through the day
Comes a cry ruder than the shout of shepherd lads at play.

But often from the thorny labyrinth   295
   And tangled branches of the circling wood
The stealthy hunter sees young Hyacinth
   Hurling the polished disk, and draws his hood
Over his guilty gaze, and creeps away,
Nor dares to wind his horn, or—else at the first break of day   300

The Dryads come and throw the leathern ball
   Along the reedy shore, and circumvent
Some goat-eared Pan to be their seneschal
   For fear of bold Poseidon's ravishment,
And loose their girdles, with shy timorous eyes,   305
Lest from the surf his azure arms and purple beard should rise.

On this side and on that a rocky cave,
   Hung with the yellow-bell'd laburnum, stands,
Smooth is the beach, save where some ebbing wave
   Leaves its faint outline etched upon the sands,   310
As though it feared to be too soon forgot
By the green rush, its playfellow,—and yet, it is a spot

So small, that the inconstant butterfly
   Could steal the hoarded honey from each flower
Ere it was noon, and still not satisfy   315
   Its over-greedy love,—within an hour
A sailor boy, were he but rude enow
To land and pluck a garland for his galley's painted prow,

Would almost leave the little meadow bare,
   For it knows nothing of great pageantry,   320
Only a few narcissi here and there
   Stand separate in sweet austerity,
Dotting the unmown grass with silver stars,
And here and there a daffodil waves tiny scimetars.

Hither the billow brought him, and was glad   325
   Of such dear servitude, and where the land
Was virgin of all waters laid the lad
   Upon the golden margent of the strand,

And like a lingering lover oft returned
To kiss those pallid limbs which once with intense
    fire burned,   330

Ere the wet seas had quenched that holocaust,
    That self-fed flame, that passionate lustihead,
Ere grisly death with chill and nipping frost
    Had withered up those lilies white and red
Which, while the boy would through the forest range,   335
Answered each other in a sweet antiphonal counter-change.

And when at dawn the woodnymphs, hand-in-hand,
    Threaded the bosky dell, their satyr spied
The boy's pale body stretched upon the sand,
    And feared Poseidon's treachery, and cried,   340
And like bright sunbeams flitting through a glade,
Each startled Dryad sought some safe and leafy ambuscade.

Save one white girl, who deemed it would not be
    So dread a thing to feel a sea-god's arms
Crushing her breasts in amorous tyranny,   345
    And longed to listen to those subtle charms
Insidious lovers weave when they would win
Some fencèd fortress, and stole back again, nor thought it sin

To yield her treasure unto one so fair,
    And lay beside him, thirsty with love's drouth,   350
Called him soft names, played with his tangled hair,
    And with hot lips made havoc of his mouth
Afraid he might not wake, and then afraid
Lest he might wake too soon, fled back, and then,
    fond renegade,

Returned to fresh assault, and all day long   355
    Sat at his side, and laughed at her new toy,
And held his hand, and sang her sweetest song,
    Then frowned to see how froward was the boy
Who would not with her maidenhood entwine,
Nor knew that three days since his eyes had looked
    on Proserpine,   360

Nor knew what sacrilege his lips had done,
    But said, 'He will awake, I know him well,
He will awake at evening when the sun
    Hangs his red shield on Corinth's citadel,

This sleep is but a cruel treachery   365
To make me love him more, and in some cavern of the sea

Deeper than ever falls the fisher's line
   Already a huge Triton blows his horn,
And weaves a garland from the crystalline
   And drifting ocean-tendrils to adorn   370
The emerald pillars of our bridal bed,
For sphered in foaming silver, and with coral-crownèd head,

We two will sit upon a throne of pearl,
   And a blue wave will be our canopy,
And at our feet the water-snakes will curl   375
   In all their amethystine panoply
Of diamonded mail, and we will mark
The mullets swimming by the mast of some
     storm-foundered bark,

Vermilion-finned with eyes of bossy gold
   Like flakes of crimson light, and the great deep   380
His glassy-portaled chamber will unfold,
   And we will see the painted dolphins sleep
Cradled by murmuring halcyons on the rocks
Where Proteus in quaint suit of green pastures his
     monstrous flocks.

And tremulous opal-hued anemones   385
   Will wave their purple fringes where we tread
Upon the mirrored floor, and argosies
   Of fishes flecked with tawny scales will thread
The drifting cordage of the shattered wreck,
And honey-coloured amber beads our twining limbs
     will deck.'   390

But when that baffled Lord of War the Sun
   With gaudy pennon flying passed away
Into his brazen House, and one by one
   The little yellow stars began to stray
Across the field of heaven, ah! then indeed   395
She feared his lips upon her lips would never care to feed,

And cried, 'Awake, already the pale moon
   Washes the trees with silver, and the wave
Creeps grey and chilly up this sandy dune,
   The croaking frogs are out, and from the cave   400

The night-jar shrieks, the fluttering bats repass,
And the brown stoat with hollow flanks creeps through the
        dusky grass.

Nay, though thou art a God, be not so coy,
    For in yon stream there is a little reed
That often whispers how a lovely boy   405
    Lay with her once upon a grassy mead,
Who when his cruel pleasure he had done
Spread wings of rustling gold and soared aloft into the sun.

Be not so coy, the laurel trembles still
    With great Apollo's kisses, and the fir   410
Whose clustering sisters fringe the sea-ward hill
    Hath many a tale of that bold ravisher
Whom men call Boreas, and I have seen
The mocking eyes of Hermes through the poplar's
        silvery sheen.

Even the jealous Naiads call me fair,   415
    And every morn a young and ruddy swain
Woos me with apples and with locks of hair,
    And seeks to soothe my virginal disdain
By all the gifts the gentle wood-nymphs love;
But yesterday he brought to me an iris-plumaged dove   420

With little crimson feet, which with its store
    Of seven spotted eggs the cruel lad
Had stolen from the lofty sycamore
    At day-break, when her amorous comrade had
Flown off in search of berried juniper   425
Which most they love; the fretful wasp, that earliest vintager

Of the blue grapes, hath not persistency
    So constant as this simple shepherd-boy
For my poor lips, his joyous purity
    And laughing sunny eyes might well decoy   430
A Dryad from her oath to Artemis;
For very beautiful is he, his mouth was made to kiss,

His argent forehead, like a rising moon
    Over the dusky hills of meeting brows,
Is crescent shaped, the hot and Tyrian noon   435
    Leads from the myrtle-grove no goodlier spouse

For Cytheræa, the first silky down
Fringes his blushing cheeks, and his young limbs are strong
    and brown:

And he is rich, and fat and fleecy herds
    Of bleating sheep upon his meadows lie,   440
And many an earthern bowl of yellow curds
    Is in his homestead for the thievish fly
To swim and drown in, the pink clover mead
Keeps its sweet store for him, and he can pipe on oaten reed.

And yet I love him not, it was for thee   445
    I kept my love, I knew that thou would'st come
To rid me of this pallid chastity;
    Thou fairest flower of the flowerless foam
Of all the wide Ægean, brightest star
Of ocean's azure heavens where the mirrored planets are!   450

I knew that thou would'st come, for when at first
    The dry wood burgeoned, and the sap of Spring
Swelled in my green and tender bark or burst
    To myriad multitudinous blossoming
Which mocked the midnight with its mimic moons   455
That did not dread the dawn, and first the thrushes'
       rapturous tunes

Startled the squirrel from its granary,
    And cuckoo flowers fringed the narrow lane,
Through my young leaves a sensuous ecstasy
    Crept like new wine, and every mossy vein   460
Throbbed with the fitful pulse of amorous blood,
And the wild winds of passion shook my slim stem's
       maidenhood.

The trooping fawns at evening came and laid
    Their cool black noses on my lowest boughs,
And on my topmost branch the blackbird made   465
    A little nest of grasses for his spouse,
And now and then a twittering wren would light
On a thin twig which hardly bare the weight of such delight.

I was the Attic shepherd's trysting place,
    Beneath my shadow Amaryllis lay,   470
And round my trunk would laughing Daphnis chase
    The timorous girl, till tired out with play

She felt his hot breath stir her tangled hair,
And turned, and looked, and fled no more from such
          delightful snare.

Then come away unto my ambuscade   475
     Where clustering woodbine weaves a canopy
For amorous pleasaunce, and the rustling shade
     Of Paphian myrtles seems to sanctify
The dearest rites of love, there in the cool
And green recesses of its farthest depth there is a pool,   480

The ouzel's haunt, the wild bee's pasturage,
     For round its rim great creamy lilies float
Through their flat leaves in verdant anchorage,
     Each cup a white-sailed golden-laden boat
Steered by a dragon-fly,—be not afraid   485
To leave this wan and wave-kissed shore, surely the place
          was made

For lovers such as we, the Cyprian Queen,
     One arm around her boyish paramour,
Strays often there at eve, and I have seen
     The moon strip off her misty vestiture   490
For young Endymion's eyes, be not afraid,
The panther feet of Dian never tread that secret glade.

Nay if thou wil'st, back to the beating brine,
     Back to the boisterous billow let us go,
And walk all day beneath the hyaline   495
     Huge vault of Neptune's watery portico,
And watch the purple monsters of the deep
Sport in ungainly play, and from his lair keen Xiphias leap.

For if my mistress find me lying here
     She will not ruth or gentle pity show,   500
But lay her boar-spear down, and with austere
     Relentless fingers string the cornel bow,
And draw the feathered notch against her breast,
And loose the archèd cord, ay, even now upon the quest

I hear her hurrying feet,—awake, awake,   505
     Thou laggard in love's battle! once at least
Let me drink deep of passion's wine, and slake
     My parchèd being with the nectarous feast

Which even Gods affect! O come Love come,
Still we have time to reach the cavern of thine azure home.'   510

Scarce had she spoken when the shuddering trees
   Shook, and the leaves divided, and the air
Grew conscious of a God, and the grey seas
   Crawled backward, and a long and dismal blare
Blew from some tasselled horn, a sleuth-hound bayed,   515
And like a flame a barbèd reed flew whizzing down the glade.

And where the little flowers of her breast
   Just brake into their milky blossoming,
This murderous paramour, this unbidden guest,
   Pierced and struck deep in horrid chambering,   520
And ploughed a bloody furrow with its dart,
And dug a long red road, and cleft with wingèd death
     her heart.

Sobbing her life out with a bitter cry,
   On the boy's body fell the Dryad maid,
Sobbing for incomplete virginity,   525
   And raptures unenjoyed, and pleasures dead,
And all the pain of things unsatisfied,
And the bright drops of crimson youth crept down her
     throbbing side.

Ah! pitiful it was to hear her moan,
   And very pitiful to see her die   530
Ere she had yielded up her sweets, or known
   The joy of passion, that dread mystery
Which not to know is not to live at all,
And yet to know is to be held in death's most deadly thrall.

But as it hapt the Queen of Cythere,   535
   Who with Adonis all night long had lain
Within some shepherd's hut in Arcady,
   On team of silver doves and gilded wane
Was journeying Paphos-ward, high up afar
From mortal ken between the mountains and the
     morning star,   540

511–94 *not in* M*1*, M*3*   514 Crawled] P*1*, P*2*; <Fled> <swept> crawled M*2*
515 sleuth-hound] P*1*, P*2*; sleuth͜hound M*2*   520 in] <with> in M*2*   521 its]
P*1*, P*2*; it's M*2*   523 cry,] M*2*; ~͜ P*1*, P*2*   526 raptures] <passions> raptures M*2*
531 Ere] P*1*, P*2*; E'er M*2*   534 death's] P*1*, P*2*; deaths M*2*   539 <Was journeying
Paphos-ward high up afar> On team of silver doves and gilded wane M*2*

And when low down she spied the hapless pair
    And heard the Oread's faint despairing cry,
Whose cadence seemed to play upon the air
    As though it were a viol, hastily
She bade her pigeons fold each straining plume,   545
And dropt to earth, and reached the strand, and saw
      their dolorous doom.

For as a gardener turning back his head
    To catch the last notes of the linnet mows
With careless scythe too near some flower bed,
    And cuts the thorny pillar of the rose,   550
And with the flower's loosened loveliness
Strews the brown mould, or as some shepherd lad
      in wantonness

Driving his little flock along the mead
    Treads down two daffodils which side by side
Have lured the lady-bird with yellow brede   555
    And made the gaudy moth forget its pride,
Treads down their brimming golden chalices
Under light feet which were not made for such
      rude ravages,

Or as a schoolboy tired of his book
    Flings himself down upon the reedy grass   560
And plucks two water-lilies from the brook,
    And for a time forgets the hour glass,
Then wearies of their sweets, and goes his way,
And lets the hot sun kill them, even so these lovers lay.

And Venus cried, 'It is dread Artemis   565
    Whose bitter hand hath wrought this cruelty,
Or else that mightier may whose care it is
    To guard her strong and stainless majesty
Upon the hill Athenian,—alas!
That they who loved so well unloved into Death's house
      should pass.'   570

---

541 pair$_\Lambda$] *M2*; ~, *P1*, *P2*   545 her pigeons fold each] <each> her pigeon's' fold <it's>
each *M2*   548 linnet$_\Lambda$] *M2*; ~, *P1*, *P2*   555 lady-bird] *P1*, *P2*; lady$_\Lambda$bird *M2*
556 its] *P1*, *P2*; it's *M2*   565 cried,] *P1*, *P2*; ~$_\Lambda$ *M2*   566 bitter] *P1*, *P2*; ruthless *M2*
570 pass.'] ~.$_\Lambda$ *M2*, *P1*, *P2*

So with soft hands she laid the boy and girl
   In the great golden waggon tenderly,
Her white throat whiter than a moony pearl
   Just threaded with a blue vein's tapestry
Had not yet ceased to throb, and still her breast   575
Swayed like a wind-stirred lily in ambiguous unrest.

And then each pigeon spread its milky van,
   The bright car soared into the dawning sky,
And like a cloud the aerial caravan
   Passed over the Ægean silently,   580
Till the faint air was troubled with the song
From the wan mouths that call on bleeding Thammuz
    all night long.

But when the doves had reached their wonted goal
   Where the wide stair of orbèd marble dips
Its snows into the sea, her fluttering soul   585
   Just shook the trembling petals of her lips
And passed into the void, and Venus knew
That one fair maid the less would walk amid her retinue,

And bade her servants carve a cedar chest
   With all the wonder of this history,   590
Within whose scented womb their limbs should rest
   Where olive-trees make tender the blue sky
On the low hills of Paphos, and the faun
Pipes in the noonday, and the nightingale sings on till dawn.

Nor failed they to obey her hest, and ere   595
   The morning bee had stung the daffodil
With tiny fretful spear, or from its lair
   The waking stag had leapt across the rill
And roused the ouzel, or the lizard crept
Athwart the sunny rock, beneath the grass their
    bodies slept.   600

---

573 Her] <That> Her *M2*   575 her] <that> her *M2*   577 its] *P1, P2*; it's *M2*
578 dawning] *P1, P2*; sapphire *M2*   582 night] <day> night *M2*   583 when]
<e'er> when *M2*   586 petals] <rose> petals *M2*   588 retinue,] *P1, P2*; ~. *M2*
593 faun] *P1, P2*; Faun *M2*   595–8 *not in M3*   595 Nor failed they to obey her hest,
and ere] *P1, P2*; [ ] and e'er, I *M1*; Nor failed they to obey <their queen> her hest, and e'er
M2   596 The] *M2, P1, P2*; the *M1*   597 With] *M2, P1, P2*; with *M1*   or] *M2,
P1, P2*; and *M1*   its] *M1, P1, P2*; it's *M2*   598 stag had leapt] *M2, P1, P2*; leopard
crept *M1*   rill] *M2, P1, P2*; [*illegible*] *M1*   599–606 *not in M1, M3*   599 ouzel]
<wild duck> ouzel *M2*

And when day brake, within that silver shrine
    Fed by the flames of cressets tremulous,
Queen Venus knelt and prayed to Proserpine
    That she whose beauty made Death amorous
Should beg a guerdon from her pallid Lord,   605
And let Desire pass across dread Charon's icy ford.

III

In melancholy moonless Acheron,
    Far from the goodly earth and joyous day,
Where no spring ever buds, nor ripening sun
    Weighs down the apple trees, nor flowery May   610
Chequers with chestnut blooms the grassy floor,
Where thrushes never sing, and piping linnets mate no more,

There by a dim and dark Lethæan well
    Young Charmides was lying, wearily
He plucked the blossoms from the asphodel   615
    And with its little rifled treasury
Strewed the dull waters of the dusky stream,
And watched the white stars founder, and the land was
        like a dream.

When as he gazed into the watery glass
    And through his brown hair's curly tangles scanned   620
His own wan face, a shadow seemed to pass
    Across the mirror, and a little hand
Stole into his, and warm lips timidly
Brushed his pale cheeks, and breathed their secret forth
        into a sigh.

Then turned he round his weary eyes and saw,   625
    And ever nigher still their faces came,
And nigher ever did their young mouths draw
    Until they seemed one perfect rose of flame,
And longing arms around her neck he cast,
And felt her throbbing bosom, and his breath came hot
        and fast,   630

601 when day brake] <all day long> when day brake *M2*   that] <her> that *M2*
606 And] <Should> And *M2*   Charon's] *P1*, *P2*; Charons *M2*   607–54 *not in M1, M2*
609 nor] *P1*, *P2*; or *M3*   610 Weighs] *P1*, *P2*; Weigh *M3*   nor] *P1*, *P2*; or *M3*
611 Chequers] *P1*, *P2*; Chequer *M3*   614 wearily] <listlessly> wearily *M3*
615 asphodel‿] *M3*; ~, *P1*, *P2*   618 dream.] *M3*; ~, *P1*, *P2*   619 When] <Lo!>
When *M3*

And all his hoarded sweets were hers to kiss,
    And all her maidenhood was his to slay,
And limb to limb in long and rapturous bliss
    Their passion waxed and waned,—O why essay
To pipe again of love too venturous reed!   635
Enough, enough that Erôs laughed upon that flowerless mead.

Too venturous poesy O why essay
    To pipe again of passion! fold thy wings
O'er daring Icarus and bid thy lay
    Sleep hidden in the lyre's silent strings   640
Till thou hast found the old Castalian rill,
Or from the Lesbian waters plucked drowned Sappho's
        golden quill!

Enough, enough that he whose life had been
    A fiery pulse of sin, a splendid shame,
Could in the loveless land of Hades glean   645
    One scorching harvest from those fields of flame
Where passion walks with naked unshod feet
And is not wounded,—ah! enough that once their lips
        could meet

In that wild throb when all existences
    Seem narrowed to one single ecstasy   650
Which dies through its own sweetness and the stress
    Of too much pleasure, ere Persephone
Had bade them serve her by the ebon throne
Of the pale God who in the fields of Enna loosed her zone.

56   *Ballade de Marguerite (Normande.)*

            I am weary of lying within the chase
            When the knights are meeting in market-place.

            Nay, go not thou to the red-roofed town
            Lest the hooves of the war-horse tread thee down.

639 O'er *P1, P2*; Thou *M3*   640 the] th<y>e *M3*   strings,] *M3*; ~, *P1, P2*
651 its] *P1, P2*; it's *M3*   652 ere] *P1, P2*; e'er *M3*
    56 Ballade de Marguerite. Copy text: *M*, collated with *K, P1–2*   1 chase,] *P1–2*; ~,
K, M   2 When] While *K*   knights] knyghtes *K*   3 red-roofed town,] red-roof'd
town, *K*   4 tread] <ride> tread *M*

But I would not go where the Squires ride,   5
I would only walk by my Lady's side.

Alack! and alack! thou art over bold,
A Forester's son may not eat off gold.

Will she love me the less that my Father is seen
Each Martinmas day in a doublet green?   10

Perchance she is sewing at tapestrie,
Spindle and loom are not meet for thee.

Ah, if she is working the arras bright
I might ravel the threads by the fire-light.

Perchance she is hunting of the deer,   15
How could you follow o'er hill and meer?

Ah, if she is riding with the court,
I might run beside her and wind the morte.

Perchance she is kneeling in S. Denys,
(On her soul may our Lady have gramercy!)   20

Ah, if she is praying in lone chapelle,
I might swing the censer and ring the bell.

Come in, my son, for you look sae pale,
The father shall fill thee a stoup of ale.

5 Squires ride,] squires ride: *K*   6 walk] sit *K*   Lady's] lady's *K*   7 over‸bold]
over-bold *K*   8 Forester's] *P1–2*; forester's *K*; Foresters *M*   9 me the less‸] me
less, *K*   seen‸] *K*; ~, *M*, *P1–2*   10.1–10.4 *K has:*

> But your cloak of sheepskin is rough to see,
> When your lady is clad in cramoisie.
>
> Alack! and alack! then, if true love dies,
> When one is in silk, and the other in frieze!

11 Perchance] Mayhap *K*; <But perhaps> Perchance *M*   sewing at tapestrie,] *P1–2*; working the tapestrie; *K*; sewing at tapestrie‸ *M*   13 Ah, if she is working] If it be that she
seweth *K*   bright‸] ~, *K*   15 Perchance] Mayhap *K*; <But perhaps> Perchance *M*
hunting] chasing *K*   deer,] ~; *K*   16 meer?] *K*, *P1–2*; ~. *M*   17 Ah, if she is rid-
ing] If it be that she hunteth *K*   the] <her> the *M*   court] Court *K*   18 beside her‸]
behind her, *K*   19 Perchance] Mayhap *K*; <But perhaps> Perchance *M*   kneeling]
praying *K*   S. Denys,] chapellrie‸ *K*; <chapellrie> S. Denys, *M*   20 On] To *K*
have gramercy!] *P1–2*; show gramercie! *K*; have gramercy‸ *M*   21 praying] kneeling *K*
chapelle] chapélle *K*   22 censer‸and] censer, or *K*   23 in,] *K*; ~‸ *M*, *P1–2*   you
look] thou look'st *K*   pale,] *K*, *P1–2*; ~‸ *M*   24 The father shall] *P1–2*; Thy father will
K; The Father shall *M*

But who are these knights in bright array? 25
Is it a pageant the rich folks play?

'Tis the King of England from over sea,
Who has come unto visit our fair countrie.

But why does the curfew toll sae low?
And why do the mourners walk a-row? 30

O 'tis Hugh of Amiens my sister's son
Who is lying stark, for his day is done.

Nay, nay, for I see white lilies clear,
It is no strong man who lies on the bier.

O 'tis old Dame Jeannette that kept the hall, 35
I knew she would die at the autumn fall.

Dame Jeannette had not that gold-brown hair,
Old Jeannette was not a maiden fair.

O 'tis none of our kith and none of our kin,
(Her soul may our Lady assoil from sin!) 40

But I hear the boy's voice chaunting sweet,
'Elle est morte, la Marguerite.'

Come in, my son, and lie on the bed,
And let the dead folk bury their dead.

O mother, you know I loved her true: 45
O mother, hath one grave room for two?

25 But‸] Oh, *K*   knights] knyghtes *K*   26 folks] folk *K*   27 'Tis] It's *K*; <It's>
'Tis *M*   England] France *K*; <France> England *M*   over sea] over the sea *K*; over <the>
sea *M*   28 Who] That *K*   unto] to *K*   30 a-row] *K*, *P1–2*; arow *M*   31 O 'tis]
Oh, it's *K*; O <it's> 'tis *M*   Amiens‸] Durham, *K*; <Durham> Amiens‸ *M*   son‸] ~, *K*
32 Who] That *K*   33 Nay, nay] Ah, no *K*   clear,] ~; *K*   34 who] that *K*   35
O 'tis old] Oh, it's good *K*; O <it's> 'tis old *M*   Jeannette] Alice *K*; <Janet> Jeannette *M*
hall,] Hall: *K*   37 Dame Alice was not a maiden fair; *K*   Jeannette] <Janet> Jeannette
M   gold-brown] *P1–2*; gold‸brown *M*   38 Dame Alice had not that yellow hair. *K*
Old] <Dame> Old *M*   Jeannette] J'e'an'n'et'te' *M*   39 O 'tis] Oh, it's *K*   kin,] kin;
K   40 sin!)] ~). *K*   42 Marguerite.] *P1–2*; ~! *K*; ~‸ *M*   43 in,] *K*; ~‸ *M*, *P1–2*
son,] *K*; ~‸ *M*, *P1–2*   45 O mother,] *P1–2*; Oh, mother, *K*; O mother‸ *M*   46 Oh,
mother, one grave will do for two. *K*; O mother 'hath' one grave <will do> '<hath> room' for
two? *M*

57　　　　　　*La Belle Gabrielle*

(From the French.)

Love could I charm the silver-breasted moon
　　To lie with me upon the Latmian hill
Through the hot hours of the purple noon
　　Till of strange joys my lips had drunk their fill.

Love could I change wan water into wine　　　　　　　　　5
　　To make more glad some heavy-lidded bride
Whose soul is sick with passion to entwine
　　The crimson-caftaned lover at her side.

Love could I make the lily-petals part
　　And filch the treasures of its golden seed,　　　　　　　10
Or swoon for passion in the rose's heart
　　Till its red leaves with redder pain did bleed.

Love could I see Narcissus lean to kiss
　　His laughing double in the glassy stream,
Or hear the smitten lips of Salmacis　　　　　　　　　15
　　Laugh low for pleasure of some unreal dream.

Ah what to me were silver-breasted moon,
　　Or all the sweets young Narciss' could unfold,
Or wondering lovers, or rose-chaliced swoon,
　　Or hair made golden with the lily's gold.　　　　　　　20

58　　　　　　*Humanitad*

It is full Winter now: the trees are bare,
　　Save where the cattle huddle from the cold
Beneath the pine, for it doth never wear
　　The Autumn's gaudy livery whose gold
Her jealous brother pilfers, but is true　　　　　　　5
　　To the green doublet; bitter is the wind, as though it blew

57 La Belle Gabrielle. Copy text: *M*　　　1 Love could] [*page tear*] could *M*　　4 of]
<with> of *M*　　　10 its] it's *M*　　　12 its] it's *M*
　　58 Humanitad. Copy text: *P2*, collated with *P1*, *M*

From Saturn's cave; a few thin wisps of hay
　　Lie on the sharp black hedges, where the wain
Dragged the sweet pillage of a summer's day
　　From the low meadows up the narrow lane;   10
Upon the half-thawed snow the bleating sheep
Press close against the hurdles, and the shivering
　　　　house-dogs creep

From the shut stable to the frozen stream
　　And back again disconsolate, and miss
The bawling shepherds and the noisy team;   15
　　And overhead in circling listlessness
The cawing rooks whirl round the frosted stack,
Or crowd the dripping boughs; and in the fen the
　　　　ice-pools crack

Where the gaunt bittern stalks among the reeds
　　And flaps his wings, and stretches back his neck,   20
And hoots to see the moon; across the meads
　　Limps the poor frightened hare, a little speck;
And a stray seamew with its fretful cry
Flits like a sudden drift of snow against the dull grey sky.

Full winter: and the lusty goodman brings   25
　　His load of faggots from the chilly byre,
And stamps his feet upon the hearth, and flings
　　The sappy billets on the waning fire,
And laughs to see the sudden lightening scare
His children at their play; and yet,—the Spring is in
　　　　the air,   30

Already the slim crocus stirs the snow,
　　And soon yon blanchèd fields will bloom again
With nodding cowslips for some lad to mow,
　　For with the first warm kisses of the rain
The winter's icy sorrow breaks to tears,   35
And the brown thrushes mate, and with bright eyes
　　　　the rabbit peers

From the dark warren where the fir-cones lie,
　　And treads one snowdrop under foot, and runs
Over the mossy knoll, and blackbirds fly
　　Across our path at evening, and the suns   40
Stay longer with us; ah! how good to see
Grass-girdled Spring in all her joy of laughing greenery

Dance through the hedges till the early rose,
   (That sweet repentance of the thorny briar!)
Burst from its sheathèd emerald and disclose   45
   The little quivering disk of golden fire
Which the bees know so well, for with it come
Pale boys-love, sops-in-wine, and daffadillies all in bloom.

Then up and down the field the sower goes,
   While close behind the laughing younker scares   50
With shrilly whoop the black and thievish crows,
   And then the chestnut-tree its glory wears,
And on the grass the creamy blossom falls
In odorous excess, and faint half-whispered madrigals

Steal from the bluebells' nodding carillons   55
   Each breezy morn, and then white jessamine,
That star of its own heaven, snapdragons
   With lolling crimson tongues, and eglantine
In dusty velvets clad usurp the bed
And woodland empery, and when the lingering rose
     hath shed   60

Red leaf by leaf its folded panoply,
   And pansies closed their purple-lidded eyes,
Chrysanthemums from gilded argosy
   Unload their gaudy scentless merchandise,
And violets getting overbold withdraw   65
From their shy nooks, and scarlet berries dot the leafless haw.

O happy field! and O thrice happy tree!
   Soon will your queen in daisy-flowered smock
And crown of flowre-de-luce trip down the lea,
   Soon will the lazy shepherds drive their flock   70
Back to the pasture by the pool, and soon
Through the green leaves will float the hum of murmuring
     bees at noon.

Soon will the glade be bright with bellamour,
   The flower which wantons love, and those sweet nuns
Vale-lilies in their snowy vestiture   75
   Will tell their beaded pearls, and carnations
With mitred dusky leaves will scent the wind,
And straggling traveller's joy each hedge with yellow stars
     will bind.

Dear Bride of Nature and most bounteous Spring!
   That cans't give increase to the sweet-breath'd kine,   80
And to the kid its little horns, and bring
   The soft and silky blossoms to the vine,
Where is that old nepenthe which of yore
Man got from poppy root and glossy-berried mandragore!

There was a time when any common bird   85
   Could make me sing in unison, a time
When all the strings of boyish life were stirred
   To quick response or more melodious rhyme
By every forest idyll;—do I change?
Or rather doth some evil thing through thy fair pleasaunce
     range?   90

Nay, nay, thou art the same: 'tis I who seek
   To vex with sighs thy simple solitude,
And because fruitless tears bedew my cheek
   Would have thee weep with me in brotherhood;
Fool! shall each wronged and restless spirit dare   95
To taint such wine with the salt poison of his own despair!

Thou art the same: 'tis I whose wretched soul
   Takes discontent to be its paramour,
And gives its kingdom to the rude control
   Of what should be its servitor,—for sure   100
Wisdom is somewhere, though the stormy sea
Contain it not, and the huge deep answer ''Tis not in me.'

To burn with one clear flame, to stand erect
   In natural honour, not to bend the knee
In profitless prostrations whose effect   105
   Is by itself condemned, what alchemy
Can teach me this? what herb Medea brewed
Will bring the unexultant peace of essence not subdued?

The minor chord which ends the harmony,
   And for its answering brother waits in vain   110
Sobbing for incompleted melody,
   Dies a Swan's death; but I the heir of pain,
A silent Memnon with blank lidless eyes,
Wait for the light and music of those suns which never rise.

110 vain∧] ~, *P1*   111 Sobbing] <Dying> Sobbing *M*   melody,] ~∧ *P1*, *M*
112 Swan's death;] swan's death: *M*   I∧] ~, *M*   113 eyes,] ~∧ *M*   114 which] that
M   rise.] ~∧ *M*

The quenched-out torch, the lonely cypress-gloom,   115
    The little dust stored in the narrow urn,
The gentle XAIPE of the Attic tomb,—
    Were not these better far than to return
To my old fitful restless malady,
Or spend my days within the voiceless cave of misery?   120

Nay! for perchance that poppy-crownèd God
    Is like the watcher by a sick man's bed
Who talks of sleep but gives it not; his rod
    Hath lost its virtue, and, when all is said,
Death is too rude, too obvious a key   125
To solve one single secret in a life's philosophy.

And Love! that noble madness, whose august
    And inextinguishable might can slay
The soul with honied drugs,—alas! I must
    From such sweet ruin play the runaway,   130
Although too constant memory never can
Forget the archèd splendour of those brows Olympian

Which for a little season made my youth
    So soft a swoon of exquisite indolence
That all the chiding of more prudent Truth   135
    Seemed the thin voice of jealousy,—O Hence
Thou huntress deadlier than Artemis!
Go seek some other quarry! for of thy too perilous bliss

My lips have drunk enough,—no more, no more,—
    Though Love himself should turn his gilded prow   140
Back to the troubled waters of this shore
    Where I am wrecked and stranded, even now
The Chariot wheels of passion sweep too near,
Hence! Hence! I pass unto a life more barren, more austere.

More barren—ay, those arms will never lean   145
    Down through the trellised vines and draw my soul
In sweet reluctance through the tangled green;
    Some other head must wear that aureole,
For I am Hers who loves not any man
Whose white and stainless bosom bears the sign Gorgonian.   150

Let Venus go and chuck her dainty page,
    And kiss his mouth, and toss his curly hair,
With net and spear and hunting equipage
    Let young Adonis to his tryst repair,

But me her fond and subtle-fashioned spell   155
Delights no more, though I could win her dearest citadel.

Ay, though I were that laughing shepherd boy
    Who from Mount Ida saw the little cloud
Pass over Tenedos and lofty Troy
    And knew the coming of the Queen, and bowed   160
In wonder at her feet, not for the sake
Of a new Helen would I bid her hand the apple take.

Then rise supreme Athena argent-limbed!
    And, if my lips be musicless, inspire
At least my life: was not thy glory hymned   165
    By One who gave to thee his sword and lyre
Like Æschylos at well-fought Marathon,
And died to show that Milton's England still could bear a son!

And yet I cannot tread the Portico
    And live without desire, fear, and pain,   170
Or nurture that wise calm which long ago
    The grave Athenian master taught to men,
Self-poised, self-centred, and self-comforted,
To watch the world's vain phantasies go by with
        unbowed head.

Alas! that serene brow, those eloquent lips,   175
    Those eyes that mirrored all eternity,
Rest in their own Colonos, an eclipse
    Hath come on Wisdom, and Mnemosyne
Is childless; in the night which she had made
For lofty secure flight Athena's owl itself hath strayed.   180

Nor much with Science do I care to climb,
    Although by strange and subtle witchery
She draw the moon from heaven: the Muse of Time
    Unrolls her gorgeous-coloured tapestry
To no less eager eyes; often indeed   185
In the great epic of Polymnia's scroll I love to read

How Asia sent her myriad hosts to war
    Against a little town, and panoplied
In gilded mail with jewelled scimetar,
    White-shielded, purple-crested, rode the Mede   190
Between the waving poplars and the sea
Which men call Artemisium, till he saw Thermopylæ

Its steep ravine spanned by a narrow wall,
    And on the nearer side a little brood
Of careless lions holding festival!   195
    And stood amazèd at such hardihood,
And pitched his tent upon the reedy shore,
And stayed two days to wonder, and then crept at
        midnight o'er

Some unfrequented height, and coming down
    The autumn forests treacherously slew   200
What Sparta held most dear and was the crown
    Of far Eurotas, and passed on, nor knew
How God had staked an evil net for him
In the small bay at Salamis,—and yet, the page grows dim,

Its cadenced Greek delights me not, I feel   205
    With such a goodly time too out of tune
To love it much: for like the Dial's wheel
    That from its blinded darkness strikes the noon
Yet never sees the sun, so do my eyes
Restlessly follow that which from my cheated vision flies.   210

O for one grand unselfish simple life
    To teach us what is Wisdom! speak ye hills
Of lone Helvellyn, for this note of strife
    Shunned your untroubled crags and crystal rills,
Where is that Spirit which living blamelessly   215
Yet dared to kiss the smitten mouth of his own century!

Speak ye Rydalian laurels! where is He
    Whose gentle head ye sheltered, that pure soul
Whose gracious days of uncrowned majesty
    Through lowliest conduct touched the lofty goal   220
Where Love and Duty mingle! Him at least
The most high Laws were glad of, He had sat at
        Wisdom's feast,

But we are Learning's changlings, know by rote
    The clarion watchword of each Grecian school
And follow none, the flawless sword which smote   225
    The pagan Hydra is an effete tool
Which we ourselves have blunted, what man now
Shall scale the august ancient heights and to
        old Reverence bow?

One such indeed I saw, but, Ichabod!
   Gone is that last dear son of Italy, 230
Who being man died for the sake of God,
   And whose unrisen bones sleep peacefully,
O guard him, guard him well, my Giotto's tower,
Thou marble lily of the lily town! let not the lour

Of the rude tempest vex his slumber, or 235
   The Arno with its tawny troubled gold
O'erleap its marge, no mightier conqueror
   Clomb the high Capitol in the days of old
When Rome was indeed Rome, for Liberty
Walked like a Bride beside him, at which sight pale Mystery 240

Fled shrieking to her farthest sombrest cell
   With an old man who grabbled rusty keys,
Fled shuddering for that immemorial knell
   With which oblivion buries dynasties
Swept like a wounded eagle on the blast, 245
As to the holy heart of Rome the great triumvir passed.

He knew the holiest heart and heights of Rome,
   He drave the base wolf from the lion's lair,
And now lies dead by that empyreal dome
   Which overtops Valdarno hung in air 250
By Brunelleschi—O Melpomene
Breathe through thy melancholy pipe thy sweetest threnody!

Breathe through the tragic stops such melodies
   That Joy's self may grow jealous, and the Nine
Forget a-while their discreet emperies, 255
   Mourning for him who on Rome's lordliest shrine
Lit for men's lives the light of Marathon,
And bare to sun-forgotten fields the fire of the sun!

O guard him, guard him well, my Giotto's tower,
   Let some young Florentine each eventide 260
Bring coronals of that enchanted flower
   Which the dim woods of Vallombrosa hide,
And deck the marble tomb wherein he lies
Whose soul is as some mighty orb unseen of mortal eyes.

Some mighty orb whose cycled wanderings, 265
   Being tempest-driven to the farthest rim
Where Chaos meets Creation and the wings
   Of the eternal chanting Cherubim

Are pavilioned on Nothing, passed away
Into a moonless void,—and yet, though he is dust and clay,   270

He is not dead, the immemorial Fates
    Forbid it, and the closing shears refrain,
Lift up your heads ye everlasting gates!
    Ye argent clarions sound a loftier strain!
For the vile thing he hated lurks within   275
Its sombre house, alone with God and memories of sin.

Still what avails it that she sought her cave
    That murderous mother of red harlotries?
At Munich on the marble architrave
    The Grecian boys die smiling, but the seas   280
Which wash Ægina fret in loneliness
Not mirroring their beauty, so our lives grow colourless

For lack of our ideals, if one star
    Flame torch-like in the heavens the unjust
Swift daylight kills it, and no trump of war   285
    Can wake to passionate voice the silent dust
Which was Mazzini once! rich Niobe
For all her stony sorrows hath her sons, but Italy!

What Easter Day shall make her children rise,
    Who were not Gods yet suffered? what sure feet   290
Shall find their graveclothes folded? what clear eyes
    Shall see them bodily? O it were meet
To roll the stone from off the sepulchre
And kiss the bleeding roses of their wounds, in love of Her

Our Italy! our mother visible!   295
    Most blessed among nations and most sad,
For whose dear sake the young Calabrian fell
    That day at Aspromonte and was glad
That in an age when God was bought and sold
One man could die for Liberty! but we, burnt out and cold,   300

See Honour smitten on the cheek and gyves
    Bind the sweet feet of Mercy: Poverty
Creeps through our sunless lanes and with sharp knives
    Cuts the warm throats of children stealthily,
And no word said:—O we are wretched men   305
Unworthy of our great inheritance! where is the pen

Of austere Milton? where the mighty sword
   Which slew its master righteously? the years
Have lost their ancient leader, and no word
   Breaks from the voiceless tripod on our ears: 310
While as a ruined mother in some spasm
Bears a base child and loathes it, so our best enthusiasm

Genders unlawful children, Anarchy
   Freedom's own Judas, the vile prodigal
Licence who steals the gold of Liberty   315
   And yet has nothing, Ignorance the real
One Fratricide since Cain, Envy the asp
That stings itself to anguish, Avarice whose palsied grasp

Is in its extent stiffened, monied Greed
   For whose dull appetite men waste away   320
Amid the whirr of wheels and are the seed
   Of things which slay their sower, these each day
Sees rife in England, and the gentle feet
Of Beauty tread no more the stones of each unlovely street.

What even Cromwell spared is desecrated   325
   By weed and worm, left to the stormy play
Of wind and beating snow, or renovated
   By more destructful hands: Time's worst decay
Will wreathe its ruins with some loveliness,
But these new Vandals can but make a rainproof barrenness.   330

Where is that Art which bade the Angels sing
   Through Lincoln's lofty choir, till the air
Seems from such marble harmonies to ring
   With sweeter song than common lips can dare
To draw from actual reed? ah! where is now   335
The cunning hand which made the flowering hawthorn
     branches bow

For Southwell's arch, and carved the House of One
   Who loved the lilies of the field with all
Our dearest English flowers? the same sun
   Rises for us: the seasons natural   340
Weave the same tapestry of green and grey:
The unchanged hills are with us: but that Spirit hath
     passed away.

And yet perchance it may be better so,
    For Tyranny is an incestuous Queen,
Murder her brother is her bedfellow,   345
    And the Plague chambers with her: in obscene
And bloody paths her treacherous feet are set;
Better the empty desert and a soul inviolate!

For gentle brotherhood, the harmony
    Of living in the healthful air, the swift   350
Clean beauty of strong limbs when men are free
    And women chaste, these are the things which lift
Our souls up more than even Agnolo's
Gaunt blinded Sibyl poring o'er the scroll of human woes,

Or Titian's little maiden on the stair   355
    White as her own sweet lily, and as tall,
Or Mona Lisa smiling through her hair,—
    Ah! somehow life is bigger after all
Than any painted Angel could we see
The God that is within us! The old Greek serenity   360

Which curbs the passion of that level line
    Of marble youths, who with untroubled eyes
And chastened limbs ride round Athena's shrine
    And mirror her divine economies,
And balanced symmetry of what in man   365
Would else wage ceaseless warfare,—this at least within
    the span

Between our mother's kisses and the grave
    Might so inform our lives, that we could win
Such mighty empires that from her cave
    Temptation would grow hoarse, and pallid Sin   370
Would walk ashamed of his adulteries,
And Passion creep from out the House of Lust with
    startled eyes.

To make the Body and the Spirit one
    With all right things, till no thing live in vain
From morn to noon, but in sweet unison   375
    With every pulse of flesh and throb of brain
The Soul in flawless essence high enthroned,
Against all outer vain attack invincibly bastioned,

356 lily,] ~‸ P1   tall,] P1; ~‸ P2

Mark with serene impartiality
   The strife of things, and yet be comforted,   380
Knowing that by the chain causality
   All separate existences are wed
Into one supreme whole, whose utterance
Is joy, or holier praise! ah! surely this were governance

Of Life in most august omnipresence,   385
   Through which the rational intellect would find
In passion its expression, and mere sense,
   Ignoble else, lend fire to the mind,
And being joined with it in harmony
More mystical than that which binds the stars planetary,   390

Strike from their several tones one octave chord
   Whose cadence being measureless would fly
Through all the circling spheres, then to its Lord
   Return refreshed with its new empery
And more exultant power,—this indeed   395
Could we but reach it were to find the last, the perfect creed.

Ah! it was easy when the world was young
   To keep one's life free and inviolate,
From our sad lips another song is rung,
   By our own hands our heads are desecrate,   400
Wanderers in drear exile, and dispossessed
Of what should be our own, we can but feed on wild unrest.

Somehow the grace, the bloom of things has flown,
   And of all men we are most wretched who
Must live each other's lives and not our own   405
   For very pity's sake and then undo
All that we lived for—it was otherwise
When soul and body seemed to blend in mystic symphonies.

But we have left those gentle haunts to pass
   With weary feet to the new Calvary,   410
Where we behold, as one who in a glass
   Sees his own face, self-slain Humanity,
And in the dumb reproach of that sad gaze
Learn what an awful phantom the red hand of man can raise.

389 with it in] with in *P1*

O smitten mouth! O forehead crowned with thorn!   415
   O chalice of all common miseries!
Thou for our sakes that loved thee not hast borne
   An agony of endless centuries,
And we were vain and ignorant nor knew
That when we stabbed thy heart it was our own real hearts
     we slew.   420

Being ourselves the sowers and the seeds,
   The night that covers and the lights that fade,
The spear that pierces and the side that bleeds,
   The lips betraying and the life betrayed;
The deep hath calm: the moon hath rest: but we   425
Lords of the natural world are yet our own dread enemy.

Is this the end of all that primal force
   Which, in its changes being still the same,
From eyeless Chaos cleft its upward course,
   Through ravenous seas and whirling rocks and flame,   430
Till the suns met in heaven and began
Their cycles, and the morning stars sang, and the Word was
     Man!

Nay, nay, we are but crucified, and though
   The bloody sweat falls from our brows like rain,
Loosen the nails—we shall come down I know,   435
   Staunch the red wounds—we shall be whole again,
No need have we of hyssop-laden rod,
That which is purely human, that is Godlike, that is God.

59   *Athanasia*

To that gaunt House of Art which lacks for naught
   Of all the great things men have saved from Time,
The withered body of a girl was brought,
   Dead ere the world's glad youth had touched its prime,
And seen by lonely Arabs lying hid   5
In the dim womb of some black pyramid.

59 Athanasia. Copy text: *P1–2*, collated with *Z*   2 Time] time *Z*   3 The]
A *Z*   brought,] *Z*; ~ˌ *P1–2*   4 prime,] ~; *Z*   6 dim womb] chill heart *Z*

But when they had unloosed the linen band
   Which swathed the Egyptian's body,—lo! was found
Closed in the wasted hollow of her hand
   A little seed, which sown in English ground   10
Did wondrous snow of starry blossoms bear,
And spread rich odours through our springtide air.

With such strange arts this flower did allure
   That all forgotten was the asphodel,
And the brown bee, the lily's paramour,   15
   Forsook the cup where he was wont to dwell,
For not a thing of earth it seemed to be,
But stolen from some heavenly Arcady.

In vain the sad narcissus, wan and white
   At its own beauty, hung across the stream,   20
The purple dragon-fly had no delight
   With its gold dust to make his wings a-gleam,
Ah! no delight the jasmine-bloom to kiss,
Or brush the rain-pearls from the eucharis.

For love of it the passionate nightingale   25
   Forgot the hills of Thrace, the cruel king,
And the pale dove no longer cared to sail
   Through the wet woods at time of blossoming,
But round this flower of Egypt sought to float,
With silvered wing and amethystine throat.   30

While the hot sun blazed in his tower of blue
   A cooling wind crept from the land of snows,
And the warm south with tender tears of dew
   Drenched its white leaves when Hesperos uprose
Amid those sea-green meadows of the sky   35
On which the scarlet bars of sunset lie.

But when o'er wastes of lily-haunted field
   The tired birds had stayed their amorous tune,
And broad and glittering like an argent shield
   High in the sapphire heavens hung the moon,   40

8 body,—lo!] body‸—lo, Z   found‸] ~, Z   9 hand‸] ~, Z   10 which‸] ~, Z ground‸] ~, Z   11 starry] star-like Z   12 odours] fragrance Z   air.] ~! Z 13 allure‸] ~, Z   16 he] it Z   dwell,] ~; Z   18 Arcady] Arkady Z   19 nar- cissus] narcissos Z   20 stream,] ~; Z   22 a-gleam,] ~—Z   23 Ah!] ~, Z 26 king,] ~; Z   29 float,] ~‸Z   31 his tower] the waste Z   blue‸] ~, Z   32 crept] stole Z   snows,] ~; Z   34 leaves‸] ~, Z   36 On which the scarlet] That o'er the crimson Z   37 when‸o'er the wastes of] when, through bower and Z   field‸] ~, Z 39 glittering‸] ~, Z   shield‸] ~, Z

Did no strange dream or evil memory make
Each tremulous petal of its blossoms shake?

Ah no! to this bright flower a thousand years
   Seemed but the lingering of a summer's day,
It never knew the tide of cankering fears   45
   Which turn a boy's gold hair to withered grey,
The dread desire of death it never knew,
Or how all folk that they were born must rue.

For we to death with pipe and dancing go,
   Nor would we pass the ivory gate again,   50
As some sad river wearied of its flow
   Through the dull plains, the haunts of common men,
Leaps lover-like into the terrible sea!
And counts it gain to die so gloriously.

We mar our lordly strength in barren strife   55
   With the world's legions led by clamorous care,
It never feels decay but gathers life
   From the pure sunlight and the supreme air,
We live beneath Time's wasting sovereignty,
It is the child of all eternity.   60

60   *The New Helen*

   Where hast thou been since round the walls of Troy
     The sons of God fought in that great emprise?
      Why dost thou walk our common earth again?
    Hast thou forgotten that impassioned boy,

41 dream‸or] dream, no *Z*   memory‸] ~, *Z*   42 Each tremulous petal of its] The petals of its tremulous *Z*   43 to] To *Z*   44 day,] ~; *Z*   46 grey,] gray; *Z*   49 we] *we Z*   50 again,] ~; *Z*   51 river‸] ~, *Z*   53 Counting it gain to die so gloriously, *Z*   54 Leaps lover-like into the terrible sea. *Z*   55 We] *We Z* 56 legions‸] ~, *Z*   care,] ~; *Z*   57 It] *It Z*   decay‸] ~, *Z*   58 air,] ~. *Z* 59 Time's] time's *Z*   sovereignty,] ~; *Z*   60.1–60.6 *Z has*:

    The woes of man may serve an idle lay,
      Nor were it hard fond hearers to enthral,
    Telling how Egypt's glory passed away,
      How London from its pinnacle must fall;
    But this white flower, the conqueror of time,
    Seems all too great for any boyish rhyme.

  60 The New Helen. Copy text: *P2*, collated with *Z, P1*

His purple galley, and his Tyrian men, 5
  And treacherous Aphrodite's mocking eyes?
For surely it was thou, who, like a star
  Hung in the silver silence of the night,
  Didst lure the Old World's chivalry and might
Into the clamorous crimson waves of war! 10

Or didst thou rule the fire-laden moon?
  In amorous Sidon was thy temple built
    Over the light and laughter of the sea?
  Where, behind lattice scarlet-wrought and gilt,
    Some brown-limbed girl did weave thee tapestry, 15
All through the waste and wearied hours of noon;
Till her wan cheek with flame of passion burned,
  And she rose up the sea-washed lips to kiss
Of some glad Cyprian sailor, safe returned
  From Calpé and the cliffs of Herakles! 20

No! thou art Helen, and none other one!
  It was for thee that young Sarpedôn died,
    And Memnôn's manhood was untimely spent;
  It was for thee gold-crested Hector tried
With Thetis' child that evil race to run, 25
    In the last year of thy beleaguerment;
Ay! even now the glory of thy fame
  Burns in those fields of trampled asphodel,
  Where the high lords whom Ilion knew so well
Clash ghostly shields, and call upon thy name. 30

Where hast thou been? in that enchanted land
  Whose slumbering vales forlorn Calypso knew,
    Where never mower rose at break of day
  But all unswathed the trammelling grasses grew,
And the sad shepherd saw the tall corn stand 35
    Till summer's red had changed to withered gray?
Didst thou lie there by some Lethæan stream
  Deep brooding on thine ancient memory,
  The crash of broken spears, the fiery gleam
  From shivered helm, the Grecian battle-cry? 40

7 it was thou] thou art she *Z*   10 clamorous,] ~, *Z*   21 none] no *Z*   22 young]
bright *Z*   28 Burns in those fields of trampled] Burns, torch-like, in Death's fields of *Z*
29 the] those *Z*   30 shields,] ~, *Z*   33 at break of] to greet the *Z*, *P1*   37 Didst
thou lie there] There didst thou lie *Z*   38 on] *not in Z*

Nay, thou wert hidden in that hollow hill
　　With one who is forgotten utterly,
　　　　That discrowned Queen men call the Erycine;
　　Hidden away that never mightst thou see
　　　　The face of Her, before whose mouldering shrine　　45
To-day at Rome the silent nations kneel;
　　Who gat from Love no joyous gladdening,
　　But only Love's intolerable pain,
　　　　Only a sword to pierce her heart in twain,
Only the bitterness of child-bearing.　　50

The lotos-leaves which heal the wounds of Death
　　Lie in thy hand; O, be thou kind to me,
　　　　While yet I know the summer of my days;
For hardly can my tremulous lips draw breath
　　　　To fill the silver trumpet with thy praise,　　55
　　So bowed am I before thy mystery;
So bowed and broken on Love's terrible wheel,
　　That I have lost all hope and heart to sing,
　　Yet care I not what ruin time may bring
If in thy temple thou wilt let me kneel.　　60

Alas, alas, thou wilt not tarry here,
　　But, like that bird, the servant of the sun,
　　　　Who flies before the northwind and the night,
So wilt thou fly our evil land and drear,
　　　　Back to the tower of thine old delight,　　65
　　And the red lips of young Euphorion;
Nor shall I ever see thy face again,
　　But in this poisonous garden-close must stay,
Crowning my brows with the thorn-crown of pain,
　　Till all my loveless life shall pass away.　　70

O Helen! Helen! Helen! yet a while,
　　Yet for a little while, O, tarry here,
　　　　Till the dawn cometh and the shadows flee!
For in the gladsome sunlight of thy smile
　　　　Of heaven or hell I have no thought or fear,　　75
　　　　Seeing I know no other god but thee:
No other god save him, before whose feet
　　In nets of gold the tired planets move,
　　The incarnate spirit of spiritual love
Who in thy body holds his joyous seat.　　80

67 I] we *Z*　　　68 garden-close must] garden must we *Z*; garden must I *P1*　　　69 my]
our *Z*　　　70 all my loveless] the dread cup of *Z*

Thou wert not born as common women are!
   But, girt with silver splendour of the foam,
     Didst from the depths of sapphire seas arise!
And at thy coming some immortal star,
     Bearded with flame, blazed in the Eastern skies,   85
   And waked the shepherds on thine island-home.
Thou shalt not die: no asps of Egypt creep
   Close at thy heels to taint the delicate air;
   No sullen-blooming poppies stain thy hair,
Those scarlet heralds of eternal sleep.   90

Lily of love, pure and inviolate!
   Tower of ivory! red rose of fire!
     Thou hast come down our darkness to illume:
For we, close-caught in the wide nets of Fate,
     Wearied with waiting for the World's Desire,   95
     Aimlessly wandered in the House of gloom,
Aimlessly sought some slumberous anodyne
   For wasted lives, for lingering wretchedness,
Till we beheld thy re-arisen shrine,
   And the white glory of thy loveliness.   100

61   O Golden Queen of life and joy!
          O Lily without blot or stain!
        O Loved as only loved a boy!
          O Loved in vain! O Loved in vain!

        Ah, what to thee is war or peace,   5
          Who holdest all the keys of life,
        Though the white fleets of gold should cease,
          And the blue seas be vexed with strife!

        Bring poppy flower and poppy root,
          And yellow-petaled mandragore,   10
        Bring berries of that purple fruit
          Which sleeps on Ocean's sleepless shore.

        And when remorse and ruin come,
          And the glad pulse of youth is low,
        O Helen! Helen! mingle some   15
          Divine nepenthé for my woe.

96 House] house Z, P1   98 lingering] trammelling Z
  61 O Golden Queen of life and joy. Copy text: M

Till o'er the flower-foamed fields of sea
   On violet wing night steals away,
And God's white fingers open wide
   The crimson lips of risen day.   20

62   *Panthea*

Nay, let us walk from fire unto fire,
   From passionate pain to deadlier delight,—
I am too young to live without desire,
   Too young art thou to waste this summer night
Asking those idle questions which of old   5
Man sought of seer and oracle, and no reply was told.

For, sweet, to feel is better than to know,
   And wisdom is a childless heritage,
One pulse of passion—youth's first fiery glow,—
   Are worth the hoarded proverbs of the sage: 10
Vex not thy soul with dead philosophy,
Have we not lips to kiss with, hearts to love, and eyes to see!

Dost thou not hear the murmuring nightingale
   Like water bubbling from a silver jar,
So soft she sings the envious moon is pale,   15
   That high in heaven she is hung so far
She cannot hear that love-enraptured tune,—
Mark how she wreathes each horn with mist, yon late and
        labouring moon.

20 lips] <mouth> lips *M*
   62 Panthea. Copy text: *M1 (lines 1–120)*, *M2 (lines 121–38)*, *P2 (lines 139–80)*; collated with
P1, *P2 (lines 1–138)*   1–120 *not in M2*   1 Nay, let us] <We two will> Nay, let us *M1*
4 Too young art thou] *P1*, *P2*; <And thou too fair> Too young are thou *M1*   this summer]
<one single> this summer *M1*   6 oracle,] *P1*, *P2*; ~, *M1*   9 glow,—] *P1*, *P2*; ~,ᴧ *M1*
10 Are] <Is> Are *M1*   sage:] *P1*, *P2*; ~, *M1*   11 dead] <vain> dead *M1*   13 *M1 has:*

          'Dost thou not hear the murmuring nightingale'
          <Ah! listen to yon>
          <Dost thou not hear the murmuring nightingale>

15 pale,] *P1*, *P2*; ~ᴧ *M1*   18 *M1 has:*

          <Thou hear'st it, and can'st see the pallid
               anger of the moon>
          <happier far than 'is' yon
               late and labouring moon>
        Mark, how she wreathes each horn with mist,
               yon late and labouring moon.

White lilies, in whose cups the gold bees dream,
   The fallen snow of petals where the breeze   20
Scatters the chestnut blossom, or the gleam
   Of boyish limbs in water,—are not these
Enough for thee, dost thou desire more?
Alas! the Gods will give nought else from their
     eternal store.

For our high Gods have sick and wearied grown   25
   Of all our endless sins, our vain endeavour
For wasted days of youth to make atone
   By pain or prayer or priest, and never, never,
Hearken they now to either good or ill,
But send their rain upon the just and the unjust at will.   30

They sit at ease, our Gods they sit at ease,
   Strewing with leaves of rose their scented wine,
They sleep, they sleep, beneath the rocking trees
   Where asphodel and yellow lotus twine,
Mourning the old glad days before they knew   35
What evil things the heart of man could dream, and
     dreaming do.

And far beneath the brazen floor they see
   Like swarming flies the crowd of little men,
The bustle of small lives, then wearily
   Back to their lotus-haunts they turn again   40
Kissing each other's mouths, and mix more deep
The poppy-seeded draught which brings soft
     purple-lidded sleep.

There all day long the golden-vestured sun,
   Their torch-bearer, stands with his torch a-blaze,
And, when the gaudy web of noon is spun   45
   By its twelve maidens, through the crimson haze
Fresh from Endymion's arms comes forth the moon,
And the immortal Gods in toils of mortal passions swoon.

19 lilies,] *P1*, *P2*; ~_∧ *M1*   28 or prayer] <and> or prayer *M1*   31 ease,] *P1*, *P2*; ~_∧
M1   ease,] *P1*, *P2*; ~_∧ *M1*   41 other's] *P1*, *P2*; others *M1*   42 poppy-seeded]
poppy-<laden>seeded *M1*   43 sun,] *P1*, *P2*; ~_∧ *M1*   44 torch-bearer,] *P1*, *P2*; ~_∧
M1   45 And,] *P2*; ~_∧ *M1*, *P1*   46 its] *P1*, *P2*; it's *M1*   maidens,] *P2*; ~_∧ *M1*, *P1*

There walks Queen Juno through some dewy mead
   Her grand white feet flecked with the saffron dust   50
Of wind-stirred lilies, while young Ganymede
   Leaps in the hot and amber-foaming must,
His curls all tossed, as when the eagle bare
The frightened boy from Ida through the blue Ionian air.

There in the green heart of some garden close   55
   Queen Venus with the shepherd at her side,
Her warm soft body like the briar rose
   Which would be white yet blushes at its pride,
Laughs low for love, till jealous Salmacis
Peers through the myrtle-leaves and sighs for pain of
     lonely bliss.   60

There never does that dreary north-wind blow
   Which leaves our English forests bleak and bare,
Nor ever falls the swift white-feathered snow,
   Nor ever doth the red-toothed lightning dare
To wake them in the silver-fretted night   65
When we lie weeping for some sweet sad sin, some
     dead delight.

Alas! they know the far Lethæan spring,
   The violet-hidden waters well they know,
Where one whose feet with tired wandering
   Are faint and broken may take heart and go,   70
And from those dark depths cool and crystalline
Drink, and draw balm, and sleep for sleepless souls,
     and anodyne.

But we oppress our natures, God or Fate
   Is our enemy, we starve and feed
On vain repentance—O we are born too late!   75
   What balm for us in bruisèd poppy seed
Who crowd into one finite pulse of time
The joy of infinite love and the fierce pain of infinite crime!

---

52 must,] *P1, P2*; ~ᴧ *M1*   54 frightened] <laughing> frightened *M1*   58 its] *P1,
P2*; it's *M1*   59 till] *P1, P2*; <and> while *M1*   60 sighs] <weeps> sighs *M1*
61 dreary north-wind] *P1, P2*; <dreary north wind> <bitter east wind> dreary northwind *M1*
64 Nor ever doth the red-toothed lightning] *P2*; No rain and red-toothed lightning ever
M1; Nor doth the red-toothed lightning ever *P1*   70 go,] *P1, P2*; ~ᴧ *M1*   72 balm]
<balm> <peace> balm *M1*   souls,] *P1, P2*; ~ᴧ *M1*   78 fierce] <wild> fierce *M1*
crime!] *M1*; ~. *P1, P2*

O we are wearied of this sense of guilt,
    Wearied of pleasure's paramour despair,   80
Wearied of every temple we have built,
    Wearied of every right, unanswered, prayer,
For man is weak; God sleeps: and heaven is high:
One fiery-coloured moment: one great love; and lo! we die.

Ah! but no ferry-man with labouring pole   85
    Nears his black shallop to the flowerless strand,
No little coin of bronze can bring the soul
    Over Death's river to the sunless land,
Victim and wine and vow are all in vain,
The tomb is sealed; the soldiers watch; the dead rise not again.   90

We are resolved into the supreme air,
    We are made one with what we touch and see,
With our heart's blood each crimson sun is fair,
    With our young lives each spring-impassioned tree
Flames into green, the wildest beasts that range   95
The moor our kinsmen are, all life is one, and all is change.

With beat of systole and of diastole
    One grand great life throbs through earth's giant heart,
And mighty waves of single Being roll
    From nerve-less germ to man, for we are part   100
Of every rock and bird and beast and hill,
One with the things that prey on us, and one with what we kill.

From lower cells of waking life we pass
    To full perfection; thus the world grows old:
We who are godlike now were once a mass   105
    Of quivering purple flecked with bars of gold,
Unsentient or of joy or misery,
And tossed in terrible tangles of some wild and
        wind-swept sea.

This hot hard flame with which our bodies burn
    Will make some meadow blaze with daffodil,   110
Ay! and those argent breasts of thine will turn
    To water-lilies; the brown fields men till
Will be more fruitful for our love to-night,
Nothing is lost in nature, all things live in Death's despite.

82 unanswered,] *M1*; ~‚ *P1, P2*   84 love;] *P1, P2*; ~: *M1*   88 Death's] *P1, P2*;
death's *M1*   93 heart's] *P1, P2*; hearts *M1*   104 world] *P1, P2*; World *M1*
113 to-night] *P1, P2*; tonight *M1*

The boy's first kiss, the hyacinth's first bell,   115
    The man's last passion, and the last red spear
That from the lily leaps, the asphodel
    Which will not let its blossoms blow for fear
Of too much beauty, and the timid shame
Of the young bride-groom at his lover's eyes,—these with
        the same   120

One sacrament are consecrate, the earth
    Not we alone hath passions hymeneal,
The yellow buttercups that shake for mirth
    At daybreak know a pleasure not less real
Than we do when in some fresh-blossoming wood   125
We draw the spring into our hearts and feel that life is good.

So when men bury us beneath the yew
    Thy crimson-stainèd mouth a rose will be,
And thy soft eyes lush bluebells dimmed with dew,
    And when the white narcissus wantonly   130
Kisses the wind its playmate some faint joy
Will thrill our dust, and we will be again fond maid and boy.

And thus without life's conscious torturing pain
    In some sweet flower we will feel the sun,
And from the linnet's throat will sing again,   135
    And as two gorgeous-mailèd snakes will run
Over our graves, or as two tigers creep
Through the hot jungle where the yellow-eyed huge
        lions sleep

And give them battle! How my heart leaps up
    To think of that grand living after death   140
In beast and bird and flower, when this cup,
    Being filled too full of spirit, bursts for breath,
And with the pale leaves of some autumn day
The soul earth's earliest conqueror becomes earth's last
        great prey.

O think of it! We shall inform ourselves   145
    Into all sensuous life, the goat-foot Faun,
The Centaur, or the merry bright-eyed Elves
    That leave their dancing rings to spite the dawn

---

118 Which] <That> Which *M1*   its] *P1, P2*; it's *M1*   121–38 *not in M1*   125 do_∧]
M2; ~, *P1, P2*   wood_∧] *M2*; ~, *P1, P2*   126 hearts_∧] *M2*; ~, *P1, P2*   131 its] *P1,
P2*; it's *M2*   139–80 *not in M2*

Upon the meadows, shall not be more near
Than you and I to nature's mysteries, for we shall hear   150

The thrush's heart beat, and the daisies grow,
    And the wan snowdrop sighing for the sun
On sunless days in winter, we shall know
    By whom the silver gossamer is spun,
Who paints the diapered fritillaries,   155
On what wide wings from shivering pine to pine the
        eagle flies.

Ay! had we never loved at all, who knows
    If yonder daffodil had lured the bee
Into its gilded womb, or any rose
    Had hung with crimson lamps its little tree!   160
Methinks no leaf would ever bud in spring,
But for the lovers' lips that kiss, the poets' lips that sing.

Is the light vanished from our golden sun,
    Or is this dædal-fashioned earth less fair,
That we are nature's heritors, and one   165
    With every pulse of life that beats the air?
Rather new suns across the sky shall pass,
New splendour come unto the flower, new glory to
        the grass.

And we two lovers shall not sit afar,
    Critics of nature, but the joyous sea   170
Shall be our raiment, and the bearded star
    Shoot arrows at our pleasure! We shall be
Part of the mighty universal whole,
And through all æons mix and mingle with the
        Kosmic Soul!

We shall be notes in that great Symphony   175
    Whose cadence circles through the rhythmic spheres,
And all the live World's throbbing heart shall be
    One with our heart, the stealthy creeping years
Have lost their terrors now, we shall not die,
The Universe itself shall be our Immortality!   180

63   *Phêdre*

How vain and dull this common world must seem
    To such a One as thou, who should'st have talked
    At Florence with Mirandola, or walked
Through the cool olives of the Academe:
Thou should'st have gathered reeds from a green stream   5
    For Goat-foot Pan's shrill piping, and have played
    With the white girls in that Phæacian glade
Where grave Odysseus wakened from his dream.

Ah! surely once some urn of Attic clay
    Held thy wan dust, and thou hast come again   10
    Back to this common world so dull and vain,
For thou wert weary of the sunless day,
    The heavy fields of scentless asphodel,
    The loveless lips with which men kiss in Hell.

64   *Queen Henrietta Maria*

In the lone tent, waiting for victory,
    She stands with eyes marred by the mists of pain,
    Like some wan lily overdrenched with rain:
The clamorous clang of arms, the ensanguined sky,
War's ruin, and the wreck of chivalry,   5
    To her proud soul no common fear can bring:
    Bravely she tarrieth for her Lord the King,
Her soul a-flame with passionate ecstasy.
O Hair of Gold! O Crimson Lips! O Face
    Made for the luring and the love of man!   10

63 *Phêdre.* Copy text: *M2*, collated with *Y*, *B*, *M1*, *P1–2*   1 this] our *Y*   2 a
One] a one *Y*, *M1*; an one *B*   thou] Thou *Y*   3 with] to *Y*, *B*, *M1*   or] and *Y*, *B*,
M1   4 With young Charmides in the Academe! *Y*; Through the cool olives of the
Academe. *B*; With Charmides through Plato's Academe: *M1*   6 Goat-foot] goat-foot
Y, *B*   7 glade∧] ~, *Y*   9 Ah!] ~, *Y*   some] \<an\> some *M2*   10 dust,] ~; *Y*,
B   11 common world so] world we count so *Y*; common world thus *B*, *M1*; common
world \<thus\> so *M2*   vain,] ~: *B*; ~∧ *M1*   12 weary] wearied *M1*   14 Hell] hell *Y*
    64 *Queen Henrietta Maria.* Copy text: *M*, collated with *Y*, *B*, *P1–2*   2 stands∧] ~,
Y, *B*   3 overdrenched] over-drenched *Y*, *B*   rain:] ~; *Y*; ~. *B*   6 bring:] ~; *Y*, *B*
7 Lord] lord *Y*, *B*   King,] *Y*, *P1–2*; ~—*B*; ~∧ *M*   8 soul a-flame] heart aflame *Y*; soul
aflame *B*   9 O Hair of Gold! O Crimson Lips! O Face] *P1–2*; O hair of gold! O crimson
lips! O face *Y*, *B*; O Hair of gold! O crimson lips! O Face *M*

With thee I do forget the toil and stress,
The loveless road that knows no resting place,
   Time's straitened pulse, the soul's dread weariness,
   My freedom, and my life republican!

65   *Louis Napoleon*

Eagle of Austerlitz! where were thy wings
   When far away upon a barbarous strand,
   In fight unequal, by an obscure hand,
Fell the last scion of thy brood of Kings!

Poor boy! thou shalt not flaunt thy cloak of red,   5
   Or ride in state through Paris in the van
   Of thy returning legions, but instead
Thy mother France, free and republican,

Shall on thy dead and crownless forehead place
   The better laurels of a soldier's crown,   10
   That not dishonoured should thy soul go down
To tell the mighty Sire of thy race

That France hath kissed the mouth of Liberty,
   And found it sweeter than his honied bees,
   And that the giant wave Democracy   15
Breaks on the shores where Kings lay couched at ease.

66   *Madonna Mia*

A lily-girl, not made for this world's pain,
   With brown, soft hair close braided by her ears,
   And longing eyes half veiled by slumberous tears
Like bluest water seen through mists of rain:
Pale cheeks whereon no love hath left its stain,   5
   Red underlip drawn in for fear of love,
   And white throat, whiter than the silvered dove,
Through whose wan marble creeps one purple vein.

11 toil] storm *Y*   12 <Time's straitened pulse, t> The loveless road that knows no resting place, *M*   that knows] which holds *Y*   14 republican!] ~. *Y, B*
   65 Louis Napoleon. Copy text: *P1–2*
   66 Madonna Mia. Copy text: *P1–2*

Yet, though my lips shall praise her without cease,
　　Even to kiss her feet I am not bold,   10
　　Being o'ershadowed by the wings of awe.
Like Dante, when he stood with Beatrice
　　Beneath the flaming Lion's breast, and saw
　　The seventh Crystal, and the Stair of Gold.

67   *Roses and Rue*

I

I remember we used to meet
　　By a garden seat,
And you warbled each pretty word
　　With the air of a bird,

And your voice had a quaver in it   5
　　Just like a linnet,
And shook with the last full note
　　As the thrush's throat.

And your eyes, they were green and grey,
　　Like an April day,   10
But lit into amethyst
　　When I stooped and kissed.

67 Roses and Rue. Copy text: *X*, collated with *M1, M2*　　　0.1–0.8 *M1 has:*

Could we dig up this long buried treasure
　　Were it worth the pleasure?
We never could learn love's song,
　　We are parted too long.

Could the passionate past that is <dead> fled
　　<Call back> <Raise up> Call back it's dead,
Could we live it all over again,
　　Were it worth the pain?

1–32 *not in M2*　　　1 meet‿] ~, *M1*　　　2 a garden] an ivied *M1*　　　4 bird.] ~, *M1*
5 it‿] ~, *M1*　　　7 And shook, as the blackbird's throat *M1*　　　8 With it's last big note.
M1　　　9 eyes,] *M1;* ~‿ *X*　　　12 stooped‿] *M1;* ~, *X*　　　12.1–12.4 *M1 has:*

And your mouth, it would never smile,
　　For a long, long while,
Then it rippled all over with laughter
　　Five minutes after.

And your hair—well, I never could tie it,
   For it ran all riot
Like a tangled sunbeam of gold,   15
   Great fold upon fold.

II

You were always afraid of a shower
   (Just like a flower!);
I remember you started and ran
   When the rain began.   20

I remember I never could catch you,
   For no one could match you;
You had wonderful luminous fleet
   Little wings to your feet.

Yet you somehow would give me the prize,   25
   With a laugh in your eyes,
The rose from your breast, or the bliss
   Of a single swift kiss

On your neck with its marble hue,
   And its vein of blue—   30
How these passionate memories bite
   In my heart as I write!

13–16 *M1 has these lines following line 24*   13 I remember your hair, did I tie it? *M1*
14 ran all riot,] always ran riot, *M1*   15 gold,] ~,—*M1*   16 These things are old. *M1*
17 <And> you <never could bear> were always afraid of a shower, *M1*   18 (Just] ~
M1   flower!);] ~, *M1*   19 I remember you] <So you always> I remember you *M1*
22 you;] ~, *M1*   25–32 *not in M1*   32.01–32.12 *M2 has:*

   'You have only wasted your life,'
     (Ah, there was the knife!)
   Those were the words you said,
     And you turned your head.

   'You have only yourself to blame
     That you have no fame,'—
   (Well, now I have fame enough:
     it is sorry stuff.

   For the <public> <loud world> bellows and brays
     With its blatant praise;
   it bothers the ear of each poet,
     if it only could know it.)

III

I remember so well the room,
   And the lilac bloom
That beat at the dripping pane,   35
   In the warm June rain.

And the colour of your gown,
   It was amber-brown,
And two little satin bows
   From your shoulders rose.   40

And the handkerchief of French lace
   Which you held to your face—
Had a tear-drop left a stain?
   Or was it the rain?

'You have only wasted your life'—   45
   (Ah! there was the knife!)
Those were the words you said,
   As you turned your head.

33 the] <your> the *M1*   35 pane,] pane_∧ *M1*; <pain> pane_∧ *M2*   36 rain.] ~_∧ *M2*
37 gown,_∧] ~_∧ *M1*; ~,—*M2*   38 amber-brown] amber_∧brown *M2*   39 little] yellow
M1; <little> yellow *M2*   40 rose.] ~_∧ *M2*   41–44.4 *In M1, lines 44.1–44.4 originally
preceded 41–44, but W renumbered the two stanzas*   41 the] <that> the *M1*   42 Which]
which *M2*   face_∧—] ~,—*M1*; ~; *M2*   43 tear-drop] small tear *M1, M2*
44.1–44.4 *M1 has:*

  β   <And> In your voice as it said goodbye
          Was a <bitter> petulant cry,
  α   <And> On your hand as it waved adieu
          <had> There were veins of blue.

M2 has:

        On your hand as it waved adieu,
          There were veins of blue,
        In your voice as it said goodbye
          Was a bitter cry.

45–8 *Cf. 32.01–32.04*   45 life,'—] ~,'_∧ *M1*; ~,'_∧ *M2*   46 Ah! there] Ah_∧that *M1*;
Ay! there *M2*   knife!] strife, *M2*   47 When I rushed through the garden gate_∧ *M1*;
When I rushed through the garden gate, *M2*   48 It was too late. *M1*; it was all too late.
M2   48.1–48.4 *M1 has:*

        Could we live it over again,
          Were it worth the pain?
        Could the passionate past that is fled
          Call back it's dead?

*W wrote the number '1' next to this stanza, perhaps to indicate that a version of the stanza appeared
on page 1 of M1 (cf. lines 0.5–0.8)*   48.5–48.8 *M2 has:*

I had wasted my boyhood, true,
　　But it was for you,　　　　　　　　50
You had poets enough on the shelf,
　　I gave you myself!

IV

Well, if my heart must break,
　　Dear Love, for your sake,
It will break in music, I know;　　　　55
　　Poets' hearts break so.
But strange that I was not told
　　That the brain can hold
In a tiny ivory cell
　　God's Heaven and Hell.　　　　　60

68　　　　　　　*Portia*

I marvel not Bassanio was so bold
　　To peril all he had upon the lead,
　　Or that proud Aragon bent low his head,
Or that Morocco's fiery heart grew cold:
For in that gorgeous dress of beaten gold　　5
　　Which is more golden than the golden sun,
　　No woman Veronesé looked upon
Was half so fair as Thou whom I behold.
Yet fairer when with wisdom as your shield
　　The sober-suited lawyer's gown you donned　　10
And would not let the laws of Venice yield
　　Antonio's heart to that accursèd Jew—
O Portia! take my heart: it is thy due:
I think I will not quarrel with the Bond.

Strange that a word should part
　　little heart from heart:
The age <world> is in swaddling bands,
　　no one understands.

49–52 *not in M1*　　49 true,] ~: *M2*　　50 was for you,] was <all> for you. *M2*
52 myself!] ~. *M2*　　53–60 *M1 divides these lines into two four-line stanzas; not in M2*
54 Love] love *M1*　　55 music,] ~ ∧ *M1*　　60 Heaven and Hell] heaven and hell *M1*
　　68 Portia. Copy text: *M*, collated with *Y*, *P1–2*　　3 head,] *Y*, *P1–2*; ~∧ *M*
4 cold:] ~. *Y*　　5 gold∧] ~, *Y*　　7 Veronesé] Veronese *Y*　　8 Thou] thou *Y*, *P1–2*
9 Yet fairer when∧] Ah, fairer! when, *Y*; <Ah!> 'Yet' Fairer when *M*　　shield∧] ~, *Y*
10 donned∧] ~, *Y*, *P1–2*　　13 Portia!] ~, *Y*　　heart:] ~! *Y*　　14 Bond] bond *Y*

69   *Apologia*

Is it thy will that I should wax and wane,
  Barter my cloth of gold for hodden grey,
And at thy pleasure weave that web of pain
  Whose brightest threads are each a wasted day?

Is it thy will—Love that I love so well—   5
  That my Soul's House should be a tortured spot
Wherein, like evil paramours, must dwell
  The quenchless flame, the worm that dieth not?

Nay, if it be thy will I shall endure,
  And sell ambition at the common mart,   10
And let dull failure be my vestiture,
  And sorrow dig its grave within my heart.

Perchance it may be better so—at least
  I have not made my heart a heart of stone,
Nor starved my boyhood of its goodly feast,   15
  Nor walked where Beauty is a thing unknown.

Many a man hath done so; sought to fence
  In straitened bonds the soul that should be free,
Trodden the dusty road of common sense,
  While all the forest sang of liberty,   20

Not marking how the spotted hawk in flight
  Passed on wide pinion through the lofty air,
To where some steep untrodden mountain height
  Caught the last tresses of the Sun God's hair.

Or how the little flower he trod upon,   25
  The daisy, that white-feathered shield of gold,
Followed with wistful eyes the wandering sun
  Content if once its leaves were aureoled.

But surely it is something to have been
  The best belovèd for a little while,   30
To have walked hand in hand with Love, and seen
  His purple wings flit once across thy smile.

69 Apologia. Copy text: *P2*, collated with *P1*   23 some] the *P1*

Ay! though the gorgèd asp of passion feed
 On my boy's heart, yet have I burst the bars,
Stood face to face with Beauty, known indeed
 The Love which moves the Sun and all the stars!   35

70   *Quia Multum Amavi*

Dear Heart I think the young impassioned priest
 When first he takes from out the hidden shrine
His God imprisoned in the Eucharist,
 And eats the bread, and drinks the dreadful wine,

Feels not such awful wonder as I felt   5
 When first my smitten eyes beat full on thee,
And all night long before thy feet I knelt
 Till thou wert wearied of Idolatry.

Ah! had'st thou liked me less and loved me more,
 Through all those summer days of joy and rain,   10
I had not now been sorrow's heritor,
 Or stood a lackey in the House of Pain.

Yet, though remorse, youth's white-faced seneschal,
 Tread on my heels with all his retinue,
I am most glad I loved thee—think of all   15
 The suns that go to make one speedwell blue!

71   *Silentium Amoris*

As oftentimes the too resplendent sun
 Hurries the pallid and reluctant moon
Back to her sombre cave, ere she hath won
 A single ballad from the nightingale,
 So doth thy Beauty make my lips to fail,   5
And all my sweetest singing out of tune.

70 *Quia Multum Amavi.* Copy text: *P1–2*
71 *Silentium Amoris.* Copy text: *P1–2*

And as at dawn across the level mead
  On wings impetuous some wind will come,
And with its too harsh kisses break the reed
    Which was its only instrument of song,   10
    So my too stormy passions work me wrong,
And for excess of Love my Love is dumb.

But surely unto Thee mine eyes did show
  Why I am silent, and my lute unstrung;
Else it were better we should part, and go,   15
    Thou to some lips of sweeter melody,
    And I to nurse the barren memory
Of unkissed kisses, and songs never sung.

72   *Her Voice*

The wild bee reels from bough to bough
  With his furry coat and his gauzy wing,
Now in a lily-cup, and now
    Setting a jacinth bell a-swing,
      In his wandering;   5
Sit closer love: it was here I trow
    I made that vow,

Swore that two lives should be like one
  As long as the sea-gull loved the sea,
As long as the sunflower sought the sun,—   10
    It shall be, I said, for eternity
      'Twixt you and me!
Dear friend, those times are over and done,
    Love's web is spun.

Look upward where the poplar trees   15
  Sway and sway in the summer air,
Here in the valley never a breeze
    Scatters the thistledown, but there
      Great winds blow fair
From the mighty murmuring mystical seas,   20
    And the wave-lashed leas.

    72 *Her Voice*. Copy text: *P1–2*, collated with *M*   18 Scatters the thistledown]
Scat<hes> 'ters' <the> one thistle's down *M*   19 Great] <The> Great *M*   20
seas,] ~. *M*   21 *not in M*

Look upward where the white gull screams,
    What does it see that we do not see?
Is that a star? or the lamp that gleams
    On some outward voyaging argosy,—   25
        Ah! can it be
We have lived our lives in a land of dreams!
        How sad it seems.

Sweet, there is nothing left to say
    But this, that love is never lost,   30
Keen winter stabs the breasts of May
    Whose crimson roses burst his frost,
        Ships tempest-tossed
Will find a harbour in some bay,
        And so we may.   35

And there is nothing left to do
    But to kiss once again, and part,
Nay, there is nothing we should rue,
    I have my beauty,—you your Art,
        Nay, do not start,   40
One world was not enough for two
        Like me and you.

73   *My Voice*

Within this restless, hurried, modern world
    We took our hearts' full pleasure—You and I,
And now the white sails of our ship are furled,
    And spent the lading of our argosy.

Wherefore my cheeks before their time are wan,   5
    For very weeping is my gladness fled,
Sorrow has paled my young mouth's vermilion,
    And Ruin draws the curtains of my bed.

29 say,] ~, *M*   30 But this,] I hold‿ *M*   31 Winter may follow after May *M*
32 Whose] But *M*   his frost,] the frost: *M*   36 And‿] Sweet, *M*   37 again,] ~‿ *M*
38 rue,] ~—*M*   39 You have your beauty, I my art; *M*
   73 My Voice. Copy text: *P2*, collated with *P1*   7 has paled my young mouth's] hath
paled my lips *P1*

But all this crowded life has been to thee
   No more than lyre, or lute, or subtle spell   10
Of viols, or the music of the sea
   That sleeps, a mimic echo, in the shell.

74   *ΓΛΥΚΥΠΙΚΡΟΣ · ΕΡΩΣ ·*

Sweet I blame you not for mine the fault was, had I not been made
   of common clay
I had climbed the higher heights unclimbed yet, seen the fuller air,
   the larger day.

From the wildness of my wasted passion I had struck a better,
   clearer song,
Lit some lighter light of freer freedom, battled with some Hydra-
   headed wrong.

Had my lips been smitten into music by the kisses that but made
   them bleed,   5
You had walked with Bice and the angels on that verdant and
   enamelled mead.

I had trod the road which Dante treading saw the suns of seven
   circles shine,
Ay! perchance had seen the heavens opening, as they opened to the
   Florentine.

And the mighty nations would have crowned me, who am crownless
   now and without name,
And some orient dawn had found me kneeling on the threshold of
   the House of Fame.   10

I had sat within that marble circle where the oldest bard is as the
   young,
And the pipe is ever dropping honey, and the lyre's strings are ever
   strung.

Keats had lifted up his hymenæal curls from out the poppy-seeded
   wine,
With ambrosial mouth had kissed my forehead, clasped the hand of
   noble love in mine.

74 ΓΛΥΚΥΠΙΚΡΟΣ ΕΡΩΣ . Copy text: *P2*, collated with *P1*

And at springtide, when the apple-blossoms brush the burnished
    bosom of the dove,   15
Two young lovers lying in an orchard would have read the story
    of our love.

Would have read the legend of my passion, known the bitter secret
    of my heart,
Kissed as we have kissed, but never parted as we two are fated now
    to part.

For the crimson flower of our life is eaten by the cankerworm
    of truth,
And no hand can gather up the fallen withered petals of the rose
    of youth.   20

Yet I am not sorry that I loved you—ah! what else had I a boy
    to do,—
For the hungry teeth of time devour, and the silent-footed
    years pursue.

Rudderless, we drift athwart a tempest, and when once the storm
    of youth is past,
Without lyre, without lute or chorus, Death the silent pilot comes
    at last.

And within the grave there is no pleasure, for the blind-worm
    battens on the root,   25
And Desire shudders into ashes, and the tree of Passion bears
    no fruit.

Ah! what else had I to do but love you, God's own mother was
    less dear to me,
And less dear the Cytheræan rising like an argent lily from
    the sea.

I have made my choice, have lived my poems, and, though
    youth is gone in wasted days,
I have found the lover's crown of myrtle better than the poet's
    crown of bays.   30

24 the] a *P1*

75   *The Garden of Eros*

    It is full summer now, the heart of June,
        Not yet the sun-burnt reapers are a-stir
    Upon the upland meadow where too soon
        Rich autumn time, the season's usurer,
    Will lend his hoarded gold to all the trees,   5
    And see his treasure scattered by the wild and
        spend-thrift breeze.

    Too soon indeed! yet here the daffodil,
        That love-child of the Spring, has lingered on
    To vex the rose with jealousy, and still
        The harebell spreads her azure pavilion,   10
    And like a strayed and wandering reveller
    Abandoned of its brothers, whom long since
        June's messenger

    The missel-thrush has frighted from the glade,
        One pale narcissus loiters fearfully
    Close to a shadowy nook, where half afraid   15
        Of their own loveliness some violets lie
    That will not look the gold sun in the face
    For fear of too much splendour,—ah! methinks it is a place

    Which should be trodden by Persephone
        When wearied of the flowerless fields of Dis!   20
    Or danced on by the lads of Arcady!
        The hidden secret of eternal bliss
    Known to the Grecian here a man might find,
    Ah! you and I may find it now if Love and Sleep be kind.

    There are the flowers which mourning Herakles   25
        Strewed on the tomb of Hylas, columbine,
    Its white doves all a-flutter where the breeze
        Kissed them too harshly, the small celandine,
    That yellow-kirtled chorister of eve,
    And lilac lady's-smock,—but let them bloom alone,
        and leave   30

75 The Garden of Eros. Copy text: *P1–2*, collated with *M1, M2*   1–126 *not in M1, M2*

Yon spired holly-hock red-crocketed
   To sway its silent chimes, else must the bee,
Its little bellringer, go seek instead
   Some other pleasaunce; the anemone
That weeps at daybreak, like a silly girl   35
Before her love, and hardly lets the butterflies unfurl

Their painted wings beside it,—bid it pine
   In pale virginity; the winter snow
Will suit it better than those lips of thine
   Whose fires would but scorch it, rather go   40
And pluck that amorous flower which blooms alone,
Fed by the pander wind with dust of kisses not its own.

The trumpet-mouths of red convolvulus
   So dear to maidens, creamy meadow-sweet
Whiter than Juno's throat and odorous   45
   As all Arabia, hyacinths the feet
Of Huntress Dian would be loth to mar
For any dappled fawn,—pluck these, and those fond
     flowers which are

Fairer than what Queen Venus trod upon
   Beneath the pines of Ida, eucharis,   50
That morning star which does not dread the sun,
   And budding marjoram which but to kiss
Would sweeten Cytheræa's lips and make
Adonis jealous,—these for thy head,—and for thy
     girdle take

Yon curving spray of purple clematis   55
   Whose gorgeous dye outflames the Tyrian King,
And fox-gloves with their nodding chalices,
   But that one narciss which the startled Spring
Let from her kirtle fall when first she heard
In her own woods the wild tempestuous song of
     summer's bird,   60

Ah! leave it for a subtle memory
   Of those sweet tremulous days of rain and sun,
When April laughed between her tears to see
   The early primrose with shy footsteps run
From the gnarled oak-tree roots till all the wold,   65
Spite of its brown and trampled leaves, grew bright with
     shimmering gold.

Nay, pluck it too, it is not half so sweet
   As thou thyself, my soul's idolatry!
And when thou art a-wearied at thy feet
   Shall oxlips weave their brightest tapestry,   70
For thee the woodbine shall forget its pride
And vail its tangled whorls, and thou shalt walk on
    daisies pied.

And I will cut a reed by yonder spring
   And make the wood-gods jealous, and old Pan
Wonder what young intruder dares to sing   75
   In these still haunts, where never foot of man
Should tread at evening, lest he chance to spy
The marble limbs of Artemis and all her company.

And I will tell thee why the jacinth wears
   Such dread embroidery of dolorous moan,   80
And why the hapless nightingale forbears
   To sing her song at noon, but weeps alone
When the fleet swallow sleeps, and rich men feast,
And why the laurel trembles when she sees the
    lightening east.

And I will sing how sad Proserpina   85
   Unto a grave and gloomy Lord was wed,
And lure the silver-breasted Helena
   Back from the lotus meadows of the dead,
So shalt thou see that awful loveliness
For which two mighty Hosts met fearfully in war's abyss!   90

And then I'll pipe to thee that Grecian tale
   How Cynthia loves the lad Endymion,
And hidden in a grey and misty veil
   Hies to the cliffs of Latmos once the Sun
Leaps from his ocean bed in fruitless chase   95
Of those pale flying feet which fade away in his embrace.

And if my flute can breathe sweet melody,
   We may behold Her face who long ago
Dwelt among men by the Ægean sea,
   And whose sad house with pillaged portico   100
And friezeless wall and columns toppled down
Looms o'er the ruins of that fair and violet-cinctured town.

Spirit of Beauty! tarry still a-while,
   They are not dead, thine ancient votaries,
Some few there are to whom thy radiant smile   105
   Is better than a thousand victories,
Though all the nobly slain of Waterloo
Rise up in wrath against them! tarry still, there are a few

Who for thy sake would give their manlihood
   And consecrate their being, I at least   110
Have done so, made thy lips my daily food,
   And in thy temples found a goodlier feast
Than this starved age can give me, spite of all
Its new-found creeds so sceptical and so dogmatical.

Here not Cephissos, not Ilissos flows,   115
   The woods of white Colonos are not here,
On our bleak hills the olive never blows,
   No simple priest conducts his lowing steer
Up the steep marble way, nor through the town
Do laughing maidens bear to thee the crocus-flowered
     gown.   120

Yet tarry! for the boy who loved thee best,
   Whose very name should be a memory
To make thee linger, sleeps in silent rest
   Beneath the Roman walls, and melody
Still mourns her sweetest lyre, none can play   125
The lute of Adonais, with his lips Song passed away.

Nay, when Keats died the Muses still had left
   One silver voice to sing his threnody,
But ah! too soon of it we were bereft
   When on that riven night and stormy sea   130
Panthea claimed her singer as her own,
And slew the mouth that praised her; since which time we
     walk alone,

Save for that fiery heart, that morning star
   Of re-arisen England, whose clear eye
Saw from our tottering throne and waste of war   135
   The grand Greek limbs of young Democracy
Rise mightily like Hesperus and bring
The great Republic! him at least thy love hath taught to sing,

127–32 *not in M1*   127 died,] ~, *M2*   129 But,ah!,] But, ah!, *M2*   131 own,]
~, *M2*   132 her;] ~,—*M2*   since which time we walk alone,] *not in M2*
133–74 *not in M1, M2*

And he hath been with thee at Thessaly,
   And seen white Atalanta fleet of foot   140
In passionless and fierce virginity
   Hunting the tuskéd boar, his honied lute
Hath pierced the cavern of the hollow hill,
And Venus laughs to know one knee will bow before
     her still.

And he hath kissed the lips of Proserpine,   145
   And sung the Galilæan's requiem,
That wounded forehead dashed with blood and wine
   He hath discrowned, the Ancient Gods in him
Have found their last, most ardent worshipper,
And the new Sign grows grey and dim before its conqueror.   150

Spirit of Beauty! tarry with us still,
   It is not quenched the torch of poesy,
The star that shook above the Eastern hill
   Holds unassailed its argent armoury
From all the gathering gloom and fretful fight—   155
O tarry with us still! for through the long and
     common night,

Morris, our sweet and simple Chaucer's child,
   Dear heritor of Spenser's tuneful reed,
With soft and sylvan pipe has oft beguiled
   The weary soul of man in troublous need,   160
And from the far and flowerless fields of ice
Has brought fair flowers meet to make an earthly paradise.

We know them all, Gudrun the strong men's bride,
   Aslaug and Olafson we know them all,
How giant Grettir fought and Sigurd died,   165
   And what enchantment held the king in thrall
When lonely Brynhild wrestled with the powers
That war against all passion, ah! how oft through
     summer hours,

Long listless summer hours when the noon
   Being enamoured of a damask rose   170
Forgets to journey westward, till the moon
   The pale usurper of its tribute grows
From a thin sickle to a silver shield
And chides its loitering car—how oft, in some cool
     grassy field

Far from the cricket-ground and noisy eight,   175
    At Bagley, where the rustling bluebells come
Almost before the blackbird finds a mate
    And overstay the swallow, and the hum
Of many murmuring bees flits through the leaves,
Have I lain poring on the dreamy tales his fancy weaves,   180

And through their unreal woes and mimic pain
    Wept for myself, and so was purified,
And in their simple mirth grew glad again;
    For as I sailed upon that pictured tide
The strength and splendour of the storm was mine   185
Without the storm's red ruin, for the singer is divine,

The little laugh of water falling down
    Is not so musical, the clammy gold
Close hoarded in the tiny waxen town
    Has less of sweetness in it, and the old   190
Half-withered reeds that waved in Arcady
Touched by his lips break forth again to fresher harmony.

Spirit of Beauty tarry yet a-while!
    Although the cheating merchants of the mart
With iron roads profane our lovely isle,   195
    And break on whirling wheels the limbs of Art,
Ay! though the crowded factories beget
The blind-worm Ignorance that slays the soul, O tarry yet!

For One at least there is,—He bears his name
    From Dante and the seraph Gabriel,—   200
Whose double laurels burn with deathless flame
    To light thine altar; He too loves thee well,
Who saw old Merlin lured in Vivien's snare,
And the white feet of angels coming down the golden stair,

175 *not in M2*   *M1 has:*

                    sweet long days mispent
              <up>on the river when the noisy eight
              <had> were

176–276 *not in M1, M2*

Loves thee so well, that all the World for him   205
   A gorgeous-coloured vestiture must wear,
And Sorrow take a purple diadem,
   Or else be no more Sorrow, and Despair
Gild its own thorns, and Pain, like Adon, be
Even in anguish beautiful;—such is the empery   210

Which Painters hold, and such the heritage
   This gentle solemn Spirit doth possess,
Being a better mirror of his age
   In all his pity, love, and weariness,
Than those who can but copy common things,   215
And leave the Soul unpainted with its mighty questionings.

But they are few, and all romance has flown,
   And men can prophesy about the sun,
And lecture on his arrows—how, alone,
   Through a waste void the soulless atoms run,   220
How from each tree its weeping nymph has fled,
And that no more 'mid English reeds a Naïad shows her head.

Methinks these new Actæons boast too soon
   That they have spied on beauty; what if we
Have analyzed the rainbow, robbed the moon   225
   Of her most ancient, chastest mystery,
Shall I, the last Endymion, lose all hope
Because rude eyes peer at my mistress through a telescope!

What profit if this scientific age
   Burst through our gates with all its retinue   230
Of modern miracles! Can it assuage
   One lover's breaking heart? what can it do
To make one life more beautiful, one day
More god-like in its period? but now the Age of Clay

Returns in horrid cycle, and the earth   235
   Hath borne again a noisy progeny
Of ignorant Titans, whose ungodly birth
   Hurls them against the august hierarchy
Which sat upon Olympus, to the Dust
They have appealed, and to that barren arbiter they must   240

Repair for judgment, let them, if they can,
   From Natural Warfare and insensate Chance,
Create the new Ideal rule for man!
   Methinks that was not my inheritance;

For I was nurtured otherwise, my soul   245
Passes from higher heights of life to a more supreme goal.

Lo! while we spake the earth did turn away
    Her visage from the God, and Hecate's boat
Rose silver-laden, till the jealous day
    Blew all its torches out: I did not note   250
The waning hours, to young Endymions
Time's palsied fingers count in vain his rosary of suns!

Mark how the yellow iris wearily
    Leans back its throat, as though it would be kissed
By its false chamberer, the dragon-fly,   255
    Who, like a blue vein on a girl's white wrist,
Sleeps on that snowy primrose of the night,
Which 'gins to flush with crimson shame, and die beneath
    the light.

Come let us go, against the pallid shield
    Of the wan sky the almond blossoms gleam,   260
The corn-crake nested in the unmown field
    Answers its mate, across the misty stream
On fitful wing the startled curlews fly,
And in his sedgy bed the lark, for joy that Day is nigh,

Scatters the pearléd dew from off the grass,   265
    In tremulous ecstasy to greet the sun,
Who soon in gilded panoply will pass
    Forth from yon orange-curtained pavilion
Hung in the burning east, see, the red rim
O'ertops the expectant hills! it is the God! for love of him   270

Already the shrill lark is out of sight,
    Flooding with waves of song this silent dell,—
Ah! there is something more in that bird's flight
    Than could be tested in a crucible!—
But the air freshens, let us go, why soon   275
The woodmen will be here; how we have lived this night
    of June!

76   *Ave Imperatrix*

Set in this stormy Northern sea,
    Queen of these restless fields of tide,
England! what shall men say of thee,
    Before whose feet the worlds divide?

The earth, a brittle globe of glass,   5
    Lies in the hollow of thy hand,
And through its heart of crystal pass,
    Like shadows through a twilight land,

The spears of crimson-suited war,
    The long white-crested waves of fight,   10
And all the deadly fires which are
    The torches of the lords of Night.

The yellow leopards, strained and lean,
    The treacherous Russian knows so well,
With gaping blackened jaws are seen   15
    Leap through the hail of screaming shell.

The strong sea-lion of England's wars
    Hath left his sapphire cave of sea,
To battle with the storm that mars
    The star of England's chivalry.   20

The brazen-throated clarion blows
    Across the Pathan's reedy fen,
And the high steeps of Indian snows
    Shake to the tread of armèd men.

And many an Afghan chief, who lies   25
    Beneath his cool pomegranate-trees,
Clutches his sword in fierce surmise
    When on the mountain-side he sees

The fleet-foot Marri scout, who comes
    To tell how he hath heard afar   30
The measured roll of English drums
    Beat at the gates of Kandahar.

---

76 Ave Imperatrix. Copy text: *P2*, collated with *Y*, *P1*, *M1*, *M2*   1–24 *not in M1*, *M2*
2 tide] Tide *Y*   14 The treacherous] Which the wild *Y*   22 Across the] Through the
black *Y*   25 And] and *M2*   chief,] ~ˌ *M1*, *M2*   26 pomegranateˌtrees]
pomegranate-trees *M1*   27 Clutches] Clutching *M2*   surmiseˌ] ~, *M1*   28 When]
when *M2*   mountain-side] mountainside *M1*; mountain side *M2*   29 the fleet foot marri
scouts. *M2*   Marri] marri *M1*   scout,] ~ˌ *M1*   30–2 *not in M2*   30 hath] has *M1*

For southern wind and east wind meet
    Where, girt and crowned by sword and fire,
England with bare and bloody feet   35
    Climbs the steep road of wide empire.

O lonely Himalayan height,
    Grey pillar of the Indian sky,
Where saw'st thou last in clanging flight
    Our wingèd dogs of Victory?   40

The almond-groves of Samarcand,
    Bokhara, where red lilies blow,
And Oxus, by whose yellow sand
    The grave white-turbaned merchants go:

And on from thence to Ispahan,   45
    The gilded garden of the sun,
Whence the long dusty caravan
    Brings cedar wood and vermilion;

And that dread city of Cabool
    Set at the mountain's scarpèd feet,   50
Whose marble tanks are ever full
    With water for the noonday heat:

Where through the narrow straight Bazaar
    A little maid Circassian
Is led, a present from the Czar   55
    Unto some old and bearded khan,—

Here have our wild war-eagles flown,
    And flapped wide wings in fiery fight;
But the sad dove, that sits alone
    In England—she hath no delight.   60

In vain the laughing girl will lean
    To greet her love with love-lit eyes:
Down in some treacherous black ravine,
    Clutching his flag, the dead boy lies.

33–124 *not in M1, M2*   37–40 *not in Y*   42 Bokhara,] ~ˏ *Y*   43 Oxus,] ~ˏ *Y*
44 go:] ~; *Y*   45–52 *Y reverses the two stanzas*   46 gilded garden of the] garden of
the golden *Y*   48 cedar wood] cedar *Y, P1*   vermilion;] ~,— *Y*   49 Cabool,] ~,
Y   50 Set where the plain and mountain meet, *Y*   52 heat:] ~; *Y*   53–6 *not in
Y*   61 will] shall *Y*

And many a moon and sun will see   65
   The lingering wistful children wait
To climb upon their father's knee;
   And in each house made desolate

Pale women who have lost their lord
   Will kiss the relics of the slain—   70
Some tarnished epaulette—some sword—
   Poor toys to soothe such anguished pain.

For not in quiet English fields
   Are these, our brothers, lain to rest,
Where we might deck their broken shields   75
   With all the flowers the dead love best.

For some are by the Delhi walls,
   And many in the Afghan land,
And many where the Ganges falls
   Through seven mouths of shifting sand.   80

And some in Russian waters lie,
   And others in the seas which are
The portals to the East, or by
   The wind-swept heights of Trafalgar.

O wandering graves! O restless sleep!   85
   O silence of the sunless day!
O still ravine! O stormy deep!
   Give up your prey! give up your prey!

And thou whose wounds are never healed,
   Whose weary race is never won,   90
O Cromwell's England! must thou yield
   For every inch of ground a son?

Go! crown with thorns thy gold-crowned head,
   Change thy glad song to song of pain;
Wind and wild wave have got thy dead,   95
   And will not yield them back again.

65 will] shall *Y*   70 Will kiss] Brood o'er *Y*   87 still] lone *Y*   88 your] thy
Y   your] thy *Y*   91 Cromwell's] Milton's *Y*

Wave and wild wind and foreign shore
   Possess the flower of English land—
Lips that thy lips shall kiss no more,
   Hands that shall never clasp thy hand.   100

What profit now that we have bound
   The whole round world with nets of gold,
If hidden in our heart is found
   The care that groweth never old?

What profit that our galleys ride,   105
   Pine-forest-like, on every main?
Ruin and wreck are at our side,
   Grim warders of the House of pain.

Where are the brave, the strong, the fleet?
   Where is our English chivalry?   110
Wild grasses are their burial-sheet,
   And sobbing waves their threnody.

O loved ones lying far away,
   What word of love can dead lips send!
O wasted dust! O senseless clay!   115
   Is this the end! is this the end!

Peace, peace! we wrong the noble dead
   To vex their solemn slumber so;
Though childless, and with thorn-crowned head,
   Up the steep road must England go,   120

Yet when this fiery web is spun,
   Her watchmen shall descry from far
The young Republic like a sun
   Rise from these crimson seas of war.

101 profit] boots it *Y*   103 If⌃] ~, *Y*   heart⌃] hearts, *Y*   105 profit] boots it *Y*
122 Her watchmen] Some watchman *Y*   123 The young] Her new *Y*

77 *Pan. Double Villanelle*

I

O Goat-foot God of Arcady!
  This modern world is grey and old,
Ah what remains to us of Thee?

No more the shepherd lads in glee
  Throw apples at thy wattled fold,   5
O Goat-foot God of Arcady!

Nor through the laurels can one see
  Thy soft brown limbs, thy beard of gold,
Ah what remains to us of Thee?

And dull and dead our Thames would be   10
  For here the winds are chill and cold,
O Goat-foot God of Arcady!

77 Pan. Copy text: *M3. Because the differences between N, M2, and M3 involve switching lines and rhymes as well as adding new material, the changes are too complicated to list as variants, and so N and M2 have been reproduced in full rather than collated against M3. M1, however, is an indiscriminate assemblage of miscellaneous jottings over time that are rough versions of lines found in N, M2, and M3. Variants from M1 are recorded separately for N, M2, and M3.*   N *reads:*

O Goat-foot God of Arcady!
  Cyllene's shrine is grey and old;
This northern isle hath need of thee!

No more the shepherd lads in glee
  Throw apples at thy wattled fold,   5
O Goat-foot God of Arcady!

Nor through the laurels can one see
  Thy soft brown limbs, thy beard of gold:
This northern isle hath need of thee!

Then leave the tomb of Helicé,   10
  Where nymph and faun lie dead and cold,
O Goat-foot God of Arcady;

For many an unsung elegy
  Sleeps in the reeds our rivers hold:
This northern isle hath need of thee.   15

And Thine our English Thames shall be,
  The open lawns, the upland wold,
O Goat-foot God of Arcady,
This northern isle hath need of thee!

Variants for N: 1 Goat-foot] Goatfoot *M1*   Arcady!] ~_∧_ *M1*   2 Cyllene's]
Cyllenes *M1*   old;] ~: *M1*   3 northern isle] {modern world} mighty age *M1*
thee!] ~. *M1*   4 No more the shepherd lads [   ] *M1*   5–19 *not in M1*

Then keep the tomb of Helicé,
    Thine olive-woods, thy vine-clad wold,
Ah what remains to us of Thee?   15

Though many an unsung elegy
    Sleep in the reeds our rivers hold,
O Goat-foot God of Arcady!
Ah what remains to us of Thee?

M2 reads:

Ah what remains to us of Thee,
    This modern world is dull and old,
O goat-foot God of Arcady!

No more the shepherd lads in glee
    Throw apples at thy wattled fold;   5
Ah what remains to us of Thee?

Nor through the laurels can one see
    Thy soft brown limbs, thy beard of gold,
O goat-foot God of Arcady!

Yet leave the tomb of Helicé   10
    Though here the winds are chill and cold;
Ah what remains to us of Thee?

For many an unsung elegy
    Sleep in the reeds our rivers hold,
O goat-foot God of Arcady!   15

And thine the silent Thames shall be,
    And all the glades thou shalt behold;
Ah what remains to us of Thee,
O goat-foot God of Arcady!

Variants for M2:   1 Ah₍ₐ₎] ~! *M1*   5 fold;] ~, *M1*   9 O <shepherd> goat
[   ] *M1*   10-19 *not in M1*   *Variants for M3:*   1 Goat-foot] goat-foot *M1*
Arcady!] ~—*M1*   2 This northern isle is chill and cold *M1*   3 Thee?] thee. *M1*
4-9 *M1 has:*

Still in the laurels can one see
    Thy soft brown limbs thy beard of gold
O goat foot God of Arcady—

No more the shepherd lads in glee
    Throw apples at thy wattled fold—
        [   ]

10-11 *M1 has:*

And thine our silent Thames shall be
        and
    Here shall thou build thy wattled fold—

12 *not in M1*   13 Then keep] Yet leave *M1*   Helicé] Helice *M1*   14 Though here
the winds are chill [   ] *M1*   15 *not in M1*   16 Though] For *M1*   17 hold,]
~₍ₐ₎ *M1*   18-19 *not in M1*

II

Ah leave the hills of Arcady,   20
    Thy satyrs and their wanton play,
This modern world hath need of Thee.

No nymph or Faun indeed have we,
    For Faun and nymph are old and grey,
Ah leave the hills of Arcady!   25

This is the land where Liberty
    Lit grave-browed Milton on his way,
This modern world hath need of Thee!

A land of ancient chivalry
    Where gentle Sidney saw the day,   30
Ah leave the hills of Arcady!

---

20 Ah] <Nay> Ah *M3*   20–2 *M1 has*:

                    Ah leave the hills of Arcady
                        For nymph [   ]
                        [   ]

M1 also has:

                    Ah leave the hills of Arkady
                        Dear Faun forget thy wanton play
                    This fiery world hath need of Thee.

M1 also has:

                    Ah leave the hills of Arcady,
                        Dear Faun forget thy wanton play,
                    This modern world hath need of thee

M1 also has:

                        [   ]
                        Thy satyrs in their wanton play
                        [   ]

23 we,] ~ₐ *M1*   24 grey,] ~ₐ *M1*   25 *not in M1*   26–8 *M1 has*:

                    This is the land where Liberty
                        lit [   ] way
                        [   ]

M1 also has:

                        [   ]
                        Lit grave-browed Milton on his way—
                        [   ]

M1 also has:

                    This is the land where Liberty
                        Lit grave-browed Milton on his way
                    This modern world hath need of thee

29 land] Land *M1*   30 day,] ~: *M1*   31 *not in M1*

This fierce sea-lion of the sea,
   This England, lacks some stronger lay,
This modern world hath need of Thee!

Then blow some Trumpet loud and free,   35
   And give thy oaten pipe away,
Ah leave the hills of Arcady!
This modern world hath need of Thee!

78   *Sen Artysty; or, The Artist's Dream*

I too have had my dreams: ay, known indeed
The crowded visions of a fiery youth
Which haunt me still.

*   *   *   *   *   *   *

                          Methought that once I lay,
Within some garden-close, what time the Spring
Breaks like a bird from Winter, and the sky   5
Is sapphire-vaulted. The pure air was soft,
And the deep grass I lay on soft as air.
The strange and secret life of the young trees
Swelled in the green and tender bark, or burst
To buds of sheathèd emerald; violets   10
Peered from their nooks of hiding, half afraid
Of their own loveliness; the vermeil rose
Opened its heart, and the bright star-flower
Shone like a star of morning. Butterflies,
In painted liveries of brown and gold,   15

32 sea-lion] sealion *M1*   sea,]~ˌ *M1*   33 England, lacks] England needs *M1*   lay,] ~ˌ
M1   34 *not in M1*   This modern] <Ah leave> This modern *M3*   35 Ah blow some
trumpet wild and free,ˌ *M1*   36 oaten] reedy *M1*   away,] ~—*M1*   37–8 *not in M1*
    78 Sen Artysty; or, The Artist's Dream. Copy text: RC, collated with *M1*, *M2*   1–19 *not
in M1*   1 ay, known indeed] ayˌknown too well *M2*   3 still.] ~ˌ *M2*   Methought]
methought *M2*   lay,] ~ˌ *M2*   4 Within] within *M2*   garden-close] *M2*; gardenˌclose
RC   garden-close, what time the] garden-closeˌwhen the new *M2*   5 Breaks] Brake *M2*
Winter] winter *M2*   5.0–5.1 *After 'winter,' M2 has:*

                        <this wide world
      Seemed <fallen> slumbering in a trance of loveliness:>

6 *M2 has:* 'and' The sky was sapphire <flame> vaulted: the 'pure' air was soft: 7 And] and
M2   9 bark,] ~ˌ *M2*   10 emerald;] ~: *M2*   11 Peered] peered *M2*   hiding,]
hiding placesˌ *M2*   12 Of] of *M2*   loveliness;] ~, *M2*   13 Opened] opened *M2*
its] it's *M2*   star-flower] starˌflower *M2*   14 Shone] shone *M2*   morning. Butterflies,]
morning—butterfliesˌ *M2*   15 In painted liveries] in burnished livery *M2*   gold,] ~ˌ *M2*

Took the shy bluebells as their pavilions
And seats of pleasaunce; overhead a bird
Made snow of all the blossoms as it flew
To charm the woods with singing: the whole world
Seemed waking to delight!

                   And yet—and yet—.   20
My soul was filled with leaden heaviness:
I had no joy in Nature; what to me,
Ambition's slave, was crimson-stainèd rose,
Or the gold-sceptred crocus? The bright bird
Sang out of tune for me, and the sweet flowers   25
Seemed but a pageant, and an unreal show
That mocked my heart; for, like the fabled snake
That stings itself to anguish, so I lay,
Self-tortured, self-tormented.

                      The day crept
Unheeded on the dial, till the sun   30
Dropt, purple-sailed, into the gorgeous East,

---

16 Took] took *M2*   shy bluebells] white lilies *M2*   17 And] and *M2*   pleasaunce;] ~—
M2   18 Made] made *M2*   all the] {all the} the peach *M2*   it] he *M2*   19 singing:] ~—*M2*   20 Seemed] seemed *M2*   delight!] ~, *M2*   And yet—and yet—.] and
yet—and yet‿*M1*; and yet and yet‿*M2*   21 My] my *M1, M2*   filled with] full of *M1, M2*
heaviness:] ~, *M1, M2*   22 I had no joy in Nature;] I had no joy {for} 'in nature—' the
[   ] *M1*; No joy had I in nature—*M2*   22–4 what . . . crocus?] *not in M2*   22–7
what . . . for,] *not in M1*   24 The] the *M2*   25 Sang] sang *M2*   flowers] flower *M2*
26 Seemed] seemed *M2*   pageant] {mockery} pageant *M2*   and an] a *M2*   27 heart; for,]
heart—for‿ *M2*   the fabled snake] that fabled worm *M1*   28 itself] its self
M2   anguish,] ~—*M1*; ~‿*M2*   so I lay,] *not in M1*   lay,] *not in M2*   28.1–28.2 *M1 has:*

          Gnawing my heart away I lay watched
          the

29 Self-tortured, self-tormented.] self tortured self tormented—*M2*   29.1–29.4 *M2 has
here a version of lines 22–5:*

                  what to me
          ambitions slave was crimson stainèd rose
          or golden sceptred lilies—the bright bird
          sang

29–30 The . . . dial,] *not in M2*   30 till] but when *M2*   30–1 *M1 has:*

          When the [   ]
          steered purple-sailed into the east

31 Dropt, purple-sailed,] dropt‿purpled sailed‿ *M2*   gorgeous East,] g. east‿ *M2* 31.1–31.5
M1 has:

            I heard [   ]
            sweeter than ever stole from shepherd pipe
            in secret vales Arcadian, or where
            The [*illegible*] lean to kiss
            The blue Sicilian waters—

When, from the fiery heart of that great orb,
Came One whose shape of beauty far outshone
The most bright vision of this common earth.
Girt was she in a robe more white than flame, 35
Or furnace-heated brass; upon her head
She bare a laurel crown, and like a star
That falls from the high heaven suddenly,
Passed to my side.

               Then kneeling low, I cried,
'O much-desired! O long-waited for! 40
Immortal Glory! Great world-conqueror!
O let me not die crownless; once, at least,

32 When,] Lo∧ *M2*   that great orb,] the gt. orb∧ *M2*   *M1 has:*

               but there
         from the clear centre of the fiery orb

33 One whose shape] one whose form *M2*   outshone] outs h *M2*   33–4 *M1 has:*

         <passed>
         came one whose [   ] far outshone
         Michael or Gabriel: <or [*illegible*]>
         or any captain of the

34 this common earth.] ts mortal earth∧ *M2*   35–9 *not in M1*   35 Girt] Clad *M2*
white than flame,] wh. than flame∧ *M2*   36 Or furnace-heated brass;] or furnace∧heated
brass, *M2*   upon] <and> {on} 'upon' *M2*   37 *M2 has:* she bare {a} 'the laurel' crown
{of laurels}—like one star   38 from] fr. *M2*   suddenly,] ~∧ *M2*   39 Passed]
passed *M2*   side.] ~: *M2*   Then kneeling low, I cried,] and leaping up∧I cried∧ *M2*
40 'O] ∧~ *M1, M2*   *M2 has:* O much [   ]   O∧] *M1, M2*; Oh, *RC*   much-desired]
much∧desired *M1*   O∧ *M1*; Oh, *RC*   long-waited] long∧waited *M1*   *M1 also has:*

         O long desired, much waited
         The waves that laugh round Sicily—and lo

40.1–40.3 *M1 has:*

         Dear Herald of glad tidings! Thou art here
         to give m{y}e my desire, [*illegible*] thy name
         is Glory—

40.1–40.5 *M1 also has:*

         Dear Herald of glad tidings. thou art here
         Lured from thy lofty seat by many a prayer
         To give me my desire which so long
         Hath with undying flame burned in my heart,
         nor suffered me to rest:

41 Great world-conqueror] the worlds conqueror *M1*   42 O∧] Oh, *RC*   42–4
M1 has:

         let me die crownless—let 'once at least' one leaf
         of thy imperial laurels bind my brow,
         <once let the>
         ignoble else—once let the clarion note
            <for the rest>

Let thine imperial laurels bind my brows,
Ignoble else. Once let the clarion-note
And trump of loud ambition sound my name,   45
And for the rest I care not.'
                              Then to me,
In gentle voice, the angel made reply:
'Child ignorant of the true happiness,
Nor knowing life's best wisdom, thou wert made
For light, and love, and laughter; not to waste   50
Thy youth in shooting arrows at the sun,
Or nurturing that ambition in thy soul
Whose deadly poison will infect thy heart,
Marring all joy and gladness! Tarry here,
In the sweet confines of this garden-close,   55
Whose level meads and glades delectable
Invite for pleasure; the wild bird that wakes
These silent dells with sudden melody
Shall be thy playmate; and each flower that blows
Shall twine itself unbidden in thy hair—   60
Garland more meet for thee than the dread weight
Of Glory's laurel-wreath.'
                           'Ah! fruitless gifts,'
I cried, unheeding of her prudent word,
'Are all such mortal flowers, whose brief lives
Are bounded by the dawn and setting sun.   65
The anger of the noon can wound the rose,
And the rain rob the crocus of its gold;
But thine immortal coronal of Fame,
Thy crown of deathless laurel, this alone
Age cannot harm, nor winter's icy tooth   70

45 And] and $M1$ sound] speak $M1$ name,] ~$_\wedge$ $M1$ 46 And] and $M1$ not.' Then to me,] not—then to me$_\wedge$ $M1$ 47 In] in $M1$ voice,] ~$_\wedge$ $M1$ reply:] ~—$M1$ Continuing from 'Glory—' in line 40.3, $M1$ also has: Then the angel answered me   48 'Child]$_\wedge$'poor' child $M1$ true] {true} right $M1$ 49 Nor] nor $M1$ life's best wisdom,] {the} Life's true wisdom—$M1$ thou] Thou $M1$ 50 for light + love + laughter not waste $M1$ 51 Thy youth] thy might $M1$ sun,] ~$_\wedge$ $M1$ 51.1 $M1$ has: <whose very brightness does but mar thy aim>   52–4 Or . . . gladness!] not in $M1$ 54 Tarry here,] tarry here$_\wedge$ $M1$ 55 In] <within> in $M1$ this garden-close,] the garden close$_\wedge$ $M1$ 55.1–55.2 $M1$ has:

    make garlands for thyself out of the rose
    whose crimson stained petals <better far> more befit

56 Whose] whose $M1$ and,] ~, $M1$ 57 Invite for pleasure; the] invite for pleasures— The $M1$ wakes] not in $M1$ 58 These] The $M1$ 59 should be thy playmates— and [   ] $M1$ 60 Shall twine] shall <wreathe> twine $M1$ hair—] ~$_\wedge$ $M1$ 60.1 $M1$ has: [   ] gentle violet [   ]   61 Garland] garland $M1$ meet] fit $M1$ dread] dull $M1$ 62 of glory's laurel wreath—[   ]$M1$ 63–71 not in $M1$

Pierce to its hurt, nor common things profane.'
No answer made the angel, but her face
Dimmed with the mists of pity.
                              Then methought
That from mine eyes, wherein ambition's torch
Burned with its latest and most ardent flame,   75
Flashed forth two level beams of straightened light,
Beneath whose fulgent fires the laurel crown
Twisted and curled, as when the Sirian star
Withers the ripening corn, and one pale leaf
Fell on my brow; and I leapt up and felt   80
The mighty pulse of Fame, and heard far off
The sound of many nations praising me!

*   *   *   *   *   *   *

One fiery-coloured moment of great life!
And then—how barren was the nations' praise!
How vain the trump of Glory! Bitter thorns   85
Were in that laurel leaf, whose toothèd barbs

72 angel,] ~∧ *M1*   73 Dimmed] dimmed *M1*   pity. Then] pity—then *M1*   74 mine]
my *M1*; mine *also M1*   eyes, wherein ambition's] eyes∧where ambitions *M1*   75 Burned
with] Had set *M1*   ardent flame,] fulgent flame,∧ *M1*   76 straightened light,] straitened
light,∧ *M1*   77 whose fulgent fires] whose fires *M1*   laurel] laurelled *M1*   77.1 *M1*
has: (so averted me my gaze, twisted and c[*page tear*]   78 Twisted] twisted *M1*
curled,] ~∧ *M1*   Sirian] fierce dog *M1*   79 Withers] withers *M1*   corn] {meadows}
corn *M1*   pale] laurel *M1*; pale *also M1*   *M1 also has:*

> the gold corn
> burns in the torrid sky and
> withers to dust ashes—

80–1 *M1 has:*

> Fell from the clusters [   ] on my brow
> and I leapt up and felt the pulse of time
> beat in my throbbing veins and heard far off

82 me!] me—*M1*   83 fiery-coloured] fiery∧coloured *M1*   life!] life,∧ *M1*   84 And
then—] Dear God∧ *M1*   the nations' praise!] their clamorous praise,∧ *M1*   85–6 *M1*
has an early fragment that reads:

> Dear God—a bitter thorn was in the leaf
> which [   ]

85 vain] dull *M1*   Glory! Bitter] glory—<bitter> for sharp *M1*   86 Were in that] were
in the *M1*   87–91 *M1 has an early fragment that reads:*

> I strove to tear it from my bleeding brow
> but all in vain for still the toothed barb
> bit
> burned and bit deep till fire and red flame
> seemed to feed full the air upon me in <O God God>
>   upon my brain and make
> the Garden a bare desert

Burned and bit deep till fire and red flame
Seemed to feed full upon my brain, and make
The garden a bare desert.
                                With wild hands
I strove to tear it from my bleeding brow,   90
But all in vain; and with a dolorous cry
That paled the lingering stars before their time,
I waked at last, and saw the timorous dawn
Peer with grey face into my darkened room,
And would have deemed it a mere idle dream   95
But for this restless pain that gnaws my heart,
And the red wounds of thorns upon my brow.

79   *Libertatis Sacra Fames*

Albeit nurtured in democracy,
      And liking best that state republican
      Where every man is Kinglike and no man
Is crowned above his fellows, yet I see,
Spite of this modern fret for Liberty,   5
      Better the rule of One, whom all obey,
      Than to let clamorous demagogues betray
Our freedom with the kiss of anarchy.
Wherefore I love them not whose hands profane
      Plant the red flag upon the piled-up street   10
      For no right cause, beneath whose ignorant reign
Arts, Culture, Reverence, Honour, all things fade,
      Save Treason and the dagger of her trade,
      Or Murder with his silent bloody feet.

87 Burned] burned *M1*   fire and red] fire red *M1*   88 Seemed] seemed *M1*   brain,]
~∧ *M1*   89 The] the *M1*   desert. With] desert—with *M1*   wild] vain *M1*; wild *also*
M1   90 it] them *M1*   brow,] ~∧ *M1*   91 But] but *M1*   vain;] ~. *M1*
dolorous] bitter *M1*   92 That broke the curtained silence of the night∧ *M1*   93 I
waked again—: and {would have} saw the timorous dawn *M1*   94 Peer] peer *M1*
room,] ~∧ *M1*   95 and would have deemed [   ] *M1*   96 *not in M1*   97 And
the red] Save for the *M1*   brow.] ~∧ *M1*

    79 Libertatis Sacra Fames. Copy text: *P2*, collated with *M, Y, P1*   1 nurtured in democ-
racy,] my soul still frets for liberty∧ *M*; nurtured in Democracy, *Y*   2 And liking best]
and most I love *M*   state republican] state Athenian *M*; State Republican *Y*   3 Where]
where *M*   Kinglike∧] kinglike, *Y*   4 see,] ~∧ *M*   5 Liberty,] Liberty∧ *M*; liberty, *Y*
6 Better] better *M*   One,] ~∧ *M*   obey,] ~∧ *M*   6.1–6.2 *M has two trial lines:*

                        than anarchy which in a single day
                        oer throws the mighty [   ]

7–14 *not in M*   8 anarchy.] ~! *Y*   11 cause,] ~: *Y*   12 Culture, Reverence,
Honour] culture, reverence, honour *Y*   14 Or] And *P1*   his] its *Y*

80   *Sonnet to Liberty*

Not that I love thy children, whose dull eyes
See nothing save their own unlovely woe,
Whose minds know nothing, nothing care to know,—
But that the roar of thy Democracies,
Thy reigns of Terror, thy great Anarchies,   5
Mirror my wildest passions like the sea
And give my rage a brother—! Liberty!
For this sake only do thy dissonant cries
Delight my discreet soul, else might all kings
By bloody knout or treacherous cannonades   10
Rob nations of their rights inviolate
And I remain unmoved—and yet, and yet,
These Christs that die upon the barricades,
God knows it I am with them, in some things.

81   *Tædium Vitæ*

To stab my youth with desperate knives, to wear
This paltry age's gaudy livery,
To let each base hand filch my treasury,
To mesh my soul within a woman's hair,
And be mere Fortune's lackeyed groom,—I swear   5
I love it not! these things are less to me
Than the thin foam that frets upon the sea,
Less than the thistle-down of summer air
Which hath no seed: better to stand aloof
Far from these slanderous fools who mock my life   10
Knowing me not, better the lowliest roof
Fit for the meanest hind to sojourn in,
Than to go back to that hoarse cave of strife
Where my white soul first kissed the mouth of sin.

80 Sonnet To Liberty. Copy text: *P1–2*, collated with *M*   1 children,] ~‸ *M*   2 See nothing, <but> save the face of their own woe, *M*   3 nothing,] ~,—*M*   know,—] ~, *M* 6 wildest] loftiest *M*   7 brother—! Liberty!] brother! Liberty‸ *M*   9 soul,] ~; *M*   kings] Kings *M*   10 knout‸] ~, *M*   cannonades‸] ~, *M*   12 unmoved—] ~!—*M*   13 that] who *M*   barricades,] ~,—*M*   14 them,] ~‸ *M*
81 Tædium Vitæ. Copy Text: *P1–2*

82   *Fabien dei Franchi*

To My Friend Henry Irving.

The silent room, the heavy creeping shade,
    The dead that travel fast, the opening door,
    The murdered brother rising through the floor,
The ghost's white fingers on thy shoulders laid,
And then the lonely duel in the glade,   5
    The broken swords, the stifled scream, the gore,
    Thy grand revengeful eyes when all is o'er,—
These things are well enough,—but thou wert made
    For more august creation! frenzied Lear
    Should at thy bidding wander on the heath   10
    With the shrill fool to mock him, Romeo
For thee should lure his love, and desperate fear
Pluck Richard's recreant dagger from its sheath—
    Thou trumpet set for Shakespeare's lips to blow!

83   *Serenade*

(For Music.)

The western wind is blowing fair
    Across the dark Ægean sea,
And at the secret marble stair
    My Tyrian galley waits for thee.
Come down! the purple sail is spread,   5
    The watchman sleeps within the town,
O leave thy lily-flowered bed,
    O Lady mine come down, come down!

She will not come, I know her well,
    Of lover's vows she hath no care,   10
And little good a man can tell
    Of one so cruel and so fair.

82 Fabien dei Franchi. Copy text: *M*, collated with *P1*, *P2 Subscript P2*; *not in M, P1*
13 its sheath‸—] *P1, P2*; it's sheath,—*M*
    83 Serenade. Copy text: *P1–2*, collated with *N, M*   4 thee.] ~! *N*; Thee. *M*
6 town,] ~; *N*   8 Lady mine‸] lady mine, *N*   down,] ~! *M*   down!] ~, *N*   8.1 *N*
has a refrain: O lady mine, come down.   9–32 *not in N*   9–40 *not in M*

True love is but a woman's toy,
  They never know the lover's pain,
And I who loved as loves a boy   15
  Must love in vain, must love in vain.

O noble pilot tell me true
  Is that the sheen of golden hair?
Or is it but the tangled dew
  That binds the passion-flowers there?   20
Good sailor come and tell me now
  Is that my Lady's lily hand?
Or is it but the gleaming prow,
  Or is it but the silver sand?

No! no! 'tis not the tangled dew,   25
  'Tis not the silver-fretted sand,
It is my own dear Lady true
  With golden hair and lily hand!
O noble pilot steer for Troy,
  Good sailor ply the labouring oar,   30
This is the Queen of life and joy
  Whom we must bear from Grecian shore!

The waning sky grows faint and blue,
  It wants an hour still of day,
Aboard! aboard! my gallant crew,   35
  O Lady mine away! away!
O noble pilot steer for Troy,
  Good sailor ply the labouring oar,
O loved as only loves a boy!
  O loved for ever evermore!   40

34 day,] ~; N   36 Lady mine‸away!] lady mine, away, N   37 pilot‸] ~, N
38 sailor‸] ~, N   oar,] ~; N   38.1–38.4 N has here a version of lines 29–32:

       This is the queen of life and joy,
         And we must leave the Grecian shore.
       O noble pilot, steer for Troy,
         Good sailor, ply the lab'ring oar;

39 boy!] ~, N   40 ever‸evermore!] ever, evermore. N

84   *Camma*

As one who poring on a Grecian urn
    Scans the fair shapes some Attic hand hath made,
    God with slim goddess, goodly man with maid,
And for their beauty's sake is loth to turn
And face the obvious day, must I not yearn   5
    For many a secret moon of indolent bliss,
    When in the midmost shrine of Artemis
I see thee standing, antique-limbed, and stern?

And yet—methinks I'd rather see thee play
    That serpent of old Nile, whose witchery   10
Made Emperors drunken,—come, great Egypt, shake
    Our stage with all thy mimic pageants! Nay,
    I am grown sick of unreal passions, make
The world thine Actium, me thine Antony!

84 Camma. Copy text: *M3*, collated with *M1*, *M2*, *P1–2*   *Title* Camma]
<Cleopatra> Helena *M2*   1–8 *M1 and M2 have a different octet from subsequent versions.*
M1 has:

            They say the Cornish moon was amorous
            Of so much beauty: that pale Dian's star
            Stooped for a moment from its silver car
            To listen to those sweet lips tremulous
            With all their broken music: boisterous
            <Rude> [   ] forgot to fume and fret
            When on their crags Verona's lovers met
                                    joy [*illegible*]

M2 has:

            They say the Cornish moon was amorous
            Of so much beauty, that the evening star
            Stayed all night long upon its silver ear
            To listen to those sweet lips tremulous
            With broken music, that the boisterous
            Rude 'English' seas <of England> forgot to fume and fret
            When on it's sands Verona's lovers met,
            And that the nightingale grew envious.

2 Scans] <Sees> Scans *M3*   some] <wh> some *M3*   5 must I not] <e'en <so> 'do' I>
'must I not' *M3*   6 many a secret moon] *P1–2*; <days of secret joy and> many secret
moons *M3*   9–14 *not in M1*   9 yet—] ~ˌ *M2*   methinks,] *M2, P1–2*; ~, *M3*
thee] Thee *M2*   10 old] red *M2*   Nile,] *P1–2*; ~ˌ *M2, M3*   11 drunken,—come,
great Egypt,] drunkenˌ—Come,<dear> great Egyptˌ *M2*   12 Our] <The> Our *M2*
mimic] wildest *M2*   pageants!] *not in M2*   Nay,] *P1–2*; nayˌ *M2, M3*   13 unreal]
mimic *M2*   14 Actium,] ~ˌ *M2*   Antony!] ~. *M2*

85   *Impression du Matin*

The Thames nocturne of blue and gold
    Changed to a Harmony in grey:
    A barge with ochre-coloured hay
Dropt from the wharf: and chill and cold

The yellow fog came creeping down   5
    The bridges, till the houses' walls
    Seemed changed to shadows, and S. Paul's
Loomed like a bubble o'er the town.

Then suddenly arose the clang
    Of waking life; the streets were stirred   10
    With country waggons: and a bird
Flew to the glistening roofs and sang.

But one pale woman all alone,
    The daylight kissing her wan hair,
    Loitered beneath the gas lamps' flare,   15
With lips of flame and heart of stone.

86   *In the Gold Room. A Harmony*

Her ivory hands on the ivory keys
    Strayed in a fitful fantasy,
Like the silver gleam when the poplar trees
    Rustle their pale leaves listlessly,
Or the drifting foam of a restless sea   5
When the waves show their teeth in the flying breeze.

85 Impression du Matin. Copy text: *P1–2*, collated with *Y*, *M*   1 nocturne] nocturn
Y   2 Harmony] harmony *Y*, *M*   grey:] gray: *Y*; gray‿ *M*   4 Dropt] Stirred *M*
wharf:] ~; *Y*   5 The] A *M*   6 bridges] river *M*   houses'] House's *Y*; houses *M*
7 Seemed changed to] Became like *M*   S. Paul's] St. Paul's *Y*   8 like a bubble‿] a great
bubble, *M*   town.] ~‿ *M*   9–12 *not in M*   11 waggons] wagons *Y*   12 roofs‿]
~, *Y*   13 But one] And a *Y*; And one *M*   woman‿] ~, *M*   15 gas lamps'] gaslamp's *Y*; gaslamp's *M*   16 flame‿] ~, *Y*   stone.] ~‿ *M*
        86 In the Gold Room. Copy text: *P2*, collated with *M1*, *M2*, *P1*   2 a] the *M2*   fantasy,]
~‿ *M1*   5 Or] <As the> Or *M1*   drifting] <glad white> drifting *M1*   a restless] <the
white glad> a restless *M1*   6 breeze.] ~‿ *M1*

Her gold hair fell on the wall of gold
   Like the delicate gossamer tangles spun
On the burnished disk of the marigold,
    Or the sun-flower turning to meet the sun   10
    When the gloom of the dark blue night is done,
And the spear of the lily is aureoled.

And her sweet red lips on these lips of mine
   Burned like the ruby fire set
In the swinging lamp of a crimson shrine,   15
    Or the bleeding wounds of the pomegranate,
    Or the heart of the lotus drenched and wet
With the spilt-out blood of the rose-red wine.

87   *Impressions.*
                I. Les Silhouettes

    The sea is flecked with bars of grey,
    The dull dead wind is out of tune,
    And like a withered leaf the moon
  Is blown across the stormy bay.

    Etched clear upon the pallid sand   5
    Lies the black boat: a sailor boy
    Clambers aboard in careless joy
  With laughing face and gleaming hand.

    And overhead the curlews cry,
    Where through the dusky upland grass   10
    The young brown-throated reapers pass,
  Like silhouettes against the sky.

---

7 gold$_\wedge$] ~, *M2*   11 dark blue] jealous *M1, P1*; zealous *M2*   done,] ~$_\wedge$ *M1*   13 red
lips] red <mouth> lips *M1*   15 swinging] <crimson> swinging *M1*   a crimson] <the
flame-lit> a crimson *M1*   16 pomegrante,] ~$_\wedge$ *M1*   17 lotus] lotos *M1, M2*
18 wine.] ~$_\wedge$ *M1*

87 Impressions. I. Les Silhouettes. Copy text: *M3*, collated with *M1, M2, N, P1, P2*   *Title*
Les Silhouettes] Impression du Soir *M2*; <Impression du Soir> Les Silhouettes *M3*
1 sea] sky *M1*   2 dull dead] tired *M1*   tune,] ~$_\wedge$ *M1*   3 And like] & like *M1*
4 stormy] fitful *M1*   5–8 *not in M2*; *M1 has:*

    I see the dim boat on the strand
      Tomorrow some lighthearted boy
      Will leap aboard in careless joy
    Go to seek some other land

6 Lies . . . boat] *P2;* The black boat lies *M3, P1*; A black boat lies *N*   a] some *N*   7 joy$_\wedge$]
~, *N*   8 laughing . . . gleaming] gleaming face, and waving *N*   9–12 *not in M1*
9 cry,] ~$_\wedge$ *M2*   10 grass$_\wedge$] ~, *M2*   11 Pass,] ~$_\wedge$ *M2, N*   12 sky.] ~$_\wedge$ *M2*

88   *II. La Fuite de la Lune*

To outer senses there is peace,
A dreamy peace on either hand,
Deep silence in the shadowy land,
Deep silence where the shadows cease.

Save for a cry that echoes shrill   5
From some lone bird disconsolate;
A corncrake calling to its mate;
The answer from the misty hill.

And suddenly the moon withdraws
Her sickle from the lightening skies,   10
And to her sombre cavern flies,
Wrapped in a veil of yellow gauze.

---

88 Impressions. II. La Fuite de la Lune. Copy text: *M3*, collated with *M1*, *I*, *M2*, *N*, *P1–2*
Title II. La Fuite de la Lune] *N*, *P1–2*; Le Crepuscule *M2*; <Impressions> II. La fuite de la
lune *M3*   1–4 *not in M1*   2 dreamy] dream-like *I*; Dream-like *M2*   hand,] ~; *I*
3 land,] ~∧ *M2*   4 cease.] ~, *I*   5–6 *M1 has:*

> 'Save for the cry that echoes shrill
>   Of some poor bird disconsolate—'
>   {all is still}
>   <Save for some cry disconsolate.>

6 disconsolate;] ~, *N*   7 corncrake] curlew *M1*, *M2*, *I*   its] it's *M2*   mate;] ~: *M1*; ~,
M2, *N*   8 misty] distant *M1*, *M2*, *I*, *N*; <distant> misty *M3*   hill.] ~: *M1*
9–12 *This stanza is substantially different in three early versions. M1 has:*

> With sound of streams that murmuring flow,
>   And with the winds low lullaby
>   The orbéd maiden leaves the sky
> And the white fires <grow more> dimmer grow.

I has:

> And, herald of my love to Him
>   Who, waiting for the dawn, doth lie,
>   The orbéd maiden leaves the sky,
> And the white fires grow more dim.

M2 has:

> And herald of her love to Him
>   Who in the Latmian cave doth lie,
>   The pallid Lady leaves the sky,
> And the white torches grow more dim.

11 flies,] ~∧ *N*

89   *Impression. Le Reveillon*

    The sky is laced with fitful red,
    The circling mists and shadows flee,
    The dawn is rising from the sea,
Like a white lady from her bed.

    And jagged brazen arrows fall   5
    Athwart the feathers of the night,
    And a long wave of yellow light
Breaks silently on tower and hall,

    And spreading wide across the wold
    Wakes into flight some fluttering bird,   10
    And all the chestnut tops are stirred,
And all the branches streaked with gold.

90   *Helas!*

    To drift with every passion till my soul
    Is a stringed lute on which all winds can play,
    Is it for this that I have given away
    Mine ancient wisdom, and austere control?
    Methinks my life is a twice-written scroll   5
    Scrawled over on some boyish holiday
    With idle songs for pipe and virelay,
    Which do but mar the secret of the whole.
    Surely there was a time I might have trod
    The sunlit heights, and from life's dissonance   10

---

89 Impression. Le Reveillon. Copy text: *P1–2*, collated with *M, I*   1–4 *M has:*

    See how {the} <envious East> {is} 'the distant hills are' red
      <With> <How the dark> the Envious East with gladness glows—
      Aurora blushing as the rose
    Deserts the crocus-flowered bed<—>

1 Eastward the dawn has broken red, *I*   2 flee,] ~; *I*   3 The dawn is rising] Aurora rises *I*   4 And leaves the crocus-flowered bed. *I*   5–8 *not in M*   5 Eastward the silver arrows fall, *I*   6 Splintering the veil of holy night; *I*   9 spreading wide across the] <stealing through the silent> spreading wide across the *M*   wold₌] ~, *M, I*   10 bird,] ~; *I*   11 stirred,] ~: *M*   12 gold.] ~: *M*

    90 Helas! Copy text: *M*, collated with *P1–2*   4 control?] *P1–2*; ~. *M*   7 virelay,] *P1–2*; ~₌ *M*   10 sunlit] <august> sunlit *M*

Struck one clear chord to reach the ears of God:
Is that time dead? lo! with a little rod
I did but touch the honey of romance—
And must I lose a soul's inheritance?

91 *To V. F.*

Through many loveless songless days
We have to seek the golden shrine,
But Venus taught you how to twine
Love's violets with Apollo's bays.

92 *To M. B. J.*

Green are the summer meadows,
    Blue is the summer sky,
And the swallows like flickering shadows
    Over the tall corn fly.

And the red rose flames on the thicket,   5
    And the red breast sings on the spray,
And the drowsy hum of the cricket
    Comes from the new mown hay.

And the morning dewdrops glisten,
    And the lark is on the wing,   10
Ah! how can you stop and listen
    To what I have to sing.

93 Our soul is like a kite,
That soars with ease to heavenly height,
Held by a thread invisible.

  91 To V. F. Copy text: *M*
  92 To M. B. J. Copy text: *M1*, collated with *M2*   6 spray,] ~; *M2*   8 new‸mown]
new-mown *M2*   9 glisten,] ~! *M2*   11 how can] could *M2*   12 sing.] ~? *M2*
  93 Our soul is like a kite. Copy text: *DT*

On earth through nature see,
But only feel when reaching toward infinity   5
The link that binds this life.

So frail the thread of life,
Our souls could not endure the strife
Without this link with heavenly heights.

We droop as blighted things   10
If clouds but touch our earthly wings,
Too human yet for heaven.

Our soul longs for new life,
Breaks the frail thread by constant strife,
Now ceases in unending flight.   15

94   *Impressions.*
                          I. Le Jardin

The lily's withered chalice falls
    Around its rod of dusty gold,
    And from the beech trees on the wold
The last woodpigeon coos and calls.

The gaudy leonine sunflower   5
    Hangs black and barren on its stalk,
    And down the windy garden-walk
The dead leaves scatter, hour by hour.

Pale privet-petals white as milk
    Are blown into a snowy mass,   10
    The roses lie upon the grass
Like little shreds of crimson silk.

---

94 *Impressions. I. Le Jardin. Copy text: Q,* collated with *M1, M2, SM, M3*   1–4 *M1*
has these lines after 5–8   1 lily's] lilie's *M2;* lilies *SM*   2 its] it's *M1*   dusty]
<withered> dusty *M1*   gold,] ~: *M1*   3 beech∧trees] beechtrees *M2;* beech-trees *SM;*
beechtree *M3*   4 woodpigeon] *M2, M3;* wood∧pigeon *M1, SM;* wood-pigeon *Q*
5 sunflower] sun-flower *M1;* sun flower *SM*   6 stalk,] ~: *M3*   7 garden-walk] *M1,*
M2, SM, M3; garden∧walk *Q*   8 scatter,] *M1, M3;* ~,—*Q;* ~∧ *M2, SM*   9 <And
light and white as wool or milk> <The> 'Pale' privet petals white as milk *M1*   privet-
petals∧] ~, *M2, SM, M3*   9 milk,] ~, *M2, SM, M3*   10 Are] are *M1*   mass.] *M1,*
M3; ~; *Q;* ~: *M2, SM*   11 grass∧] *M1, M2, SM, M3;* ~, *Q*

95   *II. La Mer*

A white mist drifts across the shrouds,
    A wild moon in this wintry sky
    Gleams like an angry lion's eye
Out of a mane of tawny clouds.

The muffled steersman at the wheel   5
    Is but a shadow in the gloom;—
    And in the throbbing engine room
Leap the long rods of polished steel.

The shattered storm has left its trace
    Upon this huge and heaving dome,   10
    For the thin threads of yellow foam
Float on the waves like ravelled lace.

96   *Le Jardin des Tuileries*

This winter air is keen and cold,
    And keen and cold this winter sun,
    But round my chair the children run
Like little things of dancing gold.

Sometimes about the gaudy kiosk   5
    The mimic soldiers strut and stride,
    Sometimes the blue-eyed brigands hide
In the bleak tangles of the bosk.

---

95 Impressions. II. La Mer. Copy text: *Q*, collated with *M*   1 *M has:* [   ] netted
shrouds∧   2–10 *not in M*   11–12 *M has:*

        where the thick yellow threaded foam
        <Lies> 'Floats' {on} on the wave like ravelled lace∧

96 Le Jardin des Tuileries. Copy text: *GC*, collated with *M1*, *M2*   0.1–0.4 *M1 has:*

        Against the heavy yellow <sky> skies
            The light and luminous balloons
            Dip and drift like silver moons,
        Drift like satin butterflies;

1–4 *not in M2*   1 This winter air] For though the day *M1*   2 winter] morning *M1*
3 But round] Around *M1*   run∧] ~, *M1*   5 gaudy] *M2*; painted *M1, GC*   6–20 *not*
in M2

And sometimes, while the old nurse cons
   Her book, they steal across the square,
   And launch their paper navies where   10
Huge Triton writhes in greenish bronze.

And now in mimic flight they flee,
   And now they rush, a boisterous band—
   And, tiny hand on tiny hand,   15
Climb up the black and leafless tree.

Ah! cruel tree! if I were you,
   And children climbed me, for their sake
   Though it be winter I would break
Into Spring blossoms white and blue!   20

97   The moon is like a yellow seal
           Upon a dark blue envelope;
           And down below the dusky slope
        Like a black sword of polished steel

        With flickering damascenes of gold   5
           Lies the dim Seine, while here and there
           Flutters the white or crimson glare
        Of some swift carriage homeward-rolled.

98   *The Harlot's House*

        We caught the tread of dancing feet,
        We loitered down the moonlit street,
        And stopped beneath the Harlot's house.

9 old nurse] nurse-maid *M1*   12 Huge] <The> 'Huge' *M1*   writhes] spouts *M1*
13 And now in mimic] And sometimes in shrill *M1*   14 now they] sometimes *M1*
band—] ~, *M1*   16 the] a *M1*   17 you,] ~ₐ *M1*   18 sakeₐ] ~, *M1*   19 win-
terₐ] ~, *M1*   20 Spring] spring *M1*   blue!] ~. *M1*

    97 The moon is like a yellow seal. Copy text: *M2*, collated with *M1*   2 Upon] upon *M1*
envelope;] ~, *M1*   3 And] and *M1*   down] *M1*; soon *M2*   slopeₐ] ~, *M1*   5 With]
with *M1*   6 Flows the dark Seine [   ] *M1*   7–8 *not in M1*

    98 The Harlot's House. Copy text: *V*, collated with *M1*, *M2*, *M3*   1 caught] <heard>
caught *M1*   tread] beat *M1*; tread *also M1*   feet,] ~ₐ *M1*   2 moonlit] midnight *M1*;
<midnight> empty *M2*   3 Harlot's] <Prince's> harlots *M1*; harlot's *M2*; Harlots *M3*

Inside, above the din and fray,
We heard the loud musicians play   5
The 'Treues Liebes Herz' of Strauss.

Like strange mechanical grotesques,
Making fantastic arabesques,
The shadows raced across the blind.

We watched the ghostly dancers spin   10
To sound of horn and violin,
Like black leaves wheeling in the wind.

Like wire-pulled automatons,
Slim silhouetted skeletons
Went sidling through the slow quadrille,   15

Then took each other by the hand,
And danced a stately saraband;
Their laughter echoed thin and shrill.

Sometimes a clock-work puppet pressed
A phantom lover to her breast,   20
Sometimes they seemed to try and sing,

Sometimes a horrible Marionette
Came out, and smoked its cigarette
Upon the steps like a live thing.

4 Inside,] inside‸ *M1*; Inside‸ *M3*   din and] <horrid> din and *M1*   fray,] ~‸ *M1*, *M3*
6 Treues Liebes] Treuen lieben *M1*; Trëues Liebe *M2*   Herz‸'] *M1*, *M2*, *M3*; ~,' *V*   of]
not in M1   7 Like] like *M1*; Like *also M1*   grotesques,] ~‸ *M1*, *M2*; ~, *also M1*
8 Making] in <strange> black *M1*   arabesques,] ~‸ *M1*; ~, *also M1*   9 blind.] ~, *M3*
10 We] we *M1*   ghostly dancers] {curious dancers} 'whirling shadows' *M1*; phantom
waltzers *also M1*; <phantom> {flickering} 'phantom' waltzers *M2*   spin‸] ~, *M2*
11 To] to *M1*; To *also M1*   violin,] ~‸ *M1*; ~, *also M1*   12 The shadows raced across
the blind‸ *M1*; Like {black} mad leaves whirling in the wind‸ *also M1*   wheeling]
<whirling> wheeling *M2*   13–18 *not in M1, M2*   17 a] the *M3*   19–21 *M2*
has these lines after 22–4   19 clock-work puppet] leering <puppet> wax doll *M1*; <clock-
work> ghostly puppet *M2*; phantom puppet *M3*   20 Her lover to her clock-work breast‸
M1; It's lover to a <phantom> clock work breast: *M2*; A clock-work lover to its breast, *M3*
21 they seemed to try and] {the puppets tried to} they seemed to try and *M1*   sing,] ~.
M1, *M2*   22 a] {the} a *M1*   Marionette] marionettes *M1*; marionette *M2*, *M3*
23 out,] ~‸ *M1*   its cigarette‸] <their> 'its' cigarettes, *M1*; it's cigarette, *M2*; a cigarette‸
M3   24 <Like living things,> '<Like a live thing>' upon the steps, like a live thing. *M1*
steps‸] ~, *M3*

Then turning to my love I said,   25
'The dead are dancing with the dead,
The dust is whirling with the dust.'

But she, she heard the violin,
And left my side, and entered in;
Love passed into the house of Lust.   30

Then suddenly the tune went false,
The dancers wearied of the waltz,
The shadows ceased to wheel and whirl,

And down the long and silent street,
The dawn with silver-sandalled feet,   35
Crept like a frightened girl.

99   *Fantaisies Décoratives.*
                I. Le Panneau

Under the rose-tree's dancing shade
There stands a little ivory girl,
Pulling the leaves of pink and pearl
With pale green nails of polished jade.

The red leaves fall upon the mould,   5
The white leaves flutter, one by one,
Down to a blue bowl where the sun,
Like a great dragon, writhes in gold.

25 Then] And *M2*   love_∧] ~, *M3*   said,] ~_∧ *M2*   26 'The] _∧The *M1*, *M2*, *M3*
dead are] Dead are *M1*   the dead] the Dead *M1*   27 The dust is whirling with the]
This palace is a thing of *M1*; <This palace> The dust is whirling with the *M2*   dust.'] ~._∧
M1, *M2*; ~_∧ *M3*   28 she,_∧] ~,—*M1*   violin,] ~_∧ *M1*   29 side,] ~_∧ *M3*   in;] ~,
M1; ~: *M2*   30 house] House *M2*   33 wheel] wind *M1*; <wind> wheel *M2*
whirl,] ~_∧ *M1*; ~. *M2*   34 And_∧] ~, *M2*   street,] ~_∧ *M1*, *M3*   35 silver-
sandalled] silver_∧sandalled *M1*   feet,] ~_∧ *M1*, *M3*; ~<,> *M2*   36 Crept_∧] ~, *M3*   a
frightened] a little frightened *M1*; a <little> 'wan and' frightened *M2*   girl.] ~_∧ *M2*
  99 Fantaisies Décoratives. I. Le Panneau. Copy text: *LP*, collated with *M1*, *M2*   1–4
M2 has these lines after 25–8   1 the] a *M2*   rose-tree's] rose_∧tree's *M1*   3 Pulling]
pulling *M1*   4 With] with *M1*   5 The red leaves] Some rose-leaves *M1*
6 The white leaves] and others *M1*   7 Down] down *M1*   bowl_∧] ~, *M1*   sun,] ~_∧
M1, *M2*   8 Like] like *M1*   dragon,] ~_∧ *M1*, *M2*

The white leaves float upon the air,
　　The red leaves flutter idly down, 10
　　Some fall upon her yellow gown,
And some upon her raven hair.

She takes an amber lute and sings,
　　And as she sings a silver crane
　　Begins his scarlet neck to strain, 15
And flap his burnished metal wings.

She takes a lute of amber bright,
　　And from the thicket where he lies
　　Her lover, with his almond eyes,
Watches her movements in delight. 20

And now she gives a cry of fear,
　　And tiny tears begin to start:
　　A thorn has wounded with its dart
The pink-veined sea-shell of her ear.

And now she laughs a merry note: 25
　　There has fallen a petal of the rose
　　Just where the yellow satin shows
The blue-veined flower of her throat.

With pale green nails of polished jade,
　　Pulling the leaves of pink and pearl,
　　There stands a little ivory girl 30
Under the rose-tree's dancing shade.

100 ## II. Les Ballons

Against these turbid turquoise skies
　　The light and luminous balloons
　　Dip and drift like satin moons,
Drift like silken butterflies,

9–20 *not in M1, M2*　　　21 gives a cry of fear] cries a little cry *M1, M2*　　　22 and from her
eyes the sweet tears flow: *M1*; Two tiny tears begin to flow, *M2*　　　23 A] a *M1*　　wounded
with its dart] pricked her just below *M1, M2*　　　24 <her tiny rose-shell of an> polished agate
of an eye. *M1*; The violet agate of her eye. *M2*　　　25–32 *not in M1*　　　25 merry note:] little note, *M2*　　　27 yellow] flowered *M2*　　　28 Her apple-breasts and small brown throat.
M2　　29–32 *M2 has these lines as its first stanza*　　　29 jade,] ~∧ *M2*　　　32 the] a *M2*
　　100 Fantaisies Décoratives. II. Les Ballons. Copy text: *LP*, collated with *M1, M2*
1 these turbid turquoise] the heavy yellow *M1, M2*　　skies] <sky> skies *M1*　　　3 satin]
silver *M1*　　　4 silken] satin *M1*; silky *M2*　　butterflies,] *M2*; ~; *M1*; ~. *LP*

Reel with every windy gust,   5
  Rise and reel like dancing girls,
  Float like strange transparent pearls,
Fall and float like silver dust.

Now to the low leaves they cling,
  Each with coy fantastic pose,   10
  Each a petal of a rose
Straining at a gossamer string.

Then to the tall trees they climb,
  Like thin globes of amethyst,
  Wandering opals keeping tryst   15
With the rubies of the lime.

101   *Under the Balcony*

O beautiful star with the crimson mouth!
  O moon with the brows of gold!
Rise up, rise up, from the odorous south!
    And light for my love her way,
    Lest her little feet should stray   5
On the windy hill and the wold!
O beautiful star with the crimson mouth!
  O moon with the brows of gold!

O ship that shakes on the desolate sea!
  O ship with the wet, white sail!   10
Put in, put in, to the port to me!
    For my love and I would go
    To the land where the daffodils blow
In the heart of a violet dale!
O ship that shakes on the desolate sea!   15
  O ship with the wet, white sail!

O rapturous bird with the low, sweet note!
  O bird that sits on the spray!
Sing on, sing on, from your soft brown throat!
    And my love in her little bed   20
    Will listen, and lift her head
From the pillow, and come my way!

5–16 *not in M1*   7 pearls,] ~∧ *M2*   9–16 *not in M2*
  101 Under the Balcony. Copy text: *SS*

O rapturous bird with the low, sweet note!
　　O bird that sits on the spray!

O blossom that hangs in the tremulous air!　　　　25
　　O blossom with lips of snow!
Come down, come down, for my love to wear!
　　You will die on her head in a crown,
　　You will die in a fold of her gown,
　　To her little light heart you will go!　　　　30
O blossom that hangs in the tremulous air!
　　O blossom with lips of snow!

102　　*To My Wife: With a Copy of My Poems*

　　　I can write no stately proem
　　　　As a prelude to my lay;
　　　From a poet to a poem
　　　　I would dare to say.

　　　For if of these fallen petals　　　　5
　　　　One to you seem fair,
　　　Love will waft it till it settles
　　　　On your hair.

　　　And when wind and winter harden
　　　　All the loveless land,　　　　10
　　　It will whisper of the garden,
　　　　You will understand.

103　　*Sonnet. On the Sale by Auction of Keats' Love Letters*

　　　These are the letters which Endymion wrote
　　　　To one he loved in secret, and apart.
　　　And now the brawlers of the auction mart
　　　Bargain and bid for each poor blotted note,

102 To My Wife: With a Copy of My Poems. Copy text: *G*, collated with *M*　　2 lay;] ~, *M*　3 poem∧] ~,—*M*　　4 I would dare to] This is all I *M*　　5 For] Yet *M*　　7 it∧] ~, *M*
103 Sonnet. On the Sale by Auction of Keats' Love Letters. Copy text: *M1*, collated with *V*, *SC*, *M2*, *M3*, *M4*, *M5*　　Title Sonnet.] *V*, *M2*, *M3*; not in *M1*, *SC*, *M4*, *M5*　　1–5 *not in M5*　　1 which] that *M4*　　2 secret,] ~∧ *V*, *M2*, *M4*　　apart.] ~, *V*, *M2*, *M3*; ~: *M4*　3 now∧] ~, *M4*　　auction∧mart] auction-mart *V*, *M2*, *M4*　　4 note,] *V*, *SC*, *M2*, *M3*, *M4*; ~. *M1*

Ay! for each separate pulse of passion quote   5
   The merchant's price: I think they love not Art
   Who break the crystal of a poet's heart
That small and sickly eyes may glare and gloat.

Is it not said that many years ago,
   In a far Eastern town, some soldiers ran   10
   With torches through the midnight, and began
To wrangle for mean raiment, and to throw
   Dice for the garments of a wretched man,
Not knowing the God's wonder, or his woe?

104   *The New Remorse*

The sin was mine; I did not understand.
   So now is music prisoned in her cave,
   Save where some ebbing desultory wave
Frets with its restless whirls this meagre strand.
And in the withered hollow of this land   5
   Hath Summer dug herself so deep a grave,
   That hardly can the leaden willow crave
One silver blossom from keen Winter's hand.
But who is this who cometh by the shore?
(Nay, love, look up and wonder!) Who is this   10
   Who cometh in dyed garments from the South?
It is thy new-found Lord, and he shall kiss
   The yet unravished roses of thy mouth,
And I shall weep and worship, as before.

105   *Canzonet*

   I have no store
Of gryphon-guarded gold;
   Now, as before,
Bare is the shepherd's fold.

5 Ay] Aye *V*   6 merchant's] latest *M3*   price:] ~! *V*, *M2*; ~.—*M3*; ~:—*M4*   Art‿]
M3, *M4*, *M5*; art, *M1*, *SC*; art‿ *V*, *M2*   7 heart‿] ~, *V*   8 and] or *V*, *M2*, *M5*;
<and> or *M3*   gloat.] *V*, *SC*, *M2*, *M3*, *M4*, *M5*; ~! *M1*   9–14 *not in M5*   9 said‿]
~, *M2*, *M3*   that‿] ~, *V*   9 ago,] ~‿ *M2*, *M3*, *M4*   10 town,] ~‿ *V*, *M2*, *M3*, *M4*
14 wonder,] ~‿ *M3*   his] His *SC*   woe?] *V*, *M2*, *M4*; ~. *M1*, *M3*; ~! *SC*
   104 The New Remorse. Copy text: *SL*, collated with *CS*   1 understand.] ~; *CS*   4 this]
the *CS*   7 leaden] silver *CS*   8 silver] little *CS*   9 who] that *CS*   10 wonder!)
Who] wonder,) who *CS*   11 Who cometh in] That cometh with *CS*   14 shall] will *CS*
   105 Canzonet. Copy text: *A*

Rubies, nor pearls,   5
Have I to gem thy throat;
    Yet woodland girls
Have loved the shepherd's note.

    Then, pluck a reed
And bid me sing to thee,   10
    For I would feed
Thine ears with melody,
    Who art more fair
Than fairest fleur-de-lys,
    More sweet and rare   15
Than sweetest ambergris.

    What dost thou fear?
Young Hyacinth is slain,
    Pan is not here,
And will not come again.   20
    No hornèd Faun
Treads down the yellow leas,
    No God at dawn
Steals through the olive trees.

    Hylas is dead,   25
Nor will he e'er divine
    Those little red
Rose-petalled lips of thine.
    On the high hill
No ivory Dryads play,   30
    Silver and still
Sinks the sad autumn day.

---

106   *With a Copy of 'The House of Pomegranates'*

Go, little book,
    To him who, on a lute with horns of pearl,
Sang of the white feet of the Golden Girl:
    And bid him look
Into thy pages: it may hap that he   5
May find that golden maidens dance through thee.

106 With a Copy of 'The House of Pomegranates'. Copy text: *G*, collated with *H*   1 Go,]
~ ‸ *H*   book,] Book ‸ *H*   2 who,] ~ ‸ *H*   pearl,] ~ ‸ *H*   3 white feet] wonder *H*
Girl:] ~ , *H*   5 pages:] ~ . *H*   it may hap that he] Haply it may be *H*   6 That he may
find some comeliness in Thee. *H*

107   *Symphony in Yellow*

 An omnibus across the bridge
  Crawls like a yellow butterfly,
  And, here and there, a passer-by
 Shows like a little restless midge.

 Big barges full of yellow hay   5
  Are moored against the shadowy wharf,
  And, like a yellow silken scarf,
 The thick fog hangs along the quay.

 The yellow leaves begin to fade
  And flutter from the Temple elms,   10
  And at my feet the pale green Thames
 Lies like a rod of rippled jade.

108   *La Dame Jaune*

 She took the curious amber charms
  From off her neck, and laid them down,
  She loosed her jonquil-coloured gown,
 And shook the bracelets from her arms.

 She loosed her lemon-satin stays,   5
  She took a carven ivory comb,
  Her hair crawled down like yellow foam,
 And flickered in the candle's rays.

 I watched her thick locks, like a mass
  Of honey, dripping from the pin;   10
  Each separate hair was as the thin
 Gold thread within a Venice glass.

---

107 Symphony in Yellow. Copy text: *GG*, collated with *CM*
108 La Dame Jaune. Copy text: *M* 5 stays,] ~‸ *M*

109   *Remorse*
                         (A Study in Saffron)

> I love your topaz-coloured eyes
>   That light with blame these midnight streets;
> I love your body when it lies
>   Like amber on the silken sheets.
>
> I love the honey-coloured hair   5
>   That ripples to your ivory hips;
> I love the languid listless air
>   With which you kiss my boyish lips.
>
> I love the bows that bend above
>   Those eyelids of chalcedony: 10
> But most of all, my love! I love
>   Your beautiful fierce chastity!

                                                  Ryder Street
Nov. 10. 89.   no II.

110   *In the Forest*

> Out of the mid-wood's twilight
>   Into the meadow's dawn,
> Ivory-limbed and brown-eyed
>   Flashes my Faun!

109 Remorse. Copy text: *M2*; collated with *M1 Subscript* (a study in saffron.) *M2*
1–4 *M1 has*:

> I love your mouth of vermilion,
>   Your gilded breasts, your {little} sunburnt neck
> Which is as brown as cinnamon
>   With here and there a purple fleck.

5 the] <your> the *M1*   hair,] ~, *M1*   6 hips;] <feet> hips. *M1*   7 languid] tired
M1   9–12 *M1 has*:

> I love the <wandering> little hyaline
>   Thin vein that on forehead glows
> I love your <polished> pale pink nails which <seem> shine
>   Like petals <stolen> pilfered from a rose

110 In the Forest. Copy text: *LP*

He skips through the copses singing,   5
    And his shadow dances along,
And I know not which I should follow,
    Shadow or song!

O Hunter, snare me his shadow!
    O Nightingale, catch me his strain!   10
Else moonstruck with music and madness
    I track him in vain.

III   *The Faithful Shepherd*

From the branches of the tree
    Little leaves are falling, falling,
From the daisy sprinkled lea
    Shepherd boys are calling, calling.
But my love is far away;   5
So I sing ah! well-a-day!
    well-a-day! ah! well-a-day!
So I sing ah! well-a-day.

In the dim and darkling west
    Golden lights are dying, dying,   10
And in hurried homeward quest
    Silver doves are flying, flying,
But my love is still away,
So I sing ah! well-a-day!
    well-a-day! ah! well-a-day!   15
So I sing ah! well-a-day.

Phillis, Phillis, where art thou?
    All the land grows dreary, dreary,
And upon the jasmine bough
    Philomel is weary, weary,   20
Phillis, Phillis, come my way,
And I'll sing a roundelay,
    Roundelay, a roundelay,
I will sing a roundelay.

111 The Faithful Shepherd. Copy text: *M*   6 well-a-day!] ~_∧ *M*   15 well-a-day!]
~_∧ *M*

112   *The House of Judgment*

And there was silence in the House of Judgment, and the Man came naked before God.

And God opened the Book of the Life of the Man.

And God said to the Man, 'Thy life hath been evil, and thou hast shown cruelty to those who were in need of succour, and to those who lacked help thou hast been bitter and hard of heart. The poor called to thee and thou did'st not hearken, and thine ears were closed to the cry of My afflicted. The inheritance of the fatherless thou did'st take unto thyself, and thou did'st send the foxes into the vineyard of thy neighbour's field. Thou did'st take the bread of the children and give it to the dogs to eat, and my lepers who lived in the marshes, and were at peace and praised Me, thou did'st drive forth on to the highways, and on Mine earth out of which I made thee thou did'st spill innocent blood.'

And the Man made answer and said, 'Even so did I.'

And again God opened the Book of the Life of the Man.

And God said to the Man, 'Thy life hath been evil, and the Beauty I have shown thou hast sought for, and the Good I have hidden thou did'st pass by. The walls of thy chamber were painted with images, and from the bed of thine abominations thou did'st rise up to the sound of flutes. Thou did'st build seven altars to the sins I have suffered, and did'st eat of the thing that may not be eaten, and the purple of thy raiment was broidered with the three signs of shame. Thine idols were neither of gold nor of silver that endure, but of flesh that dieth. Thou did'st stain their hair with perfumes and put pomegranates in their hands. Thou did'st stain their feet with saffron and spread carpets before them. With antimony thou did'st stain their eyelids and their bodies thou did'st smear with myrrh. Thou did'st bow thyself to the ground before them, and the thrones of thine idols were set in the sun. Thou did'st show to the sun thy shame and to the moon thy madness.'

And the Man made answer and said, 'Even so did I.'

And a third time God opened the Book of the Life of the Man.

And God said to the Man, 'Evil hath been thy life, and with evil did'st thou requite good, and with wrongdoing kindness. The hands that fed thee thou did'st wound, and the breasts that gave thee suck thou did'st despise. He who came to thee with water went away

---

112 The House of Judgment. Copy text: *FR*, collated with *SL*   7 thee∧] ~, *SL*   8 My] the *SL*   11 my] the *SL*   13 earth∧] ~, *SL*   thee∧] ~, *SL*   17–19 the Beauty . . . by.] *SL has:* thou did'st seek for the seven sins.   24 silver∧that] silver, which *SL*   25 perfumes∧] colours, *SL*   put] set *SL*   26 saffron∧] perfumes, *SL*   27 eyelids∧] ~, *SL*   29 thine] the *SL*

thirsting, and the outlawed men who hid thee in their tents at night
thou did'st betray before dawn. Thine enemy who spared thee thou
did'st snare in an ambush, and the friend who walked with thee thou
did'st sell for a price, and to those who brought thee Love thou did'st   40
ever give Lust in thy turn.'

And the Man made answer and said, 'Even so did I.'

And God closed the Book of the Life of the Man, and said, 'Surely
I will send thee into Hell. Even into Hell will I send thee.'

And the Man cried out, 'Thou canst not.'   45

And God said to the Man, 'Wherefore can I not send thee to Hell,
and for what reason?'

'Because in Hell have I always lived,' answered the Man.

And there was silence in the House of Judgment.

And after a space God spake, and said to the Man, 'Seeing that I may   50
not send thee into Hell, surely I will send thee unto Heaven. Even unto
Heaven will I send thee.'

And the Man cried out, 'Thou canst not.'

And God said to the Man, 'Wherefore can I not send thee unto
Heaven, and for what reason?'   55

'Because never, and in no place, have I been able to imagine it,'
answered the Man.

And there was silence in the House of Judgment.

113   *The Disciple*

When Narcissus died the pool of his pleasure changed from a cup of
sweet waters into a cup of salt tears, and the Oreads came weeping
through the woodland that they might sing to the pool and give it
comfort.

And when they saw that the pool had changed from a cup of sweet   5
waters into a cup of salt tears, they loosened the green tresses of their

---

43 Man] man *SL*   44 I will] I shall *SL*   thee into] thee to *SL*   Even into] Even unto
SL   will I] shall I *SL*   48 *SL has:* And the Man made answer and said, 'Because in Hell
have I always lived.'   51 into] to *SL*   will] shall *SL*   unto] to *SL*   52 will] shall
SL   54 unto] to *SL*   56–7 *SL has:* And the Man made answer and said, 'Because
never, and in no place, have I been able to imagine Heaven.'

113 The Disciple. Copy text: *FR*, compared with *SL Although the Spirit Lamp version of this
poem in prose is essentially the same anecdote, the text differs so markedly from the copy text taken
from the Fortnightly Review that the Spirit Lamp version is reproduced in full:*

When Narcissus died the Trees and the Flowers desired to weep for him.

hair and cried to the pool and said, 'We do not wonder that you should
mourn in this manner for Narcissus, so beautiful was he.'

'But was Narcissus beautiful?' said the pool.

'Who should know that better than you?' answered the Oreads. 'Us   10
did he ever pass by, but you he sought for, and would lie on your banks
and look down at you, and in the mirror of your waters he would mirror
his own beauty.'

And the pool answered, 'But I loved Narcissus because, as he lay on
my banks and looked down at me, in the mirror of his eyes I saw ever my   15
own beauty mirrored.'

114   *The Artist*

One evening there came into his soul the desire to fashion an image
of *The Pleasure that abideth for a Moment*. And he went forth into the
world to look for bronze. For he could only think in bronze.

But all the bronze of the whole world had disappeared, nor anywhere
in the whole world was there any bronze to be found, save only the   5
bronze of the image of *The Sorrow that endureth for Ever*.

And the Flowers said to the Trees 'Let us go to the River and pray it to lend us of its waters,
that we may make tears and weep and have our fill of sorrow.'

So the Trees and the Flowers went to the River, and the Trees called to the River and said,
'We pray thee to lend us of thy waters that we may make tears and weep and have our fill of
sorrow.'

And the River answered, 'Surely ye may have of my waters as ye desire. But wherefore
would ye turn my waters, which are waters of laughter, into waters that are waters of pain? And
why do ye seek after sorrow?'

And the Flowers answered, 'We seek after sorrow because Narcissus is dead.'

And when the River heard that Narcissus was dead, it changed from a river of water into a
river of tears.

And it cried out to the Trees and the Flowers and said, 'Though every drop of my waters is
a tear, and I have changed from a river of water into a river of tears, and my waters that were
waters of laughter are now waters of pain, yet can I not lend ye a tear, so loved I Narcissus.'

And the Trees and the Flowers were silent, and after a time, the Trees answered and said,
'We do not marvel that thou should'st mourn for Narcissus in this manner, so beautiful
was he.'

And the River said, 'But was Narcissus beautiful?'

And the Trees and the Flowers answered, 'Who should know that better than thou? Us did
he ever pass by, but thee he sought for, and would lie on thy banks and look down at thee, and
in the mirror of thy waters he would mirror his own beauty.'

And the River answered, 'But I loved Narcissus because, as he lay on my banks and looked
down at me, in the mirror of his eyes I saw ever my own beauty mirrored. Therefore loved I
Narcissus, and therefore must I weep and have my fill of sorrow, nor can I lend thee a tear.'

114 The Artist. Copy text: *FR*

Now this image he had himself, and with his own hands, fashioned, and had set it on the tomb of the one thing he had loved in life. On the tomb of the dead thing he had most loved had he set this image of his own fashioning, that it might serve as a sign of the love of man that dieth   10
not, and a symbol of the sorrow of man that endureth for ever. And in the whole world there was no other bronze save the bronze of this image.

And he took the image he had fashioned, and set it in a great furnace, and gave it to the fire.   15

And out of the bronze of the image of *The Sorrow that endureth for Ever* he fashioned an image of *The Pleasure that abideth for a Moment*.

115   *The Doer of Good*

It was night-time and He was alone.

And He saw afar-off the walls of a round city and went towards the city.

And when He came near he heard within the city the tread of the feet of joy, and the laughter of the mouth of gladness and the loud noise of   5
many lutes. And He knocked at the gate and certain of the gate-keepers opened to him.

And He beheld a house that was of marble and had fair pillars of marble before it. The pillars were hung with garlands, and within and without there were torches of cedar. And he entered the house.   10

And when He had passed through the hall of chalcedony and the hall of jasper, and reached the long hall of feasting, He saw lying on a couch of sea-purple one whose hair was crowned with red roses and whose lips were red with wine.

And He went behind him and touched him on the shoulder and said   15
to him, 'Why do you live like this?'

And the young man turned round and recognised Him, and made answer and said, 'But I was a leper once, and you healed me. How else should I live?'

And He passed out of the house and went again into the street.   20

And after a little while He saw one whose face and raiment were painted and whose feet were shod with pearls. And behind her came, slowly as a hunter, a young man who wore a cloak of two colours. Now the face of the woman was as the fair face of an idol, and the eyes of the young man were bright with lust.   25

115 The Doer of Good. Copy text: *FR*

And He followed swiftly and touched the hand of the young man and said to him, 'Why do you look at this woman and in such wise?'

And the young man turned round and recognised Him and said, 'But I was blind once, and you gave me sight. At what else should I look?'   30

And He ran forward and touched the painted raiment of the woman and said to her, 'Is there no other way in which to walk save the way of sin?'

And the woman turned round and recognised Him, and laughed and said, 'But you forgave me my sins, and the way is a pleasant way.'   35

And He passed out of the city.

And when He had passed out of the city he saw seated by the roadside a young man who was weeping.

And He went towards him and touched the long locks of his hair and said to him, 'Why are you weeping?'   40

And the young man looked up and recognised Him and made answer, 'But I was dead once and you raised me from the dead. What else should I do but weep?'

116   *The Master*

Now when the darkness came over the earth Joseph of Arimathea, having lighted a torch of pinewood, passed down from the hill into the valley. For he had business in his own home.

And kneeling on the flint stones of the Valley of Desolation he saw a young man who was naked and weeping. His hair was the colour of   5 honey, and his body was as a white flower, but he had wounded his body with thorns and on his hair had he set ashes as a crown.

And he who had great possessions said to the young man who was naked and weeping, 'I do not wonder that your sorrow is so great, for surely He was a just man.'   10

And the young man answered, 'It is not for Him that I am weeping,

116 The Master. Copy text: *FR*, collated with *M*   1–2 Now] And *M*   came over] <overwhelmed> came over *M*   earth‚] <world> earth, *M*   Arimathea, having lighted] Arimathea ', having' lighted *M*   2 of pinewood] <which was of pinewood> of pinewood *M*   passed down] <<and> passed 'down'> passed down *M*   the hill] <summit of the hill> the hill *M*   3 the valley] <the depths of the valley> the valley *M*   own] <own> *M*   7 hair had he] head he had *M*   9 naked and weeping,] naked: *M*   I do not wonder] I 'do not' wonder <not> *M*   11 answered,] <made> answer'ed': *M* Him] 'H' <h>im *M*

but for myself. I too have changed water into wine, and I have healed
the leper and given sight to the blind. I have walked upon the waters,
and from the dwellers in the tombs I have cast out devils. I have fed
the hungry in the desert where there was no food, and I have raised   15
the dead from their narrow houses, and at my bidding, and before
a great multitude of people, a barren fig-tree withered away. All
things that this man has done I have done also. And yet they have not
crucified me.'

117   *The Teacher of Wisdom*

From his childhood he had been as one filled with the perfect
knowledge of God, and even while he was yet but a lad many of the
saints, as well as certain holy women who dwelt in the free city of his
birth, had been stirred to much wonder by the grave wisdom of his
answers.   5

And when his parents had given him the robe and the ring of manhood he kissed them, and left them and went out into the world, that he
might speak to the world about God. For there were at that time many
in the world who either knew not God at all, or had but an incomplete
knowledge of Him, or worshipped the false gods who dwell in groves   10
and have no care of their worshippers.

And he set his face to the sun and journeyed, walking without sandals, as he had seen the saints walk, and carrying at his girdle a leathern
wallet and a little water-bottle of burnt clay.

And as he walked along the highway he was full of the joy that comes   15
from the perfect knowledge of God, and he sang praises unto God without ceasing; and after a time he reached a strange land in which there
were many cities.

And he passed through eleven cities. And some of these cities were in
valleys, and others were by the banks of great rivers, and others were set   20
on hills. And in each city he found a disciple who followed him from
each city, and the knowledge of God spread in the whole land, and
many of the rulers were converted, and the priests of the temples in

12 I‚too‚] I, too, *M*   I have healed] 'I have' healed *M*   16 houses,] ~—*M*
16–19 *Passage after* 'narrow houses,' *not in M*
  117 The Teacher of Wisdom. Copy text: *FR*

which there were idols found that half of their gain was gone, and when
they beat upon their drums at noon none, or but a few, came with pea-   25
cocks and with offerings of flesh as had been the custom of the land
before his coming.

Yet the more the people followed him, and the greater the number
of his disciples, the greater became his sorrow. And he knew not why
his sorrow was so great. For he spake ever about God, and out of the   30
fulness of that perfect knowledge of God which God had himself given
to him.

And one evening he passed out of the eleventh city, which was a city
of Armenia, and his disciples and a great crowd of people followed after
him; and he went up on to a mountain and sat down on a rock that was   35
on the mountain, and his disciples stood round him, and the multitude
knelt in the valley.

And he bowed his head on his hands and wept, and said to his Soul,
'Why is it that I am full of sorrow and fear, and that each of my disciples
is as an enemy that walks in the noonday?'   40

And his Soul answered him and said, 'God filled thee with the perfect knowledge of Himself, and thou hast given this knowledge away to
others. The pearl of great price thou hast divided, and the vesture without seam thou hast parted asunder. He who giveth away wisdom robbeth himself. He is as one who giveth his treasure to a robber. Is not   45
God wiser than thou art? Who art thou to give away the secret that God
hath told thee? I was rich once, and thou hast made me poor. Once I saw
God, and now thou hast hidden Him from me.'

And he wept again, for he knew that his Soul spake truth to him, and
that he had given to others the perfect knowledge of God, and that he   50
was as one clinging to the skirts of God, and that his faith was leaving
him by reason of the number of those who believed in him.

And he said to himself, 'I will talk no more about God. He who giveth
away wisdom robbeth himself.'

And after the space of some hours his disciples came near him and   55
bowed themselves to the ground and said, 'Master, talk to us about
God, for thou hast the perfect knowledge of God, and no man save thee
hath this knowledge.'

And he answered them and said, 'I will talk to you about all other
things that are in heaven and on earth, but about God I will not talk to   60
you. Neither now, nor at any time, will I talk to you about God.'

And they were wroth with him and said to him, 'Thou hast led
us into the desert that we might hearken to thee. Wilt thou send us
away hungry, and the great multitude that thou hast made to follow
thee?'   65

And he answered them and said, 'I will not talk to you about God.'

And the multitude murmured against him and said to him, 'Thou hast led us into the desert, and hast given us no food to eat. Talk to us about God and it will suffice us.'

But he answered them not a word. For he knew that if he spake to 70 them about God he would give away his treasure.

And his disciples went away sadly, and the multitude of people returned to their own homes. And many died on the way.

And when he was alone he rose up and set his face to the moon, and journeyed for seven moons, speaking to no man nor making any answer. 75 And when the seventh moon had waned he reached that desert which is the desert of the Great River. And having found a cavern in which a Centaur had once dwelt, he took it for his place of dwelling, and made himself a mat of reeds on which to lie, and became a hermit. And every hour the Hermit praised God that He had suffered him to keep some 80 knowledge of Him and of His wonderful greatness.

Now, one evening, as the Hermit was seated before the cavern in which he had made his place of dwelling, he beheld a young man of evil and beautiful face who passed by in mean apparel and with empty hands. Every evening with empty hands the young man passed by, and 85 every morning he returned with his hands full of purple and pearls. For he was a Robber and robbed the caravans of the merchants.

And the Hermit looked at him and pitied him. But he spake not a word. For he knew that he who speaks a word loses his faith.

And one morning, as the young man returned with his hands full of 90 purple and pearls, he stopped and frowned and stamped his foot upon the sand, and said to the Hermit, 'Why do you look at me ever in this manner as I pass by? What is it that I see in your eyes? For no man has looked at me before in this manner. And the thing is a thorn and a trouble to me.' 95

And the Hermit answered him and said, 'What you see in my eyes is pity. Pity is what looks out at you from my eyes.'

And the young man laughed with scorn, and cried to the Hermit in a bitter voice, and said to him, 'I have purple and pearls in my hands, and you have but a mat of reeds on which to lie. What pity should you have 100 for me? And for what reason have you this pity?'

'I have pity for you,' said the Hermit, 'because you have no knowledge of God.'

'Is this knowledge of God a precious thing?' asked the young man, and he came close to the mouth of the cavern. 105

'It is more precious than all the purple and the pearls of the world,' answered the Hermit.

'And have you got it?' said the young Robber, and he came closer still.

'Once, indeed,' answered the Hermit, 'I possessed the perfect 110 knowledge of God. But in my foolishness I parted with it, and divided it amongst others. Yet even now is such knowledge as remains to me more precious than purple or pearls.'

And when the young Robber heard this he threw away the purple and the pearls that he was bearing in his hands, and drawing a sharp sword of curved steel he said to the Hermit, 'Give me, forthwith, this knowledge of God that you possess, or I will surely slay you. Wherefore should I not slay him who has a treasure greater than my treasure?' 115

And the Hermit spread out his arms and said, 'Were it not better for me to go unto the outermost courts of God and praise Him, than to live in the world and have no knowledge of Him? Slay me if that be your desire. But I will not give away my knowledge of God.' 120

And the young Robber knelt down and besought him, but the Hermit would not talk to him about God, nor give him his Treasure, and the young Robber rose up and said to the Hermit, 'Be it as you will. As for myself, I will go to the City of the Seven Sins, that is but three days' journey from this place, and for my purple they will give me pleasure, and for my pearls they will sell me joy.' And he took up the purple and the pearls and went swiftly away. 125

130

And the Hermit cried out and followed him and besought him. For the space of three days he followed the young Robber on the road and entreated him to return, nor to enter into the City of the Seven Sins.

And ever and anon the young Robber looked back at the Hermit and called to him, and said, 'Will you give me this knowledge of God which is more precious than purple and pearls? If you will give me that, I will not enter the city.' 135

And ever did the Hermit answer, 'All things that I have I will give thee, save that one thing only. For that thing it is not lawful for me to give away.' 140

And in the twilight of the third day they came nigh to the great scarlet gates of the City of the Seven Sins. And from the city there came the sound of much laughter.

And the young Robber laughed in answer, and sought to knock at the gate. And as he did so the Hermit ran forward and caught him by the skirts of his raiment, and said to him: 'Stretch forth your hands, and set your arms around my neck, and put your ear close to my lips, and I will give you what remains to me of the knowledge of God.' And the young Robber stopped. 145

150

And when the Hermit had given away his knowledge of God, he fell upon the ground and wept, and a great darkness hid from him the city and the young Robber, so that he saw them no more.

And as he lay there weeping he was ware of One who was standing beside him; and He who was standing beside him had feet of brass and 155

hair like fine wool. And He raised the Hermit up, and said to him:
'Before this time thou had'st the perfect knowledge of God. Now
thou shalt have the perfect love of God. Wherefore art thou weeping?' And He kissed him.

118   *The Sphinx*

In a dim corner of my room for longer than my fancy thinks
A beautiful and silent Sphinx has watched me through the
          shifting gloom.

Inviolate and immobile she does not rise she does not stir
For silver moons are naught to her and naught to her the suns
          that reel.

Red follows grey across the air the waves of moonlight ebb and flow   5
But with the dawn she does not go and in the night-time she is there.

Dawn follows dawn and nights grow old and all the while this
          curious cat
Lies couching on the Chinese mat with eyes of satin rimmed
          with gold.

118 The Sphinx. Copy text: *M3, S*; collated with *F1, M1, F2, M2, F3, M3, M4, F4*
Collation of the poem was complicated enough to warrant listing readings that agreed with copy text
as well as those that varied. While S served as copy text for substantives and accidentals, M3 was
textual authority for capitalization since The Sphinx *was printed wholly in capital letters. The*
initial words in the second and fourth lines of each stanza in M1 and M2 were usually capitalized.
This, however, was a function of the four-line stanza in which these early versions of the poem were
written, and such capitalization is not included in the list of variants.   1 room₋] *S*; ~,
M1, M3, M4   thinks₋] *S*; ~, *M1, M3, M4*   2 Sphinx] *S*; Sphynx *M1, M3, M4*
through] *M3, M4, S*; {from} through *M1*   shifting] *M3, M4, S*; dusky *M1*   3 rise₋] *S*;
~, *M3, M4*   stir₋] *S*; ~, *M3, M4*   4 her₋ and] *S*; ~, and *M3, M4*   5 air₋] *S*; ~, *M3,
M4*   flow₋] *S*; ~, *M3, M4*   6 go₋] *S*; ~, *M3, M4*   7 Dawn follows dawn₋ and
nights grow old₋] *S*; {And all the weary hours grow old,} Dawn follows night, and Time grows
old₋ *F2*; Dawn follows dawn, and night grows old, *also F2*; Dawn follows dawn, and nights
grow old, *M3, M4*   and all the while this curious cat] *M3, M4, S*; <as> while like a curious
cat *F2*; As on the woven Chinese mat *also F2*; She heeds them not, this curious cat *also F2*
cat₋] *F2, S*; cat, *also F2*; c[*page tear*] *M3*; cat<,> *M4*   8 Lies couching on the Chinese
mat] *M3, M4, S*; she couches on the Chinese mat *F2*; She couches, like a curious cat *also F2*;
but couches on the [   ] *also F2*   mat₋] *F2, S*; ~, *M3*; ~<,> *M4*   gold.] *F2, M3, M4, S*;
gold₋ *also F2*

Upon the mat she lies and leers and on the tawny throat of her
Flutters the soft and silky fur or ripples to her pointed ears.   10

Come forth my lovely seneschal! so somnolent, so statuesque!
Come forth you exquisite grotesque! half woman and half animal!

Come forth my lovely languorous Sphinx! and put your head upon
        my knee!
And let me stroke your throat and see your body spotted like
        the lynx!

And let me touch those curving claws of yellow ivory and grasp   15
The tail that like a monstrous asp coils round your heavy
        velvet paws!

*

A thousand weary centuries are thine while I have hardly seen
Some twenty summers cast their green for autumn's gaudy liveries.

9 leers‸] *S*; ~, *M3*, *M4*   10 fur‸] *S*; ~, *M3*, *M4*   10.1 <Her> The rows of little
ivory tusks *F2*; The rows of little polished tusks *M2*   10.2–10.4 *F2 and M2 have:*

> Between her cruel crescent lips
> Are white, and bright, as when one strips
> A milky almond from it's husks.

10.5–10.8 *M2 has:*

> Close-coiled within her sombre lair,
>   I see her like a mezzotint,
>   Brown-shadowed, with a yellow glint
> Of strange reflections here and there.

11 forth‸] *M1*, *F2*, *M2*, *S*; ~, *M3*, *M4*   seneschal!] *M3*, *M4*, *S*; ~, *M1*, *F2*, *M2*   so somnolent, so statuesque] *F2*, *M2*, *M3*, *M4*, *S*; And rub your head against my desk *M1*   statuesque!] *M3*, *M4*, *S*; desk, *M1*; statuesque, *F2*, *M2*   12 forth‸] *M1*, *F2*, *S*; ~, *M2*, *M3*,
M4   you] *F2*, *M2*, *M3*, *M4*, *S*; <thou> you *M1*   grotesque!] *M4*, *S*; Grotesque, *M1*;
grotesque, *F2*, *M2*; grotesque <,>! *M3*   woman‸] *S*; ~, *M1*, *F2*, *M2*, *M3*, *M4*   animal!]
M3, *M4*, *S*; ~. *M1*, *M2*; ~‸ *F2*   13 forth‸] *M1*, *M2*, *S*; ~, *M3*, *M4*   lovely‸] *M1*, *M2*,
M4, *S*; ~, *M3*   Sphinx!] *S*; Sphynx, *M1*, *M2*; Sphynx! *M3*; Sph<y>'i'nx *M4*   head] *S*;
paws *M1*, *M2*, *M3*, *M4*   knee!] *S*; ~, *M1*, *M2*, *M3*, *M4*   14 throat‸] *S*; ears, *M1*; head,
M2, *M3*, *M4*   lynx!] *S*; ~‸ *M1*; ~. *M2*; ~, *M3*, *M4*   15 touch] *M2*, *M3*, *M4*, *S*; stroke
F2   those] *M3*, *M4*, *S*; your *F2*, *M2*   of yellow ivory‸and grasp] *S*; And let me grasp
[   ] *F2*; of ivory, and let me grasp *M2*; of yellow ivory, and grasp *M3*, *M4*   16 The tail
that‸] *S*; Her long tail‸ *F2*; <your> the tail which, *also F2*; Your tail, that‸ *M2*; The tail that,
M3, *M4*   asp‸] *F2*, *S*; ~, *also F2*, *M2*, *M3*, *M4*   coils round] *M3*, *M4*, *S*; Is curled around
F2; <coils> curls round *also F2*; curls round *M2*   your heavy velvet paws] *M2*, *M3*, *M4*, *S*;
her velvet feet *F2*; <your> heavy velvet paws *also F2*   paws!] *S*; feet, *F2*; paws‸ *also F2*;
paws. *M2*, *M3*, *M4*   17 A] *M2*, *M3*, *M4*, *S*; Ten *M1*   thine‸] *S*; ~, *M1*, *M2*, *M3*, *M4*
18 autumn's] *M2*, *M3*, *M4*, *S*; autumns *M1*

But you can read the hieroglyphs on the great sandstone obelisks,
And you have talked with Basilisks, and you have looked on
    Hippogriffs.   20

O tell me, were you standing by when Isis to Osiris knelt?
And did you watch the Egyptian melt her union for Antony

And drink the jewel-drunken wine and bend her head in mimic awe
To see the huge Proconsul draw the salted tunny from the brine?

And did you mark the Cyprian kiss white Adon on his catafalque?   25
And did you follow Amenalk, the god of Heliopolis?

And did you talk with Thoth, and did you hear the moon-horned Io
    weep?
And know the painted kings who sleep beneath the wedge-shaped
    pyramid?

*

Lift up your large black satin eyes which are like cushions where
    one sinks!
Fawn at my feet fantastic Sphinx! and sing me all your memories!   30

19 But you can] *M2, M3, M4, S*; And could you *F2*   on the great sandstone] *M3, M4, S*; on the rose-sandstone *F2*; <on the great sandstone> upon the carven *M2*   obelisks,] *M2, M3, S*; ~? *F2*; ~<,>! *M4*   20 And you have talked with] *M2, M3, M4, S*; and could you touch the *F2*   Basilisks,] *M3, S*; basilisks? *F2*; basilisks, *M2*; Basilisks<,>! *M4*   and] *M2, M3, S*; <a>And *M4*   you have looked on] *M2, M3, M4, S*; did you see the *F2*   Hippogriffs.] *M3, S*; hippogriffs. *F2, M2*; Hippogriffs<.>! *M4*   20.1–20.4 *M2 has:*

    Tell me, what memory absorbs
        Your dreams, and what analysis
        Can draw the secret forth which is
    Concealed within those caverned orbs.

21 knelt?] *M3, M4, S*; ~, *M1*   22 watch] *M4, S*; see *M1*; <see> watch *M3*   Antony͵] *M1, S*; ~, *M3, M4*   23 wine͵] *S*; ~, *M3, M4*   awe͵] *S*; ~, *M3*; ~<,> *M4*   24 To see] *M4, S*; <And make> To see *M3*   Proconsul] *S*; Pro-consul *M3, M4*   25 mark] *M3, M4, S*; see *M2*   26 follow] *M4, S*; bow to *M2*; <fawn on> follow *M3*   god] *M4, S*; God *M2*; <gold> god *M3*   27 talk] *M1, M3, M4, S*; walk *M2*   the moon-horned] *M3, M4, S*; poor roaming *M1*; the <moonfaced> horned *M2*   Io] *M3, M4, S*; Iô *M1, M2*   weep?] *M3, M4, S*; ~, *M1, M2*   28 know the painted] *S*; did you know the *M1, M2, M3, M4*   kings] *M1, M3, M4, S*; Kings *M2*   who] *S*; that *M1, M2, M3, M4*   beneath the wedge-shaped] *M3, M4, S*; Within the mighty *M1*; Beneath the porphyry *M2*   pyramid?] *M3, S*; pyramid. *M1, M2*; Pyramid? *M4*   29 eyes͵] *S*; ~, *M2, M3*; ~<,> *M4*   cushions] *M3, M4, S*; <jewels> cushions *M2*   sinks!] *S*; ~, *M2, M4*; <,>! *M3*   30 feet͵] *S*; ~, *M2, M3, M4*   Sphinx!] *S*; Sphynx, *M2*; Sphynx! *M3, M4*   memories!] *M3, M4, S*; mysteries. *M2*

Sing to me of the Jewish maid who wandered with the Holy Child,
And how you led them through the wild, and how they slept beneath
    your shade.

Sing to me of that odorous green eve when couching by the marge
You heard from Adrian's gilded barge the laughter of Antinous

And lapped the stream and fed your drouth and watched with hot
    and hungry stare   35
The ivory body of that rare young slave with his pomegranate
    mouth!

Sing to me of the labyrinth in which the twy-formed Bull
    was stalled!
Sing to me of the night you crawled across the Temple's
    granite plinth

When through the purple corridors the screaming scarlet Ibis flew
In terror, and a horrid dew dripped from the moaning mandragores,   40

And the great torpid Crocodile within the tank shed slimy tears,
And tare the jewels from his ears and staggered back into the Nile,

31 maid] *M1*, *M2*, *M3*, *M4*, *S*; girl *F1*   wandered with the] *M1*, *M2*, *M3*, *M4*, *S*; led a little
F1   Holy Child] *M3*, *M4*, *S*; holy child *F1*, *M1*, *M2*   32 how you] *M1*, *M2*, *M4*, *S*;
<that> how you *M3*   33 of that] *M3*, *M4*, *S*; on some *F1*; of the *M1*   eve,] *S*; evening,
F1; eve, *M1*, *M3*, *M4*   when,couching by the] *M3*, *M4*, *S*; from the reedy *F1*; when, couching by the *M1*   marge,] *F1*, *M3*, *S*; ~, *M1*, *M4*   34 You heard] *M1*, *M3*, *M4*, *S*; you
hear *F1*   from Adrian's] *M1*, *S*; <from> upon the Emperor's *F1*; {upon grave Hadrian's}
from Hadrian's *also F1*; from Hadrian's *M3*; from <Ha> 'A'drian's *M4*   Antinous,] *S*; ~.
F1, *M1*; ~, *M3*, *M4*   35 stream,] *S*; ~, *M3*, *M4*   drouth,] *S*; ~, *M3*, *M4*   36 *only
in M3, M4, S*   37 labyrinth] *M1*, *M3*, *S*; <L>labyrinth *M4*   twy-formed] *M3*, *M4*, *S*;
monstrous *M1*   Bull] *M3*, *M4*, *S*; bull *M1*   stalled!] *M3*, *M4*, *S*; ~, *M1*   38 you
crawled across] *M1*, *M3*, *M4*, *S*; [   ] and when you crossed *F1*   Temple's granite plinth]
M3, *M4*, *S*; temple's plinth *F1*; temple's granite plinth *M1*   plinth,] *F1*, *M4*, *S*; ~, *M1*, *M3*
39 When through the purple] *S*; Along the painted *F1*; When through the painted *M1*, *F3*,
M3, *M4*   Ibis] *M3*, *M4*, *S*; ibis *F1*, *M1*, *F3*   40 In terror, and a horrid dew dripped
from the moaning] *F1*, *M1*, *F3*, *M3*, *M4*, *S*; to sit upon your neck; for you/ <The>/ was
music drawn from *also F1*   mandragores,] *M1*, *M3*, *M4*, *S*; ~, *F1*; ~. *F3*
41–2 *F1 has:*

> <For you the little dappled deers
>   were slain a [   ] while
>   for you the monstrous crocodile
> Tore out the jewels from his ears>

41 And the great] *M1*, *M2*, *F3*, *M3*, *M4*, *S*; For you the *also F1*   torpid] *M1*, *M2*, *F3*, *M3*,
M4, *S*; {monstrous} {mailed} torpid *also F1*   Crocodile,] *M3*, *M4*, *S*; crocodile, *also F1*,
M1, *F3*, *M3*; crocodile, *M2*   within the tank,shed] *M1*, *F3*, *M3*, *M4*, *S*; That was a God,

And the priests cursed you with shrill psalms as in your claws you
    seized their Snake
And crept away with it to slake your passion by the shuddering
    palms!

*

Who were your lovers? who were they who wrestled for you in the
    dust?   45
Which was the vessel of your lust? what leman had you, every day?

Did giant Lizards come and crouch before you on the reedy banks?
Did Gryphons with great metal flanks leap on you in your trampled
    couch?

wept *also F1*; Within the tank, shed *M2*   slimy] *M1, M2, F3, M3, M4, S*; {horrid} slimy *also
F1*   42 And tare] *also F1, M1, M2 , F3, M3, S*; And t<o>'a're *M4*   his ears,ᴧ] *S*; his
ears, *also F1, M1, M2, F3, M3*; <his> its ears, *M4*   and staggered back into the] *M1, M2,
F3, M3, M4, S*; <And>/ to lure you <to his> back into reedy *also F1*   Nile,] *M1, M2, M3,
M4, S*; ~. *also F1, F3*

43 And the priests cursed you with shrill] *M2, M3, M4, S*; Or while the priests were chanting
F1; And the priests cursed you <in their> with shrill *M1*   psalmsᴧ] *F1, M3, M4, S*; ~, *M1,
M2*   as in your claws you seized their] *M3, M4, S*; Did you not seek the temple *F1*; <And
you crawled on and> As in your claws you *M1*; And in your claws you seized their *M2*
Snakeᴧ] *S*; snakeᴧ *F1*; snake, *M1, M2, M4*; Snake, *M3*   44 And crept away with it,to]
M1, M3, M4, S; Did you not crawl with him,and *F1*; And {crawled} crept away with it, to *M2*
palms!] *M3, M4*; ~. *F1, M1, M2*; ~ᴧ *S*   45 who were] *F2, M2, M3, S*; Who were *M4*
they,] *M2, M3, M4, S*; ~, *F2*   who wrestled] *M3, M4, S*; that wrestled *F2, M2*   dust?]
M2, M3, M4, S; <sand> dust: *F2*   46 what] *M3, S*; What *F2, M2, M4*   you,] *M2, M3,
M4, S*; ~ᴧ *F2*   47–8 *F2 has*:

> Did panthers with soft velvet flanks
>   <stride> toy with, <and tear,> you on your 'trampled' couch
>   did river horses come and crouch
>   before you on the slimy banks

47 giant Lizards] *M4, S*; monstrous lizards *M2*; giant <l>Lizards *M3*   reedy] *M3, M4, S*;
<river> reedy *M2*   48 Gryphons] *M3, M4, S*; gryphons *M2*   great] *M3, M4, S*; huge
M2   48.1–48.4 *F2 has*:

> Did tawny vultures wheel around
>   Your basalt cavern as you slept
>   beside the horrid Katablept
> whose eyes were chained unto the ground.

M2 has:

> Did winged horses whinny round
>   That basalt-cavern, where you slept
>   Beside the dreadful Katablept,
> Whose eyes were chained unto the ground?

Did monstrous Hippopotami come sidling toward you in the mist?
Did gilt-scaled Dragons writhe and twist with passion as you passed
      them by?   50

And from the brick-built Lycian tomb what horrible Chimaera came
With fearful heads and fearful flame to breed new wonders from your
      womb?

              *

Or had you shameful secret quests and did you harry to your home
Some Nereid coiled in amber foam with curious rock-crystal breasts?

Or did you treading through the froth call to the brown Sidonian   55
For tidings of Leviathan, Leviathan or Behemoth?

Or did you when the sun was set climb up the cactus-covered slope
To meet your swarthy Ethiop whose body was of polished jet?

Or did you while the earthen skiffs dropped down the grey
      Nilotic flats
At twilight and the flickering bats flew round the Temple's
      triple glyphs   60

Steal to the border of the bar and swim across the silent lake
And slink into the vault and make the pyramid your Lúpanar

49 *only in M3, M4, S*   50 gilt-scaled] *S*; the wild *M3, M4*   51 Chimaera] *M2, M3,
S*; <c>Chima'e'ra *M4*   came,] *M3, M4, S*; ~, *M2*   52 heads,] *M3, M4, S*; ~, *M2*
flame,] *M3, M4, S*; ~, *M2*   53 quests,] *S*; guests *F2*; quests, *M2, M3*; <g>quests, *M4*
And] *M2, M3, M4, S*; or *F2*   harry] *M2, M3, M4, S*; carry *F2*   54 [   ] the moon
bare/ her curious rock-crystal breasts,/ blue-veined with lapis lazuli—*F1*   Nereid,] *F2,
S*; ~, *also F2, M2, M3, M4*   foam,] *F2, S*; ~, *also F2, M2, M3, M4*   rock-crystal] *F2, M2,
M3, M4*; rock,crystal *S*   breasts?] *M2, M3, M4, S*; ~, *F2*; ~. *also F2*   55 you,] *S*; ~,
M3, M4   froth,] *S*; ~, *M3, M4*   Sidonian,] *M3, S*; ~, *M4*   56 *only in M3, M4, S*
57 you,] *S*; ~, *M2, M3, M4*   set,] *S*; ~, *M2, M3, M4*   slope,] *M3, M4, S*; ~, *M2*
58 Ethiop,] *S*; Ethiope, *M2*; Ethiop, *M3, M4*   59 you,] *S*; ~, *F2, M2, M3, M4*
dropped] *M3, M4, S*; dropt *F2, M2*   flats,] *M2, M3, M4, S*; ~, *F2*   60 twilight,] *S*; ~,
F2, M2, M3, M4   flickering] *M3, M4, S*; shadowy *F2*; <shadowy> flickering *M2*   Temple's] *M3, M4, S*; temples *F2*; temple's *M2*   glyphs,] *S*; ~, *F2, M2, M3, M4*   61 to the
border of the bar] *F2, M2, M4, S*; <from some torn and tortured boy> to the border of the bar
M3   bar,] *M2, S*; ~, *F2, M3, M4*   silent] *S*; stagnant *F2, M3, M4*; <stagnant> {steam-
ing} silent *M2*   lake,] *S*; ~, *F2, M2, M3, M4*   62 And slink into the vault,and make]
S; [   ] or did you make *F2*; and like the 'strange' embalmer, <take> make *also F2*; And slink
into the vault, and make *also F2, M2, M3, M4*   pyramid] *F2, M2, M3, S*; Pyramid *M4*
your] *F2, M2, M3, M4, S*; a *also F2*   Lúpanar,] *S*; lupanar, *F2*; lupanar, *also F2, M2*;
<House of Joy> Lúpanar, *M3*; Lupanar, *M4*

Till from each black sarcophagus rose up the painted swathèd dead?
Or did you lure unto your bed the ivory-horned Tragelaphos?

Or did you love the God of Flies who plagued the Hebrews and was
    splashed   65
With wine unto the waist? or Pasht, who had green beryls for
    her eyes?

Or that young God, the Tyrian, who was more amorous than
    the dove
Of Ashtaroth? or did you love the God of the Assyrian

Whose wings, like strange transparent talc, rose high above
    his hawk-faced head,
Painted with silver and with red and ribbed with rods of oreichalch?   70

Or did huge Apis from his car leap down and lay before your feet
Big blossoms of the honey-sweet and honey-coloured nenuphar?

*

How subtle-secret is your smile! Did you love none then? Nay,
    I know
Great Ammon was your bedfellow! He lay with you beside the Nile!

63 from] *F2, M3, M4, S*; in *also F2*; {in} from *M2*   sarcophagus] *F2, M2, M3, M4, S*; sar-
cophagos *also F2*   rose up the painted] *F2, M2, M3, M4, S*; Desire <waked> shook the *also
F2*; Desire shook the *also F2, also M2*   swathèd] *F2, M3, S*; swathed *also F2, also, M4*
dead?] *F2, M2, M3, M4, S*; ~, *also F2*; ~ₐ *also F2, also M2*   64 ivory-horned] *F2, M2,
M3, M4, S*; ivoryₐhorned *also F2*   Tragelaphos] *M3, S*; tragelaphos *F2, M2*; <t>Trage-
laphos *M4*   65 did you love the God of Fliesₐwho plagued the Hebrews,and] *S*; that pale
God <whose> 'with' almond eyes,/ And almond body, who *F1*; did you love the God of
Flies, / That plagued the Hebrews, and *M2*; did you love the God of Flies, who plagued the
Hebrews, and *M3, M4*   66 waist?] *M2, M3, M4, S*; ~, *F1*   or] *F1, M2, M3, S*; Or *M4*
Pasht,] *M3, M4, S*; ~ₐ *F1, M2*   had] *F1, M2, M3, M4, S*; has *also F1*   her] *M3, M4, S*;
his *F1, M2*   66.1–66.4 *M2 has:*

Or that sea-God, whose burnished nails
Were cream-blue like the turkis-stone,
And wore a twisted saffron zone
Above his gleaming fishes' scales?

67 *only in M2, M3, M4, S*   68 Ashtaroth] *M3, M4, S*; Cythera *M2*   or] *M3, S*; Or
M2, M4   Assyrianₐ] *M3, S*; Assyrian, *M2*; Assyrian<s> *M4*   69 wings, like strange
transparent talc,] *M2, M3, M4, S*; wingsₐlike <strange> 'thin' transparent talcₐ *F1*
70 redₐ] *S*; ~, *F1, M2, M3, M4*   oreichalch?] *M2, S*; ~. *F1, M3*; ~<.>? *M4*
71 downₐ] *S*; ~, *M3, M4*   72 nenuphar?] *S*; ~. *M3*; ~<.>? *M4*   73 subtle-secret]
M3, M4, S; strange and curious *M1*; strange and subtle *M2*   smile!] *M3, M4, S*; ~, *M1*; ~:
M2   knowₐ] *M1, M3, M4, S*; ~, *M2*   74 bedfellow!] *M3, M4, S*; bedfellow, *M1*;
bed-fellow, *M2*   Nile!] *S*; ~. *M1, M2, M3, M4*   74.1–74.4 *M1 has these lines after
line 90*   74.1 His feet were shod with sardonyx, *F1, M1, M2*   74.2 His throne was

The river-horses in the slime trumpeted when they saw him come   75
Odorous with Syrian galbanum and smeared with spikenard and
      with thyme.

He came along the river-bank like some tall galley argent-sailed,
He strode across the waters, mailed in beauty, and the waters sank.

He strode across the desert sand: he reached the valley where
      you lay:
He waited till the dawn of day: then touched your black breasts with
      his hand.   80

You kissed his mouth with mouths of flame: you made the hornèd
      God your own:
You stood behind him on his throne: you called him by his secret
      name.

You whispered monstrous oracles into the caverns of his ears:
With blood of goats and blood of steers you taught him monstrous
      miracles.

White Ammon was your bedfellow! Your chamber was the steaming
      Nile!   85
And with your curved archaic smile you watched his passion come
      and go.

*

wrought of cedar wood, *F1*; His throne was carved from Tyrian wood, *also F1*; His throne was made of gilded wood, *M1*; His throne was made of thyine wood, *M2*   74.3 And on his hornèd brow there stood *F1*; And on his horned <brow> head there stood *M1*; And on his horned head there stood *also F1, M2*   74.4 The {crimson} scarlet phoenicipteryx. *F1*; The scarlet phoenicopteryx. *also F1*; The crimson phoenicopteryx. *M1*; The <blood-> crimson phoenicopteryx. *M2*   74.5–74.6 *M2 has:*

> His throne was stained with terebinth,
>   And strewn with tissued tapestries;

74.7 his cloak had golden dragonflies *F2*; His cloak had gilded dragon-flies *M2* 74.8 woven on tyrian hyacinth *F2*; Inwoven on the hyacinth. *M2*

75 The river-horses in the slime trumpeted] *S*; the river‸horses <in the reeds/trumpeted> did not stir for {wonder} terror *F4*   76 smeared] *S*; <stained> smeared *F4*   thyme.] *S*; myrrh‸ *F4*   77 river-bank] *S*; river‸bank *F4*   tall] *S*; great *F4*   78 He strode across the waters, mailed in beauty, and the waters sank] *S*; {and mailed/ in monstrous beauty/} He strode across the river, mailed in beauty/ like [   ] *F4*   79–80 *only in S* 81 you made the hornèd God your own:] *S*; [   ] the hornèd God. *F4*   82–6 *only in S*

With Syrian oils his brows were bright: and widespread as a tent at
    noon
His marble limbs made pale the moon and lent the day a larger light.

His long hair was nine cubits' span and coloured like that yellow
    gem
Which hidden in their garment's hem the merchants bring from
    Kurdistan.   90

His face was as the must that lies upon a vat of new-made wine:
The seas could not insapphirine the perfect azure of his eyes.

His thick soft throat was white as milk and threaded with thin veins
    of blue:
And curious pearls like frozen dew were broidered on his flowing
    silk.

*

On pearl and porphyry pedestalled he was too bright to look upon: 95
For on his ivory breast there shone the wondrous ocean-emerald,

That mystic moonlit jewel which some diver of the Colchian caves
Had found beneath the blackening waves and carried to the
    Colchian witch.

87 Syrian oils] S; glistening <might> F4   were bright:] S; very bright, F4   87–8 and
widespread as a tent at noon/ His marble limbs made pale the moon₍ₐ₎] S; <His marble limbs
made pale the /moon, like a tent at noon.> F4; <wondrous with [   ]/ and widespread like
a tent at noon.> also F4; and, widespread like a tent at noon,/ His marble limbs made pale the
moon, also F4   88 lent the day a larger light] S; <lit the black> {lit with the lamps} paler
still the lampless night F4   89–90 M1 has these lines after line 92   89 nine cubits'] S;
a cubits F1; a cubit's M1, M2, M3, M4   span₍ₐ₎] F1, S; ~, M1, M2, M3, M4   gem₍ₐ₎] F1, M2,
M3, M4, S; ~, M1   90 Which₍ₐ₎] F1, M1, M2, S; ~, M3, M4   garment's M1, M2, M3,
S; garments F1; garments' M4   hem₍ₐ₎] F1, M1, M2, S; ~, M3, M4   bring] F1, M3, M4, S;
bear M1, M2   Kurdistan] F1, M1, M2, M4, S; Kurdistân M3   91 The <silken>
<starry> woven Tyrian broideries/ <He wore were perfect> 'were starred with gold on' hya-
line, F1   must] M1, M2, M3, S; m<a>'u'st M4   new-made] M2, M3, M4, S; newmade
M1   92 perfect] M1, M2, M3, M4, S; splendid F1   93 milk₍ₐ₎] S; ~, M3–4
94 pearls₍ₐ₎] S; ~, M3, M4   dew₍ₐ₎] S; ~, M3, M4   95–6 F1 has:

    No man could see him unappalled,
      <and> for on his ivory breast there shone
    Too bright for man to look upon
    The wondrous ocean emerald.

95 pedestalled₍ₐ₎] also F1, M1, M2, S; ~, also F1, M3, M4   upon:] S; ~, also F1, M1, M2, M3,
M4   96 on] also F1, M1, M3, M4, S; <on> from M2   ocean-emerald] also F1, M1,
M2, M3, M4, S; ocean₍ₐ₎emerald also F1   ocean-emerald,] M3, M4, S; ~. also F1, M1, M2
97 of] S; from M3; <from> of M4   98 waves₍ₐ₎] S; ~, M3, M4

Before his gilded galiot ran naked vine-wreathed Corybants,
And lines of swaying elephants knelt down to draw his chariot,   100

And lines of swarthy Nubians bare up his litter as he rode
Down the great granite-paven road between the nodding peacock-
    fans.

The merchants brought him steatite from Sidon in their painted
    ships:
The meanest cup that touched his lips was fashioned from a
    chrysolite.

The merchants brought him cedar-chests of rich apparel bound
    with cords: 105
His train was borne by Memphian Lords: young Kings were glad
    to be his guests.

Ten hundred shaven priests did bow to Ammon's altar day and
    night,
Ten hundred lamps did wave their light through Ammon's carven
    house—and now

Foul snake and speckled adder with their young ones crawl from
    stone to stone
For ruined is the house and prone the great rose-marble monolith!   110

99 gilded] *M3*, *M4*, *S*; golden *F2*, *M2* vine-wreathed] *M2*, *M3*, *M4*, *S*;
vine<leaved>'wreathed' *F2* Corybants,] *F2*, *M3*, *M4*, *S*; ~; *M2* 100 lines of sway-
ing] *M3*, *M4*, *S*; swaying lines of *F2*; rows of swaying *also F2*; herds of swaying *M2* to draw]
M2, *M3*, *M4*, *S*; <before> to draw *F2* chariot,] *M3*, *M4*, *S*; ~. *F2*, *M2* 101 litter,] *S*;
~, *M3*, *M4* 102 *only in M3, M4, S* 103–4 *M3, M4 have these lines after 105–6*
103 merchants] *M3*, *M4*, *S*; traders *M1*, *M2* Sidon,] *M3*, *M4*, *S*; ~, *M1*, *M2* ships:] *M2*,
M3, *M4*, *S*; ~; *M1* 104 *only in M1, M2, M3, M4, S* 105 merchants] *M3*, *M4*, *S*;
traders *M1*, *M2* cedar-chests] *M2*, *M3*, *M4*, *S*; cedar,chests *M1* 106 Lords] *M3*,
M4, *S*; lords *M1*, *M2* young] *S*; Great *M1*, *M2*; <great> the *M3*; the *M4* 107 Ten]
S; Three *F1*, *M2*; Five *M3*; <Two> Three *M4* altar,] *M3*, *M4*, *S*; altars, *F1*; altar, *M2*
night,] *M3*, *M4*, *S*; ~, *F1*; ~; *M2* 108 Ten] *S*; Three *F1*, *M2*; Five *M3*; <Five> Three
M4 wave] *M2*, *M3*, *M4*, *S*; shed *F1* carven house—] *S*; {ivory} marble house, *F1*; mar-
ble house,—] *M2*; cedar house—] *M3*; cedar-house—] *M4* and] *M2*, *M3*, *M4*, *S*; but *F1*
now,] *F1*, *M3*, *M4*, *S*; ~, *M2* 109 Foul snake and speckled] *S*; The scorpion and the
M2; Foul snake<s> and speckled *M3*; <Foul> Slow snake and speckled *M4* adder] *M2*,
M4, *S*; adder<s> *M3* ones crawl from stone to stone] *M3*, *M4*, *S*; one's crawl across his
Throne *M2* stone,] *S*; Throne, *M2*; stone, *M3*, *M4* 110 For] *M3*, *M4*, *S*; And *M2*
ruined is the] *M3*, *M4*, *S*; <fallen> ruined is <this> the *M2* house,] *S*; ~, *M2*, *M3*, *M4*
the great] *M3*, *M4*, *S*; <His huge> The great *M2* rose-marble monolith!] *M3*, *M4*, *S*; rose-
sandstone monolith. *M2*

Wild ass or trotting jackal comes and couches in the mouldering
    gates:
Wild satyrs call unto their mates across the fallen fluted drums.

And on the summit of the pile the blue-faced ape of Horus sits
And gibbers while the figtree splits the pillars of the peristyle.

*

The god is scattered here and there: deep hidden in the windy sand   115
I saw his giant granite hand still clenched in impotent despair.

And many a wandering caravan of stately negroes silken-shawled,
Crossing the desert, halts appalled before the neck that none can
    span.

And many a bearded Bedouin draws back his yellow-striped
    burnous
To gaze upon the Titan thews of him who was thy paladin.   120

*

Go, seek his fragments on the moor and wash them in the evening
    dew,
And from their pieces make anew thy mutilated paramour!

---

111 Wild ass‸or trotting jackal‸] S; The <grey hawk> vulture‸and the <grey owl> <wild>
'grey' hawk‸ M2; Wild ass, or trotting jackal, M3, M4   comes and couches in the mouldering gates] M3, M4, S; come/ To build upon his shattered gate M2   112 Wild satyrs call
unto their mates across the] M3, M4, S; The satyr calls unto its mate/ Across each M2
drums] M3, M4, S; drum M2   113 Horus] M3, M4, S; Nubia M2   114 And gib-
bers‸while] S; And mocks him, and M2; And gibbers, while M3, M4   figtree] M3, S; fig-
tree M2, M4   the peristyle] M3, M4, S; his peristyle M2   115 The god is scattered
here and there:] S; His temple is the jackal's lair‸ F1; His body lieth here and there, F2; His
limbs are scattered here and there, M2; <His limbs are> The god is scattered here and there:
M3; The God is scattered here and there: M4   deep hidden] M4, S; And hidden F1, F2,
M2; Ay, for hidden also F2; <and> deep hidden M3   116 I saw] F2, M3, M4, S; There
lies F1; men see also F2; Men meet M2   giant] F2, M2, M3, M4, S; great F1   despair.] F1,
F2, M2, M3, M4, S; ~‸ also F2   116.1 Behind his huge and trunkless thighs F2, M2
116.2 The goatherd with his goats has room F2; The goat-herd with his goats has room
M2   116.3 To shelter from the red simoom: F2; To shelter from the wild Simoom: M2
116.4 The jackels <crouch> sleep upon his eyes: F2; The jackals sleep upon his eyes.
M2   117 stately negroes] M3, M4, S; <Nubian merchants> Swarthy Bedouins F2;
swarthy Bedouins M2, F3   silken-shawled,] M2, M3, M4, S; {silken-turbaned} silken-
shawled, F2; ~‸ F3   118 desert,] M2, M3, M4, S; ~‸ F2   the neck] F2, S; whose thighs
also F2; the head M2; the <body> torso M3; the torso M4   that none can] S; <no man can>
they {could} {dare} can not F2; <the> ten men can hardly also F2; they dare not M2; none
can M3, M4   span.] F2, M2, M3, M4, S; ~‸ also F2   119–20 only in M3, M4, S
121 Go,] M3, M4, S; O‸ M2   moor‸] S; ~, M2, M3, M4   122 paramour!] M3, M4, S;
~. M2

Go, seek them where they lie alone and from their broken pieces
    make
Thy bruisèd bedfellow! and wake mad passions in the senseless
    stone!

Charm his dull ear with Syrian hymns! He loved your body! Oh, be
    kind,   125
Pour spikenard on his hair, and wind soft rolls of linen round his
    limbs!

Wind round his head the figured coins! Stain with red fruits those
    pallid lips!
Weave purple for his shrunken hips! and purple for his barren loins!

*

Away to Egypt! Have no fear. Only one God has ever died.
Only one God has let his side be wounded by a soldier's spear.   130

But These, thy lovers, are not dead. Still by the hundred-cubit gate
Dog-faced Anubis sits in state with lotus-lilies for thy head.

---

123 Go,] *M3, M4, S*; O∧ *F2, M2*   alone∧] *F2, S*; ~, *M2, M3, M4*   124 bruisèd] *M3, S*;
bruised *F2, M2, M4*   bedfellow!] *S*; ~, *F2, M2, M3, M4*   mad] *M4, S*; Wild *F2, M2*;
<wild> mad *M3*   stone!] *M3, M4, S*; ~. *F2, M2*   124.1 Oh sit between his ancient
knees, *F1*; Crouch down between his ancient knees, *M2*   124.2 And charm his ear with
curious songs, *F1*; Charm his dull ear with curious songs, *M2*   124.3–124.4 *F1 and M2
have:*

> He will forget his bitter wrongs,
> He will forgive thine harlotries.

125 Charm his dull] *F1, M3, M4, S*; <nay soothe his> charm his deaf *also F1*; O charm his *M2*
with Syrian hymns!] *M3, M4, S*; with <Theban> hymns, *F1*; with Theban hymns, *also F1*;
with languorous hymns, *M2*   your body! Oh,] *M3, M4, S*; thy body so *F1*; thy body—O∧
also F1; thy body, O∧ *M2*   126 on his hair] *M4, S*; in his wounds *F1*; on his neck *also F1,
M2*; on his <wounds> hair *M3*   rolls of linen round his] *M2, M3, M4, S*; linen round his
trunkless *F1*   limbs!] *M3, M4, S*; ~. *F1, M2*   127 figured coins!] *M4, S*; gilded coins,
M2; <gilded> figured coins! *M3*   Stain with red fruits those pallid lips!] *S*; Pour {oils of
Libya} odorous spikenard on his hair∧ *F1*; Pour odorous spikenard on his {hea} hair, *also F1*;
Pour odorous spikenard on his lips, *M2*; <with red paint bright> Stain with red roots those
pallid lips! *M3*; Stain with red roots those pallid lips! *M4*   128 Weave purple for] *M3,
M4, S*; Set purple on *F1*; Spread fleeces on *M2*   shrunken] *M3, M4, S*; bruisèd *F1*; sterile
M2   hips!] *S*; ~, *F1, M2, M3, M4*   and purple for his barren loins!] *M3, M4, S*; Cling to
him with [   ] *F1*; Weave purple for his barren loins. *M2*   129 Have] *M3, M4, S*; have
M2   fear.] *M3, M4, S*; ~, *M2*   died.] *S*; ~, *M2, M3*; ~<,>! *M4*   130 spear.] *M2,
M3, S*; ~<.>! *M4*   131 These] *M3, S*; these *M2, M4*   thy] *M2, M4, S*; <your>
thy *M3*   dead,] *M3, M4, S*; ~: *M2*   132 Anubis] *M2, M3, S*; An<a>'u'bis *M4*
state∧] *M3, M4, S*; ~, *M2*

Still from his chair of porphyry gaunt Memnon strains his lidless
    eyes
Across the empty land, and cries each yellow morning unto Thee.

And Nilus with his broken horn lies in his black and oozy bed   135
And till thy coming will not spread his waters on the withering corn.

Your lovers are not dead, I know. They will rise up and hear your
    voice
And clash their cymbals and rejoice and run to kiss your mouth!
      And so,

Set wings upon your argosies! Set horses to your ebon car!
Back to your Nile! Or if you are grown sick of dead divinities   140

Follow some roving lion's spoor across the copper-coloured plain,
Reach out and hale him by the mane and bid him be your paramour!

Couch by his side upon the grass and set your white teeth in his
      throat
And when you hear his dying note lash your long flanks of polished
      brass

And take a tiger for your mate, whose amber sides are flecked with
      black,   145
And ride upon his gilded back in triumph through the Theban gate,

And toy with him in amorous jests, and when he turns, and snarls,
      and gnaws,
O smite him with your jasper claws! and bruise him with your agate
      breasts!

*

133 Still,] *M2, S*; ~, *M3, M4*   porphyry,] *S*; lazuli, *M2*; porphyry, *M3, M4*   gaunt] *M3,
M4, S*; Huge *M2*   134 each yellow morning] *M3, M4, S*; each morning *M2*   Thee]
M3, M4, S; thee *M2*   135 Nilus,] *M2, S*; ~, *M3, M4*   horn,] *M2, S*; ~, *M3, M4*
bed,] *S*; ~, *M2, M3, M4*   136 only in *M2, M3, M4, S*   137 Your] *M4, S*; <Thy>
Your *M2, M3*   know.] *M3, M4, S*; ~; *M2*   up,] *S*; ~, *M2, M3, M4*   voice,] *S*; ~, *M2,
M3, M4*   138 cymbals,] *S*; ~, *M2, M3, M4*   rejoice,] *S*; ~, *M2, M3, M4*   mouth!
And so,] *M3, M4, S*; mouth,—and so, *M2*   139 only in *M2, M3, M4, S*
140 Nile!,] *M3, M4, S*; ~!, *M2*   Or, *M3, S*; or, *M2*; Or, *M4*   dead divinities,] *M3, M4, S*;
old divinities, *M2*   141 only in *F1, M2, M3, M4, S*   142 out,] *S*; ~, *F1, M2, M3,
M4*   mane,] *S*; ~, *F1, M2, M3, M4*   bid] *M3, M4, S*; make *F1, M2*   143 grass,] *S*;
~, *F1, M2, M3, M4*   and set your *M3, M4, S*; <and when he> [   ] *F1*; and fix your *M2*
throat,] *S*; ~, *M2, M3, M4*   144 note,] *M2, S*; ~, *M3, M4*   brass,] *S*; ~, *M2, M3, M4*
145 mate,] *M3, M4, S*; ~, *M2*   flecked] *M3, M4, S*; striped *M2*   146 triumph,] *M2,
S*; ~, *M3, M4*   147 only in *M2, M3, M4, S*   148 claws!] *S*; paws, *M2*; claws, *M3,
M4*   bruise] *M3, M4, S*; <wound> bruise *M2*   breasts!] *M2, M3, S*; ~, *M4*

Why are you tarrying? Get hence! I weary of your sullen ways,
I weary of your steadfast gaze, your somnolent magnificence.   150

Your horrible and heavy breath makes the light flicker in the lamp,
And on my brow I feel the damp and dreadful dews of night and
        death.

Your eyes are like fantastic moons that shiver in some stagnant lake,
Your tongue is like a scarlet snake that dances to fantastic tunes,

Your pulse makes poisonous melodies, and your black throat is like
        the hole   155
Left by some torch or burning coal on Saracenic tapestries.

Away! the sulphur-coloured stars are hurrying through the
        Western Gate!
Away! or it may be too late to climb their silent silver cars!

See, the dawn shivers round the grey gilt-dialled towers, and the
        rain
Streams down each diamonded pane and blurs with tears the
        wannish day.   160

---

149 Get] *M4, S*; get *M2*; <g>Get *M3*   hence!] *M3, M4, S*; ~, *M2*   sullen ways] *M3, M4,*
S; <awful> stony gaze *M2*   150 I weary of your steadfast gaze, your] *M3, M4, S*; And
silent mood, and sullen {gaze} ways,/ And *M2*   151 *only in M2, M3, M4, S*
152 brow] *M3, M4, S*; brows *M2*   dews of night and death.] *M3, M4, S*; dripping dews of
<night and> death, *M2*   153 fantastic moons] *S*; two <mirrored> tawny moons *M2*;
a mirrored lake *M3, M4*   shiver in some stagnant lake] *S*; shiver in some <marshy> stagnant
lake *M2*; shivers with fantastic moons *M3, M4*   154 a scarlet] *M3, M4, S*; <a> <some>
a scarlet *M2*   tunes,] *M3, M4, S*; ~, *M2*   155 Your pulse makes] *M3, M4, S*; With
pulse of *M2*   black throat is like the] *M2, M3, M4, S*; <eyes are> throat is like the blackened
F2   156 Left by some torch, or burning coal,] *S*; which <year> ages since a lighted coal,
F2; Left by some torch, or lighted coal, *also F2, M2*; Left by some torch, or <lig> burning coal,
M3; Left by some torch, or burning coal, *M4*   on Saracenic] *F2, M2, M3, M4, S*; upon Ara-
bian *also F2*; in <ancient> my *also F2*   156.1–156.8 *M2 has:*

> Your horrid claws begin to close,
>   You bind me with an iron mesh,
>   You set your teeth against my flesh,
> You tear my heart out like a rose.
>
> You tear my heart out with your claws,
>   You drink my blood like crimson wine,
>   You set your icy lips to mine,
> You <hold> mouth me in your blackened jaws,

157 Western] *S*; Eastern *M3, M4*   Gate!] *M4, S*; ~<,>! *M3*   158–9 *only in M3, M4, S*
160 pane] *M4, S*; <pain> pane *M3*   blurs] *M3, S*; Bl<ea>'u'rs *M4*

What snake-tressed Fury fresh from Hell, with uncouth gestures
    and unclean,
Stole from the poppy-drowsy Queen and led you to a student's cell?

                    *

What songless tongueless Ghost of Sin crept through the curtains
    of the night,
And saw my taper burning bright, and knocked, and bade you
    enter in?

Are there not others more accursed, whiter with leprosies than I?   165
Are Abana and Pharpar dry that you come here to slake your thirst?

Get hence, you loathsome Mystery! Hideous animal, get hence!
You wake in me each bestial sense, you make me what I would not be.

You make my creed a barren sham, you wake foul dreams of sensual
    life,
And Atys with his blood-stained knife were better than the thing
    I am.   170

False Sphinx! False Sphinx! by reedy Styx old Charon, leaning on
    his oar,
Waits for my coin. Go thou before, and leave me to my Crucifix,

Whose pallid burden, sick with pain, watches the world
                with wearied eyes,
And weeps for every soul that dies, and weeps for every soul in vain.

161–4 *M3, M4 have these lines after line 156*   161 *only in M3, M4, S*   162 Queen‚]
S; ~, *M3, M4*   163 songless] *M4, S*; song-less *M3*   164 in?] *M3, M4*; ~. *S*
165–8 *M2 has these lines after line 150*   165 Are there not others more accursed, whiter
with leprosies than I?] *M3, M4, S*; are all your horrid lemans hearsed/ That you must [   ]
F2; What <if> though your chamberers be hearsed/ in porphory sarcophagi, *M2*
166 dry‚] *F2, M2, S*; ~, *M3, M4*   167 loathsome] *M3, M4, S*; dreadful *M2*   Mystery!]
M3, S; mystery, *M2*; mystery! *M4*   Hideous] *M3, M4, S*; Fantastic *M2*   hence!] *M3, M4,*
S; ~, *M2*   168 *only in M2, M3, M4, S*   169 *only in M3, M4, S*   170 blood-
stained] *M4, S*; bloodstained *M3*   171 Sphinx . . . Sphinx] *S*; Sphynx . . . Sphynx *M3,*
M4   172 coin] *M4, S*; <soul> coin *M3*   thou] *S*; you *M3, M4*   173 watches] *S*;
looks on *M3, M4*   wearied] *S*; pallid *M3, M4*   174 *only in M3, M4, S*

119   *The Ballad of Reading Gaol*

I

He did not wear his scarlet coat,
       For blood and wine are red,
And blood and wine were on his hands
       When they found him with the dead,
The poor dead woman whom he loved,   5
       And murdered in her bed.

He walked amongst the Trial Men
       In a suit of shabby gray;
A cricket cap was on his head,
       And his step seemed light and gay;   10
But I never saw a man who looked
       So wistfully at the day.

I never saw a man who looked
       With such a wistful eye
Upon that little tent of blue   15
       Which prisoners call the sky,
And at every drifting cloud that went
       With sails of silver by.

I walked, with other souls in pain,
       Within another ring,   20
And was wondering if the man had done
       A great or little thing,
When a voice behind me whispered low,
       '*That fellow's got to swing.*'

Dear Christ! the very prison walls   25
       Suddenly seemed to reel,
And the sky above my head became
       Like a casque of scorching steel;
And, though I was a soul in pain,
       My pain I could not feel.   30

*119 The Ballad of Reading Gaol. Copy text: J2, collated with M1, Let, M2, Jp1, M3, Jp2, J1
In Let, manuscript variants are taken from letters written by W discussing changes to the poem. The
numbers that follow Let in the entries below correspond to the pages in* Letters *where the discussions
occurred. The sequencing of each Let citation in relation to M2, Jp1, and M3 was determined by the
date of the individual letter*   1–528 *not in M1*   1–174 *not in M3, Jp2*   7 Men]
men *M2*   8 gray] grey *M2, Jp1*   17 drifting] straying *M2*   went] <passed> went
M2, Jp1   18 sails of silver] ravelled fleeces *M2*   23 low,] ~∧ *M2*   25 Christ!]
God: *M2*   28 casque] cup *M2*   steel;] ~, *M2*

I only knew what hunted thought
    Quickened his step, and why
He looked upon the garish day
    With such a wistful eye;
The man had killed the thing he loved,   35
    And so he had to die.

*

Yet each man kills the thing he loves,
    By each let this be heard,
Some do it with a bitter look,
    Some with a flattering word,   40
The coward does it with a kiss,
    The brave man with a sword!

Some kill their love when they are young,
    And some when they are old;
Some strangle with the hands of Lust,   45
    Some with the hands of Gold:
The kindest use a knife, because
    The dead so soon grow cold.

Some love too little, some too long,
    Some sell, and others buy;   50
Some do the deed with many tears,
    And some without a sigh:
For each man kills the thing he loves,
    Yet each man does not die.

*

He does not die a death of shame   55
    On a day of dark disgrace,
Nor have a noose about his neck,
    Nor a cloth upon his face,
Nor drop feet foremost through the floor
    Into an empty space.   60

He does not sit with silent men
    Who watch him night and day;
Who watch him when he tries to weep,
    And when he tries to pray;
Who watch him lest himself should rob   65
    The prison of its prey.

42 sword!] ~. *M2, Jp1*   44 old;] ~, *M2*   59 feet‿foremost] feet-foremost *M2*
62 day;] ~, *M2*   64 pray;] ~, *M2*

He does not wake at dawn to see
  Dread figures throng his room,
The shivering Chaplain robed in white,
  The Sheriff stern with gloom,   70
And the Governor all in shiny black,
  With the yellow face of Doom.

He does not rise in piteous haste
  To put on convict-clothes,
While some coarse-mouthed Doctor gloats, and notes   75
  Each new and nerve-twitched pose,
Fingering a watch whose little ticks
  Are like horrible hammer-blows.

He does not know that sickening thirst
  That sands one's throat, before   80
The hangman with his gardener's gloves
  Slips through the padded door,
And binds one with three leathern thongs,
  That the throat may thirst no more.

He does not bend his head to hear   85
  The Burial Office read,
Nor, while the terror of his soul
  Tells him he is not dead,
Cross his own coffin, as he moves
  Into the hideous shed.   90

He does not stare upon the air
  Through a little roof of glass:
He does not pray with lips of clay
  For his agony to pass;
Nor feel upon his shuddering cheek   95
  The kiss of Caiaphas.

69 Chaplain] chaplain *M2*   robed] all *M2*; <robed> all *Jp1*   71 Governor all in] Governor in *M2*; Governor <all> in *Jp1*   black,] ~_∧ *M2*   75 While] With *M2*   some coarse-mouthed] the coarse-mouthed *M2*, some coarse-mouthed *Let676*; some coarse-faced *Let680*; <the coarse-mouthed> some callous *Jp1*   gloats, and notes_∧] standing by, *M2*; <straddles by,> gloats, and notes_∧ *Jp1*; straddles by, *Let686*   76 Each new and nerve-twitched pose] With his flattened bulldog nose *M2*; <With his flattened bull-dog nose> Each new and nerve-twitched pose *Jp1*; with a flattened bulldog nose *Let686*   77 a] <a> <the> a *Jp1*; the *Let686*   79 know] feel *M2, Jp1, J1*   82 Slips] Comes *M2, Jp1, J1*   padded] <open> padded *M2, Jp1*   83 leathern] buckled *M2*   86 Burial Office] dreadful Service *M2*; Funeral Service *Jp1*   87 terror] anguish *M2, Jp1, J1*   89 Cross] Pass *M2, Jp1*   94 pass;] ~, *M2, Jp1*

II

Six weeks our guardsman walked the yard,
   In the suit of shabby gray:
His cricket cap was on his head,
   And his step seemed light and gay,   100
But I never saw a man who looked
   So wistfully at the day.

I never saw a man who looked
   With such a wistful eye
Upon that little tent of blue   105
   Which prisoners call the sky,
And at every wandering cloud that trailed
   Its ravelled fleeces by.

He did not wring his hands, as do
   Those witless men who dare   110
To try to rear the changeling Hope
   In the cave of black Despair:
He only looked upon the sun,
   And drank the morning air.

He did not wring his hands nor weep,   115
   Nor did he peek or pine,
But he drank the air as though it held
   Some healthful anodyne;
With open mouth he drank the sun
   As though it had been wine!   120

And I and all the souls in pain,
   Who tramped the other ring,
Forgot if we ourselves had done
   A great or little thing,
And watched with gaze of dull amaze   125
   The man who had to swing.

97 Six weeks] <One month> Six weeks *M2*   our] the *M2, Jp1, J1*   98 gray] grey *M2,*
Jp1   100 seemed] was *M2, Jp1, J1*   107 wandering] sailing *M2*   trailed] passed
M2   108 Its ravelled fleeces] With streaming pennons *M2*   119 sun‸] ~<,> *Jp1*
120 wine!] ~. *M2;* ~<.>! *Jp1*   121 pain,] ~‸ *M2;* ~',' *Jp1*

And strange it was to see him pass
   With a step so light and gay,
And strange it was to see him look
   So wistfully at the day,   130
And strange it was to think that he
   Had such a debt to pay.

*

For oak and elm have pleasant leaves
   That in the spring-time shoot:
But grim to see is the gallows-tree,   135
   With its adder-bitten root,
And, green or dry, a man must die
   Before it bears its fruit!

The loftiest place is that seat of grace
   For which all worldlings try:
But who would stand in hempen band   140
   Upon a scaffold high,
And through a murderer's collar take
   His last look at the sky?

It is sweet to dance to violins   145
   When Love and Life are fair:
To dance to flutes, to dance to lutes
   Is delicate and rare:
But it is not sweet with nimble feet
   To dance upon the air!   150

So with curious eyes and sick surmise
   We watched him day by day,
And wondered if each one of us
   Would end the self-same way,
For none can tell to what red Hell   155
   His sightless soul may stray.

*

127 And] For *M2*, *Jp1*, *J1*   pass] walk *M2*   132 debt] sin *M2*   133 For] The *M2*,
J1   134 spring-time] forest *M2*   137 And] For *M2*   138 fruit!] ~. *M2*, *Jp1*
139 that] <that> the *Jp1*; the *J1*   140 all] <we> all *M2*; <the> all *Jp1*   141 who
would] <'tis ill to> who would *M2*   144 His] <One's> His *M2*   sky?] ~. *M2*
146 Love and Life] Life and Love *Let653*   147 lutes,] ~, *Let653*   150 air!] ~.
Let653, *M2*; ~<.>! *Jp1*   151 sick] dread *M2*   155 red] <red> <hidden> red
Let671; <hidden> red *Jp1*

At last the dead man walked no more
  Amongst the Trial Men,
And I knew that he was standing up
  In the black dock's dreadful pen,   160
And that never would I see his face
  In God's sweet world again.

Like two doomed ships that pass in storm
  We had crossed each other's way:
But we made no sign, we said no word,   165
  We had no word to say;
For we did not meet in the holy night,
  But in the shameful day.

A prison wall was round us both,
  Two outcast men we were: 170
The world had thrust us from its heart,
  And God from out His care:
And the iron gin that waits for Sin
  Had caught us in its snare.

III

In Debtor's Yard the stones are hard,   175
  And the dripping wall is high,
So it was there he took the air
  Beneath the leaden sky,
And by each side a Warder walked,
  For fear the man might die.   180

Or else he sat with those who watched
  His anguish night and day;
Who watched him when he rose to weep,
  And when he crouched to pray;
Who watched him lest himself should rob   185
  Their scaffold of its prey.

158 Men] men *M2*   162 In God's sweet world] <for weal or woe again> in God's sweet
world again *Let698*; For weal or woe *J1*   166 say;] ~, *M2*   169 prison‸wall] prison-
wall *M2*   171 heart,] ~: *M2*; ~<:>, *Jp1*   173 Sin] sin *M2*   175–210 *not in Jp1*,
although the proof has a note at this point reading 'Take in "A" here', directing the inclusion of
stanzas that were on separate sheets, presumably corresponding to those in M3   176 dripping]
weeping *M2*   179 by] on *M2*   Warder] warder *M2, M3, Jp2, J1*   walked,] ~‸ *M2,*
M3; ~',' *Jp2*   180 might] would *M2, M3*; <would> might *Jp2*   181–6 *not in M2*
181 those who watched] silent men *M3*; <silent men> those who watched *Jp2*   182 His
anguish] Who watched him *M3*; <Who watched him> His anguish *Jp2*   day;] ~, *M3*
183 rose] <rose> <crouched> rose *M3*   184 crouched] <crouched> <knelt> crouched
M3   pray;] ~, *M3*   186 Their scaffold] <Their hangman> <Our prison> The scaffold
M3; <The> Their scaffold *Jp2*   its] <his> its *M3*

The Governor was strong upon
    The Regulations Act:
The Doctor said that Death was but
    A scientific fact: 190
And twice a day the Chaplain called,
    And left a little tract.

And twice a day he smoked his pipe,
    And drank his quart of beer:
His soul was resolute, and held   195
    No hiding-place for fear;
He often said that he was glad
    The hangman's hands were near.

But why he said so strange a thing
    No Warder dared to ask: 200
For he to whom a watcher's doom
    Is given as his task,
Must set a lock upon his lips,
    And make his face a mask.

Or else he might be moved, and try   205
    To comfort or console:
And what should Human Pity do
    Pent up in Murderers' Hole?
What word of grace in such a place
    Could help a brother's soul?   210

*

With slouch and swing around the ring
    We trod the Fools' Parade!
We did not care: we knew we were
    The Devil's Own Brigade:
And shaven head and feet of lead   215
    Make a merry masquerade.

---

187 strong] strict *M3*; <strict> strong *Let684, Jp2*   188 Regulations] Regulation *Let635*   190 fact:] ~; *Let635*   191 called,] ~ₐ *Let635*; ~; *M3* 192 tract] Tract *Let635*   193–204 *not in M3*   193–654 *not in Jp2*   196 hiding-place] hiding‿place *M2*   fear;] ~: *M2*   198 hangman's] <dreadful> hangman's *M2*   hands were] day was *M2, J1*   199–210 *M2 has these lines as handwritten insertions in the typescript*   200 Warder] warder *J1*   205 and] or *M3*   206 comfort] <pity> comfort *M2*   210 Could] Can *M3*   211–654 *not in M3*   212 Parade!] ~: *M2, Jp1*

We tore the tarry rope to shreds
    With blunt and bleeding nails;
We rubbed the doors, and scrubbed the floors,
    And cleaned the shining rails: 220
And, rank by rank, we soaped the plank,
    And clattered with the pails.

We sewed the sacks, we broke the stones,
    We turned the dusty drill:
We banged the tins, and bawled the hymns,   225
    And sweated on the mill:
But in the heart of every man
    Terror was lying still.

So still it lay that every day
    Crawled like a weed-clogged wave: 230
And we forgot the bitter lot
    That waits for fool and knave,
Till once, as we tramped in from work,
    We passed an open grave.

With yawning mouth the yellow hole   235
    Gaped for a living thing;
The very mud cried out for blood
    To the thirsty asphalte ring:
And we knew that ere one dawn grew fair
    Some prisoner had to swing.   240

Right in we went, with soul intent
    On Death and Dread and Doom:
The hangman, with his little bag,
    Went shuffling through the gloom:
And each man trembled as he crept   245
    Into his numbered tomb.

*

218 nails;] ~: *M2*   230 weed-clogged] windless *M2*   233 tramped] came *M2, Jp1*
235 yellow] horrid *M2, Jp1, J1*   236 thing;] ~: *M2*   238 asphalte] asphalt
M2   239 one] the *M2, Jp1*   240 Some prisoner] One of us *M2, Jp1*; The fellow *J1*
243 little] leathern *M2*   244 shuffling through] <by us in> shuffling through *M2, Jp1*
245 each man trembled as he crept] I trembled as I groped my way *J1*   246 his] my *J1*

That night the empty corridors
   Were full of forms of Fear,
And up and down the iron town
   Stole feet we could not hear,   250
And through the bars that hide the stars
   White faces seemed to peer.

He lay as one who lies and dreams
   In a pleasant meadow-land,
The watchers watched him as he slept,   255
   And could not understand
How one could sleep so sweet a sleep
   With a hangman close at hand.

But there is no sleep when men must weep
   Who never yet have wept: 260
So we—the fool, the fraud, the knave—
   That endless vigil kept,
And through each brain on hands of pain
   Another's terror crept.

               *

Alas! it is a fearful thing   265
   To feel another's guilt!
For, right within, the sword of Sin
   Pierced to its poisoned hilt,
And as molten lead were the tears we shed
   For the blood we had not spilt.   270

The Warders with their shoes of felt
   Crept by each padlocked door,
And peeped and saw, with eyes of awe,
   Gray figures on the floor,
And wondered why men knelt to pray   275
   Who never prayed before.

---

248 Fear] fear *M2*; <f>'F'ear *Jp1*   250 Stole] <Went> Stole *M2, Jp1*   258 a] the
M2, Jp1   262 endless] fearful *M2*; <arid> {ceaseless} endless *Let671*; <arid>
<another's> endless *Let680*; <arid> endless *Jp1*   265 Alas!] ~<:>! *M2*   fearful]
dreadful *M2*   266 guilt!] ~: *M2*; ~<:>! *Jp1*   267 For] And *Jp1*   Sin] sin *M2*;
<s>'S'in *Jp1*   271 Warders] warders *M2, Jp1, J1*   272 padlocked] iron *M2*;
<iron> padlocked *Jp1*   274 Gray] Grey *M2, Jp1*

All through the night we knelt and prayed,
   Mad mourners of a corse!
The troubled plumes of midnight were
   The plumes upon a hearse: 280
And bitter wine upon a sponge
   Was the savour of Remorse.

*

The gray cock crew, the red cock crew,
   But never came the day:
And crooked shapes of Terror crouched,   285
   In the corners where we lay:
And each evil sprite that walks by night
   Before us seemed to play.

They glided past, they glided fast,
   Like travellers through a mist: 290
They mocked the moon in a rigadoon
   Of delicate turn and twist,
And with formal pace and loathsome grace
   The phantoms kept their tryst.

With mop and mow, we saw them go,   295
   Slim shadows hand in hand:
About, about, in ghostly rout
   They trod a saraband:
And the damned grotesques made arabesques,
   Like the wind upon the sand!   300

With the pirouettes of marionettes,
   They tripped on pointed tread:
But with flutes of Fear they filled the ear,
   As their grisly masque they led,
And loud they sang, and long they sang,   305
   For they sang to wake the dead.

---

278 Mad mourners of] Like watchers round *M2*; Like mourners with *Jp1*   corse!] ~: *M2*,
Jp1   279 troubled] purple *M2*   were] shook *Jp1*, *J1*   280 The] Like the *Jp1*, *J1*
281 And bitter] And as bitter *Jp1*, *J1*   283 gray] Grey *M2*; grey *Jp1*   285 Terror]
terror *M2*; <t>'T'error *Jp1*   290 travellers] figures *M2*   292 delicate] <curi-
ous> delicate *M2*; <dainty> delicate *Jp1*   294 phantoms] antics *M2*   296 Slim]
Pale *M2*   298 a] their *M2*   saraband:] ~, *M2*, *Jp1*   300 Like the wind] Like 'the'
wind *Jp1*   sand!] ~. *M2*; ~<.>! *Jp1*   302 pointed] dainty *M2*   303 But] And *M2*;
<And> But *Jp1*   304 their] the *M2*

'*Oho!*' they cried, '*The world is wide,*
   But fettered limbs go lame!
And once, or twice, to throw the dice
   Is a gentlemanly game,   310
But he does not win who plays with Sin
   In the secret House of Shame.'

*

No things of air these antics were,
   That frolicked with such glee:
To men whose lives were held in gyves,   315
   And whose feet might not go free,
Ah! wounds of Christ! they were living things,
   Most terrible to see.

Around, around, they waltzed and wound;
   Some wheeled in smirking pairs;   320
With the mincing step of a demirep
   Some sidled up the stairs:
And with subtle sneer, and fawning leer,
   Each helped us at our prayers.

*

The morning wind began to moan,   325
   But still the night went on:
Through its giant loom the web of gloom
   Crept till each thread was spun:
And, as we prayed, we grew afraid
   Of the Justice of the Sun.   330

The moaning wind went wandering round
   The weeping prison-wall:
Till like a wheel of turning steel
   We felt the minutes crawl:
O moaning wind! what had we done   335
   To have such a seneschal?

---

307 Oho!] Oho<:>! *M2*   308 go lame!] are lame, *M2, Jp1*   313 antics] phantoms
M2   317 Ah!] O∧ *M2*   Christ!] ~<:>! *M2*   320 pairs;] ~: *M2*   324 Each]
They *M2*   327 Through its giant loom∧] Across its loom, *M2*   328 Crept∧]
Crawled, *M2*   330 Sun.] ~∧ *M2*   331–6 *not in M2*   334 crawl:] ~. *Let668*
335 moaning wind] <wind of woe> moaning wind *Let668*

At last I saw the shadowed bars,
　　Like a lattice wrought in lead,
Move right across the whitewashed wall
　　That faced my three-plank bed,　　　　　　340
And I knew that somewhere in the world
　　God's dreadful dawn was red.

*

At six o'clock we cleaned our cells,
　　At seven all was still,
But the sough and swing of a mighty wing　　　345
　　The prison seemed to fill,
For the Lord of Death with icy breath
　　Had entered in to kill.

He did not pass in purple pomp,
　　Nor ride a moon-white steed.　　　　　　350
Three yards of cord and a sliding board
　　Are all the gallows' need:
So with rope of shame the Herald came
　　To do the secret deed.

*

We were as men who through a fen　　　　　355
　　Of filthy darkness grope:
We did not dare to breathe a prayer,
　　Or to give our anguish scope:
Something was dead in each of us,
　　And what was dead was Hope.　　　　　　360

For Man's grim Justice goes its way,
　　And will not swerve aside:
It slays the weak, it slays the strong,
　　It has a deadly stride:
With iron heel it slays the strong,　　　　　365
　　The monstrous parricide!

*

339 right across] slowly on *M2*　　　345 mighty] giant *M2*; \<flapping\> \<monstrous\>
mighty *Jp1*　　　349 pass] come *M2*　　　350 steed.] ~: *M2*　　　351 board,] ~\<,\> *Jp1*
352 gallows'] gallows *M2*　　　353 the Herald] God's Angel *M2*; the \<Angel\> herald
Jp1　　　354 secret] awful *M2*　　　355–66 *not in M2*　　　356 filthy] dreary *Jp1*
361 Man's] man's *Let661*, *Jp1*　　way] road *Let661*　　　362 will] may *Let661*
363 strong,] ~; *Let661*　　　366 The] This *Let661*, *Jp1*　　parricide!] ~\<.\>! *Jp1*

We waited for the stroke of eight:
　　Each tongue was thick with thirst:
For the stroke of eight is the stroke of Fate
　　That makes a man accursed,　　　　　　370
And Fate will use a running noose
　　For the best man and the worst.

We had no other thing to do,
　　Save to wait for the sign to come:
So, like things of stone in a valley lone,
　　Quiet we sat and dumb:　　　　　　375
But each man's heart beat thick and quick,
　　Like a madman on a drum!

*

With sudden shock the prison-clock
　　Smote on the shivering air,　　　　　380
And from all the gaol rose up a wail
　　Of impotent despair,
Like the sound that frightened marshes hear
　　From some leper in his lair.

And as one sees most fearful things　　　385
　　In the crystal of a dream,
We saw the greasy hempen rope
　　Hooked to the blackened beam,
And heard the prayer the hangman's snare
　　Strangled into a scream.　　　　　　390

And all the woe that moved him so
　　That he gave that bitter cry,
And the wild regrets, and the bloody sweats,
　　None knew so well as I:
For he who lives more lives than one　　　395
　　More deaths than one must die.

375 So,] ~ ᴧ *M2*　　lone,] ~ ᴧ *M2*　　　377 thick and quick] <horribly> thick and quick *M2*
378 drum!] ~. *M2*; ~<.>! *Jp1*　　383 that] the *J1*　　frightened marshes] silent hunters
M2　　384 leper] wild beast *M2*　　his] its *M2*　　393 wild] vain *M2*; <vain> wild
Jp1

IV

There is no chapel on the day
   On which they hang a man:
The Chaplain's heart is far too sick,
   Or his face is far too wan,
Or there is that written in his eyes   400
   Which none should look upon.

So they kept us close till nigh on noon,
   And then they rang the bell,
And the Warders with their jingling keys   405
   Opened each listening cell,
And down the iron stair we tramped,
   Each from his separate Hell.

Out into God's sweet air we went,
   But not in wonted way,   410
For this man's face was white with fear,
   And that man's face was gray,
And I never saw sad men who looked
   So wistfully at the day.

I never saw sad men who looked   415
   With such a wistful eye
Upon that little tent of blue
   We prisoners called the sky,
And at every careless cloud that passed
   In happy freedom by.   420

But there were those amongst us all
   Who walked with downcast head,
And knew that, had each got his due,
   They should have died instead:
He had but killed a thing that lived,   425
   Whilst they had killed the dead.

404 rang] banged *M2*   405 Warders] warders *M2*, *Jp1*, *J1*   412 gray] grey *M2*;
gr<e>'a'y *Jp1*   419 careless] wandering *M2*; idle *Jp1*; happy *J1*   420 In happy
freedom] With sails of silver *M2*; <With such strange> In happy freedom *Jp1*; In such strange
freedom *J1*   421 But] And *M2*; <And> But *Jp1*   424 instead;] ~: *M2*

For he who sins a second time
    Wakes a dead soul to pain,
And draws it from its spotted shroud,
    And makes it bleed again,   430
And makes it bleed great gouts of blood,
    And makes it bleed in vain!

*

Like ape or clown, in monstrous garb
    With crooked arrows starred,
Silently we went round and round   435
    The slippery asphalte yard;
Silently we went round and round,
    And no man spoke a word.

Silently we went round and round,
    And through each hollow mind   440
The Memory of dreadful things
    Rushed like a dreadful wind,
And Horror stalked before each man,
    And Terror crept behind.

*

The Warders strutted up and down,   445
    And kept their herd of brutes,
Their uniforms were spick and span,
    And they wore their Sunday suits,
But we knew the work they had been at,
    By the quicklime on their boots.   450

For where a grave had opened wide,
    There was no grave at all:
Only a stretch of mud and sand
    By the hideous prison-wall,
And a little heap of burning lime,   455
    That the man should have his pall.

---

431 And goes for ever through the land *M2*; <[   ] goes for ever through the land> *Let667*
432 With the red feet of Cain. *M2*; <with the red feet of Cain> And binds it with a chain
Let667   vain!] ~. *Jp1*   436 asphalte‸yard;] asphalt-yard, *M2*   441 Memory]
memory *M2, Jp1*   443 stalked] <ran> stalked *M2*   445 Warders] warders *Jp1, J1*
446 kept] watched *Jp1, J1*

For he has a pall, this wretched man,
    Such as few men can claim:
Deep down below a prison-yard,
    Naked for greater shame,   460
He lies, with fetters on each foot,
    Wrapt in a sheet of flame!

And all the while the burning lime
    Eats flesh and bone away,
It eats the brittle bone by night,   465
    And the soft flesh by day,
It eats the flesh and bone by turns,
    But it eats the heart alway.

*

For three long years they will not sow
    Or root or seedling there:
For three long years the unblessed spot   470
    Will sterile be and bare,
And look upon the wondering sky
    With unreproachful stare.

They think a murderer's heart would taint   475
    Each simple seed they sow.
It is not true! God's kindly earth
    Is kindlier than men know,
And the red rose would but blow more red,
    The white rose whiter blow.   480

Out of his mouth a red, red rose!
    Out of his heart a white!
For who can say by what strange way,
    Christ brings His will to light,
Since the barren staff the pilgrim bore   485
    Bloomed in the great Pope's sight?

*

458 claim:] ~, *M2*; ~<,>: *Jp1*   462 flame!] ~. *M2, Jp1*   472 sterile] <barren> sterile *M2, Jp1*   477 true!] ~. *M2*; ~<.>! *Jp1*   481 red, red] red∧red *M2*   rose!] ~<:>! *M2, Jp1*   482 white!] ~<:>! *M2, Jp1*   483 way,] ~∧ *M2*   484 His] his *M2*   485 barren] <sterile> barren *Jp1*

But neither milk-white rose nor red
   May bloom in prison air;
The shard, the pebble, and the flint,
   Are what they give us there: 490
For flowers have been known to heal
   A common man's despair.

So never will wine-red rose or white,
   Petal by petal, fall
On that stretch of mud and sand that lies   495
   By the hideous prison-wall,
To tell the men who tramp the yard
   That God's Son died for all.

            *

Yet though the hideous prison-wall
   Still hems him round and round,   500
And a spirit may not walk by night
   That is with fetters bound,
And a spirit may but weep that lies
   In such unholy ground,

He is at peace—this wretched man—   505
   At peace, or will be soon:
There is no thing to make him mad,
   Nor does Terror walk at noon,
For the lampless Earth in which he lies
   Has neither Sun nor Moon.   510

            *

They hanged him as a beast is hanged:
   They did not even toll
A requiem that might have brought
   Rest to his startled soul,
But hurriedly they took him out,   515
   And hid him in a hole.

488 air;] ~: *M2*   492 common] wretched *M2*, *Jp1*   504 ground,] ~<.>, *Jp1*
506 soon:] ~, *M2*   509 Earth] earth *M2*, *Jp1*   510 Sun] sun *M2*, *Jp1*   Moon]
moon *M2*, *Jp1*   511 beast] dog *M2*; <dog> beast *Jp1*   512 even] care to *M2*, *Jp1*
514 Rest] <Peace> Rest *M2*

They stripped him of his canvas clothes,
  And gave him to the flies:
They mocked the swollen purple throat,
  And the stark and staring eyes: 520
And with laughter loud they heaped the shroud
  In which their convict lies.

The Chaplain would not kneel to pray
  By his dishonoured grave:
Nor mark it with that blessed Cross   525
  That Christ for sinners gave,
Because the man was one of those
  Whom Christ came down to save.

Yet all is well; he has but passed
  To Life's appointed bourne: 530
And alien tears will fill for him
  Pity's long-broken urn,
For his mourners will be outcast men,
  And outcasts always mourn.

                    V

I know not whether Laws be right,   535
  Or whether Laws be wrong;
All that we know who lie in gaol
  Is that the wall is strong;
And that each day is like a year,
  A year whose days are long.   540

But this I know, that every Law
  That men have made for Man,
Since first Man took his brother's life,
  And the sad world began,
But straws the wheat and saves the chaff   545
  With a most evil fan.

517–22 M2 has these lines as handwritten insertions in the typescript   517 They] The
warders M2, Jp1, J1   his canvas clothes] his clothes M2, Jp1, J1   520 eyes:] ~, M2
521 laughter loud] <lime> laughter loud Jp1   heaped] <made> heaped Jp1   the shroud]
the <bitter> shroud Jp1   522 their] the M2; <the> their Jp1; the J1   convict] dead
man M2   523 would] did M2   525 Nor] He would not M2   that blessed Cross]
the Cross M2   529 Yet∧] ~, M1   well;] ~∧ M1   530 Life's appointed] mans
appointed M1; each man's certain M2; <each man's certain> Life's appointed Jp1
bourne:] ~∧ M1   535 Laws] laws M1   right,] ~∧ M1   536 Laws] laws M1
wrong;] ~: M1; ~, M2, Jp1   538 strong;] ~, M1, M2   541 know,] ~∧ M2   Law]
law M1   545 saves] <hoards> saves M1

This too I know—and wise it were
    If each could know the same—
That every prison that men build
    Is built with bricks of shame,   550
And bound with bars lest Christ should see
    How men their brothers maim.

With bars they blur the gracious moon,
    And blind the goodly sun:
And they do well to hide their Hell,   555
    For in it things are done
That Son of God nor son of Man
    Ever should look upon!

*

The vilest deeds like poison weeds
    Bloom well in prison-air: 560
It is only what is good in Man
    That wastes and withers there:
Pale Anguish keeps the heavy gate,
    And the Warder is Despair.

For they starve the little frightened child   565
    Till it weeps both night and day:
And they scourge the weak, and flog the fool,
    And gibe the old and gray,
And some grow mad, and all grow bad,
    And none a word may say.   570

546.1–546.6 *M1 has*:

        With front of brass and feet of lead
           We tramp the prison yard.
        We tramp the slippery asphalte ring
           With soul and body marred,
        And each man's brain grows sick with hate,
           And each man's heart grows hard.

547–654 *not in M1*   547 know—] ~: *M2*   548 same—] ~: *M2*   557 That Christ, whom sun and moon obey, *M2*   Man] <m>'M'an *Jp1*   558 Ever should] Should never *M2*; <Should ever> Ever should *Jp1*   upon!] ~. *M2, Jp1*   559 Like poison weeds, the vilest deeds *M2*   561 Man] man *M2*   568 gibe] mock *M2*; <strike> gibe *Let668*   gray] grey *M2, Jp1*

Each narrow cell in which we dwell
   Is a foul and dark latrine,
And the fetid breath of living Death
   Chokes up each grated screen,
And all, but Lust, is turned to dust   575
   In Humanity's machine.

The brackish water that we drink
   Creeps with a loathsome slime,
And the bitter bread they weigh in scales
   Is full of chalk and lime,   580
And Sleep will not lie down, but walks
   Wild-eyed, and cries to Time.

*

But though lean Hunger and green Thirst
   Like asp with adder fight,
We have little care of prison fare,   585
   For what chills and kills outright
Is that every stone one lifts by day
   Becomes one's heart by night.

With midnight always in one's heart,
   And twilight in one's cell,   590
We turn the crank, or tear the rope,
   Each in his separate Hell,
And the silence is more awful far
   Than the sound of a brazen bell.

And never a human voice comes near   595
   To speak a gentle word:
And the eye that watches through the door
   Is pitiless and hard:
And by all forgot, we rot and rot,
   With soul and body marred.   600

574 grated] iron *M2*   583 lean] Grey *Let680*   green] Green *Let680*   586 chills
and kills] <slays the soul> chills and kills *M2, Jp1*   592 his] our *Jp1*   594 brazen]
dreadful *M2*

And thus we rust Life's iron chain
　　Degraded and alone:
And some men curse, and some men weep,
　　And some men make no moan:
But God's eternal Laws are kind　　　　　　605
　　And break the heart of stone.

＊

And every human heart that breaks,
　　In prison-cell or yard,
Is as that broken box that gave
　　Its treasure to the Lord,　　　　　　　610
And filled the unclean leper's house
　　With the scent of costliest nard.

Ah! happy they whose hearts can break
　　And peace of pardon win!
How else may man make straight his plan　　615
　　And cleanse his soul from Sin?
How else but through a broken heart
　　May Lord Christ enter in?

＊

And he of the swollen purple throat,
　　And the stark and staring eyes,　　　　620
Waits for the holy hands that took
　　The Thief to Paradise;
And a broken and a contrite heart
　　The Lord will not despise.

The man in red who reads the Law　　　　625
　　Gave him three weeks of life,
Three little weeks in which to heal
　　His soul of his soul's strife,
And cleanse from every blot of blood
　　The hand that held the knife.　　　　　630

604 some] most *M2*; all *Jp1*　　　no] their *Jp1*　　　614 win!] ~<:>! *M2, Jp1*　　　615 may]
can *M2, Jp1*　　　616 Sin] sin *M2*　　　618 May] Can *M2, Jp1*　　　622 Paradise;] ~, *M2*
625 the Law] <the Law> one's doom *Let684*

And with tears of blood he cleansed the hand,
  The hand that held the steel:
For only blood can wipe out blood,
  And only tears can heal:
And the crimson stain that was of Cain   635
  Became Christ's snow-white seal.

VI

In Reading gaol by Reading town
  There is a pit of shame,
And in it lies a wretched man
  Eaten by teeth of flame,   640
In a burning winding-sheet he lies,
  And his grave has got no name.

And there, till Christ call forth the dead,
  In silence let him lie:
No need to waste the foolish tear,   645
  Or heave the windy sigh:
The man had killed the thing he loved,
  And so he had to die.

And all men kill the thing they love,
  By all let this be heard,   650
Some do it with a bitter look,
  Some with a flattering word,
The coward does it with a kiss,
  The brave man with a sword!

                                          C. 3. 3.

634 heal:] ~, *M2*, *Jp1*   644 lie:] ~<:>! *M2*   654 sword!] ~. *M2*, *Jp1*

APPENDIX

QUESTIONABLE TEXTS

Many of Wilde's contemporaries testified to his impressive gift for story-telling and claimed to have recorded his narratives. The best known of these are the four poems in prose which were included by Vyvyan Holland in *Son of Oscar Wilde* (1954; revised edn. London: Robinson, 1999): 'The Poet', 'The Actress', 'Simon of Cyrene', and 'Jezebel'. According to Rupert Hart-Davis (*Letters* 809 n.3) Holland's source was a privately printed twelve-page pamphlet entitled *Echoes*. In 1948 the then British Museum Library was presented with a copy of this very rare document by Mrs Gabrielle Enthoven (1868–1950), the theatre historian and collector who had been a friend of Wilde. Included with this copy are two letters (one bearing the date of 19 March 1948) from Mrs Enthoven to G. E. Oldman, then the Museum's Principal Keeper of Printed Books. In them she claims that Wilde had told her stories and that she sometimes recorded them after he had left; she further explains that 'a friend' had printed five or six copies of the stories (the *Echoes* pamphlet) for her, at some point between 1890 and 1893. There is no evidence to link Wilde with the printing of *Echoes*, nor to suggest that Enthoven's texts matched Wilde's or had his authority.

Some years later, between January and October 1912, these stories—'almost word for word the same', according to Holland (*Son of Oscar Wilde*, 279)—appeared in *Mask: A Quarterly Journal of the Art of the Theatre*, edited by the scene designer and author Gordon Craig and published in Florence. Each piece was entitled 'An Unpublished Story by Oscar Wilde', and each was prefaced by the following: 'This story was told by Wilde to Miss Aimée Lowther when a child and written out by her. A few copies were privately printed but this is the first time it has been given to the public' (*Son of Oscar Wilde*, 278). Aimée Lowther (1871–1935) was known to both Wilde and Enthoven. The epigraph she uses to authorize her stories is confusing. She may have heard the stories at first hand; however, according to Hart-Davis, she too possessed a copy of *Echoes*. She could thus have corrected her versions against it (if indeed it originated from Enthoven's transcription rather than her own). In a letter to Lowther, tentatively dated by Hart-Davis as August 1899, Wilde had warned her against publishing 'the little poem in prose I call "The Poet"' because it was to appear 'next week in a Paris magazine above my own signature' (*Letters*, 809). This magazine has never been traced. Although his letter indicates that Wilde knew his stories had been recorded by others, it does not provide authority for the texts printed in either *Mask* or *Echoes*.

Recently a photocopy of an untitled MS in Wilde's hand, apparently a draft fragment of 'The Poet', was made available to the editors through the good offices of Merlin Holland, Wilde's grandson. The date of the MS cannot be determined; it could be a draft from the early 1890s, or it could be a remnant from Wilde's efforts in 1899 to publish the poem in the unlocated Paris magazine. The fragment reads:

Every morning the P<p>oet {went} passed out <into> of the gate of the city, and went into the waste land and wandered <there> through it.

And at evening he returned to the city and the people met him at the gate and said to him what [   ]

And he told them of wonderful things, saying that he had seen them.

Now one day as he was sitting [   ]

There are substantial differences between the text of the fragment and those of *Echoes* and *Mask*. The comparable passage, reprinted by Vyvyan Holland in *Son of Oscar Wilde*, reads:

The poet lived in the country amongst the meadows and the woods; but every morning he went into the great city which lay many miles away over the hills in the blue mist. And every evening he returned. And in the dusky twilight the children and the people would gather round him while he told them of all the wonderful things that he had seen that day in the woods, and by the river, and on the hill-tops. (257)

In summary, while the fragment supports the claim that the text of 'The Poet' in *Echoes* and *Mask* was indeed derived from a story told by Wilde— and by extension adds credence to this claim for the other three poems in those collections—it does not essentially alter the textual status of any of the four. Their texts remain without Wilde's authority.

Other reported poems in prose, such as those in Gide's memoirs of Wilde (first published in *L'Ermitage*, June 1902), bear some resemblance to those that Wilde published in the *Fortnightly Review* (July 1894), which Henry-D. Davray translated in *La Revue blanche* (1 May 1899). Gide could have consulted the translations of the poems in prose to impart greater accuracy to his memoir. However, those stories generated by Guillot de Saix in, for example, his 'Oscar Wilde: Contes et propos recueillis par Guillot de Saix' in *Les Œuvres libres* (15 Sept. 1949) remain virtuoso performances but thoroughly unreliable since he creates brief stories from remarks attributed to Wilde concerning possible works that he never wrote (indeed, de Saix even includes his own creation of the last act of a play on Beau Brummell, whose life Wilde had allegedly expressed interest in dramatizing).

COMMENTARY

[In the headnotes and annotations, line numbers follow the titles of poems.]

1 YE SHALL BE GODS

MS: Written in Lady Wilde's notebook (*M*, location: Berg) some time between 1871 and 1874, while W was a student at Trinity College, Dublin.

Not published in W's lifetime.

Modelled after a speech by the Chorus in Swinburne's poetic drama *Atalanta in Calydon*, W's poem employs the form of a Greek choral song, divided into strophes and antistrophes (W uses Greek orthography in designating one section sung and danced in one direction, the next in the opposite direction). Like Swinburne's metre, W's is anapaestic trimeter with liberal substitution of other poetic feet; Swinburne's lyric of three stanzas has only one stanza of twelve lines, whereas W employs the twelve-line stanza throughout his poem. Both poets use the rhyme scheme *ababcdcdefef*.

Title. Cf. the serpent's words to Eve regarding the forbidden fruit in Genesis 3: 5: 'For God doth know that in the day ye eat thereof, then your eyes shall be opened, and ye shall be as gods, knowing good and evil'.

1. Echoes the first line of the Chorus's speech in *Atalanta in Calydon*, 322: 'Before the beginning of years . . .'.

3. Echoes Genesis 2: 7: 'And the Lord God formed man of the dust of the ground . . .'.

8. Echoes Genesis 1: 26: 'And God said, Let us make man in our image, after our likeness . . .'.

21–4. *O gods ever wrathful*: in Swinburne's lyric passage 'Before the beginning of years' in *Atalanta in Calydon*, the gods of wrath are overthrown and Aphrodite (or, in W's poem, Love in line 41) is enthroned, an expression of Swinburne's romantic Hellenism and his disdain for Christian pieties.

45–6. *Iapygian . . . Lampsacene's shrine*: Iapygia, a district of Italy, was a centre for the worship of Aphrodite; 'Lampsacene's shrine' refers to that of the god Priapus, symbolized by a phallus, who was worshipped as a fertility god in Lampsacus, Asia Minor. His cult spread to Greece and eventually to Italy, where he was revered as the protector of gardens and orchards. In some myths, he is said to be the son of Dionysus and Aphrodite.

56. *Lady of Lust*: akin to Swinburne's *femme fatale*, the 'Lady of Pain', in 'Dolores'.

57. *Cyprian Mother*: Aphrodite, patron goddess of the island of Cyprus.

59–60. To maintain the rhyme scheme, W takes liberties with Swinburne's passage in 'Hymn to Proserpine', 76: 'Thou art throned where another was king; where another was queen she is crowned'.

2 CHORUS OF CLOUD-MAIDENS

MS and Publishing History:
   No MS is known to exist. Since W matriculated at Oxford in October 1874, the poem was probably written in his first term. See Addendum.
   First published in *Dublin University Magazine* 86 (Nov. 1875), 622 (*D*); rev. in A. W. Pollard, ed., *Odes from the Greek Dramatists* (Chicago: A. C. McClurg & Co., 1890), 149–50 (*O*), as 'Nubes' ('Clouds'), the author and title in the Greek omitted. In Pollard's edition this poem was placed according to the Greek plays on which it was based. This is W's first published poem; repr. in *Poems* (1908).
   This free translation is based on two songs—denoted as 'strophe' and 'antistrophe'—from Aristophanes' *The Clouds* (423 BC).

Title. Taken from the version in the *Dublin University Magazine* with its Greek subscript naming the author and title of the play. However, the lines cited from Aristophanes' play (275–90; 298–313) are from Pollard's edition, in which all translations are keyed to the Greek texts in Wilhelm Dindorf's *Poetae Scenici Graeci* (1841).

   3. *our Sire's loud river*: the currents of their father Ocean.

   16. *Pallas-loved land*: Athens, the scene of Aristophanes' play. The goddess Athena, protector of the city, was known as 'Pallas Athena'.

   18. *Kekrops*: the mythical founder and first king of the ancient region of Attica, of which Athens was the principal city. Also known as Cecrops (half human, half serpent), he is said to have invented writing, and to have taught his subjects how to build cities and bury the dead.

   20. *mysteries*: the secret Eleusinian rites in honour of the earth-goddess Demeter and the queen of the Underworld, Proserpine (also known as Persephone), were initially associated with the town of Eleusis, later amalgamated with Athens, where the Eleusinion, a temple below the Acropolis, was built to house the sacred objects of the mysteries. An initiate into the Eleusinian mysteries learned how to cross safely to the Underworld after death and live happily thereafter.

   21–2. Cf. Shelley's 'The Cloud', 78: 'The pavilion of Heaven is bare'.

   28–32. Spring festivities at Elaphebolion, the 'Great Dionysia', where tragedies and comedies competed for honours and at which *The Clouds* was placed third (i.e. last). Aristophanes later rewrote the play.

   29–30. *wine-god . . . Bacchanal dance*: Bacchus (the equivalent of the Greek Dionysus) was the Roman god of the vineyards, often depicted as an effeminate youth with grapes or a wine-cup; Bacchantes were women inspired to ecstasy, wearing skins of panthers or fawns.

   Postscript. Though the postscript to the 1890 version gives the date of composition as 1874, this was added 15 years after the poem was written.

3 FROM SPRING DAYS TO WINTER

MS and Publishing History:
   No MS is known to exist.

First published in *Dublin University Magazine* 87 (Jan. 1876), 47 (*D*); repr. in *Poems* (1908); collected thereafter. See Addendum.

In this lyric poem, W employs the well-worn convention of love blossoming in the spring, followed by the death of the speaker's love in the bleakness of winter. Paralleling the joy and grief of the speaker in his devotion to his loved one, the thrush and dove—after their joyous song of spring—conclude the poem in winter with the thrush's sad song and the dove's death suggesting the continuity of human experience and natural law.

2. *Throstle*: song-thrush.

14. *Blown . . . desire*: blossoming, perhaps with a hint of 'overblown'.

20. Echoes Swinburne's 'Fragoletta', 67: 'O broken singing of the dove!'

22. *Fond Dove*: traditionally, the dove—as symbol of purity, peace, and spirit—has been associated in religious iconography with the Holy Ghost (as in John 1: 32). Also, St Benedict is said to have seen his dead sister's soul ascend to Heaven as a dove. By capitalizing 'dove', W suggests the bird's transcendent significance.

4 REQUIESCAT

MS and Publishing History:

W's poem was most likely written in his early Oxford years. First published in *P1*, rev. in *P2*; collected thereafter. A presentation holograph (*M*, location: Clark 2478) is extant.

W's sister Isola, who died on 23 February 1867, aged 9, was, her doctor reportedly said, 'the most gifted and lovable child' he had ever seen. W was then 'an affectionate, gentle, retiring, dreamy boy' of 12 at the Portora School. His 'lonely and inconsolable grief' sought expression in 'long and frequent visits to his sister's grave in the village cemetery' (quoted in Mason 295).

The similarity between W's poem and Thomas Hood's 'The Bridge of Sighs' has often been noted: 'Take her up tenderly | Lift her with care; | Fashion'd so slenderly, | Young, and so fair!'. Matthew Arnold's 'Requiescat' may also have been an inspiration: 'Strew on her roses, roses, | And never a spray of yew! | In quiet she reposes; | Ah, would that I did too!'.

Title. Translated: 'May She Rest'.

19–20. Echoes another brother's grief, that of Laertes, when he leaps into Ophelia's grave in *Hamlet*, V. i. 251: 'Now pile your dust upon the quick and dead'.

Postscript. W may have visited Avignon while en route to Italy in 1875 (see No. 5, 'San Miniato', and No. 6, 'By the Arno'). His Roman Catholic preoccupations during that period may have inspired the poem. W often appended the names of places to poems perhaps for effect rather than for accuracy.

5 SAN MINIATO

MS and Publishing History:

A MS (*M*, location: Hyde; printed in Mason 64), entitled 'San Miniato (June 15th)', contains versions of lines 1–4 of 'San Miniato', and lines 1–4 and 9–24 of No. 6, 'By the Arno'. W probably began writing this poem while travelling in Italy during June 1875. See Addendum.

First published in *Dublin University Magazine* 87 (March 1876), 297–8 (*D*), as 'Graffiti d'Italia: I. San Miniato (June 15)'; rev. in *P1* as two poems: 'San Miniato' (originally section one) and 'By the Arno' (originally sections two and three); 'By the Arno' was further revised in *P2*; both poems collected thereafter. See No. 6, 'By the Arno'.

Title. A reference to one of the hills overlooking Florence.

2. *holy house of God*: the 12th-century Romanesque church of San Miniato al Monte.

3. *Angel-Painter*: Fra Angelico, né Guido di Pietro (*c.*1400–55), the Florentine painter and Dominican monk, all of whose subjects were religious. After his death, he was given the name 'Angelico' ('angelic') in praise of his moral virtues.

4–6. Cf. Walter Pater's *Studies in the History of the Renaissance* (1873; rev. 1893), in the essay on Winckelmann: 'a characteristic work of the middle age, Angelico's *Coronation of the Virgin*, in the cloister of *Saint Mark's* at Florence [now in the Uffizi Gallery]. In some strange halo of the moon Jesus and the Virgin Mother are seated, clad in mystical white raiment, half shroud, half priestly linen.'

10. *mystic wife*: cf. Rossetti's 'Ave', 7: 'And wife unto the Holy Ghost . . .'.

15–16. A similar fear of exposure to the morning light is expressed in No. 118, *The Sphinx*, 159–66. The final line echoes Tennyson's *In Memoriam*, 48: 11–12, in alluding to sorrow: 'And holds it sin and shame to draw | The deepest measure from the chords'.

6 BY THE ARNO

MS and Publishing History:
See No. 5, 'San Miniato', for MS and publication data.

12. *lonely nightingale*: for the Romantics, a recurrent symbol of the poet's isolation and capacity for song, as in Keats's 'Ode to a Nightingale'.

16. *Splinter . . . moon*: an allusion to Artemis (also known as Diana), the moon-goddess and goddess of the hunt. W's line echoes Matthew Arnold's 'Mycerinus', 99: 'Splintered the silver arrows of the moon'. The image reappears in No. 18, 'Heart's Yearnings', 39.

7 ROME UNVISITED

MSS and Publishing History:

A draft of lines 45–56 (*M1*, location: Hyde; printed in Mason 115–16) appears in *More Letters* 23, suggesting revisions incorporated into subsequent versions. A working draft titled 'Graffiti d'Italia / II. Arona. July 10th 1875' (*M2*, location: Huntington HM 469) contains a note: 'The first of this series has already appeared in the *Dublin University Magazine* for March 1876, entitled *San Miniato*' (quoted in Mason 113–15). Since W seems no longer to have been in Arona on 10 July 1875, the date presumably records this draft of the poem. See Addendum.

First published in the *Month and Catholic Review* 9 (Sept. 1876), 77–8 (*C*), as 'Graffiti d'Italia / Arona. Lago Maggiore'; rev. as 'Rome Unvisited', in *P1*; further rev. *P2*; collected thereafter. The poem, reprinted in the Boston *Pilot* (23 Sept. 1876), was W's first publication in America.

On 25 June 1875, W wrote to his mother of his travels with his former Trinity College tutor in Classical studies, the Revd John Pentland Mahaffy (1839–1919), and William Goulding (1856–1925), a Cambridge University undergraduate whose father engaged Mahaffy to act as the young Goulding's companion / guide on a grand tour of the Classical world: 'I write this at Arona on the Lago Maggiore, a beautiful spot. Mahaffy and young Goulding I left at Milan and they will go on to Genoa. As I had no money I was obliged to leave them and feel very lonely' (*Letters* 10). W's poem was not completed, as the Huntington MS indicates, until 1876.

9–11. *Blessed Lady . . . Mother*: Rome (see line 13).

12. *crowns of triple gold*: tiaras worn by the popes. Cf. No. 34, 'Easter Day', 7.

20–4. *Fiesole . . . Apennines*: Fiesole, a town near Florence, is noted for its Roman ruins and its paintings by Fra Angelico at the Church of San Domenico, which W most likely visited. The mountain range of the Apennines runs the entire length of the Italian peninsula.

27. *drear Campagna's way*: 'drear' perhaps because of the marshes surrounding Rome.

28. *dome*: St Peter's Basilica, the 'wondrous Temple' in line 31.

32. *awful keys*: that is, the keys, which symbolize the authority of the Pope, inspire awe. See Christ's words to Peter, who later became the first Pope: 'And I will give unto thee the keys of the kingdom of heaven' (Matthew 16: 19).

35–6. For all solemn entries into St Peter's, the pope was customarily carried in on an armchair borne by footmen.

38. *God-anointed King*: reappears in No. 36, 'Italia', 11.

39. *silver trumpets ring*: echoed in No. 34, 'Easter Day', 1.

41. *brazen-pillared shrine*: surmounted by a canopy resting on bronze columns, the high altar of the basilica rests on the reputed burial site of St Peter the Apostle.

52. *wold*: a poetic form of 'weald', referring to a wooded region or open country.

53. *race*: cf. 1 Corinthians 9: 24: 'Know ye not that they which run in a race run all, but one receiveth the prize? So run, that ye may obtain.'

55–6. Cf. Psalm 30: 7–8: 'thou didst hide thy face, and I was troubled. I cried to thee, O Lord; and unto the Lord I made supplication.'

8 CHOIR BOY

MS: A single holograph is extant (*M*, location: Clark 2426).

Not published in W's lifetime.

This lyric poem, probably written during W's first years at Oxford, suggests, by its incomplete state, his dissatisfaction with it.

9–12. *S. Michael . . . lily*: Possibly, W has conflated St Michael with St Gabriel, both archangels. St Michael, the protector of the Church Militant, is generally depicted with a sword in hand and a dragon or serpent (the emblem for Satan) under foot, symbolizing Christendom's victory over evil. He also has an important role in the legends of the Virgin Mary, including his charge to inform her of her approaching death. The lily, however, is associated with St Gabriel, who, as God's chief messenger, is sent to inform the Virgin of the forthcoming birth of Jesus (Luke 1: 26–31). In late medieval and Renaissance depictions of the Annunciation Gabriel often holds a lily, or a vase of lilies appears between Gabriel and the Virgin, symbolizing their purity and chastity.

9 LA BELLA DONNA DELLA MIA MENTE

MS and Publishing History:

No MS is known to exist.

First published in *Kottabos* 2 (Trinity Term 1876), 268–9 (*K*),'Δηξίθυμον 'Ερωτος 'Ανθος' (The Rose of Love, And with a Rose's Thorns), from Aeschylus' *Agamemnon*, 720, which refers to Helen, a 'soul-wounding flower of love'; rev., divided into two poems (the other is No. 10, 'Chanson') in *P1*; unchanged in *P2*; collected thereafter. See Addendum.

W employs the late medieval and Renaissance poetic conventions of courtly love, depicting a knight consumed by his lady's beauty, which inspires him to noble deeds worthy of her adoration. The use of such conventions by such Pre-Raphaelite poets as William Morris, Swinburne, and Dante Gabriel Rossetti provided models for W.

Title. Translated: 'Lovely Lady of My Memory'.

17. Echoes Morris's 'Praise of My Lady', 41: 'Her full lips being made to kiss'.

21. *melilote*: a variety of clover with clusters of fragrant white or yellow flowers.

29–32. Cf. Swinburne's 'Dolores', 3–4, 7–8: 'The heavy white limbs, and the cruel | Red mouth like a venomous flower . . . | O mystic and sombre Dolores, | Our Lady of Pain . . .'.

31. *House of love*: echoes the title of Dante Gabriel Rossetti's sonnet sequence, *The House of Life* (1870), which traces the effects of love on body and spirit.

10 CHANSON

MS and Publishing History:

See No. 9, 'La Bella Donna della mia Mente', for publication data. A presentation holographic MS entitled 'Lily-Flower' (*M*, location: Texas) is extant, and collation indicates that it comes between the version of the poem in *Kottabos* and that in *P1–2*.

The title 'Lily-Flower' could have been bestowed in honour of Lillie Langtry (see headnote to No. 60, 'The New Helen').

The parenthetical asides in 'Chanson' suggest a debt to Dante Gabriel Rossetti, who used the device in 'Troy Town' and 'Sister Helen'. The poem proceeds by a series of contrasts between symbols of felicity and symbols of death.

2. Echoes Swinburne's 'The Triumph of Time', 176: 'gifts are goodly'.

5. *House of Ivory* | *Roses are white*: an allusion to the Virgin Mary, referred to in the 'Litany of Loreto' as a 'Tower of Ivory' and associated with the white rose, symbols of her beauty and purity.

11 'SEE! THE GOLD SUN HAS RISEN'

MS: A MS (*M*, location: Clark 2426) is extant.

Not published in W's lifetime.

W uses the ballad stanza and traditional rhyme scheme (*abab*) to express romantic love.

20. *Turning my blood to wine*: the reverse of the sacrament of the Mass (celebrating the Passion of Christ), W's metaphor is used to suggest the transforming power of human passion.

12 'SWEET I WENT OUT IN THE NIGHT'

MS: A MS is extant (*M*, location: Clark 2426).

Not published in W's lifetime.

Title. The epigraph, from Elizabeth Barrett Browning's *Aurora Leigh*, 5: 434–47, is, in fact, a paraphrase. In a letter to an Oxford friend, W wrote of *Aurora Leigh*: 'It is one of those books that, written straight from the heart—and from such a large heart too—never weary one: because they are sincere. We tire of art but not of nature after all our aesthetic training. I look upon it as much the greatest work in our literature' (*Letters* 21).

13 'SHE STOLE BEHIND HIM WHERE HE LAY'

MSS: Four extant leaves contain jottings (location: Clark 2498): *M1* contains lines 29–32 at the top, lines 1–8 at the bottom; *M2*, lines 1–20; *M3*, lines 21–8; and *M4*, lines 27–8.

Not published in W's lifetime.

6. *Colin . . . clout*: A name traditionally used for rustics, as in John Skelton's *Collyn Clout* (1521) and Edmund Spenser's *Colin Clouts come home againe* (1595).

14 THE DOLE OF THE KING'S DAUGHTER

MS and Publishing History:

An untitled MS (*M1*, location: Berg; printed in Mason 66), consists of lines 17–32. First published in *Dublin University Magazine* 87 (June 1876), 682–3 (*D*). A complete MS of the poem (*M2*, location: Buffalo) was the text from which *P1–2* were set. *P1–2* added '(Breton)' as a subtitle; collected thereafter. See Addendum.

W's poem is modelled in tone, style, and even title after Swinburne's 'The King's Daughter'.

Title. Dole is an archaic word for *grief.* By adopting '(Breton)' as a subtitle to suggest the presumed origin of the tale, W follows Swinburne in his 'May Janet (Breton)'. W's original subtitle in *D* was '(For a Painting.)'.

1. *Seven stars*: cf. Dante Gabriel Rossetti's 'The Blessed Damozel', 6: 'And the stars in her hair were seven'.

7. Cf. Swinburne's 'The King's Daughter', 43–4: 'A grass girdle for all the rest, | A girdle of arms for the king's daughter'; and Morris's 'The Eve of Crécy', 2–3: 'gold where the hems of her kirtle meet, | And a golden girdle round my sweet'.

15 LOVE SONG

MSS: Two MSS are extant (location: Clark 2464 and 2489): *M1* entitled 'Love Song', consisting of two leaves with lines 1–21 and 27–8; and *M2*, untitled, consisting of one sheet with verses on both sides consisting of lines 17–44. The postscript indicates that the poem was written during W's Oxford years.

Not published in W's lifetime.

In this Swinburnian poem, W's rhyme scheme follows Swinburne's 'Dolores' in *Poems and Ballads*—that is, an eight-line stanza rhyming *ababcdcd*.

15–16. *cumber*: presumably, the verb form should be 'cumbers' (meaning 'distresses') to agree with 'sorrow'. W suggests that sorrow is of little significance when sensual pleasures predominate.

17. *the idlest singer*: the phrase is probably drawn from Morris's 'Apology' to *The Earthly Paradise*, 7: 'The idle singer of an empty day'.

34. *red flag . . . piled-up street*: echoed in No. 79, 'Libertatis Sacra Fames', 10.

16 ΑΙΛΙΝΟΝ, ΑΙΛΙΝΟΝ ΕΙΠΕ, ΤΟ ΔΕΥ ΝΙΚΑΤΩ

MS and Publishing History:

A MS (*M*, location: Dartmouth) exists entitled 'Tristitiae' (printed in Mason 67). First published in *Dublin University Magazine* 88 (Sept. 1876), 291 (*D*); rev. in William MacIlwaine, ed., *Lyra Hibernica Sacra* (Belfast: M'Caw, Stevenson and Orr; London: Geo. Bell & Sons; and Dublin: Hodges, Foster, & Figgis, 1878), 324 (*L*), as 'O well for Him' (MacIlwaine customarily gave titles to poems from their first lines); repr. in *Poems* (1908); the original title, 'Tristitiae', was used in

Methuen's 12th edition in April 1913, but later reprintings of the poem have restored the present title. See Addendum.

Title. Taken from Aeschylus' *Agamemnon*, 121: 'Sing the song of woe, the song of woe, but may the good prevail'. In a letter to his Oxford friend William Ward (1854–1932) on 6 August 1876, W referred to the epigraph / title of his poem as 'that great chaunt' (*Letters* 22). In another letter to Ward, he describes this poem and No. 17, 'The True Knowledge', as 'brief and Tennysonian'.

1. Cf. Horace, *Epodes*, 2: 1: 'Happy the man who far away from business cares . . .'. Also, cf. Tennyson's 'Break, Break, Break', 5 and 7: 'O well for the fisherman's boy . . .' and 'O well for the sailor lad . . .'.

11–12. Cf. Sarah Adams's hymn 'Nearer, my God, to Thee': 'Out of my stony griefs, | *Bethel* I'll raise: | So by my woes to be | Nearer, my God, to thee—'. W's poem and Adams's hymn allude to Jacob at Beth-el ('the house of God'), where 'he dreamed, and behold a ladder set up on the earth, and the top of it reached to heaven: and behold the angels of God ascending and descending on it' (Genesis 28: 12).

17 THE TRUE KNOWLEDGE

MS and Publishing History:
No MS is known to exist. See Addendum.

First published in the *Irish Monthly* 4 (Sept. 1876), 594 (*I*); rev. in William MacIlwaine, ed., *Lyra Hibernica Sacra*, 325 (*L*) as 'Unto one Dead' (see No. 16 for publishers and for MacIlwaine's customary practice regarding titles; MacIlwaine also omitted the Greek epigraph and the postscript from the *Irish Monthly* version, both of which have been restored); repr. in *Poems* (1908); collected thereafter.

Epigraph. From a fragment of Euripides' play *Hypsipyle*, 6: 'like the grassy leas | In the morning, Life is mown; and this man is, | And that man is not' (G. Murray, *Euripides* (1902), 326).

1. *Thou*: possibly an invocation to Sir William Wilde, W's father, who had died on 19 April 1876: see the headnote to No. 23, 'Lotus Leaves'.

1–2. *I seek . . . to till or sow*: cf. Micah 6: 15: 'Thou shalt sow, but thou shalt not reap'.

4. *falling tears*: cf. Psalm 126: 5: 'They that sow in tears shall reap in joy'.

6. Cf. Psalm 38: 10: 'my strength faileth me: as for the light of mine eyes, it also is gone from me'.

7–8. In the biblical Jewish temple in Jerusalem, a veil barred entrance into the Holy of Holies, the inner sanctuary and dwelling place of God, where only the High Priest—on the Day of Atonement—was permitted access to the Ark of the Covenant, into which Moses had placed the tablets of the law given to him by God on Mount Sinai. Cf. Tennyson's *In Memoriam*, 56: 28: 'What hope of answer, or redress? | Behind the veil, behind the veil'. For variations on the veil image, see No. 23, 'Lotus Leaves', 47–8; No. 32, 'The Grave of Keats', 2; and No. 48, *Ravenna*, 64.

18 HEART'S YEARNINGS

MSS: A version of lines 1–5 is in W's Trinity College, Dublin, notebook dating from 1873 (*M1*, location: Clark 2449); a facsimile of a signed MS (*M2*) was printed in a Sotheby Parke-Bernet catalogue listing items for sale from the library of Gordon A. Block, Jr., on 29 January 1974.

Not published in W's lifetime.

The conventional lover's lament, which informs this poem, is also central to others written in 1876, when W was at Oxford: see, for example, No. 3, 'From Spring Days to Winter'; No. 9, 'La Bella Donna della mia Mente'; and No. 10, 'Chanson'.

Epigraph. Translated: 'Love of the Impossible', which Wilde may have derived from the Greek proverb, 'To desire impossible things is a disease of the soul', attributed to Bias, one of the Seven Sages, by Diogenes Laertius in his *Lives of the Eminent Philosophers* (I. v. 86). The Greek phrase in the epigraph also appears with the French equivalent in Part I of 'The Critic as Artist': 'that *Amour de l'Impossible*, which falls like a madness on many who think they live securely and out of reach of harm, so that they sicken suddenly with the poison of unlimited desire, and in the infinite pursuit of what they may not obtain, grow faint and swoon or stumble'. In chapter 7 of *The Picture of Dorian Gray*, the idea reappears: Dorian (like Théophile Gautier's D'Albert in *Mademoiselle de Maupin*) is stirred by the 'passion for impossible things'. See, also, *Letters* 185. Wilde probably derived the juxtaposition of the Greek and French phrases for 'Love of the impossible' from John Addington Symonds's *Studies of the Greek Poets* (1873), 292–3.

6. *out of tune*: a traditional metaphor of psychological or social disharmony, as in Ophelia's lament over Hamlet's apparent madness in *Hamlet*, III. i. 159: 'Like sweet bells jangled, out of tune and harsh'. For other appearances of the phrase, see No. 51, 'The Burden of Itys', 38; No. 71, 'Silentium Amoris', 6; and No. 87, 'Impressions. I. Les Silhouettes', 2 and note.

39. Echoes No. 6, 'By the Arno', 16.

19 THE LITTLE SHIP

MS: A MS is extant (*M*, location: Clark 2463), probably written during W's Oxford years.

Not published in W's lifetime.

26. K. C. B.: Knight Commander of the Bath (a high order of British knighthood, so called from the purifying bath which knights took before they were installed).

20 ΘPHNΩIΔIA

MS: A MS (*M*, location: Hyde, printed in Mason 94), contains lines 52–67.

First published in *Kottabos* 2 (Michaelmas Term 1876), 298–300 (*K*); repr. in *Poems* (1908); collected thereafter. See Addendum.

Achilles' wrath, as depicted in the *Iliad*, is directed against Agamemnon, who had taken the Trojan captive Briseis, Achilles' concubine, as his own. As a result, dishonoured Achilles, brooding in his tent, had refused to join the Greeks in their struggle against the Trojans.

Title. Translated: 'Lamentation'—a choral song translated from Euripides' *Hecuba*, 444–83, with the terms 'strophe' and 'antistrophe' in Greek orthography (see headnote to No. 1, 'Ye Shall be Gods').

8. *Dorian strand*: the Peloponnese in southern Greece, the realm of Agamemnon and his younger brother Menelaus, whose wife, Helen, was carried off by Paris, thus bringing about the Trojan War.

10. *Apidanus*: a river of Thessaly in northern Greece.

12. *Phthian sand*: Achilles' home in Thessaly.

17. *distant shore*: Delos (see lines 23–4), the central island of the Kyklades archipelago (see line 26), located in the Aegean east of Greece. There Leto gave birth to Apollo and Artemis (see lines 20 ff.).

46. *Time*: Kronos (or Cronus), a member of the first divine generation of the Titans, whose rule the Olympians, led by Zeus, eventually overthrew. Because of his name, which approximates in sound to the Greek word for 'time', Kronos is sometimes referred to as its personification.

59. *Tall Troy is down*: echoes the refrain of Dante Gabriel Rossetti's 'Troy Town': '(*O Troy's down, | Tall Troy's on fire!*)'.

21 LOTUS LAND

MS and Publishing History:
   One MS is extant (*M*, location: Berg). W sent this sonnet and an early version of another, No. 22, 'Desespoir', to Robert Yelverton Tyrrell, Fellow of Trinity College, Dublin, and editor of *Kottabos*, but neither appeared there. Since W signed it 'O. F. O'F. W. W.'—the 'F.' standing for 'Fingal', which he began using around July 1876 and which he dropped after December—it is likely that both poems were written in that year (see *Letters* 15, 30 n.).
   First published in Bobby Fong, 'Oscar Wilde: Five Fugitive Poems', *ELT* 22: 1 (1979), 7–8.

9–10. Echoes Book 9 of Homer's *Odyssey* and Tennyson's 'The Lotus-Eaters', both of which depict the wish for forgetfulness on the part of the eaters of the lotus tree: 'In the hollow Lotos-land to live and lie reclined | On the hills like gods together, careless of mankind' ('The Lotus-Eaters', 154–5).

11. Cf. No. 22, 'Desespoir', 1.

13. *War in Europe*: since July 1875, Serbia had supported the insurrection against the Turkish occupation of Herzegovina and Bosnia. On 30 June 1876, Serbia formally declared war on Turkey, and on 2 July, Montenegro joined Serbia as an ally. During this time, the Bulgarians had also been rebelling against severe Turkish rule: see No. 33, 'Sonnet on the Massacre of the Christians in Bulgaria'.

Postscript. Illaunroe (in Galway) was W's fishing lodge on land jutting into Lough Fee. His father, who had bought the lodge in 1853, left it to him and his half-brother, Dr Henry Wilson, in his will.

22 DESESPOIR

MSS: Mason transcribed the text of this poem from a MS sold at the Sotheby auction on 11 April 1927. The transcription is written in his interleaved personal copy of the *Bibliography of Oscar Wilde* (*M1*, location: Clark), opposite p. 91, its title 'Tacitis senescimus annis' (from Ovid's *Fasti*, 6: 771: 'we grow old with silent lapse of years'). A later autograph MS, entitled 'Desespoir', has also survived (*M2*, location: Texas). See the headnote to No. 21, 'Lotus Land', which was sent with *M1* to the editor of *Kottabos*.

Not published in W's lifetime.

In the octave of this sonnet, W contrasts the regenerative capacity of nature with the dead memories of human experience in the sestet.

Title. Translated: 'Despair'. W's MS does not have an accent mark over the first 'e' in the title.

2. *narciss*: W uses the short form of 'narcissus' (see *OED*) to retain the iambic pentameter line.

4. *blow*: bloom.

6–8. Echoed in No. 58, 'Humanitad', 32–3.

8. Echoed in No. 48, *Ravenna*, 308.

23 LOTUS LEAVES

MSS and Publishing History:

An untitled MS (*M1*, location: Clark 2426) is a working draft with versions of lines 1–12, 29–32, 21–4, 33–6, and 13–16 in that order (printed in Mason 83–4). One line, 'Alas! Alas! To me the day . . .', which follows what is now line 36, appears to be an aborted beginning to a new stanza.

First published in five parts in the *Irish Monthly* 5 (Feb. 1877), 133–5 (*I*); portions revised for *P1*, appearing as 'Impressions. II. La Fuite de la Lune' and 'Impression. Le Réveillon' (see Nos. 88 and 89).

A MS (*M2*, location: Dartmouth) exists, entitled 'Selene', consisting of three quatrains that represent a later reworking of part one of 'Lotus Leaves' (printed in Mason 85–6).

In admiration of Tennyson's *In Memoriam*, W used its stanzaic structure (a quatrain with rhyming lines *abba* in iambic tetrameter) in much of his early verse. 'Lotus Leaves' uses not only this stanzaic form but also Tennyson's elegiac theme—the loss of a beloved male figure. Though unnamed, the figure is probably W's father, Sir William, who had died on 19 April 1876 (see No. 17, 'The True Knowledge', which also touches on his father's death). W's sense of loss is expressed in a letter to his Oxford friend William Ward in early July of that year: 'I think that God has dealt very hardly with us. It has robbed me of any real pleasure in my First [at Oxford], and I have not sufficient faith in Providence to believe it is all for the best—I know it is not. I feel an awful dread of going home to our old house, with everything filled with memories' (*Letters* 15–16). The Greek epigraph and footnote to line 76 are persuasive evidence of W's mourning over his father's death.

Epigraph. From Homer's *Odyssey*, 4: 195–8, specifically Peisistratus' speech as

Odysseus, feared dead, is lamented by his son Telemachus and by Menelaus and Helen: 'I count it indeed no blame to weep for any mortal who has died and met his fate. Yea, this is the only due we pay to miserable mortals, to cut the hair and let a tear fall from the cheeks.'

15. *Aurora*: the Latin name for the personification of the dawn, also known in Greek myth as Eos, one of the Titans and sister of Helios (Sun) and Selene (Moon)—the latter goddess is the subject of one of W's MSS described above. Aurora opened, with her rosy fingers, the gates of heaven to the chariot of the Sun.

17–18. Echoes No. 6, 'By the Arno', 15–6 (see also note). In 'Lotus Leaves', however, the arrows are the dawn's, not the moon's.

19–20. *yellow light . . . tower and hall*: cf. Tennyson's *In Memoriam*, 8: 5–6: 'all the magic light | Dies off at once from bower and hall . . .'.

21–4. *wold . . . gold*: cf. Tennyson's *In Memoriam*, 11: 5–8: 'Calm and deep peace on this high wold . . . | That twinkle into green and gold'.

34. *waiting for the dawn*: refers to the dead waiting for the dawning of the day of Resurrection.

35. *orbèd maiden*: cf. Shelley's 'The Cloud', 45–6: 'That orbèd maiden with fire laden . . .'.

47–8. *veil of blue*: echoed in No. 32, 'The Grave of Keats', 2; also No. 17, 'The True Knowledge', 7–8 (see also note).

54–5. *hawthorn-blossoms . . . yew*: symbols of rebirth and death respectively.

68. *wild wind's play*: in his verse and prose, W often puns on his own name, most obviously in *The Picture of Dorian Gray*, in which 'wild', 'wilder', and 'wildly' appear 34 times in contexts that suggest his autobiographical signature.

71. *half divine*: cf. Tennyson's *In Memoriam*, 14: 10, where the poet's dead friend, the poet Arthur Hallam, is also so described.

75. *none shall gather fruit*: echoed in No. 42, 'Wasted Days', 14. Derived from the final lines of Meleager's last speech in Swinburne's *Atalanta in Calydon*: 'And let me go; for the night gathers me, | And in the night shall no man gather fruit'.

76. *sailing on the barren sea*: the Greek phrase referred to in W's footnote is from Homer's *Odyssey*, 2: 369–70, in which Eurycleia begs Telemachus not to go in search of his father, who must be dead: 'Nay abide here in charge of what is thine; thou hast no need to suffer ills and go a wanderer over the unresting sea'.

24 'O LOVED ONE LYING FAR AWAY'

MS: One untitled MS is extant (*M*, location: Yale), which appeared in facsimile in Donald G. Wing, 'The Katherine S. Dreier Collection of Oscar Wilde', *Yale University Library Gazette* 28 (Oct. 1953), 83.

Not published in W's lifetime.

The elegiac theme, the *In Memoriam* stanza (see headnote to No. 23, 'Lotus Leaves'), and an echo in lines 3–4 from No. 4, 'Requiescat', 13–4, suggest that this lyric poem was also written soon after the death of W's father in 1876.

11–12. *glory round thy head*: the gloria, sometimes called an 'aureole' or 'nimbus', is usually depicted as a gold disk or radiant circle of light—that is, a halo surrounding the head of a god (pagan or Christian) or a saint. It is usually described as 'cloud-like light', hence W's wish that it has kept the loved one's 'eyes from seeing clear'.

18–19. Cf. No. 90, 'Helas!', 1–2.

25 A FRAGMENT FROM THE AGAMEMNON OF AESCHYLOS

MS and Publishing History:
No MS is known to exist.

First published in *Kottabos* 2 (Hilary Term 1877), 320–2 (*K*); repr. in *Poems* (1908). The plot summary in square brackets is W's. See Addendum.

Enamoured of Kasandra (as W spells her name, following Greek orthography), Apollo had provided her with the powers of prophecy. When she resisted his overtures, however, he cursed her powers, rendering her prophecies unbelievable. In Aeschylus's *Agamemnon*, Kasandra (a captured Trojan princess and Agamemnon's concubine) foresees the murder of Agamemnon and herself at the hands of the enraged Klytaemnestra, whose daughter, Iphigenia, had been sacrificed by her husband to enable the Greek fleet to sail to Troy. In W's translation, the Chorus, which speaks first, is designated in Greek orthography.

5–8. For the myth involving the nightingale, see the title note to No. 51, 'The Burden of Itys'.

23. *bitter bridegroom*: Paris—see No. 20, 'Θρηνῳδία', note to line 8.

25. *Skamander*: a river near Troy.

29. *dark land*: the Greek Underworld, ruled over by Hades, where flow the River Acheron (see line 32)—which souls have to cross in order to reach the kingdom of Hades—and its tributary Kokutos (see line 31), also spelled 'Cocytus', the 'River of Groans', which runs parallel to the River Styx.

45. *Sire*: Priam, king of Troy and father of Kasandra.

50–1. See No. 20, 'θρηνῳδια', note to line 59.

26 A VISION

MS and Publishing History:
First published in *Kottabos* 2 (Hilary Term 1877), 331 (*K*), as 'A Night Vision'; rev. in *P1* as 'A Vision'; unchanged in *P2*; collected thereafter. See Addendum.

Mason 96 prints a MS (*M*) of this sonnet that, on the basis of changes in the text, clearly postdates *K*.

W's inspiration for this 'vision' is Dante's *Divine Comedy*, as line 11 indicates, but Elizabeth Barrett Browning's 'A Vision of Poets', in which Aeschylus, Sophocles, and Euripides also appear, probably provided additional inspiration.

1–2. Aeschylus and Sophocles were frequent victors at the annual Dionysian dramatic competitions, but 'One that stood alone', Euripides, whose plays provocatively criticized contemporary institutions, seldom won the crown of laurel wreaths.

4–5. Euripides scoffed at attempts to placate the gods and was reportedly prosecuted for impiety.

8. *broken stone*: according to legend, Euripides' cenotaph was struck by lightning, a sign of the gods' displeasure.

11. *Beatricé*: Dante's inspiration. In the *Kottabos* version, Beatrice is not named: 'Then she who lay beside me: 'Who are these?' | And I made answer . . .'.

27 SONNET ON APPROACHING ITALY

MS and Publishing History:
   No MS is known to exist.
   First published in the *Irish Monthly* 5 (June 1877), 415 (*I*), as 'Salve Saturnia Tellus' (Virgil's phrase in his *Georgics*, 2: 173: 'Hail . . . Land of Saturn'); rev. in *Biograph and Review* 4 (Aug. 1880), 135 (*B*), as 'Sonnet Written at Turin'; further rev. in *P1* and *P2* with the present title; collected thereafter.
   In late March 1877, W departed for Rome in the hope of celebrating Easter in the Holy City. He had written to his Oxford friend Reginald Harding (1857–1932): 'This is an era in my life, a crisis. I wish I could look into the seeds of time and see what is coming' (*Letters* 34). On this journey, he composed a series of occasional sonnets, of which 'Sonnet on Approaching Italy' was presumably the first, written either at Genoa, according to the postscript to the 1877 version, or at Turin, according to subsequent versions. W had travelled through Turin, then Genoa, within days of entering Italy. See Addendum.

1–5. Cf. Byron's *Childe Harold's Pilgrimage*, Canto 4 and stanzas 42–96.

3. *mountain's heart*: crossing the Alps by train from France to Italy, W would have passed through the Mount Cenis Tunnel, built in 1871.

5. *great prize had earned*: see No. 7, 'Rome Unvisited', note to line 53.

7–8. Lines used later in No. 48, *Ravenna*, 28–9.

9. Cf. No. 2, 'Chorus of Cloud-Maidens', 5.

10. *every twining spray*: also used in No. 48, *Ravenna*, 158.

13. Pope Pius IX refused to recognize the united kingdom of Italy, which has wrested Rome away from ecclesiastical control in 1871. As a result, he considered himself 'imprisoned' in the Vatican. See No. 31, 'Urbs Sacra Æterna', 14.

28 SONNET WRITTEN IN HOLY WEEK AT GENOA

MS and Publishing History:
   No MS is known to exist.
   First published in the Dublin *Illustrated Monitor: A Monthly Magazine of Catholic Literature* 4 (July 1877), 186 (*U*), as 'Sonnet, Written During Holy Week'; rev. in *P1* and *P2* with current title; collected thereafter. See Addendum.

Title. An indication that W was in Genoa during the last week of March in 1877 since Easter fell on 1 April in that year. He remembered the port as 'a beautiful city of palaces over the sea' (*Letters* 35).

1. *Scoglietto's far retreat*: presumably a locale near Genoa. There is an islet of that name just outside Elba's Portoferraio bay, but no evidence exists that W visited the site of Napoleon's first exile.

2–3. Echoes Andrew Marvell's 'Bermudas', 17–18: 'He hangs in shades the Orange bright, | Like golden Lamps in a green Night'. W used the phrase 'golden lamps in a green night' in a Grosvenor Gallery review that appeared in the *Dublin University Magazine* (July 1877) in a discussion of Spencer Stanhope's painting *Eve Tempted*. The association of 'bright lamps' with ripening fruit also occurs in No. 48, *Ravenna*, 21–2.

4–6. Lines also used in No. 48, *Ravenna*, 155–7.

12. *dear Hellenic hours*: a revision in *Poems* (1881). In the *Illustrated Monitor* version, W lamented the 'sweet and honied hours' since he had not yet been to Greece at that point.

29 IMPRESSION DE VOYAGE

MS and Publishing History:

First published in the Boston *Pilot* 40 (28 July 1877), 4 (*T*), as 'Hellas! Hellas!'; rev. in *Waifs and Strays* 1 (March 1880), 77 (*W*), with the present title.

A single MS of this sonnet is extant (*M*, location: Berg), from which the revised text for *P1* was set; further rev. in *P2*; collected thereafter. See Addendum.

On his tour of the Continent in March 1877 (see headnote to No. 27, 'Sonnet on Approaching Italy'), W suddenly changed his plans to continue to Rome from Genoa. On 2 April 1877, he wrote from Corfu to Reginald Harding: 'I never went to Rome at all! What a changeable fellow you must think me, but Mahaffy my old tutor [see headnote to No. 7, 'Rome Unvisited'] carried me off to Greece with him to see Mykenae and Athens. I am awfully ashamed of myself but I could not help it and will take Rome on my way back. We [including George Macmillan (1855–1936), later a partner in the publishing firm, and William Goulding: see headnote to No. 7, 'Rome Unvisited'] went to Genoa, then to Ravenna and left Brindisi last night, catching sight of Greece at 5. 30 this morning. We go tomorrow to Zante and land near Olympia and then ride through Arcadia to Mykenae' (*Letters* 34–5).

6. *Zakynthos*: Zante, one of the Ionian islands.

7. *Ithaca*: Odysseus' Ionian island home. Mt. Lycaon in Arcadia is associated with the king, Lycaon, who, having served human flesh to Zeus, was turned into a wolf for his offence.

8. *Arcady*: also known as Arcadia, the central area of the Peloponnese, the inhabitants of which regarded themselves as the most ancient people of Greece. The region was treated by poets as a pastoral paradise. Pan and Hermes (the messenger god known to the Romans as Mercury) are particularly associated with Arcadia.

Postscript. W's party had sailed past the Ionian islands and landed on the west coast of the Peloponnesian peninsula at Katakolo, where athletes bound for the Olympic Games once disembarked.

30 THE THEATRE AT ARGOS

MS and Publishing History:
First published in the Boston *Pilot* 40 (21 July 1877), 4 (*T*). See Addendum.

A transcription of a MS, now unaccounted for, appears in Mason's interleaved personal copy of his *Bibliography of Oscar Wilde* (*M*, location: Clark), opposite p. 177.

For a discussion of emendations to the poem, see Bobby Fong, 'Oscar Wilde: Five Fugitive Poems', *ELT* 22: 1 (1979), 8–9.

After arriving in Greece (see headnote to No. 29, 'Impression de Voyage'), W and his travelling companions proceeded by horseback across the Peloponnese to Argos, the ancient city that for centuries rivalled Sparta, Athens, and Corinth, until Sparta captured it around 494 BC.

7. *Danae*: the daughter of Acrisius, king of Argos, who imprisoned her in an underground chamber because of a prophecy that she would bear a son who would kill him. Zeus, however, visited the girl in a shower of gold and impregnated her. Their offspring was Perseus, who later decapitated Medusa the Gorgon, whose head was entwined with snakes and whose eyes could turn one to stone.

14. W still had his mind on Rome: see No. 27, 'Sonnet on Approaching Italy', 12–14.

31 URBS SACRA ÆTERNA

MS and Publishing History:
No MS is known to exist. See Addendum.

First published in the Dublin *Illustrated Monitor: A Monthly Magazine of Catholic Literature* 4 (June 1877), 130 (*U*); rev. in *P1* and *P2*; collected thereafter.

The structure of the octave contains rhyming words—'Queen', 'seen', 'green'—later used in No. 36, 'Italia'.

Title. Translated: 'Sacred and Eternal City'. As intended, W returned to Italy from Athens in mid-April 1877 and visited Rome (see headnote to No. 29, 'Impression de Voyage').

2. *sword republican*: during the period of the Republic (509–mid-first century BC), the Romans came to dominate the entire Mediterranean region.

5. *the bearded Goth*: in AD 410, the Visigoths (a division of the Goths, or Germanic tribes) sacked Rome, exposing a fatal weakness of the empire.

7. *discrowned by man*: also used in No. 48, *Ravenna*, 189.

8. *The hated flag*: of united Italy. See No. 27, 'Sonnet on Approaching Italy', note to line 13.

10. *eagles . . . double sun*: the first allusion is to the standard borne by the Roman legions; the second to Cicero's *De Natura Deorum*, II. v. 14: 'the doubling of the sun, which my father told me had happened in the consulship of Tuditanus and Aquilius'. The consuls served together in 129 BC, when the Republic was at its zenith. For Cicero, however, the celestial sign portended the domestic troubles that soon followed.

11. *shuddered at thy rod*: the fasces were a 'bundle of rods' bound together by red thongs and carried before important Roman magistrates by lictors, or attendants, to symbolize their power.

14. See No. 27, 'Sonnet on Approaching Italy', note to line 13.

Postscript. Monte Mario is in Vatican City.

32 THE GRAVE OF KEATS

MS and Publishing History:

First published in the *Irish Monthly* 5 (July 1877), 478 (*I*), as 'Heu Miserande Puer' (from Virgil's *Aeneid*, 6: 882, translated: 'Ah, child of pity . . .'), the sonnet concluding W's article titled 'The Tomb of Keats'. See Addendum.

A MS entitled 'Keats' Grave' (*M1*, location: Harvard), included with a letter written in mid-June 1877, to Richard Monckton Milnes, Lord Houghton (1809–85), is printed in *Letters* 41–2. The poem was subsequently revised and published in the *Burlington: A High-Class Monthly Magazine* (in Jan. 1882, a new subtitle was added: *A New Aesthetic Magazine*) 1 (Jan. 1881), 35 (*R*), with the present title.

A partially illegible facsimile of a MS (*M2*) in the Anderson Galleries catalogue of the John B. Stetson sale (23 April 1920, p. 43) had previously been transcribed in Mason 11; a transcription was printed in the Parke-Bernet Galleries catalogue of the A. Edward Newton Collection sale (14–16 May 1951, p. 173). According to Mason, this was the MS from which *Poems* was set. Further revised in *P1*; unchanged in *P2*; collected thereafter.

A facsimile from the American Art Association–Anderson Galleries catalogue (13–14 Nov. 1935, p. 252) was the autograph copy of the poem included with W's letter (*M3*), written on 21 March 1882, from Omaha, Nebraska, to Emma Speed (1823–83), daughter of George Keats, the poet's younger brother (see *Letters* 108–9).

In his *Irish Monthly* article, W used the characteristic metaphors associated with the Religion of Art—which used religious imagery for aesthetic effects—in writing of his visit to the Protestant Cemetery in Rome in mid-April 1877:

As I stood beside the mean grave of this divine boy, I thought of him as of a Priest of Beauty slain before his time; and the vision of Guido's St. Sebastian came before my eyes as I saw him at Genoa, a lovely brown boy, with crisp, clustering hair and red lips, bound by his evil enemies to a tree, and though pierced by arrows, raising his eyes with divine, impassioned gaze towards the Eternal Beauty of the opening heavens.

The painting of St Sebastian alluded to by Wilde is by the early Italian Baroque painter Guido Reni (1575–1642), noted for his religious and mythological subjects. The martyred St Sebastian (*c*. AD 3), who, according to tradition, was an officer in the Praetorian guards and a favourite of the Emperor Diocletian, was killed when he was discovered to be a Christian. From the late 19th century, Sebastian was the chosen saint of homosexuals; W adopted the name after his release from prison.

1. *world's injustice . . . pain*: in his letter to Lord Houghton, W—echoing the means by which St Sebastian was martyred—comments that Keats was 'killed by

the arrows of a lying and unjust tongue' (*Letters* 41). Byron had attributed the poet's early death to two articles that had unfairly attacked him and his work.

2. *veil of blue*: the phrase had been used in No. 23, 'Lotus Leaves', 47, and re-appears in No. 48, *Ravenna*, 64.

3. This line later appears in No. 48, *Ravenna*, 63, and is partially echoed in No. 119, *The Ballad of Reading Gaol*, 146. It is derived from Byron's 'To Thyrza', 42: 'When love and life alike were new!'

4. *youngest of the Martyrs*: Keats died at the age of 25.

6. The cypress and yew trees are traditional emblems of death, but since they are evergreens they also symbolize eternal life. As W suggests, Keats's grave was indeed in the open.

7. *violets weeping*: in his essay 'The Tomb of Keats', W writes: 'when I saw the violets and the daisies and the poppies that overgrow the tomb, I remembered how the dead poet had once told his friend that he thought the "intensest pleasure he had received in life was in watching the growth of flowers", and how another time, after lying a while quite still, he murmured in some strange prescience of early death, "I feel the flowers growing over me".'

10. *Mitylene*: chief city of Lesbos, which in 6 BC boasted Sappho and Alcaeus known for their poetry of intense personal feeling.

11. *poet-painter . . . English Land*: see No. 5, 'San Miniato', note to line 3. When the editor of the *Irish Monthly*, the Revd Matthew Russell (1834–1912), objected to 'our English Land', W wrote in mid-June 1877: 'It is a noble privilege to count one-self of the same race as Keats or Shakespeare. However I have changed it. I would not shock the feelings of your readers for anything' (*Letters* 40). W changed 'our' to 'the' for the *Irish Monthly* but restored 'our' in all subsequent versions.

12. Keats, according to Lord Houghton's 1848 biography (2: 91), had requested that his epitaph simply read 'Here lies one whose name was writ in water'—from Shakespeare's *Henry VIII*, IV. ii. 45–6: 'Men's evil manners live in brass, their virtues | We write in water'.

13. Echoes Thomas Moore's 'Oh! Breathe Not His Name', 7–8: 'And the tear that we shed, though in secret it rolls, | Shall long keep his memory green in our souls'.

14. Cf. Keats's 'Isabella; or, The Pot of Basil', 425–6, where the woman hides her murdered lover's head in a pot of basil and 'ever fed it with thin tears, | Whence thick and green and beautiful it grew'.

33 SONNET ON THE MASSACRE OF THE CHRISTIANS IN BULGARIA

MS and Publishing History:

A MS (*M*, location: BL Add. MS 44454), titled 'On the Recent Massacres of the Christians in Bulgaria', is extant.

First published in *P1*; rev. in *P2*; collected thereafter.

The massacres alluded to occurred in May 1876, part of a series of Turkish atro-cities that inflamed the Balkans (see No. 21, 'Lotus Land', note to line 13). The rebels, principally Slavs who sought independence from Turkish rule, inspired widespread sympathy, resulting in Russia's intervention. The former Prime Minister W. E. Gladstone wrote two pamphlets on the Eastern question—*The Bulgarian Horrors and the Question of the East* (1876) and *Lessons in Massacre* (1877)—which were instrumental in uniting British opinion against the Turks.

When W returned from Italy around 28 April 1877, a month late for Trinity Term, he was promptly 'sent down' (that is, 'rusticated'), during which time he apparently revised the sonnets he had written on his tour, composed others, and submitted a number of poems to editors and prominent men of the day. In mid-May 1877, W sent his 'Massacre' sonnet to Gladstone, accompanied by the following note: 'Your noble and impassioned protests, both written and spoken, against the massacres of the Christians in Bulgaria have so roused my heart that I venture to send you a sonnet which I have written on the subject' (*Letters* 37). However much Gladstone's protests had inspired W, the sonnet itself was obviously modelled after Milton's 'On the Late Massacre in Piedmont'.

1–2. *thy bones | Still straitened*: that is, still confined in the sepulchre.

3–4. *thy Rising only dreamed by Her*: in a subsequent letter to Gladstone, W wrote that 'the allusion is of course to *Mary Magdalen* being the first to see our Lord after his Resurrection, and bringing the news to the Disciples' (*Letters* 38). Also, cf. Luke 7: 47: 'Her sins, which are many, are forgiven; for she loved much'.

5–8. Cf. Milton's Sonnet XVIII: 'On the Late Massacre in Piedmont', 5–8:

> in thy book record their groans
> Who were thy Sheep and in their ancient Fold
> Slain by the bloody *Piedmontese* that roll'd
> Mother with Infant down the Rocks.

9. *incestuous gloom*: gloom begetting gloom.

11. *Crescent moon*: the crescent moon and star, ancient Byzantine symbols, were adopted by the Ottoman Turks after they captured Constantinople in 1453.

12. *didst burst the tomb*: that is, rose from the dead.

13. Cf. Matthew 27: 40, where the onlookers at the Crucifixion cry out: 'If thou be the Son of God, come down from the cross'. Also, cf. No. 38, 'E Tenebris', 1.

34 EASTER DAY

MSS and Publishing History:

Two MSS are extant (*M1*, location: BL Add MS 44454; and *M2*, location: Clark 2570a).

First published *Waifs and Strays: A Terminal Magazine of Oxford Poetry* 1 (June 1879), 2 (*W*); rev. in *P1*; unchanged in *P2*; collected thereafter.

W sent a version of this sonnet to Gladstone in mid-May 1877, soon after the statesman had received W's draft of 'On the Recent Massacres of the Christians in Bulgaria' (see No. 33). In an accompanying note, W wrote: 'The idea of *your* reading anything of mine has so delighted me, that I cannot help sending you a second sonnet. I am afraid you will think it a poor return for your courtesy to repeat the offence, but perhaps you may see some beauty in it' (*Letters* 38). Apparently encouraged by Gladstone, W submitted the poem, together with No. 35 (see below), in July to the Revd Donald Macleod (1832–1916), the editor of *Good Words*, who rejected both of them (*Letters* 44).

The octave of this sonnet is a reworking of details from No. 7, 'Rome Unvisited'. The tone of the sestet is new to W in its reproach of papal splendour—a sentiment expected in a poem sent to Gladstone and to the editor of *Good Words*, both of whom were Protestant.

Title. W could not have written the poem on Easter Day in Rome, for he was in Brindisi en route to Greece (see the headnote to No. 29, 'Impression de Voyage').

1. *The silver trumpets rang . . . Dome*: echoes No. 7, 'Rome Unvisited', 39. The Dome is presumably that of St Peter's Basilica in Vatican City.

3–4. For a similar image of the pope borne in procession, see 'Rome Unvisited', 35–6.

6. *king-like*: cf. 'Rome Unvisited', 38.

8. *Three crowns of gold*: cf. 'Rome Unvisited', 12.

11–13. Cf. Luke 9: 58: 'Foxes have holes, and birds of the air have nests, but the Son of man hath not where to lay his head'. This passage also appears in Matthew 8: 20. A similar sentiment appears in W's prison letter, *De Profundis*: 'Society, as we have constituted it, will have no place for me, has none to offer' (*Letters* 510).

14. *bruise my feet*: cf. God's words to the serpent in Eden, Genesis 3: 15: 'And I will put enmity between thee and the woman, and between thy seed and her seed; it shall bruise thy head, and thou shalt bruise his heel'.

35 SONNET. ON HEARING THE DIES IRÆ SUNG IN THE SISTINE CHAPEL

MSS and Publishing History:

In July 1877, W included this poem (*M1*, location: Clark 2570a), titled 'Sonnet. (Written after hearing Mozart's "Dies Irae" sung in Magdalen Chapel.)', in a letter to the editor of *Good Words*, with No. 34, 'Easter Day', but neither was accepted.

First published in William MacIlwaine, ed., *Lyra Hibernica Sacra* (see No. 16 for publishers and for MacIlwaine's practice of retitling poems), 325 (*L*), as 'Nay, Come not thus'. A MS with further revisions (*M2*, location: Jeremy Mason Collection) contains the present title. The poem was revised for *P1*; further rev. for *P2*; collected thereafter.

Title. 'Dies Irae': translated as 'The Day of Wrath', the first words of the sequence, or hymn, which is part of the Roman Catholic Requiem Mass for the dead. A poetical description of the Last Judgement, it is neither joyful nor triumphant but concerned with suffering souls.

7. See No. 34, 'Easter Day', note to lines 11–13.

12–14. Cf. Joel 3: 13: 'Put ye in the sickle, for the harvest is ripe: come, get you down; for the press is full, the vats overflow'. W's poem is a response to the traditional belief that, at the Lord's return to judge humanity, heaven and earth will pass away in fire.

36 ITALIA

MS and Publishing History:

No MS is known to exist.

First published in *P1*, unchanged in *P2*. Mason noted in his interleaved personal copy of *Bibliography of Oscar Wilde* (location: Clark), opposite p. 177, that this poem was first published in the Boston *Pilot* in 1877 as 'To Italy', along with No. 29, 'Impression de Voyage', and No. 30, 'The Theatre at Argos'. But since existing runs of the paper are incomplete, this version has not come to light.

As a sonnet, 'Italia' is similar to No. 27, 'Sonnet on Approaching Italy', in which W implies that the magnificence of modern Italy has been soiled by its anti-clericalism. The structure of the octave reprises that of No. 31, 'Urbs Sacra Æterna', in which 'Queen' (line 3), 'seen' (line 4), and 'green' (line 8) are also rhyming words.

2. *battle-spears*: spears and galleys (see line 7) were not used by the 19th-century Italian navy, but these weapons do recall the earlier military glory of the Romans, who, like their descendants, also persecuted the Church.

3. Echoed in No. 48, *Ravenna*, 211.

4. *the nations hail thee Queen*: cf. No. 31, 'Urbs Sacra Æterna', 4.

6. *thy sapphire lake*: Venice, a naval port, lies in the Lagune, a shallow bay of the Adriatic.

7. *thy myriad galleys ride*: reappears in No. 48, *Ravenna*, 192.

8. *flag . . . green*: previously used in No. 31, 'Urbs Sacra Æterna', 8.

10. *desecrated town*: see No. 27, 'Sonnet on Approaching Italy', note to line 13.

11. *God-anointed King*: previously used in No. 7, 'Rome Unvisited', 38.

13. *flame-girt Raphael*: named in the apocryphal Book of Tobit, Raphael is one of seven archangels who stand before God.

14. *sword of pain*: cf. Milton's *Paradise Lost*, 6: 320–1, 326–7: 'the sword | Of Michael . . . deep ent'ring shear'd | All his right side; then Satan first knew pain'.

Postscript. 'Venice' is misleading, for there is no evidence that W visited the city during his 1877 tour, though he did stay there in 1875. 'Italia', then, was probably not composed in Italy, though it makes use of impressions from W's 1875 and 1877 trips.

37 VITA NUOVA

MS and Publishing History:

No MS is known to exist.

First published in the *Irish Monthly* 5 (Dec. 1877), 746 (*I*), as 'Πόντος Ἀτρύγετος' ('The Unfruitful or Barren Sea'), taken from Homer's *Odyssey*, 2: 370; rev. in William MacIlwaine, ed., *Lyra Hibernica Sacra* (for publishers and for MacIlwaine's practice of retitling poems, see No. 15, 'Αἴλινον, αἴλινον εἰπέ, τὸδ᾽ εὖ νικάτω'), 324 (*L*), as 'The Unvintageable Sea'; further rev. in *P1* and *P2* as 'Vita Nuova' (probably derived from Dante's similarly titled work) in the 'Rosa Mystica' section; collected thereafter.

Title. Translated: 'New Life'. For the earlier title of this sonnet, 'The Unvintageable Sea', in MacIlwaine's anthology, see No. 23, 'Lotus Leaves', 76 and W's footnote.

1. *unvintageable*: a neologism that W uses to reinforce the metaphor of the sea as a fallow field (see lines 7–8).

6–7. Cf. No. 42, 'Wasted Days', 13–14.

9–11. These lines echo an incident in Luke 5: 5–6, where Jesus commands his disciples to make one more cast with their nets: 'And Simon answering said unto him, Master, we have toiled all the night, and have taken nothing: nevertheless at thy word I will let down the net. And when they had this done, they inclosed a great multitude of fishes: and their net brake.'

10. *Nathless*: an archaic form of 'nevertheless'.

14. *white limbs*: that is, of Venus, born from the foam of the sea. The *Irish Monthly* has a different version of lines 12–14: 'and I saw | Christ walking on the waters: fear was past; | I knew that I had found my perfect friend'.

38 E TENEBRIS

MS and Publishing History:
   No MS is known to exist.
   First published in *P1*; rev. in *P2*; collected thereafter. Though 'E Tenebris' remained unpublished until 1881, the religious ardour of this sonnet suggests that it belongs with those poems written in the spring of 1877 and published intermittently during the subsequent years.

Title. Translated: 'Out of Darkness'.

1–3. Cf. Matthew 14: 29–31, where one of Jesus's original twelve disciples, Simon Peter, having seen Jesus walking on the water, obtains his permission to join him: 'he walked on the water, to go to Jesus. But when he saw the wind boisterous, he was afraid; and beginning to sink, he cried, saying, Lord, save me. And immediately Jesus stretched forth his hand, and caught him . . .'. Also, cf. No. 33, 'Sonnet on the Massacre of the Christians in Bulgaria', 9 and 13, and No. 116, 'The Master', 14–15.

4. *wine of life*: from *Macbeth*, II. iii. 95.

9–11. Cf. 1 Kings 18: 27, where an ironic voice counsels despair after the fashion of the prophet Elijah, who had taunted the priests of Baal for their god's impotence: 'Cry aloud: for he is a god; either he is talking, or he is pursuing, or he is in a journey, or peradventure he sleepeth, and must be awaked'.

13. The phrase 'feet of brass' is derived from Revelation 1: 15: 'And his feet like unto fine brass, as if they burned in a furnace'. The images of 'furnace-heated brass' and 'robe more white than flame' appear in No. 78, 'Sen Artysty; or, the Artist's Dream', 35–6.

39 QUANTUM MUTATA

MS and Publishing History:
   No MS is known to exist.
   First published in *P1*; unchanged in *P2*; collected thereafter.
   Despite the furore caused by Turkish atrocities against the Christian rebels, the

Disraeli government remained committed to a non-interventionist stance through-out 1877 because it feared that interference would further weaken Turkish hegem-ony and pave the way for Russian expansion into the Balkans, a development that could have threatened the influence of the British in the region. Disraeli's policy was widely reviled as condoning Turkish excesses.

The political sentiments of W's poem suggest a close relationship to No. 33, 'Sonnet on the Massacre of the Christians in Bulgaria'; hence it was probably writ-ten sometime after May 1877, when No. 33 was sent to Gladstone, who opposed the government's stand.

Title. Translated: 'How Much Changed'.

6–9. In 1655, the Catholic Duke of Savoy harried the Protestant Vaudois from their homes in Piedmont. The persecution of this sect met with no objection from Pope Alexander VII, but the series of massacres (the subject of Milton's sonnet 'On the Late Massacre in Piedmont') aroused the indignation of Oliver Cromwell, who summoned the Protestant powers of Europe to a united front. Diplomatic pressure, along with the threat of an English fleet in the Mediterranean, forced restitution to the surviving Vaudois.

40 TO MILTON

MS and Publishing History:

An untitled MS (*M1*, location: Clark 2487) is merely a rough draft. A MS titled 'Milton' (*M2*, location: Hyde) is also a draft of the poem.

First published in *P1*; unchanged in *P2*; collected thereafter.

This sonnet owes a general debt to Wordsworth's 'Sonnets Dedicated to Liberty' in *Poems* (1807), where England's loss of moral fortitude is mourned in such poems as 'O Friend! I know not which way I must look' and 'London, 1802' ('Milton! Thou shouldst be living at this hour'). Within the W canon, 'To Milton' belongs with No. 33, 'Sonnet on the Massacre of the Christians in Bulgaria', and No. 39, 'Quantum Mutata', as his response to the Balkan crisis of 1876–8. Like its com-panions, 'To Milton' is dated from 1877.

1. A similar invocation of Milton appears in No. 58, 'Humanitad', 306–7.

3. *fiery-coloured world*: a favourite phrase of W, who uses it with variations in many of his works and letters.

6–7. Echoes Wordsworth's sonnet 'The World Is Too Much with Us', 2: 'Getting and spending, we lay waste our powers'.

10. *sea-lion*: in heraldry, a lion with a fish's tail, combining the traditional symbol of England with an allusion to its naval supremacy, which enabled Britannia to rule the waves. The image also appears in No. 76, 'Ave Imperatrix', 17.

11. *ignorant demagogues . . . held in fee*: the latter phrase, derived from feudal law, refers to property occupied by a liegeman on condition of fidelity to his lord. Hence the 'ignorant demagogues' were the Turkish rulers, whose continued resistance to Russian incursions was thought vital to British security. This consideration deterred the British from interfering with the Turks' suppression of the Balkan rebels.

13–14. *triple empire . . . Democracy*: by 1652, the Commonwealth forces under Cromwell controlled England, Ireland, and Scotland. The association of the term 'Democracy' with Cromwell is ironic since he had been regarded by many as a virtual dictator (despite the fact that he encouraged religious toleration and contributed to the development of constitutional government).

41 AVE MARIA PLENA GRATIA

MS and Publishing History:
No MS is known to exist.
First published in the *Irish Monthly* 6 (July 1878), 412 (*I*), titled 'Ave Maria Gratia Plena'; rev. in *Kottabos* 3 (Michaelmas Term 1879), 206 (*K*), as 'Ave! Maria'; further rev. as 'Ave Maria Plena Gratia' in *P1* and *P2*; collected thereafter. The speaker in the poem appears to be contemplating a painting of the Annunciation.

Title. Translated: 'Hail Mary, full of grace', the first words of the Catholic prayer that continues: 'blessed art thou amongst women, and blessed is the fruit of thy womb'. Mason notes that in Methuen's 1908 edition of *Poems* and in following editions, the original title 'Ave Maria Gratia Plena' was restored 'as being the more correct' (90 n.); however, we retain W's title.

3–4. *great God . . . Danae*: see No. 30, 'The Theatre at Argos', note to line 7.

5. *Semele*: a paramour of Zeus, she desired him to visit her in all his godly splendour. When he did so, she was destroyed by his lightning. Their offspring was Dionysus.

13. *An angel with a lily*: see No. 8, 'Choir Boy', note to lines 9–12.

14. *Dove*: symbol of the Holy Ghost, so regarded because of its mention at the baptism of Christ (John 1: 32). In Christian iconography, the Annunciation scene often includes an image of the dove.

Postscript. In the *Irish Monthly* version, W's designation—'Vatican Gallery, Rome, 1877'—implies that a painting by Raphael or Baraccio had inspired the sonnet. Subsequent publications of the poem, however, give 'Florence' as the postscript; the *Kottabos* version cites S. Marco, which housed paintings and frescoes by Fra Angelico (referred to as the 'Angel-painter' in No. 5, 'San Miniato', 3). In none of the paintings of the Annunciation by the artists mentioned, however, are the details of the kneeling girl, the angel with a lily, and the dove all present. This fact suggests that the poem was a recollected experience and was not composed in either Rome or Florence.

42 WASTED DAYS

MS and Publishing History:
No MS is known to exist.
First published in *Kottabos* 3 (Michaelmas Term 1877), 56 (*K*). Two errata slips, containing revisions of the sestet of this sonnet, were later included with the periodical: one for line 12 of the poem, included with the second issue of *Kottabos* (*E1*);

the other for lines 9–14, included with later issues of this number of *Kottabos* (*E2*). For *Poems* (1881), this sonnet was extensively rewritten as No. 66, 'Madonna Mia', the gender of the central figure changed from the 'fair slim boy' to the 'lily-girl'.

Title. The subscript—'(From a Picture Painted by Miss V. T.)'—alludes to a painting on a tile, six inches square, by Violet Troubridge, later Mrs Walter Gurney (1858–1931), who had probably met W in 1877. Two scenes are depicted: on the left, a boy in the winter snow gazes longingly into the home of a feasting family; on the right, the same boy reclines against a tree, idly watching autumn harvesters at work. The scenes are united by the motto: 'He must hunger in frost that will not worke in heate' (see Mason 96 and facing illustration).

1. Echoes No. 32, 'The Grave of Keats', 1.

14. *no man gathers fruit*: see No. 23, 'Lotus Leaves', note to line 75.

43 THE GRAVE OF SHELLEY

MSS and Publishing History:
Inspired by the same visit to the Protestant Cemetery, Rome, that inspired No. 32, 'The Grave of Keats' (see headnote), 'The Grave of Shelley' was probably written at Oxford during 1877–8. The early version (*M1*) and autograph fair copy (*M2*) MSS (location: Jeremy Mason Collection) have been reproduced in facsimile in Jeremy Mason's privately printed pamphlet, *Oscar Wilde and the Grave of Shelley* (Edinburgh: Tragara Press, 1992), with his Introduction and Notes. *M1* is printed in Stuart Mason's bibliography, 309–10.

First published in *P1*; unchanged in *P2*; collected thereafter.

6. *yon pyramid*: as an object of playful speculation in these lines, the pyramid—W had written in 'The Tomb of Keats'—was closer to Keats's grave than to Shelley's and the resting place of 'one Caius Cestius, a Roman gentleman of small note [actually, he was a praetor, a high elected magistrate, ranking just below the consuls], who died about 30 BC'.

7. *Sphinx*: W began writing his long poem *The Sphinx* around 1877 at Oxford, spelling it in the early drafts as 'Sphynx', the same spelling in the early draft of 'The Grave of Shelley'. Possibly the sonnet was written at this time—that is, between 1877 and 1878.

10. *great mother*: a characteristic Shelleyan epithet for Earth and Nature.

11–12. In 'Alastor', 304–5, Shelley seems to have foreseen his own death by drowning: 'A restless impulse urged him to embark | And meet lone Death on the drear ocean's waste'.

44 SANTA DECCA

MS and Publishing History:
A MS (*M*, location: Huntington HM 44182) of this sonnet is extant. W probably wrote it around 1877–8 after he had visited Corfu, an Ionian island, while en route to Greece in 1877 (see headnote to No. 29, 'Impression de Voyage'). In a letter to his mother from Corfu, W described the island as 'full of idyllic loveliness' (*Letters* 36).

First published in *P1*; rev. in *P2*; collected thereafter.

Title. Santa Decca (now named Mt. Pantokrator) is a mountain on Corfu.

2. *Pallas crowns of olive leaves*: the olive tree was Pallas Athena's gift to Athens; therefore, she favoured its leaves.

3. *Demeter's child . . . sheaves*: Proserpine (also known as Persephone), the goddess of fertility and of the Underworld, was the daughter of Demeter, the earth goddess, and of Zeus. She was the wife of Hades, who had carried her off from the fields of Enna (in central Sicily) and made her captive.

5. Cf. Elizabeth Barrett Browning's 'The Dead Pan', 211, in her *Poems* (1844), which extols the sacrifice of Christ that forever silenced the 'vain false gods of Hellas'. According to a well-known tradition, mentioned in Plutarch's *De Oraculorum Defectu* (*On the Cessation of Oracles*), at the hour of Christ's agony 'a cry of "Great Pan is dead!" swept across the waves in the hearing of certain mariners,— and the oracles ceased' (quoted from Mrs Browning's headnote to her poem). W's sonnet, like his other poems written after his 1877 tour of Greece and Italy, expresses a yearning for the return of the pagan past.

7. *Hylas*: King Theiodamas's beautiful young son, whom Heracles abducted and with whom he fell in love. Hylas accompanied him and the Argonauts (heroes on the ship *Argo*), who set sail to recover the Golden Fleece. On the coast of Mysia, Hylas, sent to search for water, was lured away by water-nymphs, who, in love with his beauty, drew him into the spring.

11. The Plain of Asphodel (or daffodil), traditionally regarded as an immortal flower in the Homeric Underworld, is described in the *Odyssey*, 11: 539.

45 THEORETIKOS

MSS and Publishing History:

An untitled MS (location: Clark 2486) is extant, which also contains lines for No. 46, 'Amor Intellectualis'. Early fragments (*M1*, written on one side of the sheet) and a complete version of the sonnet (*M2*, written on the obverse probably around 1877) are printed in Mason 292–3.

First published in *P1*; unchanged in *P2*; collected thereafter.

Title. Translated: 'The Contemplative'.

1–4. As in his other political sonnets, such as No. 39, 'Quantum Mutata', and No. 40, 'To Milton', W condemns England's reluctance to interfere in Turkish misrule in the Balkans. Despite the protests of Gladstone and others, the Disraeli government stood firm against pressure to intervene on behalf of the revolutionaries, and anti-Turkish demonstrations subsequently lost momentum. In 'Theoretikos', disillusionment leads W to abandon politics for art.

5–6. *that voice . . . Which spake of Freedom*: that is, Wordsworth's voice, for example in 'London, 1802', which, in invoking the name of Milton, deplores England's moral and political decline: 'Oh! raise us up, return to us again; | And give us manners, virtue, freedom, power', 6–8: see the headnote to No. 40, 'To Milton'. In the early fragments of 'Theoretikos' (see Mason 293), Wordsworth is mentioned.

14. W's sardonic reference to God suggests a cooling of Catholic fervour so obviously several months before. The allusion to God's 'enemies' refers to the Turkish Muslims against whom the Christian revolutionaries were struggling in the Balkans.

46 AMOR INTELLECTUALIS

MSS and Publishing History:
 There exist two early MS drafts of this sonnet, written around 1877–8: *M1* (location: Clark 2486) contains lines 1–11 (printed in Mason 308–9); *M2* (location: Clark 2418) contains lines 9–14.
 First published in *P1*; unchanged in *P2*; collected thereafter.

Title. Translated: 'Intellectual Love'.

1. Cf. the opening of Keats's 'On First Looking into Chapman's Homer', which provides a model for W's sonnet: 'Much have I travelled . . .'. Castaly, the area around Mt. Parnassus, is the location of a spring sacred to Apollo and the nine Muses: see No. 51, 'The Burden of Itys', note to line 256.

1–3. The Romantic vision of nature as a potent force in human development, both moral and spiritual, is echoed here: cf., for example, Shelley's 'Epipsychidion', 200–1, which depicts a 'Being' associated with the forces of nature, encountered by the speaker's spirit 'on its visioned wanderings': 'In solitudes | Her voice came to me through the whispering woods . . .'.

5. Cf. Keats's 'On First Looking into Chapman's Homer', 4: 'Which bards in fealty to Apollo hold . . .'.

10–12. Browning's *Sordello* (1840) is based on a story of a 13th-century troubadour who abducted the wife of his master. The mythical Endymion (see No. 54, 'Endymion') is here an allusion to Keats, the author of his own 'Endymion' and the sonnet 'Written on a Blank Space at the end of Chaucer's Tale "The Floure and the Leafe" ', 11–12: 'The honeyed lines do freshly interlace | To keep the reader in so sweet a place'. In *Tamberlaine the Great*, Part 2, IV. iii. 1, Christopher Marlowe writes of the 'pampered jades of Asia'.

13. *seven-fold vision*: in the 'Paradiso' of *The Divine Comedy*, Dante envisions a hierarchy of the seven planetary heavens from the Moon to Saturn (the eighth heaven being the fixed stars; the ninth, the Primum Mobile).

47 AT VERONA

MS and Publishing History:
 A photocopy (location: Clark 2458) of the first page in a notebook, now unaccounted for, has a table of contents listing a poem entitled 'With Can Grande at Verona', possibly an early version of 'At Verona'.
 First published in *P1*; unchanged in *P2*; collected thereafter.

1–2. Dante, the speaker, had been banished in 1302 by political intriguers in Florence on pain of death if he returned. His subsequent wanderings taught him the inconstancy of patrons and the cruelties of fellow exiles. During his Italian tour in 1875, W wrote to his mother that, when in exile in Verona, Dante grew 'weary of trudging up the steep *stairs*, as he says, of the *Scali*geri' (a pun on the Italian word *scali*, 'stairs', in this allusion to the powerful family ruling the city-state of Verona; *Letters* 9), an echo of Dante's passage in the 'Paradiso', 17: 59–60. W's sonnet makes Dante's experience a paradigm for the isolation of the artist, a theme sounded earlier in No. 45, 'Theoretikos'.

3–4. Cf. Matthew 15: 27: 'the dogs eat of the crumbs which fall from their masters' table'. The 'Hound's table' is presumably an allusion to Can Grande della Scala in Verona, whose courtesy won Dante's respect and admiration (indeed, Dante dedicated the 'Paradiso' to him). Commentators also believe that Can Grande was the 'Hound . . . that abased Italy shall save' ('Inferno', 1: 101–6)—the word 'Hound' playing on the word 'Cane' (Dog). In Dante's vision, the Hound was regarded as a national redeemer who would harry the 'She-Wolf'—that is, the political opportunists ravaging Italy—back to Hell. W's view also draws from an apocryphal tradition expressed by Dante Gabriel Rossetti's 'Dante at Verona', in which the levity of the Veronese court affronts the melancholy of the poet. Dante becomes the butt of jokes in which Can Grande takes part:

> Then smiled Can Grande to the rest:-
> 'Our Dante's tuneful mouth indeed
> Lacks not the gift on flesh to feed!'
> 'Fair host of mine', replied the guest,
> 'So many bones you'd not descry
> If so it chanced the *dog* were I.'   (301–6)

5. *red ways of war*: Dante had fought in the battle of Campaldino in 1289.

9. *Curse God and die*: In Job 2: 9, Job's wife encourages him to do the same. A similar expression of despair occurs in No. 38, 'E Tenebris', 9–11.

14. Echoes the concluding line of *The Divine Comedy*: 'The Love that moves the sun and the other stars', which appears as the last line of No. 69, 'Apologia'.

48 RAVENNA

MS and Publishing History:
   No MS is known to exist.
   First published by Thomas Shrimpton & Son (Oxford, 1878); repr. in *Poems* (1908).
   Ravenna was the Newdigate Prize poem for 1878, the award for which was 20 guineas (previous winners included John Ruskin in 1839, Matthew Arnold in 1843, and John Addington Symonds in 1860). W recited excerpts before the Vice-Chancellor and other notables in the Sheldonian Theatre at Oxford on 26 June, the day of its publication. W informed the Revd Matthew Russell, the editor of the *Irish Monthly*, that the subject for the 1878 competition, Ravenna, had been announced in June 1877:

> It was originally limited to fifty lines, and the subject used to be necessarily taken from some *classical* subject, either Greek or Latin, and generally a work

of art. The metre is heroic couplets, but as you have seen perhaps from my poem, of late years laxity is allowed from the horrid Popeian jingle of regular heroics, and *now* the subject may be taken from any country or time and there is no limit to the length. . . .

There was a strange coincidence about my getting it. On the 31st of March 1877 (long before the subject was given out) I entered Ravenna on my way to Greece, and on 31st March 1878 I had to hand my poem in . . . (*Letters* 53–4)

Title. Ravenna, a strategic harbour of the Roman Empire, became the chief residence of the Western Emperors in the 4th century and served as the capital of Italy under the Ostrogoths. By the time of W's visit, however, its glory had long since passed, and large sections of the city were deserted.

Dedication. On p. iii, the dedication reads: TO MY FRIEND | GEORGE FLEMING, | AUTHOR OF 'THE NILE NOVEL', AND 'MIRAGE'. 'George Fleming' was the pseudonym of Julia Constance Fletcher (1858–1938), who met W in Rome in the spring of 1877 and whose *Mirage* (1877) contains a character named Claude Davenant, a young Oxford poet, aesthete, and devotee of Greek paganism—most likely modelled after W: 'a pale, large-featured, individual; a peculiar, an interesting countenance, of singularly mild yet ardent expression. Mr Davenant was very young—probably not more than one or two and twenty; but he looked younger. He wore his hair rather long, thrown back, and clustering about his neck like the hair of a mediaeval saint' (see *Letters* 46 n.). A copy of the novel was among the books auctioned in the sale of W's possessions in 1895.

4. *throstle*: song-thrush.

6. Echoes No. 49, 'Magdalen Walks', 1.

8. *The primrose . . . uncomforted*: echoes *The Winter's Tale*, IV. iv. 120–3: ' . . . pale primroses | That die unmarried'; and Milton's 'Lycidas', line 142: '. . . the rathe Primrose that forsaken dies'.

22. *bright lamps . . . glow*: for the association of 'bright lamps' and ripening fruit, see No. 28, 'Sonnet Written in Holy Week at Genoa', 2–3 and note.

25–6. David Hunter-Blair, whose *In Victorian Days* (1939) contains his memoirs of his trip with W, once reproached him for claiming—in lines 25–6—to have entered Ravenna on horseback: '"And, Oscar—that prize poem of yours on Ravenna. I liked it: it was fine; but a lot of humbug in that too". "What do you mean?" asked Oscar. "I wrote it *ex imo corde*, from the bottom of my heart, red-hot from Ravenna itself". "Yes, but you went there lounging on the cushions of a stuffy railway carriage. . . . You know you never mounted a horse in your life; you would tumble off at once if you did" ' (136–7).

28–9. These lines were previously used in No. 27, 'Sonnet on Approaching Italy', 7–8.

33. Cf. No. 7, 'Rome Unvisited', 12. In 1509, after the Venetians had, for a time, dominated Ravenna, the city returned to papal control.

36. Cf. No. 29, 'Impression de Voyage', 14.

41–4. With slight differences, these lines were previously used in No. 21, 'Lotus Land', 9–12.

49. *Proserpine, with poppy-laden head*: see No. 44, 'Santa Decca', note to line 3. W

may be playing on the Latin 'Persephone' (as Proserpine was also known) and the word for wild poppy, *persephonium*.

60. *Gaston de Foix*: leader of the French siege of Ravenna in 1512, he was killed in the course of defeating the Spanish and Italian army sent to relieve the city. The Colonne dei Francesi was erected on the spot where he fell.

63. This line was previously used in No. 32, 'The Grave of Keats', 3; altered in No. 119, *The Ballad of Reading Gaol*, 116. W took it from Byron's 'To Thyrza', 42: 'When love and life alike were new'.

64. *veil of blue*: previously used in No. 23, 'Lotus Leaves', 47, and in No. 32, 'The Grave of Keats', 2.

69–72. Amalasuntha, the daughter of Theodoric, king of the Ostrogoths and conqueror of the city in 493, erected the 'lordly tomb' when her father died and she subsequently became regent.

76. *king and clown*: cf. Keats's 'Ode to a Nightingale', 63–4: 'The voice I hear this passing night was heard | In ancient days by emperor and clown . . . '.

80–1. *Dante*: exiled from Florence, he died in Ravenna. He was interred in the church of S. Francesco, but later, when a mausoleum embellished with a half-length relief of the poet was built next to the church, his remains were reburied.

82. *cunning sculptor's hands*: Giotto designed Dante's mask for the shrine next to the church of S. Francesco.

92–3. As architect to Florence, Giotto began the bell tower to La Cathedrale di S. Maria del Fiore, so-called from the lily that adorns Florence's coat of arms.

95. This line was previously used in No. 47, 'At Verona', 1.

102. *empty tomb*: a monument was erected to Dante in Florence's S. Croce, where Michelangelo had once been commissioned to design a tomb for the poet. Ravenna, however, has steadfastly refused to give up Dante's remains.

113. *Byron*: while in Ravenna, he resided at the Palazzo Guiccioli. His political activism led him from Italy to Greece, where, while assisting in the Greek war of independence from the Turks, he died of a fever in 1824.

114–15. *a second Anthony*: Mark Antony's dalliance with Cleopatra alienated him from Rome. Although his supporters managed to control the port at Ravenna, Octavian (later known as Augustus, the first Roman emperor) forced a confrontation at Actium, where, in 31 BC, the lovers were defeated.

128–33. The sites named here refer to places where the Greeks had fended off the Persian invasion in 5 BC.

141. *red cross*: in 1862, Jean Henry Dunant, a Swiss, urged the formation of voluntary societies to aid war victims. When the Red Cross was founded in 1863, it honoured Dunant by adopting as its international emblem the cross of the Swiss flag with colours reversed—that is, a red cross on a white background.

142–3. See No. 50, 'Cypriots or Folk Making for Malta', 1–2.

146. *Sapphic Mitylene*: see No. 32, 'The Grave of Keats', note to line 10.

148. *Castaly*: see No. 45, 'Amor Intellectualis', note to line 1.

154–8. Lines previously used in No. 28, 'Sonnet Written in Holy Week at Genoa', 4–6.

164. *gods we fancied slain*: see No. 44, 'Santa Decca', 1 and note.

173. *Hylas*: see No. 44, 'Santa Decca', note to line 7.

178. *these sweet and honied hours*: see No. 28, 'Sonnet Written in Holy Week at Genoa', note to line 12.

184. *Cæsar*: that is, Augustus (see note to lines 114–15), who made Ravenna the main naval base for the upper Adriatic.

187–9. Lines previously used in No. 31, 'Urbs Sacra Æterna', 4–5, 7.

192. *thy myriad galleys ride*: phrase previously used in No. 36, Italia', 7.

193–6. Sediment carried by the Po River silted up the estuary so that at the time of W's visit Ravenna lay six miles inland.

200. *Italia's royal warrior*: Victor Emmanuel II (1820–78), king of united Italy, who entered Rome and made it his capital in 1871 (see No. 27, 'Sonnet on Approaching Italy', note to line 13). Hunter-Blair regarded W's favourable sentiments toward the king as 'humbug': '"You know that all your sympathies were with the dethroned Pope, not with the invading and usurping King. You know they were". "Don't be angry, Dunsky", urged Oscar. "You must know that I should never, never have won the Newdigate if I had taken the Pope's side against the King's"' (*In Victorian Days*, 137).

205–12. Victor Emmanuel II became King of Naples in 1860—after the city had deposed its Bourbon ruler, Francis II—and wrested Venice from the Austrians in 1866. His occupation of Rome fulfilled Dante's dream of an Italy free of foreign domination.

211. Echoes No. 36, 'Italia', 3.

222. *ice-crowned citadels*: the Alps.

226–7. Battlefields on which Italian armies met defeat during the struggle for the unification of Italy.

231. *immortal Star*: of martial valour, as in Virgil's *Aeneid*, 9: 641, where Apollo praises Ascanius's feat of arms: 'A blessing, child, on thy young valour, so man scales the stars'.

238. Cf. No. 7, 'Rome Unvisited', 53–4, on the similar images of the torch and race. Despite W's view, in 1859 Ravenna was one of the first cities to vote in favour of Italian unity.

246–9. A view of Ravenna's past history: Adria was the name of the town originally settled by the Thessalians, Greek traders who had crossed the Adriatic. Under the Caesars, Ravenna's navy helped to maintain the Empire's sovereignty (see note to line 184 above). Finally, after the deaths of Theodoric and Amalasuntha, the Emperor Justinian of the Eastern Empire sent Belisarius to regain control of the Western Empire from the Ostrogoths. The latter's success established Ravenna as the seat of Byzantine domination in Italy. In this sense, the city was—as line 248 suggests—the 'Queen of double Empires'.

259. *wars and fears*: Russia and Turkey had just signed a treaty, in March 1878, which only partly defused the Balkan conflict (see the headnote to No. 33, 'Sonnet on the Massacre of the Christians in Bulgaria').

270–1. These lines echo No. 7, 'Rome Unvisited', 27–8.

273. *city of the violet crown*: that is, Athens, which, in Pindar's fragment 76: 1, is called 'the gleaming, and the violet-crowned'.

275. *'myriad laughter' of the sea*: John Addington Symonds, alluding to Aeschylus' *Prometheus Bound*, 89, refers to 'Prometheus, when he described the myriad laughter of the dimpling waves . . . ' (*Studies of the Greek Poets*, 1st series, 1873, 9: 281).

276. A slightly different version of this line had previously been used in No. 29, 'Impression de Voyage', 8, and later in No. 51, 'The Burden of Itys', 41.

280. Echoed in No. 118, *The Sphinx*, 18.

281. *Autumn's livery*: see No. 58, 'Humanidad', 4.

295. *lone chapel . . . marshy plain*: the church of S. Maria in Porto Fuori lay two miles from the city on the site of the old harbour.

298–301. Lines echoed in No. 23, 'Lotus Leaves', 61–4.

308. Echoed in No. 22, 'Desespoir', 8.

310–12. Lines later used in No. 75, 'The Garden of Eros', 4–6.

49 MAGDALEN WALKS

MS and Publishing History:

No MS is known to exist. Written around 1877–8, the same time as No. 48, *Ravenna*, both poems containing similar passages.

First published in the *Irish Monthly* 6 (April 1878), 211 (*I*); rev. in *P1*; further rev. in *P2*; collected thereafter. Mason (89) notes that the final three stanzas in the first published version in the *Irish Monthly*, omitted in *Poems* (1881), 'are restored [presumably by Ross] in Methuen's edition of the *Poems*, 1908, 103–104, but cancelled again in the editions of 1909, etc.'

In a letter to a friend on 13 May 1878, W described the intent in his lyric poem of five quatrains:

I have tried, in the metre as well as the words, to mirror some of the swiftness and grace of the springtime.

And though I know but too well that in this, like in everything that I do, I have failed, yet after all Nature lies out of the reach of even the greatest masters of song. She cannot be described, she can only be worshipped: and there is more perfection of beauty, it seems to me, in a single white narcissus of the meadow than in all the choruses of Euripides, or even in the *Endymion* of Keats himself. (*Letters* 51)

In some of his later work, such as 'The Decay of Lying' (1891), W emphasized the superiority of art to nature, but in *De Profundis* (written 1897, published in *Letters* (1962)) he turned to nature to provide him with refuge and solace for his suffering. Aware of inconsistencies in his aesthetic views, W had remarked in his essay 'The Truth of Masks' (1891): 'A Truth in art is that whose contradictory is also true.'

Title. When reprinted in the Boston *Pilot* (8 June 1878), it was entitled 'Primavera' (translated: 'Spring').

1–4. Echoes No. 48, *Ravenna*, 3–6.

10–12. More echoes from *Ravenna*, 9–11.

13. In the *Irish Monthly* version, W noted the source of this line: Aristophanes' *The Clouds*, 1008, 'When the plane whispers love to the elm in the grove . . .'.

17–20. Again, echoes from *Ravenna*, 14–17.

50 CYPRIOTS OR FOLK MAKING FOR MALTA

MS: This fragmentary poem was found in a notebook (*M*, location: Clark 2499), which also contains a draft of *Vera; or, The Nihilists* and jottings for the uncompleted play *Beatrice and Astone Manfredi*. Since the draft of *Vera* was completed in 1880, the poem was presumably written between 1878 and 1879: W had jotted down 'Cypriots', later reversed the notebook to write his draft of *Vera*, then later turned the notebook over again and, returning to where the poem left off, began writing passages for *Beatrice and Astone Manfredi*.
Not published in W's lifetime.

1–2. Echoes No. 48, *Ravenna*, 142–3.

3. *beaten from their course*: the sailors were proceeding west from Cyprus to Malta, but, blown awry, they drifted past their destination and continued across the Mediterranean to Gibraltar, as indicated in line 11.

11. *Calpé and the cliffs of Herakles*: both overlook the straits of Gibraltar, the entrance to the Atlantic (see line 15) from the Mediterranean Sea.

22. *great Genoan*: Christopher Columbus.

24. *Cortes*: W may be echoing Keats's 'On First Looking into Chapman's Homer,' 11–12: 'Or like stout Cortez when with eagle eyes | He stared at the Pacific . . .' (though, of course, Balboa actually discovered the Pacific in 1513).

51 THE BURDEN OF ITYS

MSS and Publishing History:
Three MSS are extant: *M1* (location: Clark 2496) is a working draft consisting of lines 25–42; *M2* (location: Hyde) is a draft of lines 217–22, 253–8, and 293–4; and *M3* (location: Clark 2425) is an early draft of four fragmentary lines that correspond to lines 271–4.
First published in *P1*; rev. in *P2*; collected thereafter.
While recalling W's 1877 tour of Greece and Italy, this poem displays a marked preference for Hellenism over Christian ritual, a significant reversal for the erstwhile devotee of the Church. In the present version, the speaker muses: 'strange, a year ago | I knelt before some crimson Cardinal' (lines 27–8); the early draft (Clark 2496), however, reads: 'strange: a month ago . . .'. This passage suggests that W began the poem in 1877, perhaps during his rustication (see headnote to No. 33, 'Sonnet on the Massacre of the Christians in Bulgaria'), and substantially completed it in 1878. Even allowing for revisions up until publication in 1881, the poem represents W's state of mind during his final year at Oxford, to which allusion is made in the final stanzas.

'The Burden of Itys' perhaps also reveals W's hopes for himself as a poet; since the poem was too long for a periodical, he may have been contemplating the publication of a volume of poems. The stanzaic form of the poem (five lines in iambic pentameter, the sixth in heptameter) was eventually used in all of the other long poems that first appeared in *Poems* (1881): 'The Garden of Eros', 'Charmides', 'Panthea', and 'Humanitad'. With the exception of 'Charmides', these works recall such 18th-century poems as James Thomson's *The Seasons* (1736–30), in which the poet's meditations are evoked by the beauties of a specific time of year. In July 1881, W wrote to the novelist Violet Hunt (1862–1942), whom he called 'the sweetest Violet in England': 'The poem I like best is "The Burden of Itys" and next to that "The Garden of Eros". They are the most lyrical, and I would sooner have any power or quality of "song" writing than be the greatest sonnet writer since Petrarch' (*Letters* 64, 79).

By alluding to Swinburne, Arnold, and Rossetti (see lines 151–68), W not only associated himself with poets whom he admired and with whom he wished to be regarded but also found, in Swinburne and Arnold, two poets who had anticipated his enthusiasm for the Greek past. W also admired Keats's vision of ancient Arcadia, a symbol of the pastoral ideal in the 'Ode on a Grecian Urn'.

Title. Derived from Greek myth, the story of Itys involves the rape of Philomela by Tereus, king of Thrace and husband to her sister, Procne. Seeking revenge by killing her son, Itys, Procne serves the flesh of his body to her husband. Determined topunish the sisters, who have fled, Tereus finds them in the city of Daulis. Responding to their pleas, the gods transform Procne into a nightingale, which forever mourns for her son, and Philomela into a swallow. W follows the Latin authors, however, in having Philomela rather than Procne transformed into a nightingale.

6. *crystal-hearted star*: the monstrance, which holds the Blessed Sacrament during the Mass, is a glass-framed shrine, in the form of a sun emitting its rays to all sides, so that the Eucharistic Host is exposed to view.

9. *monsignores*: a title of distinction reserved for minor prelates of the papal court who are entitled to wear violet vestments. In line 7, the 'violet-gleaming butterflies' are associated with these churchmen.

10–12. *pike . . . in partibus*: the association of the pike with 'some mitred old Bishop' is ironic since the symbol of the fish, for early Christians, signified their secret resistance to pagan rule (each letter in the Greek word for 'fish'—*ichtus*— begins a word in the phrase 'Jesus Christ, Son of God, Saviour'). In the poem, the modern bishop is one who is dressed in 'gaudy scales' like the 'lazy' pike. The Latin phrase *in partibus* is from *in partibus infidelium* ('in the region of infidels'), used by the Roman Catholic Church to refer, as in this case, to a titular bishop located in a region controlled by those who have not accepted the Church's authority.

14. *Palæstrina*: Giovanni Pierluigi da Palestrina (*c.*1525–94), the Italian composer and choirmaster in various churches, was appointed by Pope Julius III in 1551 as master of the Julian Chapel Choir.

17–18. Cf. No. 34, 'Easter Day', 3–6.

29. *Esquiline*: one of the hills of Rome.

36. *God's body*: the Blessed Sacrament.

37–9. *Fra Giovanni*: not a specific person but a general type, perhaps one of the 'pale monks' in line 6, Brother John sings 'out of tune' (see No. 18, 'Heart's Yearnings', note to line 6) compared to the 'small brown bird' (the nightingale), which sings in harmony with nature, though with a 'throbbing throat', evoking the memory of the Philomel myth in the following lines.

41. This line—in a slightly different form—had been used in No. 29, 'Impression de Voyage', 8 (also, see note), and in No. 48, *Ravenna*, 276. 'Arcady' is a variation of 'Arcadia', both used in the poem.

42. *Salamis*: an island in the bay of Eleusis, which W had passed on his way to Athens in 1877.

57. *Daphnis*: in Greek myth, a shepherd who was the son of the god Hermes and a nymph, who exposed him under a laurel bush (in Greek, *daphne*), hence his name. He is traditionally regarded as the originator of pastoral poetry.

58. *song of Linus*: a Greek dirge containing the refrain *ailinon, ailinon* (as in the title of No. 16), interpreted as *ai, Linus* or 'alas for Linus!' According to one myth, Linus was the music teacher of Heracles, who, having been reprimanded, killed him with his own lyre. Since Homeric times, the song of Linus has been sung at harvest time.

61. *Lycoris*: the pseudonym of the famous actress Cytheris, who had been the mistress celebrated in the elegiac verse of the Roman poet Gaius Cornelius Gallus (*c.*69–26 BC).

62. *Illyrian valley far away*: the north-west region of the Balkan peninsula, once a rustic and untamed Roman province.

63. *herbs amaracine*: an aromatic plant.

69. *Nuneham meadows*: south of Oxford.

78. *coronal*: a wreath or garland that crowns the head of a poet or singer in recognition of achievement.

80. *vales Æolian*: in ancient times, the name of the area in the northern part of the west coast of Asia Minor.

84. *Ilissus*: a stream which flowed past Athens.

88. *that little weed of ragged red*: a wild flower called 'ragged robin'.

93. *Syrinx*: a nymph who transformed herself into a reed-bed to escape from Pan's erotic pursuit. When the wind made the reeds sigh, Pan constructed a pipe from them, calling it a 'Syrinx' in memory of the nymph.

95–6. *Cytheræa*: an island off the south coast of Laconia in the Peloponnese. In some Greek myths, Aphrodite landed there after being born from sea-foam; hence, she is sometimes called 'Cytheraea'.

100. *star*: Hesperus, the evening star.

103. *leman Danae*: the loved one ('leman') of Zeus (here, the Roman equivalent, Jove). For Danae, see No. 30, 'The Theatre at Argos', note to line 7.

105–6. *Mercury . . . Dis*: Mercury, the Roman god equivalent to the Greek Hermes, acted as the messenger of the gods (his winged hat and sandals symbolizing this function) and guided the souls of the dead to the Underworld, where Dis reigned—the Roman god also known as Pluto and in Greek myth as Hades.

110. *Arachne's silver tapestry*: Arachne (Greek: 'spider') challenged Athena to a weaving contest (hence, the 'silver tapestry'), but when she depicted the erotic lives of the gods in her web, the goddess destroyed it and beat her. When Arachne hanged herself, Athena saved her but then transformed her, quite appropriately, into a spider.

114. *Heliconian glades*: Mount Helicon, the largest mountain in Boeotia, Greece, was sacred to Apollo and the Muses.

115. *vale at Tempe*: in north-east Thessaly, Greece, a valley sacred to Apollo. Laurel for the wreaths crowning victors in the Pythian games at Delphi was gathered there.

116. *Narcissus*: Ovid's account in his *Metamorphoses* (AD 8) is the best-known version of this myth: having rejected the attentions of a young woman called Echo, Narcissus is consumed by passion for a beautiful young man, whose image he sees in a pool; when he discovers that he himself is the source of the reflection, he nevertheless continues to yearn for it until he dies on the bank. In many of his works, W either alludes to or dramatizes this self-destructive homosexual fable.

120–1. *Salmacis*: a fountain nymph who loved Hermaphroditus, the son of Hermes and Aphrodite, and who prayed to the gods, when she embraced him, to make her and the young boy one body; hence, ancient art portrays Hermaphroditus as a beautiful youth with breasts.

126. *Oreads*: nymphs of the mountains.

127. *Ariadne*: she helped Theseus, the hero of Athens who had slain the Minotaur, by giving him the thread by which he found his way out of the labyrinth. After fleeing with her, he deserted her on the island of Naxos, where Dionysus discovered her, married her, and made her immortal.

131. *amber pard*: a reference to a leopard (sometimes a panther), associated with Dionysus, who, in his Indian journeys with an army of followers, travelled in a chariot drawn by panthers and bedecked with vine leaves. In line 181, the speaker indicates his devotion to Dionysus by donning a leopard skin.

132. *Maeonia's bard*: Homer—supposedly born in Maeonia, though modern scholars believe that either Chios or Smyrna is more likely.

135. *red-lipped boy*: Paris—see No. 20, '*Θρηνῳδία*', note to line 8.

137. *moil*: turmoil or confusion.

138. *Hector . . . Ajax*: in Book 6 of Homer's *Iliad*, Hector, the eldest son of Priam, king of Troy, engages Ajax, son of Telamon, king of Salamis, in single combat during the Trojan War, but the result is inconclusive. Eventually, Hector is killed by Achilles.

139–40. *Perseus . . . witch* see No. 30, 'The Theatre at Argos', note to line 7.

141–2. *tales . . . urns*: undoubtedly, W had in mind Keats's 'Ode on a Grecian Urn'.

149. *Daulian waters*: the river near Daulis, whence Tereus reigned over Thrace. The nightingale—associated with the myth involving Tereus (see the title note above)—is sometimes called the 'Daulian bird'.

153–6. *wondrous boy . . . Attic poets' spring*: the 'boy' is Swinburne, whose verse play *Atalanta in Calydon* (1865) depicts mythic events involving Artemis, goddess of the hunt, and the huntress Atalanta. The Cumner (Cumnor) hills and Bagley wood are south-west of Oxford, where Swinburne had been a student.

155. *Cumner*: In the three editions of *Poems* (1881, 1882, 1892), this misspelling of 'Cumnor' persists.

159–62. *the shepherd . . . mossy Sandford*: Matthew Arnold, as the shepherd Corydon, mourned the loss of his friend, the poet Arthur Hugh Clough, in 'Thyrsis', a pastoral elegy, in which Sicilian shepherds have 'lost a mate' and Dorian shepherds sing to Proserpine (queen of the Underworld), for 'she herself had trod Sicilian fields . . . ', 81–97. Sandford, also mentioned in 'Thyrsis', is south of Oxford.

165. *One of that little clan*: Dante Gabriel Rossetti, one of the founders of the Pre-Raphaelite Brotherhood (1848–53), artists who rejected contemporary academic painting in favour of the art before Raphael (1483–1520). They sought to return to nature and the simplicity of the 14th- and 15th-century Tuscan artists.

172. *garths . . . crofts*: both terms refer to small enclosed fields—the former to fields beside a building, yard, or garden, the latter to fields used for tillage or pasture.

173. *son of Leto*: Apollo, the sun god and embodiment of the Greek ideal of culture, was a handsome young figure associated with the arts; he was also the protector of herds and flocks. His mother, the Titan goddess Leto, gave birth to both Apollo and Artemis, whose father was Zeus.

175–6. *Bacchus . . . Indian throne*: elements of the Dionysus/Bacchus myth originated in ancient cults that emerged in Asia Minor. Some versions of the myth trace Dionysus' expedition (with a warlike following) to India, which he conquered. See No. 2, 'Chorus of Cloud-Maidens', note to lines 29–30.

179. *the wanton Bassarid*: a male votary of Dionysus. The name apparently means 'one who wears fox-skins'.

182. *Ashtaroth*: the Hebrew name for Astarte (also known as 'Ashtareth'), the Semitic goddess of fertility, love, and war, alluded to (and condemned) in several biblical passages, such as Judges 2: 13; 10: 6. A prominent Phoenician and Egyptian deity, she is sometimes identified with the Greek Aphrodite.

184. *Cithæron*: a mountain range in central Greece, between Boeotia in the north and Attica in the south.

185. *Faun*: that is, Faunus, who, in Roman myth, is a woodland deity, the protector of herbs and crops. Half man, half goat, he was the Roman version of the Greek Pan.

189. *Mænad girl*: one ecstatically inspired by Dionysus. See No. 2, 'Chorus of Cloud-Maidens', note to lines 29–30.

190. *Pans*: referring to the goatish satyrs (see line 195) devoted to Dionysus, as well as to Pan, the 'hornèd master' (see line 197), whose lusts were legendary.

200. *Apollo's lad*: the beautiful Hyacinthus, with whom Apollo fell in love, was accidentally killed when a gust of wind caught a discus they had been practising

with. The grieving Apollo transformed the boy's blood into a new flower, the bell-shaped hyacinth (or jacinth), to immortalize his name. The petals are flecked with the Greek *Ai, Ai* ('Woe, Woe'). W associated Hyacinthus with Lord Alfred Douglas in a letter to him in January 1893, later used by blackmailers and quoted in W's trials: 'Your slim gilt soul walks between passion and poetry. I know Hyacinthus, whom Apollo loved so madly, was you in Greek days' (*Letters* 326).

201. *Tyrian prince*: the beautiful god Adonis, of Phoenician origins (*adon* means 'lord'), is here associated with Tyre, the ancient city of Phoenicia, now Sur in Lebanon. When Adonis was killed by a boar, Aphrodite, his lover, pleaded with Zeus to permit him to leave the Underworld and spend part of each year with her (see lines 205–7).

204. *virgin maid*: Artemis. See note above to lines 153–6.

205–7. *dying boy . . . overweighs the jacinth*: see note above to line 200.

208. *Cyprian*: see No. 1, 'Ye Shall be Gods', note to line 57.

213. *Drops poison in mine ear*: the method by which Claudius killed Hamlet's father (*Hamlet*, I. v. 62–4).

214. *To burn one's old ships*: proverbial expression for cutting oneself off from the past.

216. *Proteus*: a Homeric sea-god, servant to Poseidon, who can assume different forms to avoid answering questions about the future; only when held captive does he resume his original form.

217–18. *Medea . . . Colchian shrine*: Medea, a sorceress who was the daughter of the king of Colchis, enabled Jason to take the Golden Fleece (originally on a ram that had the power of flight) by casting a spell on the dragon guarding it.

219. *asphodel*: see No. 44, 'Santa Decca', note to line 11.

220. *Proserpine*: see No. 44, note to line 3.

223. *golden-girdled bee*: phrase taken from Swinburne's *Atalanta in Calydon*, 1: 417.

225–6. *sombre Lord . . . pomegranate seed*: because Hades had bidden Proserpine to eat the seeds of a pomegranate (traditional symbol of fertility) during her captivity in the Underworld, she had to live there forever, but Zeus decreed that she would divide her time between the Underworld and the world above.

230. *Venus . . . Melian farm*: the statue (now in the Louvre) commonly called the *Venus de Milo*, or *Melos*, was unearthed on the island of Melos in 1820.

231–2. This fantasy is central to No. 55, 'Charmides'.

233. *The Dawn at Florence*: *Dawn*, an allegorical figure sculpted by Michelangelo for one of the Medici chapels in the Church of S. Lorenzo. In June 1875, W visited the chapels, which he describes in a letter to his father (*Letters* 4).

238. *riven veil . . . Gorgon eyes*: the veil of the Temple (see No. 17, 'The True Knowledge', note to lines 7–8) was rent in two on the day that Christ died. For the Gorgon eyes, see No. 30, 'The Theatre at Argos', note to line 7.

241. *Niobe*: though mythic stories of Niobe differ radically, the best-known account depicts her as so proud of her children that a goddess asked Apollo and

Artemis to punish her. After her children were slain, Niobe was transformed into a stone, the eyes of which continued to shed tears. W may have seen the statue of Niobe's children in Florence's Uffizi Gallery, which he visited in 1875.

245. *untented wounds*: too deep for cleansing with a roll of absorbent or medicated material (i.e. 'tent'). Cf. *King Lear*, I. iv. 300: 'Th' untented woundings of a father's curse'.

252. *dishonoured House*: the 'house' image occurs in Jesus's farewell sermon to his disciples: 'Let not your heart be troubled: ye believe in God, believe also in me. In my Father's house are many mansions . . .' (John 14: 2). In W's phrase, God's house has been dishonoured by those who crucified Christ.

254. *Melpomene*: the Muse of tragedy.

256. *limpid Castaly*: the spring more commonly called 'Castalia' after the nymph, who, when pursued by Apollo, threw herself into its waters. It was sacred to the god and the Muses on Mt. Parnassus, near Delphi, the site of Apollo's oracle.

266. See No. 54, 'Endymion', title note.

269. *Naiad*: a water nymph. Water nymphs embodied the divinity of the spring or stream in which they lived. Pan's sexual pursuits were legion: see note to line 93.

272. *silver daughter*: Aphrodite, born of the sea.

273. *gyves*: an archaic term for shackles, especially for the legs.

274. *Dryope*: the daughter of a king, Dryope was transformed into a tree after she picked flowers from the branches of a tree that began to bleed: unknown to Dryope, this tree was the transfigured body of the nymph Lotis, who, in anger, transformed Dryope as she herself had been changed.

278. *Daphne*: the nymph, whose name means 'laurel', was a river god's daughter, transformed into a laurel tree by her father when she prayed for protection from the amorous Apollo.

279. See note to lines 120–1.

282. *Antinous*: a youth (*c.*110–30) whose striking beauty made him the favourite of Hadrian (AD 76–138), the Roman emperor, and who—according to legend—drowned in the Nile in order to preserve Hadrian's life. Antinous appears in numerous literary works by late 19th-century homosexuals. See No. 118, *The Sphinx*, 34–6, where W refers to 'Adrian' and Antinous.

291. *Dryad*: a tree nymph, from the Greek *drys* ('tree').

293–4. *Marsyas . . . songs of pain*: a satyr who (with his flute) challenged Apollo (on the lyre) to a musical contest, the Muses acting as judges. By a prior agreement, the victorious Apollo tied the satyr to a tree and flayed him alive.

301–3. The image of the human heart breaking 'in music' reappears in W's lecture 'The English Renaissance', delivered on his American lecture tour in 1882, and in No. 67, 'Roses and Rue', 53–6.

306. *Pandion*: the father of Philomela and Procne.

307–8. After the rape, Tereus cut out Philomela's tongue to prevent her from exposing him. However, she revealed to Procne what had happened by weaving a tapestry depicting the events.

316. *racing eight*: rowers in a light racing boat. Races between crews from the different colleges were—and are—an important feature of Oxford University sporting life.

320. *swinked*: archaic for 'wearied with toil'.

321. *wattled sheep-cotes*: sheepcotes are small shelters for sheep; 'wattled' refers to their construction, of interlaced twigs or flexible boughs.

322. *Sandford*: see note to lines 159–62.

336. *Drifting with every wind*: cf. No. 90, 'Helas!', 1.

52 THEOCRITUS. A VILLANELLE

MS and Publishing History:

An untitled MS (*M*, location: Clark 2471) is an early draft of lines 1, 3, 16–17, 7–10, 13–15, and 10–11 in that order. Written *c*.1878, when W composed No. 51, 'The Burden of Itys', and No. 55, 'Charmides', at the time when his enthusiasm for Greek culture was dominant.

First published in *P1*; unchanged in *P2*; collected thereafter.

Title. In 3 BC, Theocritus was the founder of the Greek pastoral tradition in his poems, which the Romans called his 'Idylls', implying an idealized world of shepherds and shepherdesses. W uses the French fixed form of the villanelle, which was originally also concerned with pastoral subject matter (a *villa* was a farm or country house), its form consisting of five three-line stanzas and a concluding quatrain, all on two interlocking rhymes.

1–2. *Persephone*: see No. 44, 'Santa Decca', note to line 3.

3. *Sicily*: Theocritus' earliest idylls were composed there.

5. *Amaryllis*: in Idyll 3, the mistress of the young goatherd whose gifts of love she rejects.

7. *Simætha . . . Hecate*: in Idyll 2, Simaetha casts a spell to draw her lover back to her, calling upon Hecate, closely associated with Artemis, the moon–goddess, to help with magic. Hecate was also goddess of the crossroads, where monthly offerings of dog's flesh were presented to her (cf. Idyll 2: 35–6: 'Hark . . . where the dogs howl in the town. Sure the Goddess is at these cross-roads').

11. *Polypheme . . . fate*: a cyclops, or one-eyed giant, the son of the sea-god Poseidon, in Homer's *Odyssey* Polyphemus rears sheep and goats on an island. Imprisoned by him in a cave, Odysseus destroys his eye with a stake. In Idylls 6 and 11, Theocritus depicts Polyphemus in love with the nymph Galatea, who rejects him.

14. *Daphnis*: in Idyll 6, a legendary Sicilian shepherd (see No. 51, 'The Burden of Itys', note to line 57), who challenges his friend Damoetas to a song contest.

16. *Lacon*: in Idyll 5, Comatas and Lacon engage in a song competition, a sheep to be awarded the winner from the loser's flock. Comatas wins: in W's poem, Lacon still waits to pay his debt.

53 NOCTURNE

MSS: Three MSS (location: Clark 2432 and 2433) consisting, in *M1*, of jottings, of which only relevant variants are listed; in *M2*, of a draft of the poem with the present title; and in *M3*, of a fragment of lines 21-4.

Not published in W's lifetime.

An early version of No. 54, 'Endymion', 'Nocturne', was probably written around 1877-8. Different in form and treatment from 'Endymion', this poem warrants consideration as a separate work.

Title. When James McNeill Whistler adopted the musical term 'nocturne' for the titles of several paintings completed in the 1870s, poets followed his intent to emphasize the artifice of art as well as the interrelationship of the arts in order to discourage the public from expecting moral instruction.

1-2. Echoes No. 54, 'Endymion', 39.

3-4. Echoes 'Endymion', 41-2.

10. Echoes 'Endymion', 40.

21-2. *Acheron*: the river that ran through the domain of Hades, whose wife was Proserpine (also known as Persephone: see No. 44, 'Santa Decca', note to line 3).

54 ENDYMION

MS and Publishing History:

Probably written in 1878, when W was particularly involved with Classical subject matter, one MS fragment (*M*, location: Clark 2433) is extant, containing only lines 29-42. See No. 53, 'Nocturne', which is an early attempt at 'Endymion'.

First published in *P1*; unchanged in *P2*; collected thereafter.

Title. Though the Greek myth of Endymion has many versions, the best-known tells of his relationship with Selene, the personification of the Moon (sometimes confused with Artemis, also known as Diana, goddess of the hunt and moon-goddess). Selene falls in love with the beautiful young shepherd Endymion and seduces him. At her request, Zeus grants Endymion his wish to sleep eternally and thus remain young forever. The subtitle—'(For Music)'—appears in all printings. (See the headnote to No. 23, 'Lotus Leaves', describing a MS titled 'Selene'.)

1. The speaker, a shepherdess, is in love with Endymion.

2. *Arcady*: see No. 29, 'Impression de Voyage', note to line 8.

4. *wold*: see No. 7, 'Rome Unvisited', note to line 52.

10. *shoon*: archaic form of 'shoes'.

16-17. Cf. No. 55, 'Charmides', 33-4.

18. *seneschal*: one who has control of domestic arrangements in the home of a nobleman or other high personage.

21-2. *moon . . . Helice*: an invocation to the moon to rise above Helice, the constellation of the Great Bear, and spread her rays in order to locate the speaker's 'own true love'. In one mythical account, Kronos pursued Helice and another nymph for having raised Zeus, who transformed them into constellations, Helice becoming the

Great Bear. Another version holds that the jealous Hera, Zeus's wife, effected the transformation.

42. This line is echoed in No. 52, 'Nocturne', in the final line of each stanza.

55 CHARMIDES

MSS and Publishing History:

Written between 1878 and 1879, three fragmentary MSS have survived: *M1* (location: Clark 2493) contains jottings for lines 595–8; *M2* (location: Huntington HM 464) is a fair copy of lines 511–606; and *M3* (location: Hyde) is a fair copy of lines 607–54. *M2* and *M3* are the MSS from which lines were set for *Poems*.

First published in *P1*; rev. in *P2*; collected thereafter.

This narrative poem—with its numerous Classical allusions reminiscent of No. 51, 'The Burden of Itys' (particularly lines 231–4)—has, as its major source, Lucian's *Essays in Portraiture*, 4, in which an unnamed boy falls in love with the statue [in Aphrodite's temple], remains behind when others leave, and embraces the statue 'to the best of his endeavours'. The boy later drowns by jumping from a cliff into the sea.

While W was on his American lecture tour, a reporter from the San Francisco *Daily Examiner* (27 March 1882) asked him to name his favourite poem: 'Charmides', he reportedly said, was his 'most finished and perfect'.

Title. W took the name Charmides from Plato's *Charmides*, in which Socrates describes the young man—who was born into an aristocratic Athenian family and who died in 403 BC—as 'a marvel of stature and beauty; and all the rest, to my thinking, were in love with him. . . . I noticed that none of them, not even the smallest, had eyes for anything else, but that they all gazed at him as if he were a statue'. W's first use of the name had occurred in the first version of No. 63, 'Phêdre': see variants to line 4.

4. Echoes Keats's *Endymion*, 2: 562: 'Those same dark curls blown vagrant in the wind'.

13–14. *Corinthian hills . . . sandy bay*: Charmides landed near Athens in the late afternoon. The Corinthian hills would have been south and west.

22. *Tyrian*: see No. 51, 'The Burden of Itys', note to line 201.

26. *high hill*: the Acropolis.

27. *fane*: a temple, presumably the Parthenon, which housed a statue of Athena by Phidias (*c.*510–432 BC).

33–4. *Her*: Athena was protectress of the city and its environs.

37. *beechen cup*: made from the wood of the beech tree.

65–72. Athena, in preparing for battle, was usually depicted with a helmet, carved with such images as griffins, rams, horses, and sphinxes; a shield (or breastplate, called a 'cuirass') with the image of Medusa, the Gorgon; and a spear. Her sacred bird, an owl, symbol of her wisdom, was often at her side.

74. *Sunium*: a cape forming the southernmost point of Attica, on which was built a temple dedicated to Athena.

75. *tunnies*: tuna.

75–6. *brazen tramp | Of horses*: belonging to the sea-god Poseidon. Apparently all the gods take notice of this sacrilege: see the reaction of the moon-goddess and goddess of the hunt, Diana (for the Greeks, Artemis) in line 81.

86. *twelve Gods*: the Greek pantheon of deities, sculpted around the frieze of the Parthenon, which also included reliefs of Poseidon vying with Athena for possession of Athens.

95. *wight*: archaic for 'person'.

96. *shepherd prince*: Paris, the son of King Priam of Troy, had been brought up by shepherds: see No. 25, 'A Fragment from the Agamemnon of Aeschylos', note to line 23.

103. *crocus gown*: decorated with colours associated with crocus flowers—that is, deep yellow or purple.

105. *peplos*: a long robe woven annually for Athena's statue and ritualistically carried in procession to her temple.

108. *bossy hills*: swelling in rounded form—Athena's buttocks.

118. *argent*: silvery white.

121. *Numidian*: Numidia was an ancient country in north-west Africa, approximating to modern-day Algeria.

141. *grebe*: a diving bird.

151–60. W's description suggests an English landscape, much like that in No. 51, 'The Burden of Itys', 43–54.

152. *wattled cotes*: see No. 51, note to line 321.

159. *weald*: see No. 7, 'Rome Unvisited', note to line 52.

164–6. *Hylas . . . Herakles*: see No. 44, 'Santa Decca', note to line 7.

165. *Naiad*: see No. 51, 'The Burden of Itys', note to line 269.

167. *Narcissus*: see No. 51, note to line 116.

170. *Dionysos*: see No. 2, 'Chorus of Cloud-Maidens', note to lines 29–30.

172. *Bassarid*: see No. 51, 'The Burden of Itys', note to line 179.

181. *neat-herd's lad*: a cattle-herder's helper.

198. *wether*: a castrated ram.

207. *ousel-cock*: archaic for the blackbird (or 'ouzel').

243. *casque*: helmet.

244. *seven-cubit spear . . . targe*: the spear held by the colossal statue of Athena in the Parthenon was approximately eleven and a half feet in length (each cubit around 20 inches). A targe is a light shield, usually carried by archers or footmen.

252. *to luff*: to steer or sail a ship nearer to the wind.

271–6. These lines, concluding the first part, are reminiscent of the ending of Arnold's 'The Scholar-Gipsy', where the Tyrian trader sails away from trespassers and, when he reaches safe harbour, undoes his baled goods. The Symplegades were rocks guarding the Dardanelles, the entrance to the Hellespont.

277. *Triton-god*: the son of Poseidon (or, in Roman myth, Neptune), often depicted as half human, half fish, holding a trident and a shell horn.

282. *halcyon*: this fabled bird, identified with the kingfisher, had the power to charm the wind and waves in order to restore serenity to the sea.

289. *Colonos*: a hill one mile north of Athens, the legendary place where Oedipus died and Sophocles was born.

292. *Hymettus*: a mountain east of Athens, famous for its honey and marble.

297. *Hyacinth*: see No. 51, 'The Burden of Itys', note to line 200.

301. *Dryads*: see No. 51, note to line 291.

303. *seneschal*: see No. 54, 'Endymion', note to line 18.

317. *enow*: archaic for 'enough'.

332. *lustihead*: an archaic form of 'lust'.

338. *bosky*: covered with bushes or undergrowth.

342. *ambuscade*: literally an ambush, or here a concealed place.

360. *Proserpine*: see No. 44, 'Santa Decca', note to line 3.

363–4. Echoes of lines previously used in No. 48, *Ravenna*, 296–7.

364. *Corinth's citadel*: on Acrocorinth, a mountain overlooking the city.

376. *panoply*: a complete suit of armour.

379. *bossy gold*: raised ornamentation, as in 'embossed'.

384. *Proteus*: see No. 51, 'The Burden of Itys', note to line 216.

404. *reed*: see No. 51, 'The Burden of Itys', note to line 93.

405. *lovely boy*: Eros, known to the Romans as Cupid.

409. *laurel*: see No. 51, 'The Burden of Itys', note to line 278.

413. *Boreas*: the god of the North Wind, who abducted Orithyia, daughter of Erechtheus, king of Athens, and made her his wife in Thrace.

414. *Hermes*: see No. 29, 'Impression de Voyage', note to line 8.

437. *Cytheræa*: see No. 51, 'The Burden of Itys', note to line 96.

455. *mimic moons*: apparently derived from Shelley's 'mimic moon' in 'The Witch of Atlas', 283.

470–1. *Amaryllis . . . Daphnis*: see No. 52, 'Theocritus', notes to lines 5 and 14.

478. *Paphian myrtles*: trees of Cyprus, a centre for the worship of Aphrodite.

487. *Cyprian Queen*: see No. 1, 'Ye Shall be Gods', note to line 57.

490–2. *moon . . . Endymion's eyes . . . Dian*: see No. 54, 'Endymion', the title note.

495. *hyaline*: something transparent, a poeticism for the smooth sea.

498. *Xiphias*: Latin for 'swordfish'.

502. *cornel bow*: made from the wood of the cornelian cherry tree.

517–18. Cf. Swinburne's 'Ballad of Death', 85–6: 'Even where her parted breast-flowers have place, | Even where they are cloven apart—who knows not this?'

536. *Adonis*: see No. 51, 'The Burden of Itys', note to line 201.

538. *doves . . . wane*: Aphrodite rides on the waning moon (see line 572), which, in certain phases, takes on a golden hue (hence, 'gilded') from the reflection of the sun.

542. *Oread*: see No. 51, 'The Burden of Itys', note to line 126.

555. *lady-bird . . . brede*: also called a 'lady-bug', a small red or yellow beetle with black spots.

567. *may*: archaic for 'maid', as used by Chaucer and by such later writers as William Morris and Algernon Swinburne, important influences on W. For the *Collected Edition* (1908), Robert Ross 'corrected' *may* to *maid*.

573. This line was later echoed in No. 66, 'Madonna Mia', 7.

577. *van*: archaic for 'wing'.

582. *Thammuz*: a Syrian deity, identified with the Phoenician Adon, or Adonis.

602. *cressets*: receptacles designed to hold burning oil or grease.

605. *guerdon*: a favour or reward.

606. *Charon's icy ford*: the ferryman who conveyed the dead across the river Styx in the Underworld.

607. *Acheron*: see No. 25, 'Fragment from the Agamemnon of Aeschylos', note to line 29.

613. *Lethæan well*: the waters of forgetfulness in the Underworld.

619-21. A description reminiscent of the Narcissus myth (see No. 51, 'The Burden of Itys', note to line 116), though with a different outcome.

639. *O'er daring Icarus*: the son of the great artificer Daedalus, both of whom escaped from the Cretan labyrinth on wings made of wax and feathers. Ignoring his father's warning, Icarus soared too close to the sun and drowned when the wax in his wings melted and he fell into the sea. W addresses 'poesy' in line 637 to protect the daring Icarus—an indirect reference, perhaps, to Charmides, another overreacher in his unrestrained passion.

641. *Castalian rill*: see No. 51, 'The Burden of Itys', note to line 256. Those wishing to consult the Delphic Oracle had to purify themselves first in its waters. The Romans regarded 'drinking the waters of Castalia' as signifying poetic inspiration since Apollo was the god of poetry.

642. *Sappho's golden quill*: the legend that the Greek lyric poet Sappho, born in Lesbos in late 7 BC, drowned herself is pure fiction, for she left Lesbos because of political difficulties and died in Sicily.

654. *Enna . . . zone*: see No. 44, 'Santa Decca', note to line 3. *Zone* is a poetic term for a girdle or any encircling band.

56 BALLADE DE MARGUERITE (NORMANDIE.)

MS and Publishing History:
  First published in *Kottabos* 3 (Hilary Term 1879), 146–7 (*K*), entitled ' "La Belle Marguerite." Ballade du Moyen Age.' Extant is the MS with the subscript

'(Normande)'—(*M*, location: Jeremy Mason Collection)—from which type was set for *Poems*. Published in *P1*; unchanged in *P2*; collected thereafter.

W's poem—in stanzaic structure, situation, and style—appears to be modelled after Dante Gabriel Rossetti's 'John of Tours (Old French)'. Perhaps feeling some discomfort over his imitative verse, W wrote to A. H. Miles (1848–1929), who wished to include certain of his poems in *The Poets and the Poetry of the Century* (1891–7): 'You are quite at liberty to make any use of the poems you mention, with the exception of "The Dole of the King's Daughter"; the "Ballade de Marguerite", the "Serenade", and the "La Bella Donna [della mia Mente]". These four I do not consider very characteristic of my work' (*Letters* 325).

Title. Cf. the refrain of William Morris's 'The Eve of Crécy': '*Ah! qu'elle est belle La Marguerite*'. W's use of the term *ballade*, though derived from Old French poetry, has no relation to the fixed French form, which generally has three eight- or ten-line stanzas and a concluding four-line *envoi*.

1. *chase*: unenclosed land used for breeding and hunting wild animals.

10. *Martinmas*: a feast on 11 November, honouring St Martin (*c*.316–97), who had been the bishop of Tours.

16. *meer*: a variation of 'mere', meaning 'sea' or 'lake'.

18. *wind the morte*: a hunting term, meaning to sound a horn at the death (*OED* spells the word *mort*) of a deer.

24. *stoup*: a cup or tankard.

40. *assoil*: archaic for 'absolve'.

44. Cf. Matthew 8: 22: 'But Jesus said unto him, Follow me; and let the dead bury their dead'.

57 LA BELLE GABRIELLE

MS: Probably written around 1878–9, a single MS (*M*, location: Clark 2424) is extant.

Not published in W's lifetime.

Title. The French title recalls No. 56, 'Ballade de Marguerite' (see the title note). Despite the subscript, no original has been found for the poem.

2. *Latmian hill*: in the Greek myth, Endymion, beloved of the moon-goddess, sleeps everlastingly in a cave on Mt. Latmos. See No. 54, 'Endymion', the title note.

5–6. Cf. the incident in John 2: 1–10, in which Jesus, at a wedding in Cana, transforms water into wine.

8. *crimson-caftaned*: a caftan is a Turkish or Persian garment, with a long tunic underneath, tied with a girdle at the waist.

13–14. *Narcissus*: see No. 51, 'The Burden of Itys', note to line 116.

15. *Salmacis*: see No. 51, note to line 120.

58 HUMANITAD

MS and Publishing History:

First published in *P1*; rev. in *P2*; collected thereafter.

A MS (*M*, location: Hyde), containing only lines 109–14, is extant. It is a presentation verse, an extract of poetry given to an admirer. W was prone to giving such verses during his 1882 American lecture tour (cf. headnote to No. 76, 'Ave Imperatrix').

Probably written around 1878–9, when Swinburne's influence on W was most apparent, this poem echoes the sentiments of Swinburne's *Songs before Sunrise* (1871), in which praise of great men builds to a general exaltation of humanity's universal divinity in 'The Hymn of Man': 'Glory to Man in the highest! for Man is master of things'. Swinburne once wrote that 'God is no more than man: *because* man is no less than God'. In a radical reversal of his former Roman Catholic enthusiasm, W accepts this credo and embraces Swinburne's hero-worship of Giuseppe Mazzini (1805–72), the Italian revolutionary prominent in the Risorgimento ('Resurgence'), which led in 1870 to the unification of Italy (see lines 230–87).

Title: Probably modelled after Whitman's 'Libertad' in *Leaves of Grass*, 'Humanitad' is an apparent combination of the Latin *humanitatis* and the Spanish *humanidad* in referring to humanity.

1. *It is full Winter now*: echoed in No. 75, 'The Garden of Eros', 1.

4. *Autumn's gaudy livery*: previously used in No. 48, *Ravenna*, 281.

7. *Saturn's cave*: in Keats's *Hyperion*, Book Two, the Titans, overthrown by the Olympians, gather in a cave where they, with Saturn as their leader, bemoan their fate.

8. *wain*: a wagon.

19. *bittern*: a long-legged wading bird that utters a 'boom' during the mating season.

23. *seamew*: any of the gulls near coastal areas.

26. *byre*: a cowshed or barn.

28. *billets*: suitable lengths of firewood, from the French *bille* ('trunk of a tree').

32–3. Echoes of No. 22, 'Desespoir', 6–8.

48. *boys-love, sops-in-wine*: 'boy's love' is also known as 'lad's love' or southernwood, a deciduous shrub with a fragrant odour but a sour taste. 'Sops-in-wine' is the clove-gillyflower, coloured pink with a clove scent, related to the carnation.

50. *younker*: youngster.

66. *haw*: the hawthorn bush with its scarlet berries.

67. Cf. Keats's 'Ode on a Grecian Urn', 21: 'Ah, happy, happy boughs!'

69. *flowre-de-luce*: W's spelling for the 'flower-de-luce', an archaic term for the 'fleur-de-lis' ('lily flower').

72. *the hum of murmuring bees*: the device of onomatopeia, borrowed from Tennyson's song 'Come Down, O Maid' in *The Princess*, 7: 207: 'murmuring of innumerable bees'.

75. *Vale-lilies*: better known as 'lilies of the valley' (see note above to line 69).

83. *nepenthe*: a drug of Egyptian origin, mentioned in Homer's *Odyssey*, that obliterates present grief or the troubled past.

84. *mandragore*: the mandragora, related to the poisonous mandrake plant, has narcotic and emetic properties.

85–9. Cf. Wordsworth's 'Ode: Intimations of Immortality', 1–5: 'There was a time when meadow, grove, and stream, | The earth, and every common sight, | To me did seem | Apparelled in celestial light, | The glory and the freshness of a dream'.

96. Cf. No. 34, 'Easter Day', 14.

103. *To burn with one clear flame*: echoes Pater's *Studies in the History of the Renaissance* (1873), 210: 'To burn always with this hard gem-like flame, to maintain this ecstasy, is success in life'.

107. *Medea*: see No. 51, 'The Burden of Itys', note to lines 217–18.

112. *Swan's death*: according to legend, a swan that has lost its mate calls for it to the end of its days. It also foresees its own imminent death and cries out—its proverbial 'swan song'—in lamenting its end.

113. *Memnon*: an Ethiopian prince slain by Achilles in the Trojan War. A colossal statue, standing before a temple in Egyptian Thebes and supposedly representing Memnon (but, in fact, that of an Egyptian king), allegedly sang, or at least emitted harmonious sounds, at dawn when struck by the rays of the rising sun. The palace of Memnon in Ethiopia is mentioned in No. 118, *The Sphinx*, 133.

115–16. Echoes No. 43, 'The Grave of Shelley', 1–2.

117. *XAIPE*: This Greek greeting allows the meanings of 'Farewell' and 'Welcome', the ambiguity seemingly appropriate as an inscription on a tomb.

121. *poppy-crownèd God*: Hades, the god of the Underworld.

149. *Hers*: Athena, the virgin goddess, who wears on her shield the Gorgon's head, which had the power of turning to stone every living thing that looked at it.

151. *dainty page*: Cupid.

154. *Adonis*: see No. 55, 'Charmides', note to line 536.

157. *shepherd boy*: Paris. See No. 55, note to line 96.

159. *Tenedos and lofty Troy*: the former, an island off the coast of Troy, was associated with the heroic Tenes, whose stepmother fell in love with him. When he refused to return her love, she accused him publicly of improper advances towards her. Tenes was set adrift in a chest by his outraged father, and he eventually landed at Tenedos. Troy, of course, recalls Paris and Helen.

160. *the Queen*: Aphrodite.

166–8. *One . . . a son!*: presumably Byron, who died in 1824 while involved in the Greek struggle for independence from the Turks. W's phrase—'Like Aeschylos at well-fought Marathon'—suggests an analogy with Byron, though Aeschylus did not die in the Greek defeat of the Persian invaders at Marathon, near Athens, in 490 BC. W had used lines 166–7 in No. 48, *Ravenna*, 132–3.

169. *Portico*: of the Academy in Athens, the school founded by Plato as early as 380 BC, where Socrates, 'the grave Athenian master' (see line 172), conducted his legendary dialogues.

177. *Colonos*: see No. 55, 'Charmides', note to line 289.

178. *Mnemosyne*: the goddess of memory, who, by coupling with Zeus for nine nights, gave birth to the nine Muses.

180. *Athena's owl*: see No. 55, 'Charmides', note to lines 65–72.

183. *Muse of Time*: Clio, the Muse of history.

186. *Polymnia's scroll*: according to some accounts, Polymnia (or Polyhymnia) was regarded among the Greeks (whom W follows) as the Muse of history, among other functions, although to the Romans she was the Muse only of lyric poetry or of hymns to the gods.

186–204. These lines depict the Persian invasion of Greece in 480 BC.

188. *little town*: Athens.

190. *Mede*: W here identifies Xerxes I (d. 465 BC), king of the Persians (486–65), as a Mede (the Medes, however, were an ancient people related to the later Persians). Xerxes scored a victory over the Greeks at Thermopylae in 480 but then suffered a naval defeat at Salamis in the same year (see line 204).

192. *Artemisium . . . Thermopylæ*: the Greek fleet was stationed in the Gulf of Artemisium. Thermopylae was a hot spring adjacent to a pass through which the Persians hoped to gain entry to the Grecian lowlands. In the ensuing action, Leonidas, king of Sparta, ordered a retreat but remained with 300 followers to fight against overwhelming odds until all were killed.

202. *Eurotas*: the river on the banks of which Sparta was built.

206. *time too out of tune*: W conflates two well-known quotations: Hamlet's complaint, 'The time is out of joint' (I. v. 188), and Ophelia's lament over Hamlet's apparent madness (III. i. 159), 'Like sweet bells jangled, out of tune and harsh'— traditional metaphors of psychological or social disharmony. For other uses of 'out of tune', see No. 18, 'Heart's Yearnings', 6; No. 71, 'Silentium Amoris', 6; and No. 87, 'Impressions. I. Les Silhouettes', 2.

207. *Dial's wheel*: that is, a sun-dial, whose 'wheel' marks the hours when the sun's shadow falls upon it.

213. *hills | Of lone Helvellyn*: in the Lake District, the lifelong haunt of Wordsworth, 'that Spirit' (line 215).

217. *Rydalian laurels*: from 1813 Wordsworth lived at Rydal Mount, near Ambleside.

221. *Love and Duty mingle*: a central theme of Wordsworth's 'Ode to Duty'.

226. *Hydra*: a many-headed, seemingly indestructible monster that Heracles decapitated with his sword.

229. *Ichabod*: in 1 Samuel 4: 21, a name that may be translated as 'There is no glory', for when Phineas's wife heard that the Philistines had seized the ark of God and that her husband and father-in-law were dead, she named her new-born son Ichabod because 'the glory is departed from Israel . . .'.

230. *last dear son of Italy*: Mazzini.

233–4. Mazzini was not buried in Florence near Giotto's tower but in Genoa.

237. *conqueror*: because of his revolutionary views, Mazzini lived most of his life

as an exile outside of Italy. When Pope Pius IX abandoned Rome to the rebels in 1848, Mazzini entered the city in triumph and in February 1849 was elected head of the republic ('the great triumvir' in line 246).

242. *old man . . . rusty keys*: a derisive allusion to Pius IX. See No. 7, 'Rome Unvisited', note to line 32. 'Grabbled' means groped about or searched with his hands.

249. *empyreal dome*: the dome of La Cathedrale di S. Maria del Fiore in Florence, renowned in the 15th century as a feat of engineering genius by the Florentine architect Filippo Brunelleschi (1377–1446).

250. *Valdarno*: name given to the valley cut by the Arno River.

251. *Melpomene*: the Muse of tragedy.

254–5. *the Nine . . . their discreet emperies*: in Roman mythology, each Muse had her own defined area of patronage.

257. *Marathon*: a symbol of free men opposing the armies of an invading despot, so named after the battle at Marathon. See note to lines 166–8. In 1849, the republic under Mazzini quickly came under attack by French and Austrian forces supporting the pope.

259. *Giotto's tower*: see note to lines 233–4.

262. *Vallombrosa*: a monastery and town south-west of Florence.

273. Echoes Psalm 24: 7: 'Lift up your heads, O ye gates; and be ye lift up, ye everlasting doors; and the King of glory shall come in'.

275. *vile thing*: presumably a further reference to the pope. Even after the unification of Italy under Victor Emmanuel II, the papacy refused to recognize the legitimacy of the state. Rome had been taken from Church control in 1871, and the political sovereignty of the pope was reduced to the environs of Vatican City.

278. *mother of red harlotries*: in Revelation 17: 3–4, the whore of Babylon is described as sitting 'upon a scarlet coloured beast, full of names of blasphemy, having seven heads and ten horns'—a figure which Protestants have traditionally identified allegorically as the Roman Catholic Church.

279–82. The *Aeginetans*, a pediment group from a Doric temple on the island of Aegina that was removed to the Glyptothek (Sculpture Gallery) in Munich. The sculpture shows combatants before the walls of Troy.

287. *Niobe*: see No. 51, 'The Burden of Itys', note to line 241.

291. *graveclothes folded*: in John 20: 5–7, the disciples ran to the tomb of the risen Christ to find the graveclothes empty and the napkin which covered his head 'wrapped together in a place by itself'.

298. *Aspromonte*: in Calabria, on the peninsula of southern Italy, where republicans, led by Garibaldi, attempted to march to Rome but met defeat in a battle on 29 August 1862 at the hands of the Italian army.

301. *gyves*: see No. 51, 'The Burden of Itys', note to line 273.

302–5. W assails an indifferent society, in which poverty and cruelty are widespread—no doubt the influence of John Ruskin is at work in these lines, which reappear in Act I of W's play *The Duchess of Padua* (1883).

306–7. *where is the pen | Of austere Milton?*: W again invokes Milton's name—as in No. 40, 'To Milton'—to lament the moral decline of England, just as Wordsworth did in 'London, 1802': see No. 45, 'Theoretikos', note to lines 5–6.

307–8. *mighty sword . . . righteously*: the sword as metaphor for pen alludes to Milton's publication of *The Tenure of Kings and Magistrates* (1649), which argued, in support of the Independents who had imprisoned King Charles I, that subjects may depose and execute an unjust king.

310. *voiceless tripod*: according to legend, the ancient Greek oracles, which spoke from flaming tripods, were silenced by the death of Christ (see No. 44, 'Santa Decca', note to line 5).

321–2. *the seed | Of things which slay their sower*: for a variation of this line, see line 421 and note.

325. *What even Cromwell spared*: during the English civil war of 1642–8, the Puritan army often defaced monuments and buildings.

330. *new Vandals*: an allusion to the English restoration societies, which frequently destroyed the distinctiveness of old buildings by modernizing them. The Vandals, an ancient Germanic tribe powerful in the 4th and 5th centuries, plundered even Rome and hence have come to be a byword for senseless destruction.

331–2. *the Angels sing . . . lofty choir*: the Angel Choir of Lincoln Cathedral, built between 1256 and 1280, which is carved with 28 angels in the spandrels of the gallery windows, some of them holding musical instruments.

337–8. *Southwell's arch . . . the House of One*: Southwell Minster, Nottinghamshire, whose late 13th-century chapter house (hence 'House') is beautifully and naturalistically sculpted with native English flowers and foliage, including hawthorn branches. The 'arch' is its doorway. The 'One' is Jesus, who loved the lilies of the field (see Matthew 6: 28).

342. Cf. No. 40, 'To Milton', lines 1–2.

349 ff. In these lines, the contrast between 'gentle brotherhood' and the masterpieces of Renaissance art recalls Ruskin's comparison of the Gothic and Renaissance spirits in *The Stones of Venice*, 3 vols. (1851–3).

353–4. *Agnolo's | Gaunt blinded Sibyl*: Michelangelo's Persian Sibyl in the Sistine Chapel. The 'blind' Sibyl, whose name is Erythraea, is depicted by Michelangelo as turning the page of a book, presumably containing the prophecy of the Last Judgement.

355. *Titian's little maiden*: *The Presentation of the Virgin in the Temple* at Venice's Accademia, a painting of the child Mary mounting the stairs.

357. *Mona Lisa*: In his chapter on Leonardo da Vinci in *Studies in the History of the Renaissance* (1873), Walter Pater regards Leonardo's *La Gioconda* (also called the *Mona Lisa*) as a depiction of a *femme fatale*, 'the symbol of the modern idea'. Quoting the passage in 'The Critic as Artist', part I (1891), W concludes: 'the music of the mystical prose is as sweet in our ears as was that flute–player's music that lent to the lips of La Gioconda those subtle and poisonous curves'.

363. *Athena's shrine*: the Parthenon, with a sculptured frieze around the temple.

372. *House of Lust*: reappears in No. 98, 'The Harlot's House', 30.

373–90. W's expression of pantheistic monism: see the title note to No. 62, 'Panthea'.

403–8. Another lament over the loss of divine presence in the modern world, echoing Wordsworth's 'Ode: Intimations of Immortality'. See note to line 85.

411–12. *one . . . face*: cf. James 1: 23: 'he is like unto a man beholding his natural face in a glass'.

421. *sowers and the seeds*: cf. Christ's parable of the sower and the seeds in Matthew 13: 3 ff.

432. *the Word was Man*: W's alteration of the biblical passage in John 1: 1 to glorify Man rather than God: 'In the beginning was the Word, and the Word was with God, and the Word was God'.

437. *hyssop-laden rod*: during the crucifixion a sponge dipped in vinegar was 'put upon' hyssop (an aromatic herb) and offered to Jesus (John 19: 29).

438. Cf. Swinburne's 'Hymn of Man' in *Songs before Sunrise*, 44: 'But God, if a God there be, is the substance of men which is man'.

59 ATHANASIA

MS and Publishing History:
   No MS is known to exist.
   First published in *Time: A Monthly Miscellany of Interesting and Amusing Literature* 1 (April 1879), 30–1 (*Z*), as 'The Conqueror of Time'; rev. in *P1* with the present title; unchanged in *P2*; collected thereafter.
   The original title and theme seem to have been designed for the inaugural issue of the new monthly magazine. Scientific archaeology had come into its own during this period, and the public's imagination had been fired by discoveries in both Greece and Egypt (Heinrich Schliemann's *Mycenae* had been published in 1877, and a new edition of J. G. Wilkinson's *Manners and Customs of the Ancient Egyptians* had appeared in 1878). It is not surprising, then, that to evoke the agelessness of the flower in the poem, W mixed Egyptian with Hellenic allusions. Written with the same stanzaic form and rhyme scheme as the king's speech in Arnold's 'Mycerinus', 'Athanasia', set in Egypt, deals with the brevity of life.

Title. Translated: 'Immortality'.

1. *House of Art*: probably the British Museum, which, in the 19th century, was one of the great repositories of Egyptian and Greek artifacts. Cf. Dante Gabriel Rossetti's 'The Burden of Nineveh', in which the poet's reflections are inspired by his seeing sculptures being unloaded at the British Museum.

5–6. Cf. No. 43, 'The Grave of Shelley', 6–7.

10–12. Cf. Shelley's 'The Witch of Atlas', 301–4, in which a 'strange seed' is sown in the planet Venus and watered until it blooms.

24. *eucharis*: a bulbous plant from South America, blooming with white bell-shaped flowers.

25–6. *nightingale. . .cruel king*: see No. 51, 'The Burden of Itys', title note.

34. *Hesperos*: see No. 51, 'The Burden of Itys', note to line 100.

50. *ivory gate*: cf. Homer's *Odyssey*, 19: 562–5: 'For two are the gates of shadowy dreams, and one is fashioned of horn and one of ivory. Those dreams that pass through the gate of sawn ivory deceive men, bringing words that find no fulfilment.' The two gates appear in W's 'The Decay of Lying'.

51–2. Cf. Arnold's 'The Future', 50–4: 'This tract which the river of Time | Now flows through with us, is the plain. | Gone is the calm of its earlier shore.'

55–6. Cf. Arnold's 'Dover Beach', 35–7: 'And we are here as on a darkling plain | Swept with confused alarms of struggle and flight, | Where ignorant armies clash by night'.

60 THE NEW HELEN

MS and Publishing History:
No MS is known to exist.
First appeared in *Time: A Monthly Miscellany of Interesting and Amusing Literature* 1 (July 1879), 400–2 (*Z*); rev. in *P1*; further rev. in *P2*; collected thereafter.
Written in celebration of the actress Lillie Langtry, who caused great excitement on her entrance into society in 1876 and rapidly became a favourite subject of such artists as Millais, Burne-Jones, Watts, and Frank Miles, who introduced W to her in the summer of 1877. Lord Ronald Sutherland-Gower (1845–1916), author, art critic, politician, and sculptor—later, a possible model for Lord Henry Wotton in *The Picture of Dorian Gray*—recalled Miles's boast that 'he with his pencil, and his friend Oscar Wilde with his pen, will make [Langtry] the Joconde [Leonardo da Vinci's *La Gioconda*, better known as the *Mona Lisa*] and the Laura [Petrarch's beloved inspiration] of this century!' (*My Reminiscences*, 1883, 2: 153). Lillie later relied on W as her amanuensis and arbiter of things cultural. In a copy of *Poems*, which he gave her in 1881, he wrote, 'To Helen, formerly of Troy, now of London' (quoted in *Letters* 65 n.3).
'The New Helen' recalls Swinburne in its romantic treatment of Classical materials, its celebration of physical beauty, and its contempt for Christian orthodoxy. Probably written between 1878 and 1879, when W was active in London society.

2. *emprise*: archaic for 'enterprise'.

4. *impassioned boy*: Paris. See No. 20, 'Θρηνῳδία', note to line 8.

12. *Sidon . . . thy temple*: Sidon, a town in Phoenicia, had a shrine dedicated to Astarte, the Canaanite and Egyptian fertility goddess.

19–20. *Cyprian . . . Herakles*: for Cyprian, see No. 1, 'Ye Shall be Gods', note to line 57. For Calpe and the 'cliffs of Herakles', see No. 50, 'Cypriots or Folk Making for Malta', 11 and note.

22–3. *Sarpedôn . . . Memnôn*: allies of the Trojans. The former was killed by Patroclus, the latter by Achilles. See No. 58, 'Humanitad', note to line 113.

24–6. Cf. *Iliad*, 22, where Hector runs from Achilles ('Thetis' child') for the safety of Troy's walls. However, he fails to elude his pursuer and is killed. Troy was taken in the same year.

32. *Calypso*: the daughter of Atlas, she lived on the island of Ogygie at the 'navel of the sea' (Homer's *Odyssey*, 1: 50). She held Odysseus captive for seven years, hoping to persuade him to become her husband.

37. *Lethæan stream*: see No. 55, 'Charmides', note to line 613.

41. *hollow hill*: an allusion to the legend of Tannhäuser, who enjoyed pagan pleasures with Venus in the cave of the Venusberg. See No. 119, 'The Ballad of Reading Gaol', note to lines 485–6.

43. *discrowned Queen . . . Erycine*: Aphrodite, surnamed the Erycine from a temple dedicated to her on Mt. Eryx in Sicily. In Swinburne's 'Hymn to Proserpine', 73–6, the 'throned Cytherean' (Aphrodite) has fallen and the Virgin Mary is now 'crowned'.

49. Cf. Simeon's words to Mary in Luke 2: 35: 'Yea, a sword shall pierce through thy own soul also'.

57. *broken . . . wheel*: echoes Swinburne's 'Laus Veneris', 63: 'My body broken as a turning wheel'. Cf. *King Lear*, IV. vii. 45–6: 'I am bound | Upon a wheel of fire . . .'.

62. *bird . . . sun*: the swan was the sacred bird of Apollo, the sun god: it was present at his birth and derived its capacity for prophecy from the god.

65–6. *thine old delight . . . Euphorion*: in one of the many Greek myths concerning Achilles, after his death he is said to have lived with Helen in the Islands of the Blessed, where she gave birth to Euphorion, a supernatural winged creature.

68–70. Later echoed in No. 76, 'Ave Imperatrix', 93.

73. *Till the dawn . . . shadows flee*: an allusion to the Song of Solomon (Song of Songs), 2: 17: 'Until the day break, and the shadows flee away'.

77. *No other god save him*: that is, Eros. The allusion is to the Platonic notion that Love governed the motions of the universe ('the tired planets' moved by 'spiritual love', lines 78–9).

78. *nets of gold*: used in No. 76, line 102.

82–3. The birth of Aphrodite: see No. 37, 'Vita Nuova', note to line 14.

87. *asps of Egypt*: the snakes that brought about Cleopatra's death.

89–90. *poppies: . . . eternal sleep*: the poppies' narcotic effects suggest the symbolism of Lethean oblivion in the Greek mythology of the Underworld.

91–2. *Lily of love . . . Tower of ivory*: the flower symbolizes the purity of the Virgin Mary. For the 'Tower of ivory', see No. 10, 'Chanson', note to line 5.

95. *the World's Desire*: an epithet for Christ.

99–100. Cf. No. 37, 'Vita Nuova', 13–14.

61 'O GOLDEN QUEEN OF LIFE AND JOY'

MS: One untitled MS (*M*, location: Clark 2433) is extant.

Not published in W's lifetime.

Because the beseeching appeals to Helen recall No. 60, 'The New Helen', the present poem, probably written between 1878 and 1880, may also have been intended for Lillie Langtry. Several lines, however, were later scavenged for No. 83, 'Serenade', also about Helen of Troy.

1. Echoed in No. 83, 'Serenade', 31.

2. Cf. No. 60, 'The New Helen', 91.

3–4. Echoed in No. 83, 'Serenade', 15–16.

10. *mandragore*: see No. 58, 'Humanitad', note to line 84.

11. *purple fruit*: lotus flowers are alluded to in No. 21, 'Lotus Land', 9–10 (also see note).

15. *O Helen! Helen!*: A similar rhetorical device is used in No. 60, 'The New Helen', 71.

16. *nepenthé*: see No. 58, 'Humanitad', note to line 83.

17. Cf. Swinburne's 'A Forsaken Garden', 42–3: ' "look forth from the flowers to the sea"; | For the foam-flowers endure when the rose-blossoms wither . . .'.

62 PANTHEA

MSS and Publishing History:

A partial MS (*M1*, location: Hyde) has lines 1–120. Another MS (*M2*, location: Huntington HM 44181) contains lines 121–38. These comprise parts of the text from which *Poems* was set.

First published in *P1*; rev. in *P2*; collected thereafter. Most likely W wrote this meditative poem around 1879–80, when he was establishing himself as an Aesthete and was regarded by many as a disciple of Walter Pater.

Title. Panthea, an Oceanid (an ocean spirit reminiscent of the nymphs in Classical myths), appears in Shelley's *Prometheus Unbound* as an expression of pantheism.

30. Echoes Matthew 5: 45, where Jesus avers that God 'sendeth rain on the just and on the unjust'; cf. *The Merchant of Venice*, IV. i. 184–5: 'The quality of mercy is not strain'd, | It droppeth as the gentle rain from heaven . . .'.

31–6. Cf. Tennyson's 'The Lotus-Eaters', 155–6, 169–70: 'On the hills like gods together, careless of mankind. | For they lie beside their nectar . . . | . . . others in Elysian valleys dwell, | Resting weary limbs at last on beds of asphodel'. See also No. 44, 'Santa Decca', note to line 11.

42. *purple-lidded sleep*: cf. Keats's 'Eve of St. Agnes', 262: 'azure-lidded sleep'.

46. *twelve maidens*: a reference to The Hours, twelve maidens who are the daughters of Zeus and Themis and who govern and personify the seasons as well as human life. Frequently, they are depicted as figures associated with the sun-god Eos.

47. *Endymion's arms*: see the headnote to No. 54, 'Endymion'.

49. *Queen Juno*: in Roman mythology, Jupiter's wife (the equivalent of Zeus's wife, Hera), symbolically representing fertility and marriage.

51. *Ganymede*: in his *Metamorphoses* (Book X), Ovid describes Ganymede as a beautiful young boy, born to the Trojan royal family, whom an eagle (or, in other accounts, Zeus himself) bore away from the mountains of Ida, where he was guarding his father's flocks, to Olympus, where he became Zeus's cupbearer.

52. *must*: new wine in the process of fermentation.

59. *Laughs low for love . . . Salmacis*: the phrase echoes Swinburne's 'Laus Veneris', 108: 'Laughs low for love's sake'; for Salmacis, see No. 51, 'The Burden of Itys', note to lines 120–1.

67. *Lethæan spring*: see No. 55, 'Charmides', note to line 613.

84. *fiery-coloured*: see No. 40, 'To Milton', note to line 3.

85–8. *ferry-man*: Charon transported the souls of the dead across the river Styx to the 'sunless land' of the Underworld, provided they had received proper burial and paid their fare by having a 'coin of bronze' placed in their mouths.

97–102. This stanza echoes the Romantic Neoplatonism of Wordsworth's 'A Slumber Did My Spirit Seal', 7–8: 'Rolled round in earth's diurnal course, | With rocks, and stones, and trees'; and Shelley's 'Adonais', 381–3: 'the one Spirit's plastic stress | Sweeps through the dull dense world, compelling there, | All new successions to the forms they wear'.

108. *tangles*: seaweed.

128. *crimson-stainèd mouth*: cf. Keats's 'Ode to a Nightingale', 18: 'purple-stained mouth'.

139. *How my heart leaps up*: echoes Wordsworth's 'My Heart Leaps Up'.

155. *diapered fritillaries*: A species of butterfly with geometrically patterned wings.

157–62. Cf. Keats's 'Endymion', 1: 835–42: 'who, of men, can tell | That flowers would bloom, or that green fruit would swell . . . | If human souls did never kiss and greet?'

164. *dædal-fashioned earth*: echoes Shelley's 'Mont Blanc', 86: 'Within the daedal earth . . .'. 'Daedal' means cunningly fashioned.

168. Echoes Wordsworth's 'Ode: Intimations of Immortality', 179: 'Of splendour in the grass, of glory in the flower'.

172–80. Cf. Wordsworth's *The Excursion*, 9: 15, where the spirit is 'Soul of all the worlds' and Shelley's 'Epipsychidion', 565–87: 'One Heaven, one Hell, one immortality, | And one annihilation. . .'.

63 PHÈDRE

MSS and Publishing History:

First published in the *World: A Journal for Men and Women* 10 (11 June 1879), 18 (*Y*), as 'To Sarah Bernhardt'; rev. in the *Biograph and Review* 4 (Aug. 1880), 135 (*B*), as 'Sara [*sic*] Bernhardt'.

One MS (location: Huntington HM 462) has survived. The MS's recto (*M1*) contains a scored-out version entitled 'Sara [*sic*] Bernhardt'; the verso contains the poem (*M2*), entitled 'Phèdre', from which type was set for *Poems*.

Published in *P1*; unchanged in *P2*; collected thereafter. In *Poems* (1908), Robert Ross added 'To Sarah Bernhardt' as the dedication.

On 2 June 1879, the Comédie Française gave a series of performances at the Gaiety Theatre, London, during which time W probably wrote his sonnet. Bernhardt appeared in Racine's *Phèdre* as the heroine consumed with love for her stepson. Years later, W remarked in *Woman's World* (Jan. 1888): 'For my own part, I must confess that it was not until I heard Sarah Bernhardt in *Phèdre* that I absolutely realised the sweetness of the music of Racine'.

Title. Though W placed a circumflex over the first 'e', the accent should be *grave*. In *Poems* (1908), Ross corrected it.

3. *Mirandola*: Giovanni Pico della Mirandola (1463–94), Italian philosopher and exponent of Neoplatonism, settled in Florence in 1484, where he was associated with Lorenzo di Medici's Platonic Academy.

4. *Academe*: see No. 58, 'Humanitad', note to line 169.

7–8. A reference to Homer's *Odyssey*, 6, where the shipwrecked Odysseus meets Nausicaa, daughter of the king of the Phaeacians. She and her maidens had been playing ball near the bushes where Odysseus lay when their cries awakened him.

13–14. *asphodel . . . Hell*: see No. 44, 'Santa Decca', note to line 11.

64 QUEEN HENRIETTA MARIA

MS and Publishing History:
First published in the *World: A Journal for Men and Women* 11 (16 July 1879), 18 (*Y*), with the subscript '(*Charles I, act iii.*)'; rev. in *Biograph and Review* 4 (Aug. 1880), 135 (*B*).

The MS exists (*M*, location: Huntington HM462), from which type was set for *Poems*.

Revised in *P1*, without the subscript; further rev. in *P2*; Mason (227) notes: 'A manuscript has "Written at the Lyceum Theatre", which is added [presumably by Ross] for the first time in Methuen's edition, 1908, p. 178, with the dedication "To Ellen Terry".'

This sonnet was written for Ellen Terry, who appeared as the queen in W. G. Wills's *Charles I* (1872), revived at the Lyceum Theatre, London, on 27 June 1879. In her autobiography, Terry writes: 'Some people thought me best in the camp scene in the third act. . . . I was proud of it myself when I found that it had inspired Oscar Wilde to write me this lovely sonnet. . . . That phrase "wan lily" [in line 3] represented perfectly what I had tried to convey' (*The Story of My Life*, 1908, 181).

3. *wan lily . . . rain*: echoes No. 9, 'La Bella Donna della mia Mente', 32.

9–10. These lines previously appeared in W's privately printed *Duchess of Padua* (1883), Act V, in which the hero Guido Ferranti addresses the Duchess.

14. *life republican*: Terry writes of the dramatic rendering of Cromwell: 'Wills has been much blamed for making Cromwell out to be such a wretch. . . . But in plays the villain must not compete for sympathy with the hero, or both fall to the ground!' (*The Story of My Life*, 198). Cf. No. 39, 'Quantum Mutata', 1–9, where Cromwell and republicanism are spoken of more approvingly.

65 LOUIS NAPOLEON

MS and Publishing History:
    No MS is known to exist.
    First published in *P1*; unchanged in *P2*; collected thereafter.
    W composed this elegy for the son of Napoleon III, who was deposed as emperor
of France in 1870, during the Franco-Prussian War. With the conclusion of the
war, Napoleon III retired with his family to England, where he died in 1873. His
only son, Louis, studied at the Royal Naval Academy at Woolwich and in 1879
joined the British expedition against the Zulus in Zululand. While out on a recon-
naissance mission on 1 June, he was killed in a surprise attack. His death at the age
of 23 marked the end of hopes for a Bonapartist revival in France. This poem
was written sometime after 20 June 1879, when the news of Louis's death first
reached England.

    1. *Eagle of Austerlitz*: epithet attached to Napoleon Bonaparte, after his victory at
Austerlitz in 1805.

    2. *barbarous strand*: South Africa.

    5. *flaunt thy cloak of red*: that is, threaten republican France with Louis's claim to
the throne.

    6–7. *ride in state . . . thy returning legions*: an allusion to Napoleon Bonaparte's
triumphant return to Paris after his escape from Elba in 1815.

    12. *mighty Sire*: Napoleon Bonaparte.

66 MADONNA MIA

MS and Publishing History:
    No MS is known to exist.
    First published in *P1*; unchanged in *P2*; collected thereafter. This sonnet is an
extensive revision of No. 42, 'Wasted Days', which had appeared in 1877. W's revisions changed the theme, the treatment, and even the sex of the central figure in the
poem. Thus, it seems appropriate to regard 'Madonna Mia' as a different poem
rather than merely a variant version of 'Wasted Days'.
    The 'lily-girl' in line 1 suggests that the poem may have been rewritten for Lillie
Langtry (see headnotes to No. 60, 'The New Helen', and No. 61, 'O Golden Queen
of life and joy'). Moreover, in *Poems* (1881), the sonnet acts as a bridge between the
religious poems celebrating the Church and 'the New Helen', written for Langtry.
Thus, 'Madonna Mia' suggests a turning from spiritual devotion to a more tangible
object of adoration. It has been placed with the poems of 1879, but it could have
been written any time between 1878 and 1880.
    Title. W borrows the title from Swinburne's 'Madonna Mia' in *Poems and
Ballads* (1866).

    3. Cf. Shelley's 'The Triumph of Life', 514–16: 'like tears, they were | A veil to
those from whose faint lids they rained | In drops of sorrow'.

    12–14. Cf. Dante's 'Paradiso', 21, where the poet and his Beloved have ascended
to Saturn, the seventh heaven beneath the constellation Leo, and see a golden

ladder reaching on above them out of sight. W returns to this moment in No. 74, 'Γλυκύπικρος Έρως', 7–8.

67 ROSES AND RUE

MSS and Publishing History:

An untitled MS (*M1*, location: Hyde) was first published in W's *Poems* (1908) in the *Collected Edition* edited by Robert Ross under the title 'To L. L.', of which Mason thought 'Roses and Rue' was an earlier draft (202). 'Roses and Rue' is indeed shorter in length, but it has also incorporated most of the revisions made by W to the holograph draft of 'To L. L.'. This suggests that 'Roses and Rue' is the later, more finished version of the poem, not 'To L. L.'. A partial MS (*M2*, printed in Mason 205–6) contains versions of lines 33–52, as well as some unpublished stanzas.

First published in *Society: A Journal of Fact, Fiction, Fashion and Finance*, 'Midsummer Dreams' (summer issue) (June 1885), 25 (*X*).

'L. L.' was Lillie Langtry (see headnote to No. 60, 'The New Helen'); the situation of the poem is reminiscent of the parting in No. 72, 'Her Voice' and No. 73, 'My Voice'. W and Langtry remained friends into the 1880s, but it seems unlikely that he would have addressed such a poem to her after he began courting Constance Lloyd (1857–98), whom he met in 1881 and married in 1884. Furthermore, the poem's emphasis on the woman's physical charms seems appropriate to the late 1870s, when Langtry was the leading 'professional beauty' of London.

53–6. For a previous instance of the poet's heart breaking in music, see No. 51, 'The Burden of Itys', 301–2 and note.

68 PORTIA

MS and Publishing History:

First published in the *World: A Journal for Men and Women* 12 (14 Jan. 1880), 13 (*Y*).

A single MS (*M*, location: Huntington HM 462) is extant, from which type was set for *Poems*.

Published in *P1*; unchanged in *P2*; collected thereafter. Mason (228) notes: 'In Methuen's editions of 1908, p. 177 and 1909, etc., p. 157, "Written at the Lyceum Theatre" with the dedication "To Ellen Terry" is added [presumably by Ross] from a manuscript version.'

This sonnet was written for Ellen Terry, who performed the role of Portia in *The Merchant of Venice*, which opened on 1 November 1879 at the Lyceum Theatre, London. W was a guest at the Lyceum Theatre banquet on 14 February 1880 to celebrate the 100th performance.

1–2. *Bassanio . . . lead*: Bassanio, the friend of the merchant Antonio in *The Merchant of Venice*, from whom he borrows money to woo Portia in Belmont, chooses the leaden casket and wins her.

3. *Aragon*: W misspells Arragon, the prince, who is one of Portia's unsuccessful suitors.

4. *Morocco's fiery heart*: the Prince of Morocco is another unsuccessful suitor. The 'fiery heart' reappears in No. 75, 'The Garden of Eros', 133.

7. *Veronese*: Paolo Veronese (1528–88), Italian painter of the Venetian school who was born Paolo Caliari but called 'Il Veronese' after his birthplace, Verona.

10. *sober-suited lawyer's gown*: Portia dons the lawyer's gown to plead Antonio's case. The phrase here echoes one in No. 51, 'The Burden of Itys', 157.

69 APOLOGIA

MS and Publishing History:
  No MS is known to exist.
  First published in *P1*; rev. in *P2*; collected thereafter.

This poem and the following four in *Poems* (1881)—that is, Nos. 70–3: 'Quia Multum Amavi', 'Silentium Amoris', 'Her Voice', and 'My Voice'—tell a story of love celebrated, then lost. The suitor, a poet who is willing to sacrifice his art for his passion, encounters the beautiful woman's unwillingness to return his love; instead, she urges him to take consolation in his art.

Both the continuity in these poems and their general style suggest that they were composed within a brief period of time. No evidence exists to suggest that the poems were written to a specific person; the essential formula, or 'plot', is common enough. On the other hand, W could have had two women in mind during the years 1878–81, when he probably wrote these poems. One was the daughter of a retired lieutenant-colonel, Florence Balcombe (1858–1937), a beautiful Irish woman whom W had courted during his Oxford years. Her marriage in 1878 (to Bram Stoker, author of *Dracula*, 1897) left him deeply disappointed, but he continued to cherish his feelings for her. When, in 1881, Florence was an extra in a production of *The Cup*, which starred Ellen Terry (see No. 84, 'Camma'), W wrote to Ellen before the opening night on 3 January:

> I send you some flowers—two crowns. Will you accept one of them, whichever you think will suit you best. The other—don't think me treacherous, Nellie—but the other please give to Florrie *from yourself*. I should like to think that she was wearing something of mine the first night she comes on the stage, that anything of mine should touch her. Of course if you think—but you won't think she will suspect? How could she? She thinks I never loved her, thinks I forget. My God how could I? (*Letters* 74)

The other woman W had in mind in the late 1870s was Lillie Langtry, to whom he had written No. 60, 'The New Helen' and 'To L. L.', an early draft of No. 67, 'Roses and Rue', which describes a final parting similar to that of 'Her Voice' and 'My Voice'.

2. *hodden grey*: a coarse woollen cloth, made on hand looms from various fleeces without any dyes.

4. *wasted day*: Cf. No. 42, 'Wasted Days', which was revised and retitled 'Madonna Mia' (No. 66), apparently in honour of Langtry.

8. Cf. Mark 9: 44: 'Where their worm dieth not, and the fire is not quenched'.

10. *sell ambition at the common mart*: cf. No. 45, 'Theoretikos', 9.

14. *made my heart a heart of stone*: here, the speaker denies that he is unfeeling; the phrase 'heart of stone' reappears in No. 85, 'Impression du Matin', 16, where the depiction of a prostitute loitering 'beneath the gas lamps' flare' suggests her forsaken, fallen state; however, in No. 119, *The Ballad of Reading Gaol*, 606, God's compassion has the power to transform 'the heart of stone'. Cf. Ezekiel 11: 19: 'And I will give them one heart, and I will put a new spirit within you; and I will take the stony heart out of their flesh, and will give them an heart of flesh'.

24–6. *Sun God's hair . . . daisy*: an allusion to Apollo and the flower sacred to him.

36. A translation of the final line of Dante's *Divine Comedy*. The line is echoed at the conclusion of No. 47, 'At Verona', 14.

70 QUIA MULTUM AMAVI

MS and Publishing History:
  No MS is known to exist.
  First published in *P1*; unchanged in *P2*; collected thereafter.
  For this poem's relationship to others forming a sequence, see the headnote to No. 69, 'Apologia'.

Title. Translated: 'Because I Have Loved Much'. The title may have been taken from Swinburne's 'Quia Multum Amavis' ('Because You Have Loved Much') in *Songs before Sunrise* (1871).

2. *hidden shrine*: the tabernacle, in which the monstrance containing the Host is kept.

13. *remorse, youth's white-faced seneschal*: having wearied his loved one with 'Idolatry' and having been 'a lackey in the House of Pain' (line 12), the speaker alludes to remorse as his 'seneschal', one in charge of a retinue of servants.

16. *speedwell*: a small blue wild flower of the genus *Veronica officinalis*.

71 SILENTIUM AMORIS

MS and Publishing History:
  No MS is known to exist.
  First published in *P1*; unchanged in *P2*; collected thereafter.
  For this poem's relationship to others forming a sequence, see the headnote to No. 69, 'Apologia'.

Title. Translated: 'The Silence of Love'.

6. *out of tune*: see No. 18, 'Heart's Yearnings', 6 and note.

72 HER VOICE

MS and Publishing History:
  A typescript by Robert Ross of a MS (*M*, located: Clark 2491), titled 'It Is For Nothing', is an early draft of 'Her Voice', consisting of three stanzas with versions of lines 36–42, 29–35, and 15–21 in that order. 'Her Voice' and No. 73, 'My Voice',

were apparently once one poem entitled 'A Farewell', for they were so listed in the table of contents to the MS from which *Poems* (1881) was set (see headnote to No. 90, 'Helas!').

First published in *P1*; unchanged in *P2*; collected thereafter.

For this poem's relationship to others forming a sequence, see the headnote to No. 69, 'Apologia'.

36–7. Echoes Michael Drayton's *Idea*, sonnet 61, 1: 'Since there's no help, come let us kiss and part'.

73 MY VOICE

MS and Publishing History:
See No. 72, 'Her Voice'.
First published in *P1*; rev. in *P2*; collected thereafter.

9–10. Echoes Pater's description of the Mona Lisa in *Studies in the History of the Renaissance* (1873), 119: 'and all this has been to her but as the sound of lyres and flutes'.

74 ΓΛΥΚΥΠΙΚΡΟΣ · ΕΡΩΣ ·

MS and Publishing History:
No MS is known to exist.
First published in *P1*; rev. in *P2*; collected thereafter.
In this lyric poem, the lovers' parting recalls similar scenes in No. 67, 'Roses and Rue'; No. 72, 'Her Voice'; and No. 73, 'My Voice'.

Title. Translated: 'Bittersweet Love'. Cf. Sappho, fragment 81: 'Love the looser of limbs stirs me, that creature irresistible, bitter-sweet'. The error in the title in *P1* (*ΓΛΥΚΥΠΙΚΡΟΣ · ΕΡΩΣ*) for *ΓΛΥΚΥΠΙΚΡΟΣ · ΕΡΩΣ* was retained in *P2*. It was silently corrected by Robert Ross in his 1908 edition of the *Poems*.

4. *Hydra-headed*: see No. 58, 'Humanitad', note to line 226.

5. Echoes Swinburne's 'Ballad of Death', 16–17: 'O smitten lips where through this voice of mine | Came softer with her praise'.

6. *Bice*: an allusion to Beatrice, who, followed by elders and angels, meets Dante in the earthly paradise of 'Purgatorio', 30–3. See No. 48, 'Ravenna', line 105.

7–8. Dante sees the rising and setting of the sun while climbing the seven circles of Purgatory. The heavens open for him in the 'Paradiso'.

13–14. In a letter dated 21 March 1882 to Emma Speed (see headnote to No. 32, 'The Grave of Keats'), W quotes these lines (with errors), which Rupert Hart-Davis erroneously identifies as taken from 'Flower of Love' in *Poems* (1881): see *Letters* 108. However, this title is a half-title of the section in *Poems* (1882), of which the poem comprises the single work.

19. *flower . . . cankerworm*: cf. Blake's 'The Sick Rose' in *Songs of Experience*, 1–6: 'O Rose, thou art sick. | The invisible worm . . . | Has found out thy bed | Of crimson joy . . .'.

23–4. Cf. Shelley's 'Adonais', 488–9: 'my spirit's bark is driven, | Far from the shore . . .'.

28. *Cytheræan rising . . . from the sea*: echoes No. 31, 'Vita Nuova', 14. The Cytheraean is Aphrodite: see No. 51, 'The Burden of Itys', note to lines 95–6.

75 THE GARDEN OF EROS

MS and Publishing History:

A rough jotting exists for line 175 (*M1*, location: Clark 2493). The poem was first published in *P1*; unchanged in *P2*; collected thereafter. W wrote presentation verses to admirers during his 1882 American lecture tour (cf. No. 76, 'Ave Imperatrix'): a MS exists of lines 127–32, signed and dated 'March 82' (*M2*, quoted in an American Art Association catalogue for 7–8 May 1928).

1. *It is full summer now*: W had used this pattern of expression as the opening of No. 58, 'Humanitad', 1.

4–6. Lines previously used in No. 48, *Ravenna*, 310–12.

11. *a strayed and wandering reveller*: recalls Arnold's 'The Strayed Reveller', which also has a classical, mythical setting.

16–18. Lines echoed in W's *The Duchess of Padua*, Act II.

19–20: *Persephone . . . Dis*: see No. 44, 'Santa Decca', note to line 3; and No. 51, 'The Burden of Itys', note to lines 105–6.

25–6. *Herakles . . . Hylas*: see No. 44, note to line 7.

31. *crocketed*: a term borrowed from Gothic architecture to describe a floral ornament, such as buds or curled leaves, on a pinnacle.

50. *Ida, eucharis*: for Ida, see No. 62, 'Panthea', note to line 51; the eucharis is a South American plant that bears white bell-shaped flowers.

53–4. *Cytheræa's lips . . . Adonis*: see No. 51, 'The Burden of Itys', notes to lines 96 and 201.

56. *Tyrian King*: Adonis's flower, an anemone, said to have sprung from his blood when he was gored fatally by a wild boar during a hunt.

76–8. The hunter Actaeon was transformed into a stag and killed by his own hounds because he had surprised Artemis, the virgin goddess of the hunt, who was disrobing for her bath.

79. *jacinth*: see No. 51, 'The Burden of Itys', note to line 200.

81–3. See No. 51, the title note.

84. *laurel*: see No. 51, note to line 278.

87. *Helena*: Helen of Troy. See No. 60, 'The New Helen', note to lines 65–6.

89. *awful loveliness*: echoes Shelley's 'Hymn to Intellectual Beauty' 71: 'O awful LOVELINESS . . .'.

92. *Cynthia*: an epithet of the Greek goddess Artemis (taken from Mount Cynthus). See headnote to No. 54, 'Endymion'.

98. *Her face*: Athena's. The Parthenon, her shrine, suffered damage and pillaging in the wars that ravaged Athens. Thomas Bruce, 7th Earl of Elgin (1766–1841), a diplomat in Constantinople, removed, without authorization, many of Phidias's sculptures from the frieze of the Parthenon and brought them to England in 1806. The violent controversy over the rightness of Elgin's actions and later the government's purchase of the marbles surfaced periodically during the century. In the *Nineteenth Century* (December 1890), Frederic Harrison urged the return of the Elgin Marbles, 'more dear and more important [to the Greek nation] than they can ever be to the English nation' (quoted in Christopher Hitchens, *Imperial Spoils: The Curious Case of the Elgin Marbles*, 1987, p. 67).

103. *Spirit of Beauty*: the phrase, from Shelley's 'Hymn to Intellectual Beauty', 13, refers to 'The awful shadow of some unseen Power [that] | Floats though unseen amongst us' (lines 1–2). Ellmann errs in attributing to Shelley lines 103–6 of W's poem, lines inscribed in W's Tite Street library (242/257).

115. *Cephissos . . . Ilissos*: rivers which flow by Athens.

116. *Colonos*: see No. 55, 'Charmides', note to line 289.

118–19. Cf. Keats's 'Ode on a Grecian Urn', 32–3: 'To what green altar, O mysterious priest, | Lead'st thou that heifer lowing at the skies . . .'.

121–8. An allusion to Keats, buried 'beneath the Roman walls' of the Protestant Cemetery and mourned by the 'silver voice' of Shelley in his 'Adonais'—a 'threnody', or song of lamentation.

131. *Panthea*: see No. 62, 'Panthea', title note.

133. *fiery heart*: an allusion to Swinburne, whose republican sympathies stirred controversy with the publication of *Songs before Sunrise* (1871), which celebrated the revolt of Italy against Austrian rule.

137. *Hesperus*: the evening star. See No. 51, 'The Burden of Itys', note to line 100.

139–50. Swinburne's *Atalanta in Calydon* dramatizes a boar hunt in which the warrior-maid Atalanta takes part. His 'Laus Veneris' is a version of the Tannhäuser legend, and 'Hymn to Proserpine' celebrates the glories of paganism.

157–8. *Morris*: William Morris's popular *Earthly Paradise* (1868–70), set in Chaucer's time, employs archaisms reminiscent of Spenser's 'tuneful reed'. The work retells tales from Greek mythology as well as from the Old Icelandic saga literature.

163–8. The characters named are from Morris's retelling of the Icelandic stories in *Grettir the Strong* (1869) and *The Story of Sigurd the Volsung and the Fall of the Nibelungs* (1876). In the latter work, Brynhild's betrothed, Sigurd, is fed a potion that makes him forget her.

176. *Bagley*: see No. 51, 'The Burden of Itys', note to lines 153–6.

178–80. *murmuring bees*: see No. 58, 'Humanitad', note to line 72.

199–200. *One . . . Dante . . . Gabriel*: Dante Gabriel Rossetti, for whom see No. 51, 'The Burden of Itys', note to line 165.

201. *double laurels*: an allusion to Rossetti's achievements in poetry and painting.

202–4. *He*: Edward Burne-Jones (1833–98), Pre-Raphaelite painter, whose *Beguiling of Merlin* (1877) and *The Golden Stairs* (1880)—the latter first shown at the Grosvenor Art Gallery in that year—are alluded to here. In the latter painting, young girls are descending winding stairs.

209. *Adon*: see No. 51, 'The Burden of Itys', note to line 201.

216. *mighty questionings*: cf. Wordsworth's 'Ode: Intimations of Immortality', 141–2: 'those obstinate questionings | Of sense and outward things . . .'.

222. *Naïad*: see No. 51, 'The Burden of Itys', note to line 269.

223. *Actæons*: see note to lines 76–8.

227. *Endymion*: see No. 54, 'Endymion', the title note.

234. *Age of Clay*: In the first book of his *Metamorphoses*, Ovid discusses the traditional idea of the four ages in the histories of civilizations: Golden, Silver, Bronze, and Iron—in order of increasing decline—but not Clay.

237. *Titans*: the offspring of Uranus and Earth, the Titans in turn gave birth to the Olympians, by whom they were deposed in a fierce struggle.

248–50. *Hecate's boat*: Hecate, a goddess of the Underworld, is principally known for her sorcery, though she was also identified with the moon goddess Artemis. W suggests that Hecate's 'boat' is the moon, used for her journeys across the sky to end the day.

270. *the God*: Apollo, the sun god.

76 AVE IMPERATRIX

MSS and Publishing History:

A MS fragment (*M1*, location: Texas) contains lines 25–32, dated 14 January 1882, written (as a presentation copy) for the American book designer, sculptor, and artist James Edward Kelly (1855–1933), who had completed an etching of W to be used in advertising circulars during his 1882 American lecture tour. Later, Kelly was commissioned to provide five full-page designs and nine tailpieces for Rennell Rodd's *Rose Leaf and Apple Leaf* (1882), to which W contributed an introduction. A second presentation copy of lines 25–9, dated 11 April, is quoted in a Sotheby's sale catalogue for 20 July 1989 (*M2*) as 'Ave Imperatrix!'.

First published in the *World: A Journal for Men and Women* 13 (25 Aug. 1880), 12–13 (*Y*), with the subtitle 'A Poem on England'; rev. in *P1* and *P2*; collected thereafter.

Title. Translated: 'Hail, Empress'. On 1 January 1877, Queen Victoria was officially declared 'Empress of India' by virtue of the Royal Titles Bill, engineered by Disraeli. In the poem, England is identified with the queen.

5. *a brittle globe of glass*: also used in W's 1879 review entitled 'The Grosvenor Gallery'.

11–12. Recalls Milton's *Paradise Lost*, 6: 483, where the fallen angels, defeated on the first day of the war in Heaven, labour by night to fashion engines 'pregnant with infernal flame'.

13. *the yellow leopards, strained and lean*: the three golden lions on the royal coat of arms of England are sometimes called 'leopards' (from the French heraldic description *lion léopardé*) and appear as W describes them, with extended bodies.

14. *Russian*: opponent of British troops in the Crimean War, 1854–6.

17. *sea-lion*: see No. 40, 'To Milton', note to line 10. Disraeli had sent the Royal Navy to the Dardanelles in 1878 to force a Russian peace with Turkey.

22. *Pathan's reedy fen*: the Pathans—then semi-nomadic tribes known for their fierce resistance to invaders, including the British in the late 19th century—inhabited the lowlands around Kandahar, a city of south-eastern Afghanistan near what is now Pakistan.

23–4. The British invaded Afghanistan in October 1879 from India, crossing the Hindu Kush mountains by way of the Bolan, Shutergardan, and Khyber passes.

27–8. Cf. Keats's 'On First Looking into Chapman's Homer', 12–14: 'and all his men | Looked at each other with a wild surmise— | Silent, upon a peak in Darien'.

29. *Marri*: tribesman of the Yusufzai, who inhabited the mountains near Kabul and the Khyber pass.

37. *Himalayan height*: in W's day, the Hindu Kush were considered a part of the Himalayas.

40. *wingèd dogs of Victory*: during the Roman Empire, Britain was renowned for the quality of its hunting dogs, and the Imperial soldiery worshipped figures of the winged Victory. W's image combines these associations.

41–2. *Samarcand . . . Bokhara*: cities in the former khanate of Bokhara.

43–4. Cf. Arnold's 'The Strayed Reveller', 244–5: 'They see the merchants | On the Oxus stream . . .'. The river Oxus (now known as the Amu Darya) flows for some 1,600 miles through central Asia into the South Aral Sea. It was important in the history of Persia and in Alexander the Great's campaigns.

45. *Ispahan*: Isfahan, a city in central Persia famous for its gilded palaces and gardens.

54. *Circassian*: of the Muslims who lived between the Black Sea and the western side of the Caucasus. In the first half of the 19th century, when the Russians conquered their territory, many Circassians migrated to Turkey. There, many of the Circassian women, famous for their beauty, were sold into slavery.

57–8. Clearly, an overstatement by W. Through the 19th century, British missions to Bokhara, Persia, and Afghanistan failed to convince the khans that Britain would have been a stronger ally than Russia. Of the cities mentioned, only at 'Cabool' (Kabul) did the British engage in battle.

59. *sad dove*: presumably Queen Victoria, metaphorically the dove of peace as contrasted with the 'wild war-eagles' (line 57) and possibly a graceful allusion to her widowhood, the turtle-dove a symbol of her constant love.

66–7. Echoes Gray's 'Elegy Written in a Country Church-Yard', 24–5: 'No Children run to lisp their Sire's Return, | Or climb his Knees the envied Kiss to share'.

77. *Delhi*: centre of the Indian Mutiny of 1857–8, which at first involved the Bengal Army but evolved into a civil war because of widespread political and religious grievances. A force of 4,000 British troops retook the city in September 1857 and, by the spring of 1858, occupied central India.

78. *Afghan land*: during the first Afghan War of 1838–42, fought to halt alleged Russian infiltration, a British garrison at Kabul had been annihilated after it had agreed to evacuate the city.

79. *Ganges*: Kampur on the Ganges was the site of a notorious massacre of British soldiers and dependants during the Indian Mutiny.

81. *Russian waters*: during the Crimean War, from September 1854 to September 1855, combined Anglo-French forces (and later Piedmontese) suffered severe losses at the siege of Sebastopol, the main naval base for the Russian Black Sea fleet.

83. *portals to the East*: the eastern Mediterranean, the Aegean, and the Black Sea straits all provided access to various parts of the Ottoman Empire. The British navy saw action in these waters through the century.

84. *Trafalgar*: an allusion to the British naval engagement, in which Horatio Nelson achieved victory over the French and Spanish fleet on 21 October 1805, off Cape Trafalgar on the south-west coast of Spain.

100. Echoes Tennyson's *In Memoriam*, 7: 5: 'A hand that can be clasp'd no more—'.

101–2. Echoes Mark 8: 36: 'For what shall it profit a man, if he shall gain the whole world, and lose his own soul?'

105–6. Echoes lines previously used in No. 48, *Ravenna*, 192.

113. Line previously used in No. 24, 'O Loved one lying far away', 1.

116. From Tennyson's *In Memoriam*, 12: 16: ' "Is this the end? Is this the end?" '

117–20. Cf. Tennyson's *In Memoriam*, 57: 1–4: 'Peace; come away: the song of woe | Is after all an earthly song. | Peace; come away: we do him wrong | To sing so wildly; let us go'.

123. *young Republic*: W envisions the rise from 'these crimson seas of war' (line 124) of a republic (presumably replacing the British Empire) so that suffering and loss (symbolized by England's 'thorn-crowned head' in line 119 and its sacrificed 'noble dead' in line 117) may finally cease.

77 PAN. DOUBLE VILLANELLE

MSS and Publishing History:

Six pages of rough jottings exist (*M1*, location: Clark 2471), which contain lines for each of three distinct versions of the poem. The first version was published in *Pan* 1 (25 Sept. 1880), 15 (*N*), as 'Pan.—A Villanelle'. A second version, entitled 'Pan. A Villanelle', exists in MS (*M2*, location: Texas). The present version is the third form of the poem, a double villanelle, which exists in MS (*M3*, location: Berg).

Title. For the significance of the main title, see No. 44, 'Santa Decca', note to line 5; for the form of the villanelle, see No. 52, 'Theocritus', the title note.

13. *Helicé*: a daughter of Lycaon, king of Arcady.

16–17. Phrases previously used in No. 51, 'The Burden of Itys', 90–1.

26–7. Cf. No. 40, 'To Milton' (also, see the headnote), which had previously lamented England's loss of moral fortitude.

29–30. *ancient chivalry . . . Sidney*: W associates 'ancient chivalry' with the 16th-century poet Sir Philip Sidney because of his achievements as statesman, soldier, courtier, and man of letters—indeed, as the embodiment of the Renaissance ideal of chivalry, lost in the modern world. W's pastoral vision of a mythic past in 'Pan' is also Sidney's in his posthumously published *Arcadia* (1590).

32. Previously used in No. 40, 'To Milton', 10.

78 SEN ARTYSTY; OR, THE ARTIST'S DREAM

MSS and Publishing History:

Two MSS are extant: an untitled MS of four leaves (*M1*, location: Clark 1589), containing jottings of passages from line 20 to the end of the poem (printed in Dulau 4–8); and an untitled but continuous draft of lines 1–40 (*M2*, location: Clark 1588), which is printed in Mason 187–8.

First published in Clement Scott, ed., *Routledge's Christmas Annual: The Green Room* (London: George Routledge & Sons, 1880), 66–8 (*RC*), with the subscript: 'By Madame Helena Modjeska. (*Translated from the Polish* by Oscar Wilde.)'; repr. without the subscript in *Poems* (1908); collected thereafter.

This work, claimed to be a translation of a poem by the Polish actress Mme Modjeska (1844–1909), who made her London debut at the Court Theatre on 1 May 1880, was probably completed by September 1880. To the drama critic Clement Scott (1841–1904), W wrote: 'I send you the translation of Madame Modjeska's vision, which we have called *The Artist's Dream*: I read it to her last night and she was good enough to say beautiful things about it, so she was satisfied fully'. In another letter to Scott, W asserts that 'whatever beauty is in the poem is due to the graceful fancy and passionate artistic nature of Madame Modjeska. I am really only the reed through which her sweet notes have been blown' (*Letters* 69).

Despite W's reference to 'the translation' (problematic since W knew no Polish), the question remains as to how much of the poem was Mme Modjeska's. No Polish original of the poem has surfaced. Possibly, she may have offered an anecdote that W elaborated on, for the poem is not only Keatsian in its diction but in situation and theme recalls the opening sequence of 'The Fall of Hyperion'.

1. *I too have had my dreams*: cf. Keats's 'The Fall of Hyperion', 1. 4: 'Fanatics have their dreams . . .'.

3. Cf. the beginning of Keats's formal narration in 'The Fall of Hyperion', 19: 'Methought I stood where trees of every clime . . .'.

9. A line previously used in No. 55, 'Charmides', 453.

27–8. *fabled snake . . . anguish*: portions of lines previously used in No. 58, 'Humanitad', 317–18.

33. *One*: in Keats's 'The Fall of Hyperion', the guide was Moneta, mother of the Muses. Here she is Glory (see lines 41, 62), for whose favour the poet pleads.

35. *robe . . . flame*: see No. 38, 'E Tenebris', note to line 13.

51. *shooting arrows at the sun*: a proverbial act of futility, as in the case of Heracles, who, in anger over the heat of the day, once attempted to extinguish the sun.

78. *Sirian star*: in a MS version (Clark 1589), the 'fierce dog star' alludes to Sirius, the brightest star in the constellation Canis [i.e. dog] Major.

79 LIBERTATIS SACRA FAMES

MS and Publishing History:

A single untitled MS (*M*, location: Clark 2462) is extant, consisting of a sheet with random jottings (printed in Dulau 8).

First published in the *World: A Journal for Men and Women* 13 (10 Nov. 1880), 15 (*Y*); rev. in *P1*; further rev. in *P2*; collected thereafter.

In this sonnet, probably written in 1880, W is critical of the Nihilists, whose acts of terrorism were protests against the rule of Czar Alexander II, who escaped death in the February 1880 explosion in the Winter Palace's dining-room. However, in his first play, *Vera; or, The Nihilists* (1880), W romanticizes the revolutionaries despite their destructive anarchy; indeed, because of their willingness to risk their lives for the ideal of freedom, W depicts them as attractive figures. When Vera falls in love with the heir to the throne, whom she has been assigned to assassinate, she kills herself instead so that he may live to rule justly and humanely.

Title. Translated: 'The Sacred Hunger for Liberty'.

10. *red flag . . . piled-up street*: symbols of populist insurrection, previously used in No. 15, 'Love Song', 34.

12. Professing an extreme utilitarianism, the Nihilists had little use for sentiment or aesthetic refinement.

14. Echoes W's *The Duchess of Padua*, Act III: 'In its stead hath murder crept in on stealthy feet'.

80 SONNET TO LIBERTY

MS and Publishing History:

A single MS (*M*, location: Hyde) is extant.

First published in *P1*; unchanged in *P2*; collected thereafter.

In this poem, the praise of 'liberty' stands in stark contrast to the sentiments of No. 39, 'Quantum Mutata' and No. 40, 'To Milton', which deplore the decline of England. Like W's *Vera; or, The Nihilists* (see the headnote to No. 79, 'Libertatis Sacra Fames'), this sonnet characteristically expresses W's ambivalent attitudes towards liberty and the Nihilists, characterized as 'Christs that die upon the barricades, | God knows it I am with them, in some things' (lines 13–14). In 'The Soul of Man under Socialism', W endorses anarchism and, in *De Profundis*, its prominent advocate Prince Peter Kropotkin (1842–1921), that 'beautiful white Christ' (*Letters* 488).

10. *knout*: a Russian leather whip used for flogging criminals.

14. Cf. Matthew Arnold's 'To a Republican Friend, 1848', 1: 'God knows it, I am with you.'

81 TÆDIUM VITÆ

MS: No MS is known to exist.

First published in *P1*; unchanged in *P2;* collected thereafter.

Title. Translated: 'Weariness of Life'.

82 FABIEN DEI FRANCHI

MS and Publishing History:

One MS (*M*, location: Huntington HM 462) is extant, from which *P1* and *P2* were set.

First published in *P1*; rev. in *P2*, the dedication—'To My Friend Henry Irving'—was added to this sonnet in the fourth edition; collected thereafter.

In a revival of *The Corsican Brothers* (1852), an adaptation by Dion Boucicault (1822–90) of Alexandre Dumas *père*'s novel, Henry Irving performed both roles of the twin brothers Fabien and Lucien dei Franchi at the Lyceum Theatre from 18 September 1880 to 9 April 1881. In the melodrama, Lucien is killed by his rival in love, Chateau-Renaud. Lucien's apparition appears to his brother, Fabien, in a famous trapdoor scene in which the ghost seems to materialize out of the ground. Seeking revenge, Fabien finally kills Renaud in the climactic duel in the last act.

9. *frenzied Lear*: a role that Irving did not perform until 1892.

11. *Romeo*: a role that Irving performed in 1882.

13. *Richard's recreant dagger*: Irving had performed the role of the villainous Richard III in 1877.

14. Cf. Wordsworth's 'Scorn Not the Sonnet', 13–14, which praises Milton's sonnets: 'in his hand | The thing became a trumpet; whence he blew | Soul-animating strains . . .'.

83 SERENADE.

MS and Publishing History:

First published in *Pan* 1 (8 Jan. 1881), Musical Supplement (*N*), with the title 'To Helen. (Serenade of Paris)', a two-stanza version corresponding generally to lines 1–8 and 33–40; rev. in *P1* as 'Serenade. (For Music.)'; unchanged in *P2*; collected thereafter. Since a copy of *Pan* could not be located, collation was based on a transcription in Mason 171.

A facsimile of a MS containing lines 1–8 (*M*), appeared in Maggs Bros. Ltd. catalogue 1157, dated 1993. It is a presentation copy of the first stanza, signed by W.

In a letter dated 2 December 1880, the editor of *Pan*, Alfred Thompson (d. 1895), requested that W write a poem for a forthcoming issue of the publication: 'Will you do me two or 3 verses of eight lines each for a romance music by F. H. Cowen we mean to publish in PAN—as soon as possible—Title, *Happy Tears*. Subject, a young lady not certain of love discovers it exists to her delight, hinc illæ lachrymæ ['hence those tears'—from Terence's *Andria*, 126]' (Mason 171).

5. *Tyrian*: see No. 51, 'The Burden of Itys', note to line 201.

7. *lily-flowered*: the recurrence of 'lily' in the poem and the echo, in line 31, of No. 61, 'O Golden Queen of life and joy', suggests that both poems were written with Lillie Langtry in mind (see headnote to No. 61).

18–20. The image of hair like 'a tangled sunbeam of gold' is echoed in 'The Canterville Ghost', section 2, and in No. 86, 'In the Gold Room', 7–9.

29. *steer for Troy*: a re-enactment of the abduction of Helen by Paris, which precipitated the Trojan War.

84 CAMMA

MSS and Publishing History:

Three MSS are extant: the first, untitled (*M1*, location: Clark 2495), contains an early version of the octave; the second, entitled 'Helena' (*M2*, location: Clark 2451), is an early version of the sonnet; and the third (*M3*, location: Huntington HM 462) is the MS from which *P1* and *P2* were set.

First published in *P1*; unchanged in *P2*; collected thereafter.

W wrote this sonnet for Ellen Terry, who performed the leading role of Camma, a priestess of Artemis, in Tennyson's *The Cup*, produced at the Lyceum Theatre, London, on 3 January 1881. On that day, W wrote to her: 'I write to wish you *every success* tonight. *You* could not do anything that would not be a mirror of the highest artistic beauty, and I am so glad to hear you have an opportunity of showing us that passionate power which *I know you have*. You will have a great success—perhaps one of your greatest' (*Letters* 74).

In the play, Camma is desired by the unscrupulous Synorix, whose schemes to gain her favours underlie the events of the tragedy. The plot may, in part, account for the amorousness of the sonnet, the only one not mentioned in Terry's *Story of My Life* (1908) of three that W wrote for her (the others are No. 64, 'Queen Henrietta Maria', and No. 68, 'Portia').

1–8. Allusions to Keats's 'Ode on a Grecian Urn' as well as the incident involving Athena in No. 55, 'Charmides'.

10. *serpent of old Nile*: Cleopatra (*Antony and Cleopatra*, I. v. 25). Terry never did perform the role of Cleopatra.

12–13. Echoes Tennyson's 'The Lady of Shalott', 71: ' "I am half sick of shadows," said | The Lady of Shalott'. W later made use of Tennyson's line in Sibyl Vane's rejection of the stage when she professes her love to Dorian in chapter 7 of *The Picture of Dorian Gray*: 'I have grown sick of shadows. You are more to me than all art can ever be.'

14. See No. 48, *Ravenna*, note to lines 114–15.

85 IMPRESSION DU MATIN

MS and Publishing History:

First published in the *World: A Journal for Men and Women* 14 (2 March 1881), 15 (*Y*), with the title 'Impression de Matin'; rev. in *P1* as 'Impression du Matin'; unchanged in *P2*; collected thereafter.

A MS exists (*M*, location: Yale) with the title 'To my friend Luther Munday', dated January 1891 by W (a facsimile of the poem appeared in the *Picture Magazine* 5 (Feb. 1895), 101, and in Mason 176), but it lacks lines 9–12. Apparently, W wrote this poem from memory for Luther Munday (1857–1922), a theatrical producer, director of two London theatres, and, at one time, the manager for the actor Herbert Beerbohm Tree, and the secretary of the Lyric Club (1887–93). When the club was disbanded, the poem, having been written by W in the guest book, was removed (the poem facing it in the book was 'In the Garden': see No. 94, 'Impressions. I. Le Jardin').

Title. Translated: 'Impression of the Morning'. The term 'Impressionist' originated in a journalist's derisive reference to the artists who organized the 1874 Paris exhibition, which included Claude Monet's *Impression—Sunrise*.

1–2. See No. 53, 'Nocturne', title note.

7–8. *S. Paul's . . . town*: later echoed in W's 'Lord Arthur Savile's Crime', Part V (1887): 'The huge dome of St. Paul's looked like a bubble through the dusky air'.

86 IN THE GOLD ROOM. A HARMONY

MSS and Publishing History:

A MS (*M1*, location: BL, Stefan Zweig papers MS 199) had some variants reported in Mason 307. In his interleaved bibliography (*M2*, location: Clark), opposite p. 307, Mason also clipped a printed quotation of the poem from a MS in the Francis Edward catalogue No. 355 for October 1915, p. 72, which was transcribed from an 'original manuscript'.

First published in *P1*; rev. in *P2*; collected thereafter.

7–9. See No. 83, 'Serenade. (For Music.)', note to lines 18–20.

87 IMPRESSIONS.   I. LES SILHOUETTES

MSS and Publishing History:

An untitled MS (*M1*, location: Clark 2481) is an early draft, containing lines 1–8 only (printed in Dulau 7); another MS (*M2*, location: Bibliotheca Bodmeriana, Geneva), entitled 'Impression du Soir', omits lines 5–8; a third MS (*M3*, location: Hyde) is that from which *P1* and *P2* were set.

First published as 'Impressions. I. Les Silhouettes' in *Pan* 1 (23 April 1881), 4 (*N*); rev. in *P1* and *P2*; collected thereafter.

M3 was initially entitled 'Impression du Soir' before that title was deleted in favour of 'Les Silhouettes'. This places *M3* after *M2* and before *N*, *P1*, and *P2*. *M3* serves as copy text, however, since it is the MS source for *P1* and *P2*.

2. *out of tune*: see No. 18, 'Heart's Yearnings', 6 and note.

88 IMPRESSIONS.   II. LA FUITE DE LA LUNE

MSS and Publishing History:

An untitled working draft of 'Lotus Leaves' (*M1*, location: Clark 2426) contains the earliest version of lines 5–12 (printed in Mason 83–4).

First published in the *Irish Monthly* 5 (Feb. 1877), 133–5 (*I*), as the third part of No. 23, 'Lotus Leaves'.

Part three of 'Lotus Leaves' was reshaped into a MS poem (*M2*, location: Dartmouth) entitled 'Le Crépuscule' (printed in Mason 85–6), which underwent extensive changes and was published as 'Impressions. II. La Fuite de la Lune' in *Pan* 1 (23 Apr. 1881), 4 (*N*). Another MS (*M3*, location: Hyde), containing a few further revisions, is that from which *P1* and *P2* were set. *P1* and *P2* follow the text of *M3* without revisions, and the poem was collected thereafter.

Unlike the textual history for No. 87, 'Impressions. I. Les Silhouettes', *N* precedes *M3* because line 8 in *M3* contains the change of the word 'distant' to 'misty', suggesting that work on *M3* continued after the MS for *N* had been submitted to *Pan*.

Subtitle. Translated: 'The Flight of the Moon'.

9–11. These lines, which first appeared in the *Pan* version, recall the 'brown-throated reapers' of No. 87, 'Impressions. I. Les Silhouettes', 11, who pass 'like silhouettes' from the fields at the end of day. Also, cf. No. 71, 'Silentium Amoris', 1–3, for previous use of images echoed in No. 88.

89 IMPRESSION. LE REVEILLON

MS and Publishing History:

A working draft of 'Lotus Leaves' (*M*, location: Clark 2426) contains the earliest version of lines 1–4 and 9–12 (printed in Mason 83–4).

First published in the *Irish Monthly* 5 (Feb. 1877), 133–5 (*I*), entitled 'Lotus Leaves', in which lines 13–24 are an early version of the present poem.

First appeared as 'Impression. Le Reveillon' in *P1*; unchanged in *P2*; collected thereafter. Like No. 88, 'Impressions. II. 'La Fuite de la Lune', No. 89 is a revision of a section from No. 23, 'Lotus Leaves'.

Unlike No. 85, 'Impression du Matin', which attempts at an impressionistic poem but ends in the moral condemnation of a prostitute, the present poem, free of such an intrusion, focuses only on impressions that contain effects of colour and light.

Title. In painting, the French term *réveillon* refers to a strong light-effect against a sombre background, somewhat akin to the Italian term *chiaroscuro*. In the three editions of *Poems* (1881, 1882, 1892), the subtitle 'Reveillon' has no accent over the first 'e'.

90 HELAS!

MS and Publishing History:

A MS (*M*, location: Princeton), from which *P1* and *P2* set, includes the instructions: '*type*/print all in italics'. The poem was set in italics and published in *P1*; unchanged in *P2*; collected thereafter.

Printed as the introductory sonnet to *Poems* (1881), W evidently meant it as his credo. The Huntington Library has the proposed title page, motto, and table of contents from the MS of *Poems*, which W submitted to the publisher. Under the title of the volume, W wrote: 'mes premiers vers sont d'un enfant, mes seconds d'un adolescent' (a facsimile of the MS page is in Mason 285). The next page was to have contained a quote from Keats's letter to his friend John Hamilton Reynolds, dated 9 April 1818: 'I have not the slightest feeling of humility towards the Public—or to anything in existence—but the eternal Being, the Principle of Beauty,—and the Memory of great Men' (*Letters*, ed. Hyder Edward Rollins, 1958, I: 246). When *Poems* appeared, the declaration was eliminated from the title page, and the quotation from Keats's letter replaced by 'Helas!', of which no previous mention had been made. W may have written the poem just before June 1881, the date of publication of *Poems*.

Title. Translated: 'Alas!' W did not put an accent mark over the 'e' in 'Hélas!'.

1. Cf. Pater's 'Conclusion' to *Studies in the History of the Renaissance* (1873): 'Not the fruit of experience, but experience itself, is the end.' In *The Picture of Dorian Gray*, ch. 2, Lord Henry urges Dorian: 'Let nothing be lost upon you. Be always searching for new sensations.'

2. A common Romantic metaphor: cf. Coleridge's 'Eolian Harp', 15, where the 'simplest Lute' is 'by the desultory breeze caress'd'; cf., also, Shelley's 'Mutability', 5–6: 'Or like forgotten lyres, whose dissonant strings | Give various response to each varying blast . . .'.

3–4. Cf. Byron's 'Lara', 325–6: 'With thought of years in phantom chase misspent, | And wasted powers for better purpose lent'.

7. *virelay*: an Old French lyric form of two stanzas with two interlaced rhymes in each stanza.

12–14. The final three lines are derived from 1 Samuel 14: 43, in which Jonathan, Saul's son, says to his father, whose order to the Israelites to refrain from eating before battling the Philistines Jonathan had disobeyed: 'I did but taste a little honey with the end of the rod that was in mine hand, and, lo, I must die', the passage eroticized by W's replacement of 'taste a little honey' with 'touch the honey of romance'.

91 TO V. F.

MS: The inscription by W is in a gift copy of *P1* (*M*, location: Mark Samuels Lasner Collection).

Not published in W's lifetime.

Title. The initials refer to Mary Lamb Singleton (1843–1905), who published poems, essays, and novels under the pseudonym of 'Violet Fane' and for whom W wrote this poem. W's friendship had obviously deepened by 1883, when he wrote to her: 'Of course I am coming! How could one refuse an invitation from one who is a poem and a poet in one, an exquisite combination of perfection and personality, which are the keynotes of modern art' (*Letters* 150). When he became the editor of *Woman's World* in 1887, he invited Fane to contribute to the periodical. Two poems ('Hazely Heath' in Nov. 1887 and 'The Mer-Baby' in Aug. 1888) and an article ('Records of a Fallen Dynasty' in May 1888) subsequently appeared.

4. *bays*: the leaves and sprigs of the bay tree (also known as the laurel tree), forming a wreath of honour, have traditionally been bestowed on a poet or conqueror.

92 TO M. B. J.

MS; A facsimile reproduction of this poem appeared in the Parke-Bernet Galleries catalogue for the Charles C. Auchincloss sale of 29–30 Nov. 1961, 111 (*M1*). During his American lecture tour, W wrote out the poem, without title, as a presentation copy 'for my friend Mrs. Bigelow. New York. 1882—January 16th.' (*M2*, location: Johns Hopkins). Mrs Bigelow was the wife of John Bigelow (1817–1911), a former editor of the *Evening Post*, author, and, during the 1860s, appointed by Lincoln to be Envoy Extraordinary and Minister Plenipotentiary to France, in whose New York home, at 21 Gramercy Park, W had been lavishly entertained.

Not published in W's lifetime. *M1* appeared in Bobby Fong, 'Oscar Wilde: Five Fugitive Poems', *ELT* 22: 1 (1979), 11.

Title. The initials refer to Margaret Burne-Jones (1866–1954), daughter of Edward Burne-Jones (see No. 75, 'The Garden of Eros', note to lines 202–4) and later the wife of J. W. Mackail (1859–1945), the Professor of Poetry at Oxford and author of *The Life of William Morris*, 2 vols. (1899). W, who was a welcome visitor to the Grange, the Burne-Joneses' home, inscribed this poem in a copy of *Poems* (1881).

93 'OUR SOUL IS LIKE A KITE'

MS and Publishing History:
No MS is known to exist.
First published in the *New York Daily Tribune*, 23 Jan. 1882, 5 (*DT*); repr. in Bobby Fong, 'Oscar Wilde: Five Fugitive Poems', *ELT* 22: 1 (1979), 10.

The poem appeared with a letter to the editor from W. T. Mercer, who was introduced to W in London 'through the kindness of William Morris' and who interviewed W apparently in early 1882, after his first lecture in New York on 9 January. In talking about poetry, W reportedly said: 'the more beautiful its creation, the more enjoyable it is; and as I must bring our interview to a close, I will give you one of my unpublished poems, which partly illustrates my views on the longing of the soul for the beautiful and unattainable'. Such Neoplatonic views are apparent throughout this poem.

Title: Cf. Shelley's *Prometheus Unbound*, II. v. 72: 'My soul is an enchanted Boat . . .'.

94 IMPRESSIONS.   I. LE JARDIN

MSS and Publishing History:
An untitled working draft (*M1*, location: Hyde) exists, in which lines 5–8 precede lines 1–4 and in which line 10 is sketched out separately from the rest of the text (printed in Mason, facing 124, 126).

First published under the present title in the Philadelphia weekly *Our Continent* 1 (15 Feb. 1882), 9 (*Q*).

A subsequent MS of the poem, now entitled 'Autumn', appeared in facsimile in Sotheby's auction catalogue (New York), dated 1 October 1980 (*M2*). 'Autumn' was printed in *St Moritz Post, Davos and Maloja News* (Special Christmas number, 1888), 8 (*SM*).

A third MS of the poem, entitled 'In the Garden' (*M3*, location: Jeremy Mason Collection), is dated January 1891. For its provenance, see No. 85, 'Impression du Matin'.

The poem with the present title was reprinted in *Poems* (1908) and collected thereafter.

On 2 January 1882, W arrived in New York to begin a series of lectures in America (see the headnote to No. 93, 'Our soul is like a kite'). On 4 January in London, the *World: A Journal for Men and Women*, published the following:

> Practical and eccentric views the Americans take of poetry! Here is a cablegram received in London last week worthy of record by our poetasters:
>> 'Will Wilde write poem, twenty lines, terms guinea a line; *subject—sunflower or lily*, to be delivered on arrival to order of——?'
> Here follows the name of well-known publisher. The selection of the subject matter is very funny, and the terms are decidedly Transatlantic. (Mason 125)

W's poem—with its use of the Aesthete's emblems, the lily (line 1) and sunflower (line 5)—seems to be the work made to order as reported by the *World*.

Subtitle. Translated: 'The Garden'.

95 IMPRESSIONS. II. LA MER

MS and Publishing History:

A MS (*M*, location: Hyde), a working draft of No. 94, 'Impressions: I. Le Jardin', contains jottings for lines 1, 11, and 12 of the present poem (printed in Mason 126).

First published in the Philadelphia weekly *Our Continent* 1 (15 Feb. 1882), 9 (*Q*); repr. in *Poems* (1908); collected thereafter.

Subtitle. Translated: 'The Sea'. As the companion poem to No. 94, 'La Mer' was presumably inspired by W's crossing of the Atlantic in late 1881.

96 LE JARDIN DES TUILERIES

MSS and Publishing History:

Two MSS are extant: the first (*M1*, location: Huntington HM 467), entitled 'Impression de Paris. Le Jardin des Tuileries', includes, as lines 1–4, the first stanza of what is No. 100, 'Fantaisies Décoratives. II. Les Ballons' (see Mason 78, 103); the second (*M2*, location: Berg) is a note from W to the editor of *In a Good Cause*, directing that a correction be made to line 5 of the proof. The correction was never made.

First published in Margaret S. Tyssen Amherst, ed., *In a Good Cause: A Collection of Stories, Poems, and Illustrations* (London: Wells Gardner, Darton & Co., 1885), 83 (*GC*). At the foot of the page, an illustration depicting children playing on the branch of a tree is by 'L. T.'—the initials of Laura Troubridge (1853–1929), later Mrs Adrian Hope, her husband the cousin of Constance Wilde, who appointed him as a guardian of her two children when W was in prison.

After completing his American lecture tour (see the headnote to No. 94, 'Our soul is like a kite'), W returned to London in January 1883, then crossed over to Paris, where he spent three months writing and paying court to the French literati. During this time, W wrote his poem for a charity book benefiting the North-Eastern Hospital for Children (later known as the Queen's Hospital for Children, Bethnal Green).

Title. The Garden of the Tuileries, a popular promenade in Paris.

8. *bosk*: a thicket of bushes (now dialect).

12. *Triton*: see No. 55, 'Charmides', note to line 277. A statue of the sea god is located in the Garden of the Tuileries.

17–20. Cf. W's 'The Selfish Giant', in which a similar event occurs.

97 'THE MOON IS LIKE A YELLOW SEAL'

MSS: A MS (*M1*, location: Huntington HM 467), on the reverse side of the MS of No. 96, 'Le Jardin des Tuileries' (see Mason 78–9), contains jottings for lines 1–6 of No. 97. Another MS is quoted in the Anderson Galleries auction catalogue for the sale of the John C. Tomlinson library on 17–18 January 1928, item 568 (*M2*), a folio volume that contains the poem among other miscellaneous jottings. Like No. 96, some of the lines of this poem were probably written in Paris in 1883.

Not published in W's lifetime.

5. *damascenes*: metalwork ornamentations of inlaid gold or silver or a watered design, hence the reference to the Seine in line 6.

98 THE HARLOT'S HOUSE

MSS and Publishing History:

A working draft (*M1*, location: Clark 2450) exists with jottings for lines 1–12 and 19–36 (printed in Mason 56–8). A second MS (*M2*) is W's transcription of the poem but still missing lines 13–18 and containing numerous revisions: collation has been based on facsimiles of the MS from Sotheby's auction catalogue titled *English Literary History*, item 113, dated 10–11 July 1986, and Christie's (New York) catalogue, item 143, of 7 June 1990.

First published in the *Dramatic Review* 1 (11 April 1885), 167 (*V*); repr. in *Poems* (1908); collected thereafter.

A presentation copy of the poem (*M3*, location: Hyde) was made for Douglas Ainslie (1865–1948), later a poet, diplomat, and translator of Benedetto Croce. In a note accompanying the holograph, Ainslie recalled that W presented it to him shortly after W and Constance had moved into their Tite Street residence in 1885.

6. '*Treues Liebes Herz*': 'Faithful, Dear Heart', which W attributes to Strauss, presumably Johann, father or son, but no such work is known to have been written by either Strauss.

7–9 and 22–4. Echoes of these lines reappear in chapter 16 of *The Picture of Dorian Gray*, when Dorian passes a harlot's house on his way to an opium den: 'Most of the windows were dark, but now and then fantastic shadows were silhouetted against some lamp-lit blind. He watched them curiously. They moved like monstrous marionettes, and made gestures like live things.' Similar imagery also appears in No. 119, *The Ballad of Reading Gaol*, 297–9.

15. *quadrille*: a square dance, of French origin, generally performed by four couples.

16–17. Cf. Théophile Gautier's 'Bûchers et tombeaux', *Emaux et camées*, 3rd edn. (1858), 78–80: 'Le jeune au vieux donne la main; | L'irrésistible sarabande | Met en branle le genre humain' ('The young give their hand to the old | The irresistible saraband | Stirs all humanity'). A saraband is a slow, stately Spanish dance.

30. *house of Lust*: this phrase previously appeared in No. 58, 'Humanitad', 372.

99 FANTAISIES DÉCORATIVES.   I. LE PANNEAU

MSS and Publishing History:

Two MSS have been collated: one (*M1*, transcribed in Mason 103), a fragment containing versions of lines 1–8 and 21–4, is entitled 'Symphonie en Rose'; another MS (*M2*, location: Berg), containing lines 1–8 and 21–32, is entitled 'Impression Japonais. Rose et Ivoire' (printed in Mason 102).

First published in the *Lady's Pictorial* (Christmas Number 1887), 2 (*LP*); repr. in *Poems* (1908); collected thereafter.

In a letter, postmarked 24 September 1887, to the artist John Bernard Partridge (1862–1945), who illustrated several of W's poems in the *Lady's Pictorial*, W wrote:

> I send you two short poems, suitable for illustration. One is a suggestion for a design for a Japanese panel [No. 99], the other is a description of children flying balloons in the Tuileries Gardens in Paris [No. 100]. They should be set on a full page, and around them and through them should be the decorative design. Perhaps, as the girl under the rose tree is Japanese, the children who are playing with the balloons should be Japanese also. They would give a unity to the composition. Round the verses of the first poem should be fluttering rose leaves, and round the verses of the second the balloons should float, the children holding the strings from the side of the page. (*Letters* 206)

The actual illustration that accompanied 'Le Panneau' in the *Lady's Pictorial* depicts a distinctly occidental-looking woman, dressed in a kimono, standing outside a tea house, behind which her oriental lover peers. The children in the 'Les Ballons' picture, however, are neither Japanese in appearance nor in dress.

The influence of Chinese and Japanese art on Victorian artists (such as Whistler and Dante Gabriel Rossetti, who both collected such art) led to the inclusion of oriental imagery, often with Western figures, in painting as well as literature, as in the 'great dragon' writhing in gold in line 8 and the 'silver crane' with a 'scarlet neck' in lines 14–5, and in Partridge's illustration for 'Le Panneau'.

Subtitle. Translated: 'The Panel'.

8. Cf. No. 96, 'Le Jardin des Tuileries', 12.

100 FANTAISIES DÉCORATIVES.   II. LES BALLONS

MSS and Publishing History:

A MS (*M1*, location: Huntington HM 467), containing lines 1–4 of an early version of No. 96, 'Le Jardin des Tuileries', corresponds to lines 1–4 of the present poem. An early MS of 'Fantaisies Décoratives. I. Le Panneau' (*M2*, printed in Mason 103) also contains lines 1–8 of the present poem. The interrelationships of these poems suggest that W wrote drafts, at least, during his 1883 stay in Paris.

First published in the *Lady's Pictorial* (Christmas Number 1887), 3 (*LP*); repr. in *Poems* (1908); collected thereafter.

For W's suggestions concerning illustrations to No. 100 and its companion poem, see the headnote to No. 99.

16. *rubies of the lime*: the small globular fruit of the lime tree.

101 UNDER THE BALCONY

MS and Publishing History:

No MS is known to exist. A lost MS version had the title 'Rose Leaves' (see Mason 199).

First published in J. S. Woods, ed., *Shaksperean Show Book* (Manchester: George Falkner & Sons, 1884), 23 (*SS*); repr. in *Poems* (1908).

According to Mason, 'The Shaksperean Show, of which this book formed the official programme, was held at the Royal Albert Hall, Kensington, on May 29, 30, and 31, 1884, the first day of which was Oscar Wilde's wedding day' (196). The show, for charity, was staged on behalf of the Chelsea Hospital for Women, London.

Title. For the official programme of the Shakespearian 'show', W's poem was undoubtedly inspired by the balcony scene in *Romeo and Juliet* (II. ii), particularly since the prominent images in the poem—such as star, sea, bird, and flower—echo Shakespeare's in that scene.

102 TO MY WIFE: WITH A COPY OF MY POEMS

MS and Publishing History:

According to an interview entitled 'Mrs. Oscar Wilde at Home' in *To-Day* (24 Nov. 1894, 94), the inscription was written as a dedicatory poem for Constance's autograph album, which the Wildes' dinner guests were asked to sign (the poem is dated 'June' 86', after husband and wife had set up house in Tite Street). Sold at Sotheby's (London) on 15 December 1987, the album is now owned by Frederick R. Koch. Sotheby's catalogue, titled *English Literature and History*, contains a facsimile of the signed untitled page (*M*).

First published in Gleeson White, ed., *Book-Song: An Anthology of Poems of Books and Bookmen from Modern Authors* (London: Elliot Stock, 1893), 156 (*G*); repr. in *Poems* (1908); collected thereafter.

W made changes to the text and presumably chose to disguise the provenance of the poem in order to make it fit the specialized theme of the anthology in which it first appeared.

103 SONNET. ON THE SALE BY AUCTION OF KEATS' LOVE LETTERS

MSS and Publishing History:

The text of the poem, entitled 'On the Sale by Auction of Keats' Love Letters' (*M1*; location: Mark Samuels Lasner Collection), accompanied a letter, written in late 1885, from W to William Sharp (1855–1905), the Scottish poet, journalist, and biographer who also published under the pseudonym of 'Fiona Macleod'; repr. in Elizabeth Sharp's *William Sharp (Fiona Macleod): A Memoir* (New York: Duffield & Co., 1910), 115–16, and in *Letters* 182–3.

First published in the *Dramatic Review* 2 (23 Jan. 1886), 249 (*V*), as 'Sonnet. On the Recent Sale by Auction of Keats' Love Letters'. Two days later, it appeared in William Sharp, ed., *Sonnets of This Century* (London: Walter Scott, 1886), 252 (*SC*), as 'On the Sale by Auction of Keats' Love Letters' (*Letters* 182 n. 2).

W wrote out several presentation copies of the poem in subsequent years. For a Sotheby auction on 10–11 March 1952, which included property of the Marquess and Marchioness of Queensberry, the catalogue contained a facsimile of a MS (*M2*), entitled 'Sonnet. on the sale by auction of Keats love-letters', which is dated 1886 from 'Edenhurst. Torquay'.

Another extant MS (*M3*, location: Rosenbach) is entitled 'Sonnet. On the sale by auction of Keats' love-letters'. An autograph letter (*M4*, location: Hyde), post-marked 11 August 1890, from W to F. Holland Day (1864–1933), the American publisher who founded the firm of Copeland & Day in 1893 and a collector of Keats-iana, contains a version of the sonnet without a title (printed in *More Letters* 90).

In his prison letter *De Profundis* (*M5*, location: BL), W quotes lines 6–8 from the sonnet (printed in *Letters* 455).

Repr. in *Poems* (1908); collected thereafter.

Title. Because of financial difficulties, Fanny Brawne's descendants had Sotheby auction Keats's letters on 2 March 1885. W, who was present at the sale, probably drafted the sonnet soon after the event.

1. *Endymion*: an allusion to Keats's *Endymion*, an association that W also uses in No. 54, 'Endymion: (For Music)'.

2. *in secret, and apart*: Keats's relationship with Fanny was not widely known until the publication of H. Buxton Forman's edition of the letters in 1878. The final letters were written from Kentish Town in the spring and summer of 1820 as Keats was preparing to leave for Italy in the hope, ultimately vain, that he might recover his health.

7. *crystal*: in No. 51, 'The Burden of Itys', 6, the 'crystal-hearted star' refers to the monstrance in which the consecrated Host is kept.

104 THE NEW REMORSE

MS and Publishing History:

No MS is known to exist.

First published in the *Court and Society Review* 5 (13 Dec. 1887), 587 (*CS*), as 'Un Amant de Nos Jours' (translated: 'A Lover of Our Time'), printed in Mason 47; rev.

in the *Spirit Lamp* 2 (6 Dec. 1892), 97 (*SL*), with the present title; repr. in *Poems* (1908); collected thereafter.

9–11. Echoes Isaiah 63: 1: 'Who is this that cometh from Edom, with dyed garments from Bozrah?'

105 CANZONET

MS and Publishing History:
  No MS is known to exist.
  First published in *Arts and Letters* 2 (April 1888), 46–7 (*A*); repr. in *Poems* (1908); collected thereafter.

Title. Refers to a short, light, airy song that apparently developed from the longer, more serious 'canzones', love songs written by Provençal and Italian lyric poets between the 13th and 17th centuries.

2. *gryphon-guarded gold*: the griffin, a fabulous bird sacred to Apollo, had the body of a lion and the heads and wings of an eagle. It guarded Apollo's treasures in Scythia.

18. *Hyacinth*: see No. 51, 'The Burden of Itys', note to line 200.

19–20. *Pan . . . will not come again*: see No. 44, 'Santa Decca', note to line 5.

25. *Hylas*: see No. 44, 'Santa Decca', note to line 7.

30. *Dryads*: see No. 51, 'The Burden of Itys', note to line 291.

106 WITH A COPY OF 'THE HOUSE OF POMEGRANATES'

MS and Publishing History:
  An early version (*H*, location: Clark 5818) is inscribed to Justin Huntly McCarthy (1861–1936), dramatist, novelist, historian, and Irish Nationalist Member of Pariament, in a copy of *The Happy Prince and Other Tales*. Possibly, W, in writing the poem from memory for Gleeson White's anthology, erroneously noted that it had been inscribed in a copy of *A House of Pomegranates* rather than in McCarthy's copy of *The Happy Prince*.
  First published in Gleeson White, ed., *Book-Song: An Anthology of Poems of Books and Bookmen from Modern Authors* (London: Elliot Stock, 1893), 157 (*G*); repr. in *Poems* (1908), the word *A*, in the title of W's volume of fairy tales, restored by Robert Ross.
  In the unauthorized Florentine edition of Wilde's works, published by Keller-Farmer Co. (London and New York: 1907), a poem is included in Vol. 1 with the title 'An Inscription: In a Presentation Copy of His Book "A House of Pomegranates" to Richard Le Gallienne'. One of W's devoted friends, Le Gallienne (1866–1947), poet, novelist, and journalist, even provided an introduction to the volume. The source of the poem is given as *Book-Songs* [*sic*]: *An Anthology of Poems of Books and Bookmen from Modern Authors*. The poem itself, aside from several variants, is clearly a version of No. 106. Presumably, W inscribed the lines from memory for Le Gallienne in a copy of *A House of Pomegranates* which remains unlocated.

Title. W's error in the title (*The* instead of *A*) occurs twice in a letter (location: Clark) dated by Hart-Davis as June 1893, written to arrange for an American edition of *A House of Pomegranates*. In *More Letters*, pp. 121–2, Hart-Davis silently corrects the error, but we retain it here as a curiosity.

3. *Golden Girl*: McCarthy's *Serapion and Other Poems* (1883) contains a poem entitled 'The Gold Girl' (referred to twice as the 'Golden Girl'). The inspiration for McCarthy's poem may have been Whistler's painting entitled *Harmony in Yellow and Gold: The Gold Girl, Connie Gilchrist* (*c.* 1876), which depicts the 11-year-old music hall dancer (1865–1946) with her skipping rope (the painting is now in the Metropolitan Museum of Art in New York).

5–6. Cf. Swinburne's 'A Ballad of Death', 112–14: 'For haply it may be | That when thy feet return at evening | Death shall come in with thee'.

107 SYMPHONY IN YELLOW

MS and Publishing History:
No MS is known to exist.
First published in the *Centennial Magazine: An Australasian Monthly Illustrated* (Sydney) 1 (5 Feb. 1889), 437 (*CM*); repr. in Lady Constance Howard, ed., *The Golden Grain Guide to the Al Fresco Fayre and Floral Fete* (London: Clement Smith & Co., 1889), 38 (*GG*), the official programme for an exhibition held at the Royal Albert Hall, Kensington, on 29–31 May 1889, to benefit the Grosvenor Hospital for Women and Children, London; repr. in *Poems* (1908); collected thereafter.

5–8. Echoes No. 85, 'Impression du Matin', 3–6.

10. *Temple*: near Blackfriars Bridge between the Strand and the Embankment.

108 LA DAME JAUNE

MS: A MS was quoted in the American Art Association auction catalogue for the sale of the library of John Quinn, 8–9 February 1927 (*M*). The catalogue mentioned that there were some alterations in the second stanza but did not list them.

Not published in W's lifetime.

Title. Translated: 'The Yellow Lady'.

12. *Venice glass*: Venetian glassware has been renowned since the 13th century for its beauty and colour. Gold threads are often embedded in clear glass to form patterns.

109 REMORSE. (A STUDY IN SAFFRON.)

MSS: Two MSS are extant: one untitled MS (*M1*, location: Clark 2498) is an early draft of three stanzas (printed in Dulau 13), only the second of which (lines 5–8) has any correspondence to the other MS (*M2*, location: Clark 2477), a presentation poem to 'GE', who is probably Gabrielle Enthoven (1868–1950), a theatre historian who established the Enthoven Theatre Collection at the Victoria and Albert Museum. On the other side of a card containing W's autograph presentation poem is a note written by 'GE': 'Written for me by Oscar Wilde in exchange for an auto-graph Sonnett [*sic*] of Paul Verlaine. 10 November 1889.'

Not published in W's lifetime.

10. *chalcedony*: a precious stone, related to quartz, either translucent or transpar-ent, also known as agate.

110 IN THE FOREST

MS and Publishing History:

No MS is known to exist.

First published in the *Lady's Pictorial* (Christmas Number 1889), 9 (*LP*). The accompanying illustration by John Bernard Partridge (see headnote to No. 99, 'Fantaisies Décoratives') depicts a bearded man in a toga, crowned with laurel and grasping a lyre, gazing at a boy dancing in the woods in a leopard skin and carrying a staff. Since W had given specific directions for the illustrations to 'Fantaisies Décoratives', it is likely that he also suggested at least the basic layout for the picture to 'In the Forest', which was reprinted in *Poems* (1908) and collected thereafter.

11. *moonstruck . . . madness*: cf. Milton's *Paradise Lost*, 11: 486: 'moon-struck madness'.

111 THE FAITHFUL SHEPHERD

MS: A titled MS exists (*M*, location: Johns Hopkins).

First published in Karl Beckson and Bobby Fong, 'A Newly Discovered Lyric by Oscar Wilde', *Times Literary Supplement*, 17 February 1995, 9.

On the verso of the MS, W had written a note to John Mais Capel (b. 1862), an actor, composer, and musical director in the London theatre who had apparently asked him around 1892 to compose a suitable lyric for a musical accompaniment. W provided this pastoral poem, including the convention of the shepherd's lament for his absent love. Capel, who had composed settings for poems by Poe, Tennyson, and Byron in *Six Songs* (1889), perhaps found W's poem less inviting or was too pre-occupied with his theatrical work to compose the music.

Title. Derived from various pastoral works, including Giovanni Guarini's pas-toral drama *Il Pastor Fido* ('The Faithful Shepherd', 1590) and John Fletcher's *The Faithful Shepherdess* (1608).

17. *Phillis*: a conventional name for a shepherdess in pastoral verse.

20. *Philomel*: see the title note to No. 51, 'The Burden of Itys'.

22. *roundelay*: a brief, simple song with a refrain.

112 THE HOUSE OF JUDGMENT

MS and Publishing History:

No MS is known to exist.

First published in the *Spirit Lamp* 3 (17 Feb. 1893), 52–3 (*SL*); rev. in the

Fortnightly Review 54 (July 1894), 24–5 (*FR*), under the general heading 'Poems in Prose', which includes six poems in prose; repr. in *Lord Arthur Savile's Crime and Other Prose Pieces* (1908); collected thereafter.

Isobel Murray (in *Oscar Wilde*, 1989, p. 635) has suggested a partial source of 'The House of Judgment' in one of the legends in Lady Wilde's *Ancient Legends, Mystic Charms, and Superstitions of Ireland* (1887, repr. 1925). In 'The Priest's Soul', the priest, filled with the 'pride of arguing', proves 'that there was no Purgatory, and then, no Hell, and then no Heaven, and then no God'. When informed by an angel that his death is near, the priest pleads to be sent to Heaven or at least Purgatory, but since he had denied the existence of both places, the angel responds: 'You must go straight to Hell.' But the priest remarks, 'I denied Hell also, so you can't send me there either' (pp. 34–5).

Title: Cf. Genesis 28: 17: 'house of God' and Matthew 10: 15: 'day of judgment'.

3. *Book of the Life of the Man*: derived from Revelation 20: 12: 'And I saw the dead, small and great, stand before God; and the books were opened: and another book was opened, which is *the book* of life . . . '. W also uses the image in *A Woman of No Importance*, Act 1: 'The Book of Life begins with a man and a woman in a garden'.

8–9. *inheritance . . . thyself*: cf. Isaiah 10: 1–2: 'Woe unto them that decree unright-eous decrees . . . that they may rob the fatherless!'

9–10. *foxes . . . field*: cf. Song of Solomon 2: 15: 'Take us the foxes, the little foxes, that spoil the vines: for our vines have tender grapes'. Also cf. Judges 10: 4–5, where Samson puts firebrands in the tails of foxes and sets them loose to burn up the fields and vineyards of the Philistines.

10–11. *Thou . . . eat*: cf. Mark 7: 26: 'it is not meet to take the children's bread, and to cast it unto the dogs'.

13–14. *on Mine earth . . . blood*: cf. Genesis 4: 10: 'the voice of thy brother's blood crieth unto me from the ground'.

19–20. *painted . . . abominations*: cf. Ezekiel 7: 20: 'they made the images of their abominations'.

21. *seven altars . . . sins*: cf. Proverbs 26: 25: 'for there are seven abominations in his heart'. The phrase also recalls medieval Christianity's seven deadly sins: Pride, Avarice, Lechery, Anger, Gluttony, Envy, and Sloth.

23. *three signs of shame*: cf. 1 John 2: 16: 'For all that is in the world, the lust of the flesh, and the lust of the eyes, and the pride of life, is not of the Father, but is of the world'.

33–4. *with evil . . . good*: cf. 1 Samuel 25: 21: 'he hath requited me evil for good'.

37. *the outlawed men*: recalls the outlawed men of David, who in 1 Samuel 24–5 do good to Saul and to Nabal despite Saul's realization that 'thou hast rewarded me good, whereas I have rewarded thee evil' (24: 17).

113 THE DISCIPLE

MS and Publishing History:
No MS is known to exist.
First published in the *Spirit Lamp* 4 (6 June 1893), 49–50 (*SL*); rev. in the

Fortnightly Review (July 1894), 23–4 (*FR*): for further publication details, see No. 112, 'The House of Judgment'.

2. *Oreads*: see No. 51, 'The Burden of Itys', note to line 126.

114 THE ARTIST

MS and Publishing History:
No MS is known to exist.
First published in the *Fortnightly Review* (July 1894), 22 (*FR*): for further publication details, see No. 112, 'The House of Judgment'.

115 THE DOER OF GOOD

MS and Publishing History:
No MS is known to exist.
First published in the *Fortnightly Review* (July 1894), 22–3 (*FR*): for further publication details, see No. 112, 'The House of Judgment'.

11. *chalcedony*: see No. 109, 'Remorse. (A Study in Saffron.)', note to line 10.

12. *jasper*: a bright-coloured chalcedony.

18. *leper*: Jesus healed a single leper in parallel accounts found in Matthew 8: 1–4, and Mark 1: 40–5. He also healed a group of ten lepers in Luke 17: 12–19, only one of whom troubled to thank him.

29. *blind*: Jesus healed a blind man near Bethsaida by putting clay on his eyes (Mark 8: 22–6). He also healed blind Bartimaeus in parallel accounts found in Mark 10: 46–52, and Luke 18. 35–43, and a man blind from birth in John 9: 1 ff.

35. *you forgave me my sins*: Jesus has mercy on the woman taken in adultery (John 8: 3–11); and at Luke 12: 48 he says to a woman who washed his feet with tears and anointed them with ointment: 'Thy sins are forgiven'.

42. *you raised . . . dead*: the only biblical account of Jesus raising someone out of the grave is the raising of Lazarus in John 11: 1–44.

116 THE MASTER

MS and Publishing History:
An incomplete MS is extant (*M*, location: Princeton).
First published in the *Fortnightly Review* (July 1894), 24 (*FR*): for further publication details, see No. 112, 'The House of Judgment'.

10. *surely He was a just man*: in Luke 23: 47, a centurion says of the crucified Jesus, 'Certainly this was a righteous man'.

12. *changed water into wine*: Jesus's first miracle, involving water and wine, was performed at a wedding at Cana (John 2: 1–11).

13. *leper . . . blind*: see No. 115, 'The Doer of Good', notes to lines 19, 32.

13. *I have walked . . . waters*: Jesus walked on the waters of the Sea of Galilee in parallel accounts found in Matthew 14: 22–32, Mark 6: 45–51, and John 6: 15–21. Cf. No. 38, 'E Tenebris', 1–3.

14. *from the dwellers . . . devils*: Matthew 8: 28–33 depicts Jesus casting devils out of two dwellers in the tombs.

14–15. *I have fed . . . desert*: Jesus feeds the crowd in the wilderness in Matthew 15: 32–8, Mark 8: 1–9, and John 6: 1–13.

15–16. *I have raised the dead*: see No. 115, 'The Doer of Good', note to line 42.

17. *a barren fig-tree withered away*: Jesus curses a fig tree and makes it wither in parallel accounts found in Matthew 21: 18–21 and Mark 11: 12–14.

117 THE TEACHER OF WISDOM

MS and Publishing History:
   No MS is known to exist.
   First published in the *Fortnightly Review* (July 1894), 26–9 (*FR*): for further publication details, see No. 112, 'The House of Judgment'.

34. *Armenia*: the first nation officially to embrace Christianity, in the early fourth century, before it became the official religion of the Roman Empire.

40. *an enemy . . . in the noonday*: cf. Psalm 91: 6: 'the destruction that wasteth at noonday'.

43. *pearl of great price*: cf. Matthew 13: 45–6: 'Again, the kingdom of heaven is like unto a merchant man, seeking goodly pearls: Who, when he had found one pearl of great price, went and sold all that he had, and bought it'.

43–4. *vesture without seam*: in John 19: 23–4, the coat of the crucified Christ was described as being 'without seam', and, rather than rend it to divide it, the soldiers gambled for it.

63–4. *Wilt thou . . . hungry*: a counterpoint to Jesus's feeding crowds in the wilderness. See No. 116, 'The Master', note to line 16.

77. *Great River*: Euphrates. Cf. Genesis 15: 18.

78. *Centaur*: the centaur Chiron was renowned as a teacher of wisdom whose students included such Greek heroes as Heracles, Achilles, Jason, and Asclepius.

134. *Seven Sins*: see No. 112, 'The House of Judgment', note to lines 22–3.

155–6. *feet of brass . . . wool*: see Revelation 1: 14–15, which describes 'one like unto the Son of man' having hair 'white like wool . . . And his feet like unto fine brass'.

118 THE SPHINX

MSS and Publishing History:
   Manuscripts of *The Sphinx* were indiscriminately bound together over the years without regard to their provenance. It was necessary to separate them into groups based on the chronology that follows. That the poem was begun during W's Oxford

years can be inferred from a MS draft of lines 141–3, which also contains a cartoon sketch of a gowned professor (see Mason 396). 'Sphinx' was spelled 'Sphynx' in MS—as it was in the MS of No. 43, 'The Grave of Shelley', line 7, assigned the date of 1877–8.

W was in the habit of using De La Rue paper in composing his drafts. The earliest untitled MSS (*F1*, locations: Clark 2482, 2483; Hyde; and Mason 396–7) contain eleven pages of fragmentary jottings, written on folio and quarto sheets with that watermark, that correspond to lines in the earliest untitled fair copy draft MS of the poem (*M1*, location: Clark 2483), written in quatrains on three folio sheets. This early version represents the culmination of his efforts in 1877–8. Although pages are missing, W wrote in fair copy what had satisfied him to that point. In a continuous passage corresponding to lines 1–44 of the present text, however, lines 3–10, 15–16, 19–20, 23–6, 29–30, and 35–6 are still missing.

W continued work on the poem during his 1883 stay in Paris, writing to his friend and future biographer Robert Sherard (1861–1943) in April: 'The rhythmical value of prose has never yet been fully tested; I hope to do some more work in that *genre*, as soon as I have sung my Sphinx to sleep, and found a trisyllabic rhyme for catafalque' (*Letters* 144).

MSS consisting of thirteen pages of fragmentary jottings (*F2*, locations: Clark 2482, 2483; Hyde; and a facsimile tipped into the American edition of *Poems* (1909), opposite p. 286) correspond to lines found in MSS containing seventeen pages of a second untitled fair copy draft of the poem (*M2*, locations: Clark 2483, 2484; Hyde). This draft is written on De La Rue folios torn in half to make quarto sheets. On these sheets, invariably placed so that the torn edges faced the writer's left hand, W set down, four stanzas per sheet, a substantially completed version of the poem, although some pages are now unaccounted for. This version, as compared to the beginning of *M1* discussed above, contains lines 15–16, 19–20, and 25–6 (W had found his rhyme for 'catafalque' at this point).

M2 was the product of the April 1883 stay in Paris and is interesting not only because it is the first substantial draft of the poem but also because it contains thirteen stanzas later omitted in the published text. The poem was not completed at that time, however, for W complained to Sherard two months later: 'Not that I have written here—the splendid whirl and swirl of life in London sweeps me from my Sphinx' (*Letters* 147).

In July 1892, W signed an agreement with John Lane of the Bodley Head to have *The Sphinx* published with decorations by Charles Ricketts (1866–1931). Hitherto, the poem had been constructed in quatrains. (Those critics who later thought that W was using a stretched-out variant of the *In Memoriam* stanzas did not realize that *The Sphinx* was once indeed written *à la* Tennyson.) There exists a one-page untitled MS (*F3*, location: Clark 2483), consisting of jottings of lines 39–42 and 117 in two-line stanzas. The next fair copy draft MS of the poem (*M3*, location: BL Add. MS 37942) was also written in two-line stanzas with sketches by Ricketts. When W sent John Lane this MS in 1892, he requested that a TS (*M4*, location: Clark 2485) be prepared. That TS, which contains further corrections by W, is described in Mason 399, and collation reveals it to be a transcription of *M3*.

The Sphinx was essentially identical to the present text at this point, but it still lacked lines 75–88. Another untitled MS (*F4*, location: Clark 2474) consists of three pages from a notebook with fragmentary jottings of lines 75–8, 81, and 87–8. W's desire to 'make the whole poem longer' (*c.* June 1893, to Ricketts, in *Letters* 341) must refer to the inclusion of lines 75–88.

First published by Elkin Mathews and John Lane (London) on 11 June 1894 (*S*); repr. in *Poems* (1908); collected thereafter. The poem is dedicated to the French Symbolist poet Marcel Schwob (1867–1905) 'in friendship and in admiration'.

Title. In Greek myth, the sphinx was a female monster with the head and breasts of a woman, the body and paws of a lion, the wings of a bird, the tail of a serpent, and a human voice. She queried travellers on the road to Thebes, destroying all who could not answer her riddle. When Oedipus provided the correct answer, she killed herself.

11. *seneschal*: in this context, the speaker regards the Sphinx as wielding authority analogous to that of an official (a seneschal) in charge of a sovereign's household.

17–18. Echoes No. 48, *Ravenna*, 279–81.

20. *Basilisks . . . Hippogriffs*: the former, in myth, were akin to dragons, their breath and looks reputed to be fatal; the latter reputedly had the head and wings of an eagle with the hindquarters of a horse.

21. *Isis . . . Osiris*: the former, an Egyptian nature goddess, was sister and wife to Osiris, an Egyptian god of the Underworld, whose brother killed him and dismembered his corpse, the parts of which were recovered by Isis, who presumably knelt while performing a brief ceremony on recovering each part of Osiris's corpse. The mystery cults associated with Isis thus celebrated Osiris's resurrection.

22–4. Cleopatra dissolved her 'union' by placing a large pearl in wine and drinking it to impress Antony with her disdain for wealth. In 'Antony' (29), Plutarch tells of an occasion when the Proconsul, anxious to impress Cleopatra with his fishing prowess, arranged to have his servants dive into the water and attach fish to his line. Cleopatra discovered the trick and ordered her own attendants to fasten onto the hook a salted mackerel ('salted tunny' in line 24), which Antony pulled up to his embarrassment. Cf. *Antony and Cleopatra*, II. v. 15–18: ''Twas merry when | You wager'd on your angling; when your diver | Did hang a salt-fish on his hook, which he | With fervency drew up'.

25. *Cyprian . . . Adon*: see No. 1, 'Ye Shall be Gods', note to line 57, and No. 51, 'The Burden of Itys', note to line 201. A catafalque is a platform upon which a coffin rests during a state funeral.

26. *Amenalk*: also known as Amon, or Ammon, a ram-headed Egyptian deity frequently identified with Ra, the sun god, who was honoured in Heliopolis, the city of the sun.

27. *Thoth . . . Io*: the former was an Egyptian god of magic and wisdom as well as of the arts, said to have invented writing and geometry. After Zeus had made love to Io, he transformed her into a heifer (in which condition, she wept), to spare her from the rage of his wife, Hera.

34. *Adrian . . . Antinous*: see No. 51, 'The Burden of Itys', note to line 282.

36. *pomegranate mouth*: cf. No. 9, 'La Bella Donna della mia Mente', 25–6.

37. *labyrinth . . . twy-formed Bull*: within the labyrinth which he had built for King Minos on the island of Crete, Daedalus and his son, Icarus, were held prisoner by the Minotaur, a fabulous monster with a bull's head and a human body—hence, 'twy-formed', or of two forms.

39. *scarlet Ibis*: a bird (related to the heron and the stork) sacred to the Egyptians and associated with Thoth (see note to line 27), who had escaped in the guise of an ibis from the pursuit of Tryphon, a hundred-headed monster said to be the Sphinx's father. W errs in making the ibis scarlet: it has white and black plumage.

40. *moaning mandragores*: plants of the poisonous mandrake, or nightshade, family having narcotic and emetic properties. The mandrake's forked root was believed to resemble the human form and allegedly shrieked when pulled from the earth.

41. *Crocodile*: in Egyptian mythology, in which gods often took the forms of animals, the god Sebek was associated with the crocodile which was revered and, after its death, mummified.

46. *leman*: archaic for lover.

48. *Gryphons*: see No. 105, 'Canzonet', note to line 2.

51. *Lycian tomb . . . Chimaera*: born in Lycia, Asia Minor, the Chimaera was a fabulous monster with a goat's body, a lion's head, and a serpent's tail. See W's comments in 'The Decay of Lying' on Flaubert's dialogue in *La Tentation de Saint Antoine* (part 7) between the Sphinx and the Chimera.

54. *Nereid*: a sea nymph, one of the daughters of Nereus, a Greek ocean deity, regarded by mariners as beneficent. Nereids were said to have lived at the sea's bottom, spending their time in weaving and singing.

55. *Sidonian*: a native of Sidon, an ancient Phoenician seaport.

56. *Leviathan . . . Behemoth*: the former (in Hebrew, 'great serpent') personifies the evil forces of primeval chaos in various portions of the Old Testament; the Behemoth (in Hebrew, 'wild animal') most closely resembles a hippopotamus. These creatures are mentioned in Job 40: 15 and 41: 1.

59. *Nilotic*: pertaining to the Nile.

60. *glyphs*: vertical grooves in pillars.

62. *Lúpanar*: Latin for a brothel.

64. *Tragelaphos*: one of several borrowings from Flaubert's *La Tentation de Saint Antoine*, in this case referring to an animal, part stag and part goat.

65. *God of Flies*: in the Old Testament, Beelzebub (in Hebrew, 'the lord of flies'), also known as Baal, was the god of Askelon, a principal city of the Philistines. In Exodus 8: 21–31, God sends 'a grievous swarm of flies' to plague not the Hebrews but the Egyptians, their persecutors.

66. *Pasht*: Bast, a cat-headed Egyptian sun-goddess.

67. *the Tyrian*: Adonis. See No. 51, 'The Burden of Itys', note to line 201.

68. *Ashtaroth . . . God of the Assyrian*: for the former, see No. 51, 'The Burden of Itys', note to line 182. The chief Assyrian god was Assur, whose Egyptian equivalent was Horus, a hawk-headed and winged sun god.

69. *talc*: a term used by medieval writers for translucent or transparent minerals.

70. *oreichalch*: a gilded copper or brass alloy. Another of Flaubert's terms: see note to line 64.

71. *Apis*: the sacred bull of the Egyptians, commonly identified with Osiris and widely revered by the Romans.

72. *nenuphar*: a water lily.

74. *Ammon*: see note to line 26.

75. *river-horses*: a translation of the Greek *hippopotami*.

76–7. *galbanum . . . spikenard . . . thyme*: galbanum is a green resin used in incense and perfumes; spikenard is an aromatic substance used in ointments; and thyme is a herb bearing aromatic leaves.

78. *strode across the waters*: the parallel with Christ is extended later to the preparations for Ammon's burial: see lines 126–8.

82. *secret name*: traditionally, knowledge of a god's secret name diminished his powers.

92. *insapphirine*: presumably W's coinage to suggest that the seas could not make more blue the perfect azure of Ammon's eyes.

93. Echoes No. 64, 'Madonna Mia', 7–8.

98. *Colchian witch*: see No. 51, 'The Burden of Itys', note to lines 217–18.

99. *galiot . . . Corybants*: the former is a small boat; the latter were male priests in orgiastic cults devoted to the Asiatic earth goddess Cybele.

103. *steatite*: a variety of talc: see note to line 69.

104. *chrysolite*: a term which includes such green gems as zircon and topaz.

106. *Memphian*: Memphis was the ancient capital of Lower Egypt.

113. *Horus*: see note to line 68.

114. *peristyle*: a colonnade.

115–16. Cf. Shelley's 'Ozymandias' 3–5: 'Near them, on the sand, | Half sunk, a shattered visage lies, whose frown, | And wrinkled lip, and sneer of cold command . . .'.

119. *burnous*: a cloaklike garment and hood woven in one piece.

120. *Titan thews . . . paladin*: the former term refers to impressive physical prowess, the latter to a chivalric hero of great renown.

132. *Anubis*: the dog-faced Egyptian god who guarded the graves of the dead.

133. *Memnon*: see No. 58, 'Humanitad', note to lines 113–14.

135. *Nilus . . . broken horn*: Nilus was god of the Nile, which, when it overflowed its banks, created another tributary—hence a 'broken horn'.

161. *snake-tressed Fury*: an avenging spirit who was an attendant of Proserpine, the 'poppy-drowsy Queen' (line 162) of the Underworld.

166. *Abana and Pharpar*: sacred rivers of Damascus, in which Naaman, the 'captain of the host of the king of Syria', at first preferred to cure himself of leprosy instead of washing in the Jordan River, which ultimately produced a cure (2 Kings 5: 10–14).

170. *Atys*: Phrygian god of vegetation, who, legend says, died from self-inflicted castration when he broke his vow to Cybele that he would remain celibate.

171. *Styx . . . Charon*: see No. 62, 'Panthea', note to lines 85–8.

119 THE BALLAD OF READING GAOL

MSS and Publishing History:

A partial MS of lines 529–46 (and a cancelled stanza of six lines used in other parts of the poem), printed in facsimile in Mason, facing 416 (*M1*), was apparently part of a MS of the poem that W sent to his publisher Leonard Smithers (1861–1907) to be transcribed by typewriter (*Letters* 664–5). The present location of *M1* is unknown. Revisions to lines in the poem were a constant topic of discussion in W's extant correspondence for the period between 24 August 1897 and 9 January 1898 (*Letters*).

A TS of the poem with W's autograph changes and additional stanzas (*M2*, location: Clark, a new acquisition) incorporates changes discussed in correspondence up to 3 October (see *Letters* 653). This TS is evidently one of several made for W by Smithers (see *Letters* 652). *M2*, however, is not the corrected copy sent back to Smithers on 28 October because it lacks a handwritten stanza to which W later added further revisions (*Letters* 667–8).

W received the first printed proofs of the poem on 19 November (*Letters* 676–7). The proofs (*Jp1*, location: Berg), however, had inadvertently omitted lines 175–210, and the direction 'Take in "A" here' refers to the addition of these lines. *M3* consists of two lost MSS that correspond to portions of these lines: a facsimile of a MS in the Anderson Galleries auction catalogue, p. 25, for the John B. Stetson sale of 23 April 1920, contains three stanzas (lines 175–92), one of which (lines 181–6) was new to the poem; a fourth stanza (lines 205–10) was quoted in the New York Florentine edition of *The Writings of Oscar Wilde* (1907), vol. 15, p. 276.

W received a second set of printed proofs in December (*Letters* 695–6), to which he made changes, completing the version in the first edition. A facsimile of a page from the second printed proofs for lines 175–92 was found in the Christie, Mason, & Woods catalogue for the Arthur A. Houghton, Jr., sale of 11–12 June 1980 (*Jp2*). Unfortunately, these proofs were sold at auction to a dealer who subsequently died and whose stock was dispersed. Their location is unknown.

First published on 13 Feb. 1898 by Leonard Smithers, London (*J1*). Instead of W's name on the title page, his Reading Prison number appears: 'C. 3. 3.', referring to Block C, the third cell on the third floor. For the second edition (*J2*), W ordered corrections to standing type of the first edition. The text remains unchanged between the second and sixth editions, all of which were printed from the same standing type and all issued within three months of the first edition, totalling more than 5,000 copies in England alone. When the seventh edition, printed from stereotyped plates, was issued in 1899, W's name appeared on the title page in square brackets beneath his cell block number, but he did not personally oversee the printing. The new edition has four variants from the second edition in 1898, all of which are corruptions of the text. The poem was reprinted in *Poems* (1908); collected thereafter.

After W's conviction for 'acts of gross indecency' on 25 May 1895, he was sentenced to two years' hard labour, most of which was served at Reading Prison. The central narrative of the *Ballad* concerns the last days (beginning in June 1896) of a trooper in the Royal Horse Guards, Charles Thomas Wooldridge, who had been remanded to the prison to await execution for the murder of his wife. Out of jealousy, he had slit her throat three times on the road near their home, not in bed as stated in line 6 of the poem. On 7 July 1896, Wooldridge was hanged (see Mason 426–7). W included the following dedication in the published work:

In Memoriam
C. T. W.
Sometime Trooper of the Royal Horse Guards.
Obiit H. M. Prison, Reading, Berkshire,
July 7th, 1896.

After his release on 19 May 1897 from Pentonville Prison (having been transferred from Reading on the previous evening), W applied to a Jesuit monastery at Farm Street for a six-month retreat, but, on being refused, left for France on the night boat. By 1 June, he began work on the *Ballad*, which depicts the inhumane prison conditions as well as his emotional response to the trooper's execution. A first draft of the poem was finished by 24 August, when he sent the MS to Smithers with the request that it be typed. Revisions and additions to the poem continued through October, and in November W received the first printed proofs.

During the writing of the *Ballad*, W was 'keenly' aware of its departure in style from many of his mature poems, but the impulse to write a didactic poem—as a personal confession and a plea for prison reform—was so intense that he defended himself in a letter written in October 1897 to Robert Ross, who was apparently critical of the results: 'With much of your criticism I agree. The poem suffers under the difficulty of a divided aim in style. Some is realistic, some is romantic: some poetry, some propaganda. I feel it keenly, but as a whole I think the production interesting: that it is interesting from more points of view than one is artistically to be regretted' (*Letters* 654). In November, he remarked to Smithers that the 'subject' of the *Ballad* was 'all wrong' and the treatment 'too personal' (*Letters* 675). Despite such misgivings and the fear that the press would 'boycott' the work, the *Ballad* received such good reviews that he told Ross that 'really the Press has behaved very well' (*Letters* 720).

1. *scarlet coat*: Trooper Wooldridge was actually a member of the 'Blues'—that is, the Royal Horse Guards, whose uniforms were dark blue with red trimmings.

8. *shabby gray*: in November 1897, in a letter to Smithers, W wrote: 'You suggest "gray" instead of "grey" in one passage. But I have "grey" everywhere else. Is there any rule about it? I only know that Dorian *Gray* is a classic, and deservedly' (*Letters* 679).

9. *cricket cap*: like other remanded prisoners, the guardsman wore the clothes in which he was arrested.

20. *ring*: prisoners exercised in the prison yard by walking in single file in groups forming circles.

37. This famous line that becomes a refrain in the poem was probably derived from Bassanio's line in *The Merchant of Venice*, IV. i. 66: 'Do all men kill the things they do not love?'

61–2. *silent men | who watch him*: those condemned to death were placed under continuous observation.

69. *Chaplain*: the Revd Martin Thomas Friend (1843–1934), appointed to Reading Prison in 1872, where he served for some 41 years.

71. *the Governor*: Henry Bevan Isaacson (1842–1915), a retired lieutenant-colonel who had served in various prisons as a deputy governor, was governor of Reading

Prison, 1895–6. Borrowing a phrase from Tennyson's 'Lucretius', W described Isaacson in a letter to Smithers on 19 Nov. 1897 as a ' "mulberry-faced Dictator": a great red-faced, bloated Jew who always looked as if he drank, and did so' (*Letters* 676). W erred in alluding to Isaacson as a Jew, probably misled by his name. He was, in fact, the son of the Revd Stuteville William Isaacson, Rector of Bradfield St Clare, Suffolk.

83. *three leathern thongs*: a prisoner awaiting execution was bound at the wrists, elbows, and knees.

90. *hideous shed*: since public executions had long since been banned by W's time, the sentence of death was carried out within the confines of the prison (the last execution at Reading had been in 1873). In describing the shed in which the prisoner was executed, W wrote to Ross that it had 'a glass roof, like a photographer's studio on the sands at Margate. For eighteen months I thought it *was* the studio for photographing prisoners. There is no adjective to describe it. I call it "hideous" because it became so to me after I knew its use' (*Letters* 654–5).

96. *kiss of Caiaphas*: the high priest who paid Judas for betraying Jesus. On 19 Nov. 1897, W wrote to Smithers: 'By "Caiaphas" I do not mean the present Chaplain of Reading [see note to line 69]: he is a good-natured fool, one of the silliest of God's silly sheep: a typical clergyman in fact. I mean any priest of God who assists at the unjust and cruel punishments of man' (*Letters* 676).

116. *peek and pine*: presumably, W intended 'peak and pine', meaning to languish or waste away.

137. *green or dry*: cf. Luke 23. 31: 'For if they do these things in a green tree, what shall be done in the dry?'

146. *When Love and Life are fair*: see No. 32, 'The Grave of Keats', note to line 3.

155. *red Hell*: on 8 Nov. 1897, W wrote to Ross: 'The reason I altered "red Hell" into "hidden Hell" was that it seemed violent, but I now wish to go back to it. Will you alter it in the copy for me?' (*Letters* 671).

157–8. *dead man walked no more*: Wooldridge's final sentencing took place on 17 June 1896. Condemned men were customarily separated from the rest of the prisoners.

160. *black dock's dreadful pen*: on 28 Oct. 1897, W wrote to Ross: 'All your suggestions were very interesting, but, of course, I have not taken them all: "black dock's dreadful pen" for instance is my own impression of the place in which I stood: it is burned into my memory' (*Letters* 667).

162. *In God's sweet world again*: on 9 Jan. 1898, W wrote to Smithers: 'As regards your suggestion, or request, that I should revert to "in God's sweet world again", instead of "for weal or woe again" (Canto Two somewhere), certainly. . . . Second thoughts in art are always, or often, worst' (*Letters* 698).

163–6. Cf. Longfellow's 'The Theologian's Tale: Elizabeth', Part 4, in *Tales of a Wayside Inn* (1873): 'Ships that pass in the night, and speak each other in passing; | Only a signal shown and a distant voice in the darkness; | So on the ocean of life we pass and speak one another, | Only a look and a voice; then darkness again and a silence.'

173. *iron gin*: a snare or trap.

175. *Debtor's Yard*: in late November 1897, W wrote to Smithers: 'I have decided to put back the opening of Canto *Three*, because it is dramatically necessary for the telling of the story. The reader wants to know where the condemned man was, and what he was doing. I wish it were better, but it *isn't* and can't be. I think it aids the narrative immensely. So stick it in' (*Letters* 686). The Debtor's Yard was, at one time, a division of the exercise ground at the prison set aside for such prisoners.

188. *Regulations Act*: a law that placed all prisons under government supervision and prescribed humane treatment for prisoners. However, prison reformers generally regarded the Act as inadequate.

189. *The Doctor*: Dr Oliver Maurice, who, Ross said, 'resembled a bullying director of a sham city company and had a greasy white beard' (quoted in H. Montgomery Hyde, *Oscar Wilde: The Aftermath*, 1963, 43).

217. *tarry rope*: prisoners sentenced to hard labour were required to unravel the loose fibres from old rope (the unravelling of these fibres, called 'oakum', caused the skin to dry and split). The oakum was then treated with a substance, such as tar, to be used for caulking the seams of wooden vessels or as a packing for pipe joints. W performed such painful work only at Pentonville Prison at the beginning of his sentence (28 May–4 July 1895).

221. *plank*: in *De Profundis*, W writes that 'the plank-bed [designed to produce insomnia], the loathsome food, the hard ropes shredded into oakum till one's fingertips grow dull with pain . . . the harsh orders that routine seems to necessitate, the dreadful dress that makes sorrow grotesque to look at, the silence, the solitude, the shame—each and all of these things I have to transform into a spiritual experience' (*Letters* 468–9).

223. Sewing mailbags and breaking stones were the customary tasks for prisoners.

224. *the dusty drill*: one of the useless tasks assigned to prisoners was the 'crank', a narrow drum with a long handle that raised and emptied cups of sand.

226. *the mill*: the treadmill, used to pump water, was another method of punishing prisoners. Perhaps because of W's criticism of such punishments in his letter to the *Daily Chronicle* (*Letters* 723), Parliament eliminated both the crank and treadmill in the Prison Act of 1898.

237. *cried out for blood*: cf. Genesis 4: 10, where the Lord says to Cain: 'the voice of thy brother's blood crieth unto me from the ground'.

280. *plumes upon a hearse*: traditional decoration of black feathers at funerals.

281. At the time of his crucifixion, Jesus was given a sponge full of vinegar to assuage his thirst (Mark 15: 36).

283. The crowing cock recalls Peter's denial of Christ (Matthew 26: 74–5).

291. *rigadoon*: a sprightly dance for two people.

295. *mop and mow*: grimaces.

297–8. Cf. No. 98, 'The Harlot's House', 16–17, and Coleridge's 'The Rime of the Ancient Mariner', 127: 'About, about, in reel and rout . . .'.

299. Echoes No. 98, 'The Harlot's House', 7–8.

315. *gyves*: shackles.

321. *demirep*: literally, half (*demi*) a reputation, alluding to a woman whose chastity is doubtful.

330. *Justice of the Sun*: suggesting that, with sunrise (the day of the hanging), justice will have been carried out.

336. *seneschal*: see No. 54, 'Endymion', note to line 18.

345. *sough . . . mighty wing*: a sough, or rushing sound, suggests the wind created by a mighty wing—that of the angel of death (the 'Lord of Death' in line 347). The expression was used by John Bright (1811–89), the Liberal Member of Parliament who spoke on the effects of the Crimean War: 'The angel of death has been abroad throughout the land; you may almost hear the beating of his wings' (23 Feb. 1855). The image of the angel of death appears early in *Salome*, when Iokanaan tells her that he has heard 'the beating of the wings of the angel of death'; later Herod alludes to the image.

353. *Herald*: the executioner was named Billington.

367. *stroke of eight*: hangings occurred on weekdays at that hour.

371. *running noose*: a rope running through a metal eyelet so that the lack of friction ensured a sufficiently strong jolt as the noose tightened to break the neck and allow a quick death.

374. *the sign*: the tolling bell of St Lawrence's Church, Reading, fifteen minutes before the hanging and continuously thereafter.

390. *Strangled into a scream*: the *Reading Mercury* (10 July 1896), however, reported a less dramatic end: 'Billington fastened his feet, adjusted the cap, and drew the bolt, and all was over, the unfortunate man dying without a struggle and without a word'.

395–6. Cf. *Julius Caesar*, II. ii. 32–3: 'Cowards die many times before their deaths, | The valiant never taste of death but once'.

433. In his prison letter to Alfred Douglas, W remarks: 'Our very dress makes us grotesques. We are the zanies of sorrow. We are clowns whose hearts are broken. We are specially designed to appeal to the sense of humour' (*Letters* 490).

434. *crooked arrows*: marked on the prisoners' garb.

450. *quicklime*: executed prisoners were buried in lime that would quickly dissolve the corpse, in line 456 referred to as Wooldridge's pall, or covering.

485–6. Tannhäuser, the legendary troubadour, besought Pope Urban IV (1261–64) for forgiveness for having sinned with Venus, but the Pope declared that a pardon was as impossible for him as for roses to bloom on the pilgrim's staff. After Tannhäuser left, the staff burst into bloom, but the pilgrim was nowhere to be found.

489. *The shard, the pebble, and the flint*: echoes *Hamlet*, V. i. 239: 'Shards, flints, and pebbles should be thrown on her' (Ophelia).

530. *bourne*: cf. *Hamlet*, III. i. 77–9: 'the dread of something after death, | The undiscover'd country, from whose bourn | No traveller returns . . .'.

531–4. These four lines were inscribed on Jacob Epstein's monument over W's grave in Père Lachaise cemetery in Paris.

545–6. *straws the wheat . . . evil fan*: cf. Matthew 3: 12: 'Whose fan is in his hand, and he will thoroughly purge his floor, and gather his wheat into the garner; but he will burn up the chaff with unquenchable fire'.

565. *they starve . . . frightened child*: in a letter to the editor of the *Daily Chronicle*, published 28 May 1897, W protested the treatment of children at Reading and Wandsworth Prisons. At the former prison, a warder had been discharged for having given some sweet biscuits to a 'little hungry child': 'The cruelty that is practised by day and night on children in English prisons is incredible, except to those that have witnessed it and are aware of the brutality of the system.' The letter was reprinted by Murdoch & Co. as a pamphlet titled *Children in Prison and Other Cruelties of Prison Life* (1898).

606. *heart of stone*: see No. 69, 'Apologia', note to line 14.

609–12. *broken box*: cf. Mark 14: 3–9, where Christ, dining with Simon the leper, is approached by a woman carrying an alabaster box of ointment. She breaks it open and pours the precious oils upon his head. For that act of devotion, her sins are forgiven.

621–2. Cf. Luke 23: 39–43, where Christ says to the repentant thief who hangs next to him: 'Today shalt thou be with me in Paradise'.

623–4. Echoes Psalm 51: 17: 'a broken and contrite heart, O God, thou wilt not despise'.

625. *man in red*: the judge who sentenced Wooldridge to death was Mr Justice Henry Hawkins (1817–1907) at the Berkshire Assizes on 17 June; between that day and the execution on 7 July, fewer than three weeks had passed. W derived the line, as he told Ross in a letter in late November 1897, from Hugo's verse drama *Marion De Lorme* (1831), in which the final line of the play is cried out by the heroine and refers to Cardinal Richelieu, who had sentenced her lover to death: '*Voilà! l'homme rouge qui passe*'. W wrote: 'I like the expression, but "who reads *one's doom*" would I think be better. Will you alter this for me? Unless you think I have fiddled too often on the string of Doom' (*Letters* 684). Ross did not make the change.

635–6. Cain, who killed his brother, was marked by God lest he be killed in return (Genesis 4: 15). Cf. Isaiah 1: 18: 'Come now, and let us reason, saith the Lord, though your sins be as scarlet, they shall be as white as snow; though they be red like crimson, they shall be as wool'.

GENERAL INDEX

The General Index covers items in the Introduction, Editorial Introduction, Appendix, and Commentary. The Index of Titles and First Lines should be used to locate particular poems, and the running-heads in the Commentary to locate their related commentary sections. Only where a poem is referred to in another part of the book is it included in the General Index (as a subentry to 'Wilde').

INDEX OF TITLES AND FIRST LINES

Titles are shown in italic to distinguish them from first lines. References are to page- not poem-number.

ADDENDUM

(Poem numbers refer to those in the present volume.)

While the present volume was in final proofs, the existence of a scrap-book, dating from 1876 and containing references to material published as late as 1879, was made known to the editors by Merlin Holland. The scrap-book, which is in private hands, contains clippings from periodicals of some of Wilde's earliest publications, principally his poems. Sometimes these are annotated simply with the date of publication. On other occasions Wilde includes a note giving details of where they were composed. Some of the poems contain manuscript corrections to the printed texts, in some cases different from the readings of any previously known manuscript or printed version. In addition there are several lists in which Wilde orders his poems. In so far as they can be clearly interpreted, these lists broadly accord with the sequence of composition established in the present volume. Since the variants and the other information which the scrap-book supplies cannot now be inserted in their proper places in the edition, an account of them is given below. This account does not, however, attempt a complete description of the scrap-book, which contains material not related to the poems.

The folios of the scrap-book are not systematically numbered, and do not correspond to Wilde's contents list for it given below. The following account cannot therefore be tied to folio numbers.

The scrap-book contains the following contents list in Wilde's hand. The poems included are listed in chronological order of publication; with the following exceptions, the sequence accords with that established in the present volume. Poems 16 and 17 were both published in Sept. 1876, in the *Dublin University Magazine* and the *Irish Monthly* respectively; Wilde lists them in the opposite order; poems 25 and 26 were published (in that order) in the same issue of *Kottabos* in 1877; Wilde's list once more reverses this sequence. Poems 27, 28, 31, and 32 were all products of Wilde's March–April 1877 trip to Italy and Greece. Wilde's list orders them as 27, 31, 32, and 28, which accords with their sequence of publication between June and July 1877. The present volume arranges these poems according to Wilde's known travel itinerary (see pp. xxviii–xxix).

Contents

Further clippings and jottings in the scrap-book include a note in Wilde's hand (apparently apropos of poem 2): 'My first appearance in print. Translation from Aristophanes. Written November 1874[.] November 1875 published. Written in Oxford.' This note substantiates the dating given in the textual note.

There is a clipping of poem 3 from the *Dublin University Magazine*. Wilde has placed the refrains of the first three stanzas (lines 2, 5, 7, 10, 12, and 15) in brackets in MS, suggesting that he was toying with the idea of revising the poem into three tercets. However it was not republished in his lifetime.

There is a clipping of poem 5 from the *Dublin University Magazine*. Against it Wilde writes: 'Written in Florence June 1875. Published March 1876 in Dublin University Mag.' Below this he adds, but scores through: 'Second of this series refused by Editor on [?nearly] all grounds[.] See next page—and published?'

There is a clipping of a poem identified by Wilde as: 'Sent to me from New Zealand—in a copy of the New Zealand Tablet':

TO THE AUTHOR OF 'GRAFFITI D'ITALIA.'

More precious than the learning thou shalt gain,
    Thy father's name, thy wealth of youth's bright morn,
    Anew in thee thy mother's genius born,
Is the soul's yearning that doth form thy pain.

O true philosopher! who not in vain
    Hast heard the voice of wisdom, nor with scorn
    Stiflest the sighs, thine intellect that warn
Of things most high which for its search remain.

If 'steep' to thee the way, arousing fears,
    Know heavier feet than thine have gained its end,
That all the pangs of travel puts to flight.
Trust not the doubtful promptings of the years,
    Nor full assurance on each point attend.
    'Who doth the truth cometh unto the light.'

Wilde dates the clipping '1877' and writes below 'perhaps by Newman?'

There is a note in Wilde's hand apparently apropos of poem 7: 'Published in the "Month" of September. *1876*[.] Written at Arona, Ju<ne>ly, 1875'.

There is a clipping of poem 9 from *Kottabos* against which Wilde notes: 'Written

partly at Clonfin (December 1875) partly at Oxford. Published May 1876.' The first
and third lines of the third stanza (which was omitted from P1) are emended in a
hand which cannot be confirmed as Wilde's thus:

<O> Bend almond-flowers! bend adown

and

<O> Weave twining branches! weave a crown

There is a clipping of poem 14 from the *Dublin University Magazine*, with a note in
Wilde's hand that establishes its first composition: 'Written going over from Kingston
to Holyhead October 22nd 1875. Published, with some alterations, June 1876.' Line
7 is corrected in a hand that cannot be confirmed as Wilde's, from 'And where her
bosom' to 'And oh where her bosom', readings which were carried through to P1.

There are clippings of poems 17 and 16 which Wilde dates respectively as 'Irish
Monthly. September 1876' and 'Dublin Univ. Mag. September 1876'.

There is a clipping of poem 20 taken from *Kottabos*. It contains the following MS
emendations: lines 8 and 13 end with question marks; line 23, 'It may be in Delos',
becomes 'Ah! It may be in Delos'; the comma at the end of line 40 is deleted; in line
46 'son of Time' becomes 'Son of Time'; and in line 49 'the risen cloud' becomes
'the riven cloud'. The poem was not reprinted in Wilde's lifetime.

There is a clipping from *Kottabos* of poem 26, which Wilde dates '*Kottabos. 1877*'
and adds below this '*Beatrice*'. In line 11 'Then she, who lay beside me:' is deleted
and 'Then one who walked beside me;' inserted in MS. These revisions differ from
any other version of the poem.

There is a clipping of poem 25, also from *Kottabos*. In line 6 'sorrow of its dreary' is
revised in MS to 'sorrow of her dreary'. The poem was not reprinted in Wilde's lifetime.

There is a clipping of poem 27 from the *Irish Monthly* which Wilde dates as follows:
'Written after coming out of the Monte Cenis Tunnel into Italy. March 1877', thus
establishing the specific occasion on which the poem was begun. In addition there is
a clipping from an unidentified periodical which mentions the poem's publication
in the *Irish Monthly* and which quotes the sestet.

There is a clipping of poem 31 from the Dublin *Illustrated Monitor* which Wilde dates
'Written at Rome 1877. Published in the Catholic Monitor of <July> 77 June.' The
first line 'O Rome, what sights and changes hast thou seen!' is revised in MS to: 'O
Rome, a wondrous history thine has been!', a variation of what finally appeared in P1.

There are clippings of poem 29 (under the title 'Hellas! Hellas!) and poem 30, both
from the Boston *Pilot*. In the latter poem 'the East a purple sea' in line 6 becomes
'the East a purple stretch of sea'.

There is a clipping of poem 32 from the *Irish Monthly*. The following words and
phrases are underlined: 'foully' (line 5); 'catch the evening rain' (line 8); 'saddest' (line
10); 'on the sand' (line 12); 'But our tears shall' (line 13). Underneath the clipping is
a series of notes (not in Wilde's hand) numbered 1–5 and keyed to these underlinings;
they are identified by Wilde 'as corrected by the Rev. Stopford A. Brooke. M. A.' The
notes appear to be suggestions for revision which are taken up in P1. For example, the

note numbered '3' asks 'surely not "saddest"'; note '4' comments '"On the sand"— weakens Keats' expression'. Beneath his identification of the Revd Brooke, and under the heading 'corrected', Wilde writes out the first two and a half lines of the poem.

There is a clipping from poem 28 from the Dublin *Illustrated Monitor*; in line 12 'sweet and honied hours' is revised in MS to 'sweet Hellenic hours', a revision further refined in P1.

Finally, there are various lists of Wilde's poems in his own hand. The 'List of Sonnets' seems to date from July–August 1877, and appears to be a list of sonnets to be published or written. By July 1877 Wilde had published five sonnets (poems 26, 27, 28, 31, and 32); in May he had sent two (poems 33 and 34) to W. E. Gladstone which were not published until 1881 and 1879 respectively. It is not clear what Wilde's numbering in the second and subsequent lists refers to. The lists may date from 1879 or later, given that they mention poems (59, 60, and 64) which were all published in 1879. Only some of the titles in the lists can be matched to extant poems by Wilde; they may correspond to poems planned but not written, or written but lost.

List of Sonnets.
published 5.

6.	On Christian massacres		15.	Arcadia
7.	Πόντος ἀτρύγετος		16.	Argos
8.	Wasted Days		17.	Athens
9.	Tile		18.	Messina
10.	Dies Irae		19.	Pope
11.	Brindisi		20.	Χαῖρε κεχαρπωμένη
12.	Corfu		21.	Shelley's Grave
13.	Zanté		22.	Italia
14.	Olympia		23.	Bournemouth
			24.	Picture
			25.	Friendship

Love in time of Revolution	3.		San Miniato	20.
Lily Flowers			Sonnet in Holy Week	22.
Tile	5.		Italia	
Ἔρωτος ἄνθος	9.		Rome Unvisited	24.
King's Daughter	11.		Rome [?Carmel]	
Wasted Days			Dies Irae	30.
Ballade	15.		Ave Maria	
Flores Catholici			Πόντος ἀτρύγ[ετος] Patria	32.
Super flumina Babylonis	16.		Easter Day	36.

New Helen	5.		Earth [?Globe]	23.
S. B.			2. Friendship	
Keats. Corfu	9.		Messina	
<Friendship> Zante			Argos	
Conquerors of Time	13.		Night Vision	29.
Magdalen Walks	15.		France.	
Shelley.			1.	39.
Xtian Massacres.			2.	
Ellen Terry. 2.	19.		3.	

Sonnets

Keats.
Shelley.
Pope.
Rome. 2.
Ellen Terry. 2.
S. B. 1.
Dante.
Dies Irae.
Πόντ[ος] ἀτρύ[γετος]
[?Carmel].

Genoa.
Corfu.
Zante.
Argos.
Messina.
[illeg. word].
Christian M.
Tile.
Friendship. 2.
Wasted Days.